An Augustinian Christology

In *An Augustinian Christology: Completing Christ*, Joseph Walker-Lenow advances a striking christological thesis: Jesus Christ, true God and true human, only becomes who he is through his relations to the world around him. To understand both his person and work, it is necessary to see him as receptive to and determined by the people he meets, the environments he inhabits, even those people who come to worship him. Christ and the redemption he brings cannot be understood apart from these factors, for it is *through* the existence and agency of the created world that he redeems.

To pursue these claims, Walker-Lenow draws on an underappreciated resource in the history of Christian thought: St. Augustine of Hippo's theology of the "whole Christ." Presenting Augustine's christology across the full range of his writings, Joseph Walker-Lenow recovers a christocentric Augustine with the potential to transform our understandings of the Church and its mission in our world.

JOSEPH WALKER-LENOW (Ph.D., University of Virginia) is Rector of St. James' Episcopal Parish in Lothian, MD. He has previously taught at Duke Divinity School, Creighton University, and the University of Virginia, and has published research in systematic and philosophical theology in journals including the *International Journal of Systematic Theology*, *Religious Studies*, and *Political Theology*.

CURRENT ISSUES IN THEOLOGY

General Editors:
Iain Torrance
Pro-Chancellor of the University of Aberdeen

David Fergusson
University of Edinburgh

Editorial Advisory Board:
David Ford   *University of Cambridge*
Bryan Spinks   *Yale University*
Kathryn Tanner   *Yale Divinity School*

There is a need among upper-undergraduate and graduate students of theology, as well as among Christian teachers and church professionals, for a series of short, focused studies of particular key topics in theology written by prominent theologians. Current Issues in Theology meets this need.

The books in the series are designed to provide a "state-of-the-art" statement on the topic in question, engaging with contemporary thinking as well as providing original insights. The aim is to publish books which stand between the static monograph genre and the more immediate statement of a journal article, by authors who are questioning existing paradigms or rethinking perspectives.

Other titles in the series:

Holy Scripture   John Webster
The Just War Revisited   Oliver O'Donovan
Bodies and Souls, or Spirited Bodies?   Nancey Murphy
Christ and Horrors Marilyn McCord Adams
Divinity and Humanity   Oliver D. Crisp
The Eucharist and Ecumenism   George Hunsinger
Christ the Key   Kathryn Tanner
Theology without Metaphysics   Kevin W. Hector
Reconsidering John Calvin   Randall C. Zachman
God's Presence   Frances Youngman

JOSEPH WALKER-LENOW
Duke University

An Augustinian Christology
Completing Christ

CAMBRIDGE
UNIVERSITY PRESS

CAMBRIDGE
UNIVERSITY PRESS

Shaftesbury Road, Cambridge CB2 8EA, United Kingdom

One Liberty Plaza, 20th Floor, New York, NY 10006, USA

477 Williamstown Road, Port Melbourne, VIC 3207, Australia

314–321, 3rd Floor, Plot 3, Splendor Forum, Jasola District Centre,
New Delhi – 110025, India

103 Penang Road, #05–06/07, Visioncrest Commercial, Singapore 238467

Cambridge University Press is part of Cambridge University Press & Assessment,
a department of the University of Cambridge.

We share the University's mission to contribute to society through the pursuit of
education, learning and research at the highest international levels of excellence.

www.cambridge.org
Information on this title: www.cambridge.org/9781009344425

DOI: 10.1017/9781009344449

First published 2023

A catalogue record for this publication is available from the British Library

Library of Congress Cataloging-in-Publication Data
NAMES: Lenow, Joseph Walker, author.
TITLE: An Augustinian Christology : completing Christ / Joseph Walker Lenow,
Duke University.
DESCRIPTION: Cambridge, United Kingdom ; New York, NY, USA : Cambridge
University Press, 2023. | Includes bibliographical references and index.
IDENTIFIERS: LCCN 2023023830 (print) | LCCN 2023023831 (ebook) |
ISBN 9781009344425 (hardcover) | ISBN 9781009344418 (paperback) |
ISBN 9781009344449 (ebook)
SUBJECTS: LCSH: Jesus Christ – History of doctrines. | Jesus Christ – Person and
offices. | Augustine, of Hippo, Saint, 354–430. | Philosophical theology.
CLASSIFICATION: LCC BT203 .L47 2023 (print) | LCC BT203 (ebook) |
DDC 232–dc23/eng/20230823
LC record available at https://lccn.loc.gov/2023023830
LC ebook record available at https://lccn.loc.gov/2023023831

ISBN 978-1-009-34442-5 Hardback

Contents

vii

Acknowledgments

This project has been stewing for some time. That has certainly come with its share of hardships over the years, but one of the great joys it has made possible is the opportunity to discuss the ideas of this book with teachers, friends, and colleagues at many different stages of my thinking. A full accounting of those who have shaped my thinking here in large ways and small is more than I am able to provide here; even given world enough and time, my suspicion is that I would be incapable of listing all those from whom I have learned, and who have materially contributed to my ability to write this book and what I say herein. Even so, it is a true pleasure to be able to offer a word of thanks to many of those who have provided personal support, or a useful insight, or a generative question, or a welcome distraction at key moments of this project.

I am grateful to the intellectual and ecclesial communities that have supported me as I've written this book: to the University of Virginia, Creighton University, and Duke Divinity School; and to St. Paul's Memorial Episcopal (Charlottesville), Trinity Episcopal Cathedral (Omaha), and St. Mark's-on-the-Campus (Lincoln). Most recently, I am grateful to my people, staff, and colleagues at St. James' Parish (Lothian) and in the Episcopal Diocese of Maryland, who have been far more supportive of a somewhat recondite christo-logical study than a parish priest has any right to expect.

I could not have written this book without the mentorship and friendship of many teachers and colleagues, whose forbearance of my tendency to drop into their offices unannounced and seek their help with some exegetical or conceptual problem that I've fixated upon is more than I deserve. Robert Louis Wilken first introduced me to Patristic theology and to Augustine in general. Since his class in my first semester of college (and the many seminars that followed), I have progressed as a reader of early Christian thought with the help of Warren Smith, the late Judith Kovacs, and Karl Shuve. Stanley Hauerwas has been a consistent support since Divinity School and provided invaluable feedback on various drafts of this manuscript. I have learned a great deal (though not so much as I, or they, might have wished) from Larry Bouchard, Jim Childress, Nichole Flores, Jennifer Geddes, Kevin Hart, Lisa Reilly, and Heather Warren at the University of Virginia. Among my colleagues at Creighton University, all of whom I thank, I am especially grateful for conversations with Julia Feder, Peter Nguyen, and Sherri Brown.

James Wetzel hosted a manuscript symposium at Villanova University in the summer of 2021 at which an earlier draft of this book along with books recently or soon-to-be published by Emily Dumler-Winckler and Toni Alimi were read and commented upon in their entirety. Those several days were one of the most fruitful intellectual experiences I have had, and I am more grateful to Jim than I can say for organizing it and including me, as well as for all the conversations we've had since I was a master's student. John Bowlin, Eric Gregory, and Michelle Sanchez each read and provided acute and productive feedback on the whole of the manuscript, and I am grateful for their help and encouragement in the years since. Others who have read part or all of this book, and who have seen it to its publication through their assistance and friendship include Luke Bretherton, Paul Griffiths, Warren Kinghorn, Lauren Winner, and Bill Wood.

I am grateful to Beatrice Rehl and David Fergusson for their willingness to include this book in this series, in which so many of my favorite works of recent theology have been published.

Among the many friends alongside whom I have studied and learned, I wish to offer particular thanks to Laura and Bryan Alexander; Scott Bailey, Jack Bell, Matt and Emily Benton; William Boyce, Gillian Breckenridge, and Robert LeBlanc; Brandy

Daniels, Rebecca and Sarah Epstein-Levi; Nauman Faizi, Matthew Farley, Jeremy Fisher, Peter and Karen Fraser-Morris; Patrick Gardner, Charles Gillespie, Andrew and Emily Guffey; Timothy Hartman, Caleb Hendrickson, Mark and Christina Randall James; Matt Jantzen, Brian and Kim Johnson; Ross Kane, Sean Larsen, Nate Lee, Shifa Noor, Larry Perry, Travis Pickell, Ethan Prall, Justin, and Elsbeth Pritchett; Matthew Puffer, Nelson Reveley, Zac Settle, Reuben Shank, Sarah Strasen, and Peter Moench; Jonathan and Rachel Teubner; Petra Turner, A. J. Walton, Matthew Whelan, and Daniel and Leah Wise.

I could not have asked for better undergraduate teachers, doctoral advisors, and theological mentors than Chuck Mathewes and Paul Dafydd Jones. They have modeled for me a humility, kindness, rigor, and creativity that has left a permanent mark on my life and scholarship; thank you.

Throughout the last decade, there are none from whom I have learned more or have depended on as much as Ashleigh Elser, Matt Elia, Ash Faulkner, Paul Gleason, Greta Matzner-Gore, Brett and Dana McCarty, and Christina McRorie and Matt Lewis. I am more grateful than I can say to each of you, and this book could not exist without you.

In a book that wishes to attend to the ways we become who we are, in significant part, as a gift received from the hands of others, I am nowhere more conscious of how much I have received from others than when I think of my family. I don't know who I would be without Larry and Amy Lenow, or my brother John and his wife Catheryn, but I know I wouldn't be half as happy or as loved. And for an author who thought he was already aware of how an unexpected encounter can affect everything that follows, changing one's life in ways one couldn't possibly have anticipated, I have felt my life's course utterly and joyfully rerouted by meeting my brilliant wife, Rhody Walker-Lenow. Rho (who insists on me writing – accurately – that she completes me): I love you.

Abbreviations

WSA–	*Works of Saint Augustine: A Translation for the Twenty-First Century,* ed. R. Teske (Hyde Park, NY: New City Press).
ST–	Thomas Aquinas, *Summa Theologiae.* Throughout, I have used the abbreviations of the *Zentrums für Augustinus-Forschung* for the works of St. Augustine, modified with a "*v*" instead of a consonantal "*u.*"
an. et or.	*De anima et eius origine*
civ.	*De civitate dei*
conf.	*Confessionum*
corrept.	*De correptione et gratia*
div.qu.	*De diversis quaestionibus octoginta*
doctr.chr.	*De doctrina christiana*
en.Ps.	*Enarrationes in Psalmos*
ench.	*De fide spe et caritate*
ep.	*Epistulae*
ep.Io.tr.	*In epistulam Iohannis ad Parthos*
exp.prop.Rm.	*Expositio quarundam propositionum ex epistula apostoli ad Romanos*
c.Faust.	*Contra Faustum Manicheum*
Gn.litt.	*De Genesi ad litteram*
gr. et lib. arb.	*De gratia et libero arbitrio*
Io.ev.tr.	*In Iohannis evangelium tractatus CXXIV*
lib.arb.	*De libero arbitrio*
c.Max.	*Contra Maximinum Arrianum*

mor.	*De moribus ecclesiae catholicae et de moribus Manicheorum*
nat. et gr.	*De natura et gratia*
ord.	*De ordine*
persev.	*De dono perseverantiae*
praed. sanct.	*De praedestinatione sanctorum*
retr.	*Retractationum*
s.	*Sermones*
s.Dolbeau	*Sermones* a F. Dolbeau editi
c.s.Arrian.	*Contra sermonem Arrianorum*
trin.	*De trinitate*
vera rel.	*De vera religione*
virg.	*De sancta virginitatat*

Introduction

What do you have that you did not receive? It seems to me that most of the most important parts of my life are things that have happened to me, rather than things I have done. I did not choose to be born when and where I was born; I did not choose to be raised by the people who have raised me; I did not choose to be brought up in the Christian faith, or to be baptized. Yet, had any of these things been different, it seems to me that I would have been an unimaginably different person.

Consider: my understanding of the cosmos and the infinitesimally small piece of it within which I live my life; my understanding of the possibilities of human nature and our ability to move freely on land, sea, and air, or our ability to manipulate the forces of nature through technology; my hopes for my own life, and estimation of the paths open to me – so much of the unquestioned background of my life would be unrecognizable in any era but the turn of the third millennium *anno domini*. But again, at a much more fine-grained level: The way I speak, what I find funny, my personal tics, my faults in character, the things and people I love – all these seem to me more things I have been given than things I have achieved. It is unthinkable to me that I should have ended up the person that I am without having lived in a particular time and a particular place, without having been raised by my father and mother and alongside my brother, without having married the person I love, without having been surrounded by the friends and teachers and mentors who have in fact surrounded me throughout my life.

The situation is even more dramatic when one considers the possible events that have not – but might have – occurred within my life: being born into fabulous wealth or crippling poverty, childhood disease, the early loss of those I love, disability, any of the traumas of abuse or loss that can mark the entirety of one's life, finding myself in the midst of calamity or war. To a significant extent, my life has been made what it is by factors beyond my (in some cases, anyone's) control; it is something I have received, something I have been shaped by, not (or not mostly) something I have fashioned. And it seems to me that the same is true also for you.[1]

It is not that our volition and choices are meaningless. On the contrary, even taking into account the constraints that the circumstances of our lives place on their courses, a fantastic range of possibilities lies open to us. My agency, exercised within the specific contexts within which my life has unfolded, has shaped me to my very deepest levels: I would not be the person that I am had I not made certain choices about the company I keep, the ways I spend my time, and the things I value and believe. At times, these actions and patterns of action suggest a particularity or a shot of originality proper to my createdness that allows me (and you) to step beyond the limits of our social formation, a novelty that shows we are not simply passive products of external forces acting upon us.

At an inescapable level, however, the fact remains that even my volition is in great part responsive to the social world I inhabit. The activities I enjoy; my tastes in food, drink, and entertainment; the

---

[1] We are in this together, you and I; or at least I would like to think we are. A natural question, of course, is who is included (and, accordingly, who is not included) in this "we." In answer, I can do no better than Bernard Williams, who at *Shame and Necessity*, 171 n.7 writes: "The best I can say is that 'we' operates not through a previously fixed designation, but through invitation ... It is not a matter of 'I' telling 'you' what I and others think, but of my asking you to consider to what extent you and I think some things and perhaps need to think others"; Bernard Williams, *Shame and Necessity* (Berkeley, CA: University of California Press, 2008). Ideally, this dialogical "we" would be capacious enough to include even those readers who are hostile to my theological aims here, and who are rightly suspicious of how my "we" encodes the limits of my ability to know and love God and the world truly, to the detriment of others. My hope is that while this "we" will undoubtedly be at times more coercive than I intend and more blinkered than I can see, it also offers a true invitation to be corrected.

material goods I desire; the vocations I can imagine myself pursuing and my notions of the good life – all these have been profoundly influenced by the people around me, the histories in which I am enmeshed, the time in which I live. My desires, even what I want to want, have been cultivated by my relations to what is outside me, and not always for the better: My view of the world and my agency within it have been shaped powerfully by racist and patriarchal social orders, and a host of other affective deformations are attributable (to a greater or lesser extent) to features of my upbringing or the influence of others. The importance of this receptivity to the world within my life is so evident as to be inextricable from my personhood itself – to be a human person is at least in part to stand in relations of this kind, to be determined in certain respects by who and what surrounds me. What indeed have we not received?

This is, I suggest, a constitutive feature of human existence. This is what it is to be a temporal, changeable, social, embodied, thinking, and loving creature. Our lives are given their shapes through our relation to the world in which we find ourselves, both our natural environment and the other people we encounter. To have the singularity of our lives shaped through our interdependence with and vulnerability to others is simply part of what it is to be the sort of creature God has made us. We might, following Hans Frei, call this personal singularity our "identity." In contrast to more philosophically freighted terms like the "self" (with its emphasis on interiority, volition, and reflexive consciousness), "personality" (with its embedded psychological assumptions), or even "numerical identity" (with its existential implications), the term "identity" as I employ it here simply indicates whatever marks a human off as particular, all the characteristics and patterns of action that make up one's particular way of inhabiting the world.[2]

---

[2] So Hans W. Frei, *The Identity of Jesus Christ: The Hermeneutical Bases of Dogmatic Theology* (Eugene, OR: Wipf and Stock, 1997), 95: "Identity is the specific uniqueness of a person, what really counts about him, quite apart from both comparison and contrast

The fundamental claim of this study is that if the Word became truly human, then Jesus Christ also became who he is – assumed his human identity – through the contingent and unpredictable events of life, through his relations to those around him, through his relations to the whole of the created order. Christ's humanity is like ours: "When we consider the flesh, there we find Christ, and in Christ we find both him and ourselves."[3] From all eternity, the Word wills to be the Christ, but he *becomes* the Redeemer in time.[4]

If Jesus Christ is *vere homo*, then at the feet of others he learns obedience and grows in wisdom as he is nursed at the breast of the Blessed Virgin Mary, inherits and is included within the history of Israel in his circumcision, converses with the doctors of the Law in the Temple, is baptized at the hand of John, is confessed to be Lord by Peter, meets the Syrophoenecian woman, finds his friends sleeping in Gethsemane, is betrayed by his companion Judas, teaches about himself on the road to Emmaus, appears to Stephen and to Paul, is praised in hymns by Ambrose and contemplated in his suffering by Julian of Norwich, is acclaimed and worshipped in our own time – all of this marks the man Jesus Christ; all this determines him as the particular human he was and is; and it is, at least in part, *through* these very social and contingent acts that we are freed from the power of death and restored to fellowship with God. The influence of others and the effects of creaturely causes are indispensable in his coming to will as human the salvation of the world, and in his enactment of this will by giving himself over to suffering

---

to others . . . A person's identity is the self-referral, or ascription to him, of his physical and personal states, properties, characteristics, and actions."

[3] *en.Ps.* 142.3; WSA III/20, 347.

[4] The sense in which Christ becomes the Redeemer parallels Frei's description of the achievement of Christ's identity at *The Identity of Jesus Christ*, 146: "The glimpse we are provided within the story of Jesus' intentions is just sufficient to indicate the passage of intention into enactment. And what is given to us is neither intention alone nor action alone, neither inner purpose alone nor external circumstance alone. Rather, he becomes who he is in the coincidence of his enacted intention with the train of circumstances in which the story comes to a head."

and death. Human agency and finite causes are thus included within the providential ordering of God's saving work, and granted a place within the actualization of our reconciliation with Her.[5] Redemption does not occur without this creaturely agency and causality, and so we must understand them – our lives, the life of the world – in their inner unity with Christ's life.

To do so, we will attempt to think with and beyond a theological vision that is staggering in its scope and complexity, drawing together trinitarian theology, theological anthropology, soteriology, and ecclesiology; a theology frequently overlooked in standard

---

[5] The custom of writing about God without employing gendered pronouns has largely superseded the tradition of using exclusively masculine pronouns in academic theology. The case that exclusive use of masculine pronouns functions idolatrously to signify God as more properly male than female has been ably prosecuted by Elizabeth A. Johnson, in *She Who Is: The Mystery of God in Feminist Theological Discourse*, 10th Anniversary Edition (New York: The Crossroad, 2002). Yet I worry that the avoidance of gendered pronouns in theological writing may tend toward a different error: that of depersonalizing God, rendering the lively God of Abraham and Sarah somewhat inert and abstract. The God we encounter in Jesus is a God who knows us, loves us, and desires to draw us into relation with Herself. What's more, the God whom we meet in Christ is a God in whom all human particularities find their origin and to whom they exhibit a likeness – and yet, one who infinitely exceeds those particularities, and all our language. It is to Christ (I will argue in this study) that all these creaturely likenesses point, and through the very particularities of our lives that Christ's life achieves its complete redemptive shape, as the unknowable God is made known in him. For this reason, I refer here to God irregularly using both masculine and feminine pronouns, as well as, occasionally, nonbinarily gendered pronouns (for instance, Ze or the singular They). Denys Turner explains the logic of this practice at *The Darkness of God: Negativity in Christian Mysticism* (Cambridge: Cambridge University Press, 1998), 26: "If we describe God both as male and as female, then we force upon our materialistic imaginations a concrete sense of the collapse of gender-language as such ... It is in the collapse of ordinary language, brought to our attention by the necessity of ascribing incompatible attributes, that the transcendence of God above all language is best approached." Changing irregularly between the gendered pronouns used of God has the virtue of disrupting normatively male theological speech, while making the intrinsic disruptiveness of God-talk apparent in its form. It is my hope that this practice, distracting as it may be, serves a pedagogical practice even in the distracting. To facilitate clarity in light of this decision, I have also adopted the convention of capitalizing the initial letter of all personal pronouns used to refer to God.

narratives of christological development, and so far less utilized within contemporary systematic theology than its generative possibilities would suggest: St. Augustine of Hippo's theology of the *totus Christus*, the whole Christ.

***

It is tempting to portray the whole history of modern christology as an attempt to discern how we might understand Christ, true God and true human, to be implicated in creaturely contingency and human society. From at least Reimarus onward, and accelerating with the publication of D. F. Strauss' *Life of Jesus* and the kenotic christologies of the nineteenth century, modern christology has wrestled with what we might call the problem of the "historicity" of Christ – not the question of reconstructing a historical Jesus, but the question of how christology should regard the significance of history and Jesus' social context. To ask after Christ's historicity in this sense is to ask: What is Christ's debt to Jewish legal thinking, or the apocalyptic tradition of prophecy? How does Christ's ministry reflect his Roman imperial context? Are the ecosystems and environment of Galilee relevant to how we understand Christ's redemptive work? How should recognition of Christ's human inheritance of evolutionary processes shape how we regard the significance of the Cross?[6] The fundamental question of Christ's historicity – the through-line that connects all these subsidiary questions – is

---

[6] Throughout this book, I have employed somewhat idiosyncratic capitalization procedures to assist in making several different theological points. When predicating some term of God substantially – predicating some attribute of the simplicity of the divine life – I have rendered this in capital terms, though if I am simply ascribing a quality to God as a creaturely likeness, I have not. For instance: God is good, but God is also the Good. I have capitalized pronouns referring to the divine life of the Word, but have not capitalized pronouns referencing Christ as one divine-human person or the Word's human life, in recognition of the Word's humility in assuming the *forma servi*. I have also capitalized some terms of art referring exclusively to particular moments of the Word's temporal life: So I will speak at times of the Incarnation or the Cross, but will not capitalize constructions with a general referent subsequently particularized like "the incarnation of the Word" or "the cross of Christ."

this: How should we understand the union of divinity and humanity in Christ, as well as his redemptive life and ministry, in light of the relations to the created order within which he is implicated?

Rather than providing a historical overview of attempts to answer this question, let me offer instead a brief survey of the contemporary christological landscape, identifying four strategies for addressing the problem of Christ's historicity. I do not aspire to offer a detailed map of all the contemporary christological proposals on offer; rather, I hope to chart some of the currents I take to be animating christology at the present time, thus allowing me to situate my own approach within the broader discipline.

My first two strategies map roughly onto the familiar distinction between "christologies from above" and "christologies from below." Yet even here, it is not as simple as marking off the differences between theologies that begin from a "divine Son" or from a "human Jesus"; indeed, many of these contemporary christological proposals explicitly seek to overcome such an opposition of "from above" and "from below." Rather, my first two strategies are identified through attention to where they locate categories like historical becoming and relationality that are needed to account for Christ's historicity.

"Christologies of human relation" – here, roughly, "christologies from below" – foreground the social, political, and cultural context Christ inhabits and its effects upon him.[7] Thinking Christ's historicity here means seeing him as human profoundly implicated within the social and symbolic worlds of his day. This is frequently accomplished by taking research on the "historical Jesus" as the starting point of christological reflection, as, for instance – in markedly

---

[7] Cf. F. LeRon Shults' account of the development of the category of "relation" in theology and philosophy at *Reforming Theological Anthropology: After the Philosophical Turn to Relationality* (Grand Rapids, MI: Wm. B. Eerdmans, 2003), as well as Mayra Rivera's attention to "flesh" as a site of liberatory mutualistic relation at *Poetics of the Flesh* (Durham, NC: Duke University Press, 2015).

different ways – in the work of John Hick, Roger Haight, Jon Sobrino, M. Shawn Copeland, and Elizabeth Johnson.[8]

This christological trajectory has significant theoretical virtues: Of the four strategies I will consider, this first approach has arguably had the greatest success in taking on board the insights and accounting for the christological complexities introduced by modern historical research on Christ. What's more, it has demonstrated how attention to historical study of Jesus can function as a way of recovering theological awareness of Christ's creative and often subversive engagement in the oppressive sociopolitical structures of the Ancient Near East. Following Christ is thus acknowledged to entail participation in contemporary struggles for liberation from the dominative structures of our own day. All this is, in my judgment, theologically salutary.

Yet there are also potential limitations to this strategy. Most basically, it is not always clear how these thinkers correlate attention to Christ's implication in the social world with his divine identity. The methodological turn to the "historical Jesus" as a starting point for christology is often complemented by a critique of the categories of classical christology: substance,

---

[8] *The Myth of God Incarnate*, ed. John Hick (London: SCM Press, 1977); John Hick, *The Metaphor of God Incarnate: Christology in a Pluralistic Age* (Louisville, KY: Westminster John Knox Press, 2005 [1993]); Roger Haight, *Jesus, Symbol of God* (Maryknoll, NY: Orbis Books, 1999); Jon Sobrino, *Jesus the Liberator: A Historical-Theological Reading of Jesus of Nazareth*, trans. Paul Burns and Francis McDonagh (Maryknoll, NY: Orbis Books, 1991), 36–66; M. Shawn Copeland, *Knowing Christ Crucified: The Witness of African-American Religious Experience* (Maryknoll, NY: Orbis Books, 2018), and M. Shawn Copeland, "Meeting and Seeing Jesus: The Witness of African American Religious Experience," in *Jesus of Galilee: Contextual Christology for the 21st Century*, ed. Robert Lasalle-Klein (Maryknoll, NY: Orbis Books, 2011), 67–84; and Elizabeth A. Johnson, *Creation and the Cross: The Mercy of God for a Planet in Peril* (Maryknoll, NY: Orbis Books, 2019), 64–112. While Copeland and Johnson (and, to a lesser but nevertheless still significant extent, Sobrino) share a methodological starting-point with Hick and Haight in historical Jesus research, I take them to be far more successful in maintaining a Chalcedonian theology, and hope that the present project serves to supplement and nuance their christological proposals.

person, nature, and so on.[9] Yet without these categories, it can be unclear how the rich and historically situated picture of Jesus should be theologically related to the Second Person of the Trinity. Sobrino, for instance, at times seems to speak of two subjects in Christ: a human person with his own proper existence but whose life is inseparably bound to that of the Word.[10] Charitably, this suggests that Sobrino's account requires further development if it is to close off the possibility of a Nestorian interpretation – and such development will likely require exactly the christological categories (or parallel ones) that Sobrino had previously critiqued. One finds no such unclarity in Hick and Haight, by contrast; yet precision about the relation between Jesus and the Word at the expense of confession of Christ's divinity. For Hick and Haight, confession of Christ's literal divinity suggests a form of "docetism": to the extent that is the all-knowing and all-powerful God, he cannot be truly human; and if Christ is truly human as we are, we cannot in any "literal sense" say that he is God.[11] Nothing in this first strategy leads inevitably to this endpoint, of course. It does, however, suggest that those seeking to think Christ's historicity while maintaining the teachings of Chalcedonian orthodoxy may encounter difficulties if a starting point in historical research on Jesus goes unsupplemented by a more robustly developed technical christological language.

---

[9] Cf. Jon Sobrino, *Christ the Liberator: A View from the Victims*, trans. Paul Burns (Maryknoll, NY: Orbis Books, 2001), 242–243.

[10] Cf. Sobrino's statement at *Christ the Liberator*, 223: "the limited human is predicated of God, but the unlimited divine is not predicated of Jesus."

[11] The denial of a "literal sense" of Christ's divinity is found at Hick, *Metaphor of God Incarnate*, 12. Of Hick, Herbert McCabe has written, "For Professor John Hick, it is all rather simple: He writes as though no one had hitherto observed the oddness of ascribing two natures to Jesus"; McCabe, "The Myth of God Incarnate," *New Blackfriars* 58.687 (1977): 350–357, 352–353. John Cavadini has similarly critiqued Haight's theology as encoding a "principle of separation" into christology; see John C. Cavadini, "Jesus, Symbol of God," *Commonweal* 126.17 (1999): 22–24.

A second strategy, "christologies of divine relation," draws the categories of historicity – especially personhood, becoming, and relationality – into the divine life itself. As such, this christological outlook tends to operate (though not invariably so) "from above." This strategy encompasses attempts to rethink the ontology of divine personhood through the category of relation (Catherine LaCugna, John Zizioulas); often relatedly, social trinitarian theologies that view the divine essence itself as composed of the relations between the three persons (Colin Gunton, William Hasker, Jürgen Moltmann, Cornelius Plantinga, Richard Swinburne); theologies that draw historical becoming into the divine life itself (Robert Jenson, Wolfhart Pannenberg); and theologies which view the divine life as itself a process of becoming (John Cobb and David Ray Griffin, Catherine Keller).[12] Though quite diverse, this strategy takes the category of relation as central to the divine life: either an incredibly strong sense of the relations obtaining between the trinitarian persons, or an understanding of the relation between God and the created order in which some part of (in this case, usually Christ's human life) or the whole of creation are definitive of the life of God.

---

[12] See Catherine Mowry LaCugna, *God For Us: The Trinity and Christian Life* (San Francisco, CA: HarperCollins, 1991); John D. Zizioulas, *Being as Communion: Studies in Personhood and the Church* (Crestwood, NY: St. Vladimir's Seminary Press, 1985); Colin E. Gunton, *The Promise of Trinitarian Theology* (Edinburgh: T&T Clark, 1991); William Hasker, *Metaphysics and the Tri-Personal God* (Oxford: Oxford University Press, 2017); Jürgen Moltmann, *The Trinity and the Kingdom: The Doctrine of God*, trans. Margaret Kohl (Minneapolis, MN: Fortress Press, 1993 [1980]); Cornelius Plantinga, Jr., "Social Trinity and Tritheism," in *Trinity, Incarnation, and Atonement: Philosophical and Theological Essays*, eds. Ronald J. Feenstra and Cornelius Plantinga, Jr. (Notre Dame, IN: University of Notre Dame Press, 1989): 21–47; Richard Swinburne, *The Christian God* (Oxford: Oxford University Press, 1994); Robert W. Jenson, *Systematic Theology, Vol. 1: The Triune God* (Oxford: Oxford University Press, 1997), and *Systematic Theology, Vol. 2: The Works of God* (Oxford, Oxford University Press, 1999); Wolfhart Pannenberg, *Systematic Theology*, Vol. 1, trans. Geoffrey W. Bromiley (Grand Rapids, MI: Wm. B. Eerdmans, 1991 [1988]); John B. Cobb, Jr. and David Ray Griffin, *Process Theology: An Introductory Exposition* (Louisville, KY: Westminster John Knox Press, 1976); Catherine Keller, *On the Mystery: Discerning Divinity in Progress* (Minneapolis, MN: Fortress Press, 2008).

Where christologies of human relation had, at times, difficulties (or disinterest) in maintaining a full-throated confession of the one person of Christ as both *vere Deus* and *vere homo*, the principal virtue of this second strategy is in holding to Christ's full divinity without sacrificing his historicity. These theologies judge significant changes in classical teachings about the divine life to be the price of maintaining Christ's historicity, and are willing to pay it. Though my project regards these costs as finally unnecessary, and thus holds to an understanding of the divine life standing in far greater continuity with Patristic and Medieval theological reflection, I believe these theologians have accurately judged the importance of confessing Christ's historicity. More than that, I largely agree with their assessment that *something* needs to change in the classical christological tradition, for it has too often given us a Christ who seems unaffected in any serious way by the world around him. The diagnosis is correct, even if I take the treatment to be unsuccessful.

The limitations of this approach stem, on my understanding, from an insufficient apophaticism, and an attendant incaution in applying the categories of our experience of creation to the divine life. Whether these theologians of divine relation explicitly or only implicitly reject the doctrine of God's incomprehensibility, the language in which they articulate their doctrines of God uniformly oversteps the boundaries of what would be admitted within Patristic thought.[13] The question Karen Kilby poses of social trinitarianism might appropriately be put to all christologies that attempt to secure Christ's historicity by importing categories like becoming or relation into God's life: "Where exactly, one might wonder, did they acquire such a vivid feeling for the inner life of the deity?"[14] Christ's historicity is preserved, but only by making God

---

[13] For a critique of the use of Patristic theology by social trinitarians, see Sarah Coakley, "'Persons' in the 'Social' Doctrine of the Trinity: Current Analytic Discussion and 'Cappadocian' Theology," in *Powers and Submissions*, 110–129.

[14] Karen Kilby, "Perichoresis and Projection: Problems with Social Doctrines of the Trinity," *New Blackfriars* 81.956 (2000): 432–445, 439.

more like us – more like us, I worry, than is appropriate, given the Christian tradition's classical emphasis on the otherness of God and the unknowability of the divine life.

Indeed, when treated together, these first two strategies indicate a common tendency to conceive of the relationship between God and creation as competitive.[15] A competitive relation between two beings imagines them as potentially inhabiting the same theoretical "space," whether one is talking about physical space (two chairs cannot occupy exactly the same space at the same time), agency (to the extent that I am coerced to perform an action, my freedom is diminished), or use of common resources (if you redirect the river water for agricultural irrigation, there is less drinking water available for the settlement downstream). This competition can be observed in the way that attention to Christ's historicity appears as a "zero-sum" game in these first two strategies: Too strong an emphasis on Jesus' divinity will docetically undermine his full humanity (so Hick and Haight); or taking seriously the confession that this particular human is true God requires us to reconceive the divine nature so as to resemble human nature more closely, thus pushing us to attribute categories like history, temporality, and becoming to the divine life (so the various christologies of divine relation). Either the divinity of Christ must be occluded by his humanity, or divinity must be conformed to humanity such that there is no conflict between them. The common presupposition here – whether implicit or explicit – is that divinity and humanity exist on a shared ontological plane, such that the attributes of God might be thought to conflict with the attributes of humanity in Christ; or, alternatively, such that the attributes characteristic of created nature might rightly be predicated of God's life in eternity. In either case, Christ's humanity serves a regulative function here,

---

[15] This manner of phrasing the critique is obviously indebted to the work of Kathryn Tanner, whose christological approach will be considered more fully below in my discussion of the fourth strategy for addressing Christ's historicity.

to the detriment of his full divinity or at least to the end of altering a classical conception of divinity.

A third strategy, what I am calling "christologies of divine identity," attempts to overcome this contrastive picture. On this account, it is precisely the divine identity of Christ – his identity as the Word of God, the Second Person of the Trinity – that founds and exhaustively determines his human particularity. His human willing, desires, self-knowledge, sense of vocation – all these straightforwardly proceed from the willing, desire, self-knowledge, and mission that are the eternal life of the Word, for the person of Christ *is* the person of the Word. Conceived thusly, it is difficult to see what Christ's relations to the created order actually contribute to the shape of his human life. He certainly exists within created history, but the shape of his human life is given directly by the fact that he is the Word, his humanity serving as a temporal expression of the Word's life quite apart from the relationships Christ has with those around him. So, for instance, Thomas Aquinas will write that Christ has no human teachers, on account of his perfected intellect, and later Thomists will argue extensively that all Christ's human mental acts must correspond to the Word's divine intellection.[16] Karl Barth writes:

> We have a picture of the sayings and acts of Jesus Christ in His entry into and life within Galilee within the wider and narrower circle of His disciples, the multitudes, and the spiritual and (on the margin) the political leaders of the people. Jesus over against and in the midst of His disciples stands out in marked contrast to this whole world of men. He belongs to it, and He intensively addresses Himself to it, but He is a stranger within it.[17]

Christ's is an alien within this world of temporal contingency. This is not, of course, to be read as denying Christ's true entry into

---

[16] *ST* III.12.4ad.2; these points are discussed more extensively at Chapter 5, below.

[17] Karl Barth, *Church Dogmatics* IV/1, eds. Geoffrey W. Bromiley and Thomas F. Torrance, trans. G. W. Bromiley (Edinburgh: T&T Clark, 1956), 224.

created history, but rather as Barth's emphasizing the *terms on which* Christ enters into history: as Lord, as the perfect covenant-partner of God who is set against humanity's attempts at self-mastery, as the one who is perfectly obedient precisely because he is the eternal Son of God. There is little room for creaturely relation to add anything to Jesus' identity, for his identity is wholly and completely determined by his divinity. In the words of John Webster, one of Barth's most compelling successors, "The church adds nothing to the identity of the exalted Son."[18] This is not merely an ecclesiological principle: The identity of Christ must wholly depend on the Son, for anything else would undermine Christ's ability to serve as the image of God's perfection and aseity.[19] As Webster concludes, "his identity is antecedently replete; as himself *autotheos*, his identity as Son is given him by the Father in full measure."[20] Alongside many contemporary Thomists and Barthians, some followers of Hans Urs von Balthasar may be included as representatives of this third strategy, as Christ plays out in history the role he already occupies in the drama of the divine life. The Son's personhood is given wholly in obedience to the Father through the Spirit, the immediacy of the intra-triune relations utterly determining the course of his human life.[21]

---

[18] John Webster, "'In the Society of God': Some Principles of Ecclesiology," in *God without Measure: God and the Works of God*, Vol. 1 (London: Bloomsbury T&T Clark, 2016), 177–194; 186. See also a useful discussion drawing together Robert Jenson, Webster, and Augustine's doctrine of the *totus Christus* at J. David Moser, "*Totus Christus*: A Proposal for Protestant Theology and Ecclesiology," *Pro Ecclesia* 29.1 (2020): 3–30.

[19] John Webster, "The Church and the Perfection of God," in *The Community of the Word*, eds. Mark Husbands and Daniel J. Treier (Downers Grove, IL: InterVarsity Press, 2005), 75–95. See also Webster's cautions against theologies of *totus Christus* at "'In the Society of God,'" 185.

[20] Webster, "'In the Society of God,'" 187.

[21] Troy A. Stefano, "Christology after Schleiermacher: Three Twentieth-Century Christologies," in *The Oxford Handbook of Christology*, eds. Francesca Aran Murphy and Troy A. Stefano (Oxford: Oxford University Press, 2015), 362–377; 373–375. This critique is advanced more tentatively in Balthasar's case, as his thought certainly

Where the previous strategies gave Christ's humanity a regulative function in christology, this third strategy preserves God's priority in accounting for the shape of Christ's life. Christologies of divine identity are (to my mind, admirably) uncompromising in maintaining that when we have to do with the human Jesus Christ, we have to do with the God and Creator of all things. Christ's life is the perfect manifestation of the triune Lord, and the perfect accomplishment of God's redemptive will. What's more, such theologies make clear that the agency of the creaturely order – even Christ's human agency – stands in a secondary position to the agency of God. All this will be preserved in my account below.

To be clear: The person of Christ is the person of the Word. There is no human subject in him that possesses existence independently of humanity's assumption by the Word, and Jesus just is the human life of God. My critique of this third strategy does not rest upon any rejection of the fundamental christological claims underlying the theologies of Aquinas, Barth, Webster, Balthasar, or other theologians whose work might be described as christologies of divine identity. Rather, I question the ease with which these theologies move from the fact of the Incarnation to its consequences for the life of Christ.

Precisely in conceiving of Christ as a stranger in the world, christologies of divine identity exhibit a lingering tendency to conceive of the relationship between God and creation as competitive. If Christ is truly God, such accounts maintain, the particular features of his humanity can be fully accounted for by his identity as the divine Son of God. Rowan Williams, following Erich Przywara, has recently warned against conceiving of the relationship between God and creation (in Christ, no less than in more general terms) as

---

allows for a greater contribution to the redemptive form of Christ's life than does that of Thomas or Barth, particularly in his surprisingly approbative reflections on Hegel in *Theo-Logic* III. See Mark A. McIntosh, *Christology from Within: Spirituality and the Incarnation in Hans Urs von Balthasar* (South Bend, IN: University of Notre Dame Press, 1996); and Junius Johnson, *Christ and Analogy: The Christocentric Metaphysics of Hans Urs von Balthasar* (Minneapolis, MN: Fortress Press, 2013).

a "'linear' connection between a supposed finite perfection and the perfection of the infinite."[22] Such a linear connection might easily lead us "to mythologize the confession of Jesus as God, or to treat it as an identity statement of the most problematic kind."[23] A linear connection of this sort underwrites an unproblematic movement from claims about the Word's divine life to claims about Christ's human action: The Word knows, so Christ must humanly know what the Word knows or he is not truly God; the Word loves, so what Christ loves may be straightforwardly derived from the Word's eternal reality, uninfluenced by (never mind dependent upon) what he has been taught to love by the people around him or the practices in which he engages. Christ is, as Barth writes, a stranger – one whose human identity is independent of those around him, because wholly determined by the Word.

As I will argue more extensively below, this conception of Christ's human identity both misunderstands the radical difference of the divine life from anything in the created order, and underestimates the extent to which the created order has been drawn into God's redemptive work in Christ. By grace and God's providential order, the existence and agency of creation have been drawn into the life of Christ, employed to shape the human life of the Redeemer. Without abandoning the christological claims that govern christologies of divine identity, this book will argue against such approaches that Christ is not who he is – does not bear the human identity he has, with its knowledge, loves, and redemptive purpose – without us.

The fourth strategy for thinking Christ's historicity thus begins from an explicitly noncompetitive construal of the relationship between God and the created order. Following Ian McFarland, we may call it a "Chalcedonianism without reserve."[24] As Kathryn

---

[22] Rowan Williams, *Christ the Heart of Creation* (London: Bloomsbury Continuum, 2018), 235.

[23] Williams, *Christ the Heart of Creation*, 253.

[24] Ian A. McFarland, *The Word Made Flesh: A Theology of the Incarnation* (Louisville, KY: Westminster John Knox Press, 2019), 1.

Tanner writes of theological noncompetition, "God does not give on the same plane of being and activity as creatures, as one among other givers and therefore God is not in potential competition (or cooperation) with them."[25] If God is active, this does not entail that we must be passive: God's noncompetitive relation to the world means that God may freely act in creation without our freedom or activity being diminished thereby.

As seen in the works of scholars like Tanner, McFarland, Rowan Williams, Graham Ward, Aaron Riches, and Paul DeHart, this structure of noncompetition is as significant within christology as it is within broader construals of the God-world relation.[26] Our commitment to Chalcedonianism can *be* unreserved because Christ's divinity is not exclusive of his true humanity. Similarly, the distinction between these two natures is not undone: The fully historical human life of Christ poses no problem for the eternity of the divine life; we do not need to import categories like "history" into the divine life, for the Word truly lives historically in Christ's humanity. This opens a compelling new option for thinking Christ's historicity: The foundation of Christ's identity in the person of the Word is not exclusive of his human life being responsive to, or even shaped by, the people around him and the world of which he is a part. Indeed, as recent christologies of "deep incarnation" have argued the Word's assumption of flesh pushes us to see Christ's implication in all manner of relations to the nonhuman world and the processes of nature.[27] Christ's divinity does not exclude

---

[25] Kathryn Tanner, *Jesus, Humanity, and the Trinity: A Brief Systematic Theology* (Minneapolis, MN: Fortress Press, 2001), 3.

[26] Kathryn Tanner, *Christ the Key* (Cambridge: Cambridge University Press, 2010); Williams, *Christ the Heart of Creation*; Graham Ward, *Christ and Culture* (Oxford: Wiley-Blackwell, 2005); Aaron Riches, *Ecce Homo: On the Divine Unity of Christ* (Grand Rapids, MI: Wm. B. Eerdmans, 2016); Paul J. DeHart, *Unspeakable Cults: An Essay in Christology* (Waco, TX: Baylor University Press, 2021).

[27] The best entry point to theologies of "deep incarnation" remains the essays collected at *Incarnation: On the Scope and Depth of Christology*, ed. Niels Henrik Gregersen (Minneapolis, MN: Fortress Press, 2015).

his receiving in significant part his human identity through relation to the world – the very identity that is the Word's human life, the manifestation of God in creation.

The argument of this book stands resolutely within this discourse on christological noncompetition, and within the wide range of christologies arguing for an understanding of deep incarnation.[28] If I have any criticism to offer of this fourth strategy, it is that I believe these thinkers still have not gone far enough. While they offer a compelling account of the unity of divinity and humanity in Christ and make space for a real account of his implication within the created order, they have not yet fully integrated this Chalcedonianism without reserve into their accounts of Christ's redemptive work. Yet acknowledgment of the noncompetitive relation between divinity and humanity in Christ uncovers a new possibility, understanding our lives and agency as *drawn into* the work of redemption – not only as a consequence of Christ's life, the subjective outworking of what is objectively accomplished in the Cross and Resurrection, but in the very work of Incarnation itself. There are glimpses of this possibility especially in Tanner and Ward; Ward, for instance, tells us, "Jesus is the Christ only in relation to other human beings; the act of redemption is a relational act; Christology needs to pay more attention not only to the identity of the God-man, but to the redemptive operation effected in and through this complex co-abiding," and further, "Jesus Christ as God incarnate can of himself only reveal to the extent he is recognised; he can only reconcile and redeem all to the

---

[28] For my estimation of some of the ambiguities, but also the great promise, of the christological project of deep incarnation, see Joseph E. Lenow, "Christ, the Praying Animal: A Critical Engagement with Niels Henrik Gregersen and the Christology of Deep Incarnation," *International Journal of Systematic Theology* 20.4 (2018): 554–578; and Joseph E. Lenow, "Following the Deeply Incarnate Christ: Discipleship in the Midst of Environmental Crisis," in *God in the Natural World: Theological Explorations in Appreciation of Denis Edwards*, eds. Marie Turner and Ted Peters (Adelaide: ATF Theology, 2020), 313–328.

extent he is responded to. Christology begins with the operation of Christ 'between.'"[29]

These suggestions are tantalizing, perhaps even shocking – can we really say that Jesus is the Christ only in relation to other human beings? Can the historicity of Christ really be so important that redemption does not occur without Christ's relational act? A Chalcedonianism without reserve opens a pathway to answering these questions by arguing that Christ's true divinity is not exclusive of his true – and therefore profoundly relational – humanity; yet it leaves these possibilities decidedly underdeveloped. That is the project this study takes up.

***

But why Augustine? What might a *ressourcement* of his christological approach have to offer contemporary theology, as it attempts to understand Christ both truly as the incarnate Word, and truly defined by relation to the world as all human lives are? An answer emerges slowly, suggested rather than declared by moments of christological insight scattered throughout Augustine's texts: Christ telling his disciples on Mount Olivet that when they give to the poor, they are giving to him; Christ calling out from our condition of godforsakenness on the Cross; Christ identifying himself with his persecuted ecclesial Body to Saul on the Road to Damascus.

Augustine's reflection upon these Scriptural and other similar incidents are at the heart of perhaps the most distinctive feature of his christology – his teaching on the *totus Christus*, the whole Christ. In this trope, which runs throughout nearly the whole of Augustine's writings, we encounter a Christ who is distinguishable from, but also inseparable from his Body. The Church and Christ

---

[29] Ward, *Christ and Culture*, 106; 149. Cf. also Tanner, *Jesus, Humanity, and the Trinity*, 54, cited below at 92 n.47. See also John Milbank, "The Name of Jesus," in *The Word Made Strange: Theology, Language, and Culture* (Oxford: Blackwell, Ltd., 1997), 145–168.

are together one person: It is his voice that speaks in us, and our voice that we hear in him; it is he, no less than us, that suffers in our suffering, conquers in our redemption, loves as we cleave to God; it is our life that he assumes for our redemption, and his life that we will enjoy in everlasting blessedness with the triune God.

Christ's life, both before and after his resurrection and ascension, is bound to the particularities of our human lives; more strongly, Christ's human life is unintelligible apart from us. Without his union not only to human nature, but to the very concreteness of our flesh, it is unimaginable that his human life should have unfolded in the way it did. Without being united to our condition of sin, Christ cannot offer up the Cry of Dereliction from the Cross; without being united to the Church, he cannot ask Saul why he is persecuted. For Augustine, Christ's life is bound up with ours in a manner that shapes both incarnation and redemption – and it is this that allows us to see Augustine's thought as opening toward the theological question of Christ's historicity.

Tarsicius van Bavel, one of the most perceptive interpreters of Augustine's christology, sees clearly the connection between the theology of the *totus Christus* and the question of Christ's implication within created history. Writing on what he calls the "background to the notion of the 'whole Christ'," he steps to the very edge of what is sayable within the bounds of Augustine's own christology:

> Without the countless people who surround us, and their influence upon us, we would not be who we are. This includes the influence of parents, brothers and sisters, teachers, friends and all the many people that we meet during our lives. Our personality is not formed in isolation; a very large part of our thinking, our feelings, our knowledge and knowing, our attention and effort for others is thanks to others. Hence we are able to say not only that the individual constitutes the community, but also that the community constitutes the individual ... Different possible interpretations exist with regard to biblical notions of community. But the essence of each of these

interpretations is communication and relationship. A first interpretation is that of physical alliance by descent ... A second interpretation is that of a continuous influence of the whole community upon
the individual and of the individual upon the community. A third
interpretation is that of free identification through relationships
between people, in the way that these are realised through faith,
hope, and love. In this identification through love, people share in
one another's lives, thoughts, actions, feelings, dealings, skills, good
characteristics, needs etc ... I feel that these three interpretations may
be applied to the notion of the "whole Christ."[30]

From one vantage point, the whole of this book should be considered
a development of this insight. If the theology of the *totus Christus* is to
be more than a metaphor (as it clearly is within Augustine's thought),
or a hermeneutical strategy to get Augustine around some particularly sticky exegetical difficulties, or a gesture to mysticism that
forecloses further theological investigation, it must depend on something like what van Bavel proffers here. If we are truly to say that
Christ and the Church are one person, we must recognize the ways
that Christ's human life is already, from the moment of his birth,
bound up with the lives of others: the ancestors and even the evolutionary histories that are the deep history of the flesh he takes from
Mary; the communities into which he is born, and particularly the
people of Israel who are the elected covenant-partners of the God
who Christ is; the parents, friends, disciples, strangers, even the
enemies to whom Christ binds himself in love and who are subsequently bound to him by the work of the Holy Spirit.

Pursuing the course indicated by van Bavel, this book develops
Augustine's suggestive and generative christological reflections into
a theology of the whole Christ, the person of the incarnate Word
considered together with the connections he bears to the created

---

[30] Tarsicius J. van Bavel, "The Concept of the 'Whole Christ'," in *Saint Augustine*, eds.
Tarsicius van Bavel and Bernard Bruning (Brussels: Mercatorfonds/Augustinian
Historical Institute, 2007): 263–271; 266–267.

order. This Augustinian starting point will allow us to trace out a systematic project in which Christ's historicity is not only a marker of his true humanity, but is included within Christ's redemptive work itself. Our lives are not only bound to Christ through the reconciliation with God he effects through Cross and Resurrection: We become to one another the very instruments through which Christ accomplishes our redemption.

The danger, of course, is that the *totus Christus* is simply taken as a motif, disconnected from the deep structure of Augustine's thought and mobilized in service of yet another theological valorization of relationality.[31] I have chosen Augustine as interlocutor in this project not simply because I find the *totus Christus* a valuable tool for approaching Christ's historicity, but because I believe that the scope and clarity of Augustine's christological project is almost unmatched within the history of Christian thought. As we will see, Augustine's theology of the *totus Christus* draws and indeed depends upon virtually every aspect of his thought. It is impossible to understand Augustine's teaching on the Incarnation without understanding his theology of the Trinity, and his account of the distinction between God and creation. We cannot understand the many different approaches he models for thinking about the Cross without properly assessing his teaching on sin, and the moral psychology within which this teaching on sin unfolds. Augustine's account of the Church as Christ's Body must be appreciated as mutually constitutive with his political theology, his construal of our reconciliation to God can only be understood in light of his eschatology, and none of this can be done without attention to an account of predestination which can only properly be appreciated in light of God's timelessness.

---

[31] Jenson's *Systematic Theology*, for instance, puts forward the *totus Christus* as a central description of Christ's relation to the Church, but loses the theoretical resources necessary to distinguish between Head and Body precisely in his radical transformation of an Augustinian account of the divine life.

The theology of the *totus Christus* provides a kind of synecdoche of Augustine's thought: Christ is a focal point of Augustine's theological outlook, the *civitas* to which all his intellectual pathways finally lead, much as within this theology Christ is the cornerstone of humanity's eternal life with God. Recovering Augustine's teaching on the *totus Christus* thus offers us a new standpoint for evaluating his theology as a whole, uncovering both moments where his theology exhibits a greater coherence than has previously been recognized, and points of lingering ambiguity where constructive systematic theology can productively extend christological reflection beyond the limits of Augustine's own thought.

For all its richness and insight, the distinctive lines of Augustine's christology are only now beginning to come into focus within the field of Patristic theology. Within the realm of contemporary systematic theology, his christology is shockingly underutilized, largely passed over in preference for the more familiar lines of the Greek fathers, medieval scholastics, or later Protestant dogmaticians. Augustine was not a significant part of the great christological controversy that broke out in his last years. Though he was issued an invitation to the Council of Ephesus, the emperor Theodosius who summoned him was unaware that Augustine had died several months before.[32] Augustine's christological reflections have suffered for many years through comparison with the christological controversy in the East: Though Augustine's position stands at least in significant continuity with what will come to be regarded as the orthodox doctrinal position at the Councils of Ephesus and Chalcedon, the terms in which Augustine conducts his reflections on the person and work of Christ are sufficiently different than those of Cyril of Alexandria that Augustine's own perspectives may at first glance simply appear undeveloped.[33]

---

[32] George A. Bevan, "Augustine and the Western dimension of the Nestorian controversy," *Studia Patristica* XLIX (2010): 347–352; 347.

[33] Cf. Brian E. Daley, "A Humble Mediator: The Distinctive Elements in Saint Augustine's Christology," *Word and Spirit* 9 (1987): 100–117; 100–101.

This famously led Harnack to conclude that Augustine "influenced the piety of Western Christians by a doctrine of grace which met their lower inclinations, as well as by a promulgation of the immediateness of the religious relationship which failed to do justice to Christ's significance as mirror of God's fatherly heart and as the eternal mediator."[34] Later interpreters were scarcely more forgiving. Grillmeier judges that Augustine "does not always distinguish between the 'historical' and the 'mystical' person, between the individual and the total Christ. This gives his statements about the historical Christ the characteristic inconsistency which is also a feature of his picture of the *Christus totus.*"[35] For much of the hundred years that followed Harnack, Augustine's Christology was rarely a focus of research in historical study; as late as 1971, William Babcock could still write that the few existing studies were "isolated markers in a landscape that is largely blank."[36]

This situation has substantially changed in the years since Babcock's still-unpublished dissertation. Within the study of Early Christianity, a mid-century revival of interest in Augustine's christology has served as the foundation on which at least a generation of Anglophone Augustine scholarship has now built. Contemporary scholars working in the disciplines of historical, systematic, and moral theology have nurtured a vibrant Augustinian theological culture that increasingly sees christology as one of the animating forces of Augustine's thought.

---

[34] Adolph Harnack, *History of Dogma*, Vol. 5, trans. Neil Buchanan (Boston, MA: Little, Brown, 1905), 87.

[35] Aloys Grillmeier, *Christ in Christian Tradition*, Vol. 1, trans. J. S. Bowden (New York: Sheed and Ward, 1964), 327–328.

[36] William Babcock, "The Christ of the Exchange: A Study in the Christology of Augustine's Enarrationes in Psalmos" (Unpublished, Ph.D. dissertation, Yale University, 1972), 2. A much more exhaustive and incredibly illuminating discussion of the history of scholarship on Augustine's christology can be found at Dominic Keech, *The Anti-Pelagian Christology of Augustine of Hippo, 396–430* (Oxford: Oxford University Press, 2012), 9–14.

These christological reflections show him to be, in many respects, well at home among his Greek-speaking contemporaries: He speaks confidently of Christ as the one who is sent by the Father to manifest the invisible God to a creation that had turned away. He shares many enemies in common with the Cappadocian Fathers, arguing against hazily defined groups of "Arians" and "Apollinarians." In other respects, Augustine shows himself to be the inheritor of a particularly Latin christological culture, specifically employing Tertullian's "formula of the unity of person in a duality of substances" and Novatian's "principle of the distinction of operations in Christ: He does some things as God, others as man – *qua Deus, qua homo.*"[37] And again, some of what I judge to be the most insightful features of Augustine's christology emerge as he returns again and again to his own theological preoccupations: time and eternity; memory; language and signification; history and eschatology; grace and predestination. Brian Daley, in particular, has identified three distinctive features of Augustine's christology: use of the analogy of the soul's union with the body to understand the Incarnation as an "unconfused union," in which the Word is truly united to a human soul and body without change; an emphasis on Christ's humanity, and especially his humility, as the site of mediation by which God draws our loves and our intellects away from sin; and attention to the Incarnation as a work of unmerited grace, prefiguring our own gracious predestination.[38] These initial leads are held together, and indeed radiate outward through all Augustine's thought, in his theology of the *totus Christus.*

Throughout this study, I will offer my own constructive theological proposal by tracing the contours of Augustine's christological emphases. Part I roots my christological reflection in a broadly Augustinian account of God's noncompetitive relation

---

[37] John McGuckin, "Did Augustine's Christology Depend on Theodore of Mopsuestia?", *The Heythrop Journal* 31.1 (1990): 39–52, 45.

[38] Daley, "A Humble Mediator," 103–110. Paralleling, though not identical to, Daley's elucidation of the central or distinctive elements of Augustine's christology is Keech's, at *Anti-Pelagian Christology*, 10–12.

to the created order. Chapter 1 articulates this through reflection upon God's transcendence of creation – an apophatic transcendence even of theological speech – recognition of which grounds the characteristically Augustinian emphases on God's immutability, incomprehensibility, triune simplicity, and inseparable trinitarian operations toward the world. Chapter 2 considers how such a transcendent God may nevertheless become incarnate, developing a richer account of theological noncompetition through attention to God's timelessness. Part II develops this noncompetitive frame into the heart of my Augustinian christological proposal, considering and extending in Chapter 3 Augustine's theology of the *totus Christus*. Chapter 4 puts flesh on the bones of this Augustinian christology, drawing upon contemporary historical and Biblical scholarship in a manner inspired by Augustine's reflections on history and Scripture to consider Christ's human responsiveness to the nonhuman world and his sociopolitical and religious context. Chapter 5 addresses questions to which Augustine frequently returns in his christological reflections about the corruptibility of the Word's flesh, the (im)possibility of ignorance in his human life, and the perfection of his human loves. Chapter 6 attends to Christ's humanity as the point of mediation between humanity and God, considering his place as the redemptive and purifying sign that points our hearts back to God. Chapter 7 focuses especially on the Cross, in both its significatory function and as it concretely effects our liberation from the power of sin and death. Part III considers how, by the Spirit's work, Christ's Body is completed and his human life receives its full shape through the existence and agency of those united to him. Chapter 8 focuses upon the relationship between christology and the Spirit's work, particularly the gracious renovation of our loves as Christ comes to live in us. Chapter 9 expands this discussion to the level of community, asking how the reordering of our loves constitutes a community in which Christ may live. Chapter 10 takes Augustine's theology of the

Resurrection and Ascension, and the need to discern his presence even in absence, as a prompt to attend concretely to the communities in which Christ is living today, particularly the poor and oppressed. Chapter 11 situates Christ's resurrection within Augustine's eschatology, considering finally whether the Body of Christ might validly be considered an extension of the Incarnation.

When these christological concerns are foregrounded, a new Augustine emerges into view, one who has frequently been obscured in the nearly sixteen hundred years since his death. This perhaps unfamiliar, richly christocentric Augustine avoids many of the critiques commonly directed at Augustinian thought.[39] Answering those who find in Augustine a flight from worldly contingency and temporality, we find a transcendence that plunges itself into the created order, telling us that if we would be redeemed we must do the same in service to our neighbor. Addressing the concerns of those who believe Augustine's theology is governed by an antipathy for the body or sexuality, we discover that it is through love of and action within the material world – through finding our bodily particularity and mutual loving vulnerability enfolded within the body of God – that we are saved. Replying to those who find Augustine's view of history overly determined by an anti-liberal tendency toward authoritarianism and political intolerance, we reclaim a sense of the gratuity of Christ's advent, finding that our Lord often comes to us from the very individuals and communities that sin's distortive effects had previously allowed us to see only as outsiders or enemies. Recovery of Augustine's christology is not simply a plea for greater historical accuracy or a theological curio – it offers critical leverage in curbing the worst excesses of the Augustinian tradition, and

---

[39] Williams outlines them at *On Augustine*, viii: "Augustine's alleged responsibility for Western Christianity's supposed obsession with the evils of bodily experience or sexuality, or its detachment from the world of public ethics, its authoritarian ecclesiastical systems, or its excessively philosophical understanding of God's unity, or whatever else is seen as the root of all theological evils."

resources for contemporary Augustinians to respond convincingly to their detractors.

Perhaps most bracingly, concentrating on Augustine's christ-ology allows us to describe with systematic rigor a theological position that has often been treated as a *bête noire* in discussions of the intersection between christology and ecclesiology. As has long been recognized, Augustine's theology of the *totus Christus* is one of the most direct sources of the teaching that the life of the Church should be considered an "extension of the Incarnation."[40] This teaching has often been presented as a degenerate confusion of christology and ecclesiology; at the same time, it has sometimes been seen as the principal distinction between Protestant and Roman Catholic understandings of the Church. Yet beyond a vaguely articulated sense of Christ's mystical identity with the Church, it has never been clear what it might possibly mean for the Church to extend the Incarnation – at least, it is not clear what this could mean beyond an unacceptable teaching that the Church is hypostatically united to the Word as Christ's humanity is.

By returning to the source of this theological image and system-atically developing Augustine's teaching on the *totus Christus*, I will offer an account of the Body of Christ as an extension of the Incarnation that does not confuse Christ and the Church, but rather allows us to appreciate how the life of the world and the work of the Church are more intimately bound up with the Incarnation than has previously been recognized. Bound up in Christ's person: For my account directs our attention to the manifold ways that the particularity of Christ's humanity is shaped by the world around

---

[40] Thus, speaking of Augustine's anti-Pelagian writings, Emile Mersch, writes: "by reason of the hypostatic union, unparalleled grace is conferred upon the individual human nature of Christ. Then this holiness is communicated from the Head to the members. There takes place, as it were, a kind of progressive extension of the hypostatic union to all the faithful." *The Whole Christ: The Historical Development of the Doctrine of the Mystical Body in Scripture and Tradition*, trans. John R. Kelly (Milwaukee, WI: The Bruce, 1938), 407–408.

him, even to the extent that his sinless agency may not preserve him from causing harm on account of the world's sin. Attention to the Church's completion of Christ thus allows us to recover a Christ who may truly learn of the scope of his own calling from the Syrophoenician woman, even as she leaves the encounter harmed by her Lord. Bound up in Christ's work, too: For christological noncompetition, coupled with an awareness of the interdependence and receptivity inherent to human life, allows us to see the way that God's redemptive will remains irreducibly prior even as Christ's humanity opens a space for creatures to make a decisive contribution to the work of salvation. Christ saves us, in significant part, through one another.

Christ is not who he is without us, by the grace of God; and in turn, our lives are graciously included within his own, at both the foundation of God's redemptive work and in its eschatological accomplishment. The Church and Christ: one person.

***

As is hopefully clear by now, this project's primary ambitions are systematic and constructive, rather than historical and exegetical. I take this to be an entry in the long Augustinian tradition that extends across the centuries since Augustine's death. The "St. Augustine" from which this tradition derives has always had a complicated relation to Aurelius Augustinus, Bishop of Hippo Regius. Though the Christian faith's historical concern means that the two can never fully be disconnected, the scope of Augustine's thought has long meant that his intellectual inheritors tend to engage his work partially, guided by their own theological concerns. There is great value in careful and comprehensive study of Augustine, and one of the great virtues of the Augustinian scholarship of our day is its attentiveness to texts traditionally ignored by many interpreters. A faithful reading of the full scope of Augustine's writings has much to add both to our understanding of fourth- and fifth-century Christian thought, and of the development of theology in the Late Antique and early Medieval periods more broadly. Anglophone scholarship still lacks the work that might serve as the magisterial study of Augustine's christology, textured both in its account of the genesis and development of his thoughts on Christ, and in its presentation of the relation between christology and the other theological *loci* with which Augustine is occupied throughout his writings.[41]

This is certainly not that book. There are points in this study where I am conscious of saying things Augustine did not and likely would not have said. There are also points, no doubt, where I have stepped beyond Augustine without being conscious of having done so; this is, admittedly, not a boundary I have been overly careful in policing. I have drawn, for instance, freely and idiosyncratically on texts from throughout Augustine's life, without concerning myself overmuch with questions of the development of his christological thought throughout his literary career. This practice has been guided by my sense that, at various points in his writings, Augustine says things that seem to me to be true about God and Christ, and that it is desirable to have a roughly systematic account of these ostensible truths.

Particularly for a thinker with a christology as unsystematic as Augustine's, any attempt to bring coherence to what I take to be his insights on these matters across the full breadth of his theological development will undoubtedly introduce distortions into a historical accounting of his thought. I offer this as a global disavowal of the historical respectability of my project: If anyone finds my christological outlook or my exegeses of particular texts useful in the project of developing a historical narrative of what Augustine thought about Christ at various stages of his intellectual

---

[41] A significant contribution to this historical project, and the most up-to-date account of the history of study of Augustine's christology, may be found at Gregory Michael Cruess, "Augustine's Biblical Christology: A Study of the *In Ioannis Evangelium Tractatus CXXIV*" (Unpublished Ph.D. Dissertation, University of Notre Dame, 2019).

career and of the changes that occur in his thought throughout the course of his life, this is all to the good – but that project is not my own. Augustine appears in these pages less as the object of my study, than as a conversation partner. Through engagement with his texts, through learning at his feet – dissenting where he seems mistaken, and filling out the points in his writings that seem lacking – I hope to gain insight into what might be confessed of Christ today.

In this, I take myself to be stepping into a long tradition of Augustinian thought stretching through Anselm and Thomas Aquinas to the reformers and Pascal and to the present day. In each generation, parts of Augustine's thought are brought to the fore and parts suppressed; the canon of texts taken up for consideration expands or contracts; the resultant pictures of Augustine vary widely; but nevertheless, each theological perspective stands within a common Augustinian tradition, in that each takes Augustine as a central authority and constant guide. It is this very diversity of the Augustinian tradition that attracts me to it, and while I have no doubt that there are points of my thought which require, on the one hand, normative theological correction, and on the other, amendment if they are to serve as reliable interpretations of Augustine situated within his proper historical context, I hope that my own Augustinian outlook may be one minor entry in this long and impressive series of those who have understood Christ's work more deeply in conversation with the *doctor gratiae*.

While the outlook of this book remains resolutely constructive, I nevertheless hope that this study may have something to offer historical evaluations of Augustine's christology. By tracing the importance of Christ through a wide swath of the Augustinian *corpus*, by calling attention to some features of Augustine's christology that have received insufficient attention to this point, and by illustrating the fundamental consistency of the christological discussions scattered throughout Augustine's writings, I hope that this book may serve as a guide or at least a provocation for more historically oriented study of Augustine's christology. Augustine's christology *develops* throughout his life, to be distinguished from merely changing.[42] It illustrates a deep coherence that persists even as Augustine's thinking on particular points matures. We need a more textured historical account of how Augustine's christology develops and relates to more familiar areas of Augustinian study, precisely because my account is *not* the only direction in which his christology might be extended. If this study contributes to that historical project, so much the better.

***

One of the central claims of this book is that in coming to know Christ, we are able to see our connections to one another more clearly; that, in fact, we come to know ourselves as one in the one body of Christ. Love of Christ is not meant to draw us away from the world, but back into it – more specifically, back into our

---

[42] In "Did Augustine's Christology Depend on Theodore of Mopsuestia?," McGuckin has identified three distinct periods within Augustine's christological development: The first, beginning at his conversion in 386, "concentrates on the pedagogic role of Christ." He is seen here as "a somewhat remote exemplar of virtuous living" (43–44). The second stage, commencing with his ordination to the priesthood in 391, involves a new understanding of the significance of Christ's humanity; McGuckin identifies the commentary upon Psalm 21 as a conceptual turning-point (44; see also Michael Cameron, *Christ Meets Me Everywhere: Augustine's Early Figurative Exegesis* (Oxford: Oxford University Press, 2012), Chapter 6 on this point). The third stage begins in 412, the year in which Augustine first suggests that "the Christological union was itself a grace," and even that he is "the supreme example of unmerited antecedent grace" (45). This final stage marks the introduction of a new set of theological concerns to Augustine's christological reflection in light of the anti-Pelagian controversy. McGuckin's text responds to Joanne McWilliam Dewart, "The Influence of Theodore of Mopsuestia on Augustine's Letter 187," *Augustinian Studies* 10 (1979): 113–132. Joanne McWilliam also offers a more narrowly focused periodization focused specifically on the place of the Cross in Augustine's thought at "Augustine's Developing Use of the Cross: 387–400," *Augustinian Studies* 15 (1984): 15–33; while Michael Cameron, *Christ Meets Me Everywhere*, 283–284, marks the *Contra Faustum*, Augustine's exegesis of the twenty-first Psalm (as numbered by the Vulgate), and the development of his doctrine of operative grace as conceptual turning points.

concrete histories, toward the events and people that have shaped us and that we, in turn, have shaped. As Rowan Williams writes, Augustine's

> pattern of christological exposition insists that there can be no accurate discussion of the incarnation that is not itself incarnationally modeled – humble in its awareness of the inescapable context of material history, alert to the question of how *justitia* is realized, open to the dangerous and potentially humiliating solidarity of fallible and sinful human agents, and refusing prideful isolation. *Agere personam sapientiae* is for all believers the task of learning a new speech apt for the city of God, a *méthode spirituelle* that is both political, in the widest sense, and prayerful, continuous with the unbroken, transfiguring enactment of Wisdom that is Jesus Christ.[43]

Alongside the passage from van Bavel cited above, Williams' comments here might in many ways serve as a mission statement for this book. My argument is structured according to an incarnational movement, beginning with the eternal life of God in which the Word wills to take on flesh, passing through the interrelation of divine and creaturely agency as encountered in the act of assuming flesh, centered on the humanity of Christ, which is the meeting point of the life of God and the life of the world, and extending outward as our own particularity and concrete histories are incorporated within Christ. The aim of God's reconciling act is, finally, not just to return us to God, but to return us to our own flesh, learning to see all our lives as included within the life of Christ and acting in relation to others as he lives in us.

One of the central claims of this study is that sin obscures from us the truth of God, distorts our vision of the world God has created, and hides from us much of the violence we inflict on one another. There is, I trust, much error in this book; there is much here beyond

[43] Williams, *On Augustine*, 153.

my ability to recognize that contributes to the harms to which we subject one another. I offer it as the best confession I am able to make at present. I offer it seeking correction and, if necessary, rebuke; but always in the hope that, together, we might meet Christ in one another.

Part I | The Divine-Human Life

1 | The Life of God

What might it mean for a God to assume human flesh? At the risk of stating the obvious, it depends on the God who is doing the assuming.

The confession of Jesus as fully God and fully human places significant pressure on christological discourse. When Christ is hungry, Christian faith must say that this hunger is God's, for – at least on a Chalcedonian account of the Incarnation – there is no one else's hunger that it could be. Jesus Christ is the person of the Word; what it is for this human to exist is for human nature to have been assumed into unity with the hypostasis of the Word.

So also, while the Sixth Ecumenical Council distinguishes between a divine and a human will in Christ, the human will is no less God's than the divine's, for Christ is God. Maximus the Confessor's seminal interpretation of Christ's prayer in the Garden of Gethsemane is meant to underline the identity of the volitional agent: The same Christ wills divinely and humanly.[1] While Christ's human will is properly described as the Word's own, just as Christ's hunger is, there is a relevant dissimilarity between the two examples: "Will" is generally regarded as a category properly ascribed to the eternal life of God considered in itself; "hunger" is not.[2] Perhaps hunger may be used as a metaphor to describe God's desire for, for example, the

---

[1] From the immense literature treating Maximus on Gethsemane, see the especially clear treatments at Paul M. Blowers, *Maximus the Confessor: Jesus Christ and the Transfiguration of the World* (Oxford: Oxford University Press, 2016), 156–165; and Ian A. McFarland, "'Willing Is Not Choosing': Some Anthropological Implications of Dyothelite Christology," *International Journal of Systematic Theology* 9.1 (2007): 2–23.

[2] Psalm 50.12 (*If I were hungry, I would not tell you*) pushes in this direction.

salvation of the world, but (apart from Christ) we find in God no feeling of discomfort or longing produced by nutritional lack; Christ's hunger is human hunger all the way down, even if that human sensation is God's. By contrast, Christ's willing has a properly divine register and a properly human one, coordinated in what Maximus describes as a "perfect harmony (συμφυΐα) and concurrence (σύννευσις)."[3] In this respect, Christ's willing is structurally similar to his living, knowing, loving, speaking – each activity properly ascribed to God and to humanity.

So far, so good. Yet at precisely this point, the pressure placed upon Christian speech by Chalcedonian orthodoxy threatens to distort theological reflection. We know that Christ wills and knows, and loves humanly, and we also know that he is God. There is accordingly a temptation to imagine the activity of Christ's divinity through the more readily conceptualizable knowledge we possess of the activity of his human nature. We might imagine that, at the very moment Christ humanly perceives something, he perceives it divinely as well, and that as his humanity comes in the next moment to perceive something different, so does his divinity. Such an approach pictures the Word accommodating the divine life to the change and flow of temporal existence: As Christ turns in love to the hemorrhaging woman, or as he wills to walk from Capernaum to Bethsaida, there is a corresponding instance of turning in divine love, or a concurrent temporally indexed divine volition to take a stroll. Surely, we might think, this is what it means for the Word to *become* flesh – it means that God enters into history; that divinity is present in Christ, willing and knowing, and loving different things at different moments of his life. And, perhaps most importantly, that what Christ wills and knows and loves in his humanity corresponds to and is thus expressive of what he – at that very same moment – is willing and knowing and loving divinely. Such an understanding tends to authorize arguments of the following form: God knows all things divinely, and Christ is both true God and true

---

[3] *Opuscule 6*, cited at Blowers, *Maximus the Confessor*, 163.

human, so Christ must know all things humanly. More expansively, such an understanding tends toward a christological picture in which Christ's identity as the Word of God is taken, implicitly or explicitly, as a sufficient explanation of his human particularities – his emotional constitution, his desires, his decisions, and his likes and dislikes. Christ's humanity is expressive of his divinity, and that settles the majority of the most significant questions about why his human life ends up looking as it does. The person of Christ is the person of the Word, and so the sense of the Word as somehow transformed into a localized temporal agent "within" Jesus suggests itself to us.

One will not, of course, find anyone committing themselves to a christological proposal as flat-footed as this. There are innumerable qualifications that could be given, nuances and shading to be offered in the articulation of the Word's assumption of flesh. Where this temptation makes itself known is in the tendency of modern christ-ology to presume a fundamental commensurability between the life of God and the lives of human creatures at precisely the points we have been considering: in acts of knowing, or willing, or loving. We know, at least well enough to use such terms with some linguistic stability, what knowing and loving and willing are from our experi-ence of human society; we believe, on the basis of Scripture and the teaching of the Church, that such terms are rightly predicated of God and so we presume we have some understanding of the implications of the Word's knowing for Christ's human knowing.

While such a proposal attractively presents Christ as a recognizably unified agent, I believe it is untenable in light of the broadly Catholic apophatic emphasis on God's transcendence and unknowability. Compounding the error, it prematurely forecloses rich veins of christological reflection that I delve throughout this project. Far from compromising our sense of the incarnate Word's historicity by distinguishing too clearly divinity from humanity, a full-throated defense of the incomprehensibility and radical transcendence of God in Christ liberates us to imagine his enmeshment in the human and nonhuman world anew.

This chapter and the next begin this work through an exercise of ground-clearing, defamiliarizing our understanding of the Word who assumes flesh so as to open up these new lines of christological inquiry. More generally, these chapters seek to found my Augustinian christology on an Augustinian doctrine of God. At critical junctures in his doctrine of God, in his trinitarian theology, and in his writings on the Incarnation, Augustine's writings evidence a deep apophatic restraint – a restraint influential within later ancient and medieval thought, and even more remarkable when measured against the standard of contemporary systematic theology.[4] Affirming that the Word has assumed a human soul and body, Augustine refuses to peer further into God's mystery: "If a reason is asked for, it will not be miraculous; if an example is demanded, it will not be singular. Let us grant that God can do something that we cannot search out. In such cases the whole reason for what is done lies in the power of the agent."[5] Augustine's awareness of the tenuous hold our theological language has on a Lord who is unimaginably other than all things in the created world will serve us well in articulating an expansive Augustinian christological vision. The St. Augustine who serves as the wellspring of the Latin mystical tradition figures prominently in my thinking as well.

These chapters also, however, serve an apologetic aim, answering a challenge that any contemporary appropriation of Augustine's thought will face. A great deal of modern theology has made the case that the God of the Augustinian tradition is a deeply unlovely one. The problem is not so much that the Augustinian doctrine of

---

[4] On Augustine's place within the tradition of negative theology, chapters 3, 4, and 11 of Denys Turner, *The Darkness of God*, and Cyril O'Regan, "Theological Epistemology and Apophasis," in *The Oxford Handbook of Mystical Theology*, eds. Edward Howells and Mark A. McIntosh (Oxford: Oxford University Press, 2020), 369–387. See also Deirdre Carabine, "Negative Theology in the Thought of Saint Augustine," *Recherches de théologie ancienne et médiévale* 59 (1992): 5–22; Paul van Geest, *The Incomprehensibility of God: Augustine as a Negative Theologian* (Leuven: Peeters, 2011); and Susannah Ticciati, *A New Apophaticism: Augustine and the Redemption of Signs* (Leiden: Brill, 2015).

[5] ep. 137.2.8; WSA II/2, 217.

God has been compellingly rebutted, that the arguments of its incoherence have been so persuasive that belief in it is no longer really possible. Rather, there has been a significant growth in the sentiment that the final end of our loves that Augustine holds out to us is simply not a very beautiful one, and we should find another more compelling vision of God. Some of this sentiment is motivated by common criticisms that, to my mind, are closer to caricature than reflections of Augustine's own thought – that his God is "static," or overly influenced by "Greek philosophy," or privileges the oneness of God to the exclusion of his threeness.[6]

Yet those are not the only challenges raised for contemporary Augustinianism. More pressing because rooted in historical facts that could only be denied by theologians through self-deception are the objections that those committed to a broadly Augustinian conception of God, authorized and perhaps even motivated by that conception, have inflicted tremendous violence upon women, people of color, LGBTQ people, and more. Some of the more conservative tendencies of contemporary Augustinian scholarship have not helped matters, overlooking or actively marginalizing the voices raising these critical questions of the dominant theological – which is to say, in significant part, Augustinian – tradition.

In this project, then, I hope to present the beauty of a broadly Augustinian doctrine of God in compelling fashion, such that it might seem slightly more convincing to those whose fundamental theological commitments have not been settled, or at least more palatable to those previously inclined to dismiss it offhand. As part of this aim, I emphasize that the epistemic skepticism of much of the Augustinian tradition and its emphasis on a rigorously confessional conception of the Christian life offers far greater potential to support and be enriched by liberationist theological trajectories than has

---

[6] Cf. Michel René Barnes, "Augustine in Contemporary Trinitarian Theology," *Theological Studies* 56 (1995): 237–250; and Michel René Barnes, "De Régnon Reconsidered," *Augustinian Studies* 26.2 (1995): 51–79.

previously been recognized. My attention to the apophatic emphases of Augustine's thought, in particular, has been deeply informed by the work of theologies attempting to diagnose and overcome the implication of theological speech in heterosexism, patriarchy, racism, and the clerico-intellectual elitism of modern systematic theology.[7] Augustine's doctrine of God, when properly construed – not as the culmination of a metaphysical posture confidently ordering all of creation into a hierarchy with God at the top, but as an attempt to restrain the theological speech of fallen humanity from presuming it knows too much of the God who ever exceeds it – may in fact be a surprising aid to those working to undermine the sinful orders of domination of our own day.

The first part of this book, then, serves to mark off the boundaries within which a robustly Chalcedonian christology can operate – boundaries that, I will argue, are wider than we might have anticipated. If we wish to give definite theological content to claims that Christ and the Church should be considered one person, one "whole Christ" with head united to body; if we wish to describe the Church as an "extension of the Incarnation" in terms that do more than offer mysterious gestures of piety; if we wish to attend to how this theology of the *totus Christus* holds a specifically liberatory potential within the context of contemporary theology; then we will need to work out in rigorous fashion how we should, and should not (indeed, cannot), understand the Word's assumption of flesh.

∗∗∗

Whom, then, does Augustine understand the God who assumes flesh to be? In book seven of the *Confessions*, he famously describes one

---

[7] Exemplary in this respect are Linn Marie Tonstad, *God and Difference: The Trinity, Sexuality, and the Transformation of Finitude* (New York: Routledge, 2016); Elizabeth Johnson, *She Who Is*; Andrew Prevot, *Thinking Prayer: Theology and Spirituality amid the Crises of Modernity* (South Bend, IN: University of Notre Dame Press, 2015); and Karen Kilby, *God, Evil and the Limits of Theology* (London: T&T Clark, 2021).

early experience of the beauty that he would spend the remainder of his life pursuing:

> Entering within, I saw with the eye of my soul, and with a spiritual eye of some sort above my soul's eye, the immutable light far above my mind: not this common light which every carnal eye can see, nor any light of the same order but greater, as though this common light were shining much more powerfully, far more brightly, and so extensively as to fill the universe. The light I saw was not this common light at all, but something different, utterly different, from all these things. Nor was it higher than my mind in the sense that oil floats on water or the sky is above the earth; it was exalted because this very light made me, and I was below it because by it I was made. Anyone who knows truth knows it, and whoever knows it knows eternity. Love knows it.[8]

The limitations of this glimpse of God are apparent to Augustine even by the time he writes the *Confessions*. Most importantly, he recognizes that without the mediation of Christ, he is able to attain to this vision only for the "flash of one tremulous glance" (*in ictu trepidantis aspectus*).[9] This flash is a deeply ambivalent one, mirroring the *fulgur* in which Satan fell away from God, the *ictus* into which creation would collapse absent God's sustaining work, and the *in ictu oculi* in which St. Paul teaches the dead will be resurrected.[10] For a moment, Augustine is able to see both sides of the *regio dissimilitudinis*, the place of unlikeness, that he inhabits: an unlikeness to God proper to his creaturely existence, and his own unlikeness from the life he has been granted by God, as sin has distorted both his self-understanding and ability to love the

---

[8] *conf.* 7.10.16; WSA I/1, 172–3. I have modified Sr. Boulding's translation before the colon in light of Robert J. O'Connell, S. J.'s comments on this passage at *Images of Conversion in St. Augustine's Confessions* (New York: Fordham University Press, 1996), 124.

[9] *conf.* 7.17.23–18.24.

[10] Cf. *civ.* 11.13; *Gn. litt.* 4.12.22; *s.* 362.18.20; and Thomas Williams, "Augustine vs. Plotinus: The Uniqueness of the Vision at Ostia," in *Medieval Philosophy and the Classical Tradition: In Islam, Judaism, and Christianity,* ed. John Inglis (London: RoutledgeCurzon, 2002): 143–151, 149.

world.[11] Yet from far across this vacant landscape, he hears the true God cry out to him: "I am who am."[12]

What is perhaps most remarkable about this encounter is the extent to which, looking back on this baffling experience, Augustine finds continuity with the full-blooded Christian belief to which he would eventually be led. Even the bishop of Hippo Regius can affirm of this time, "I now loved your very self, and not some figment of imagination in place of you. ... I was drawn to you by your beauty but swiftly dragged away from you by my own weight."[13] He actually attains to *"That Which Is,"* even if he only carries with him "a loving memory, one that yearned for something of which I had caught the fragrance, but could not yet feast upon."[14] Augustine clearly regards this moment as formative of his understanding of God, an encounter with the very same endpoint of desire that will motivate both his youthful seeking and his mature theological reflection. The God he first comes to know and love at this moment[15] is the same one he will pursue through the remainder of his life, the one in whom he hopes finally to rest, the Love to which he hopes to point others in writing the *Confessions*.

What we find in this passage above all is Augustine's sense of God's transcendence. While we could speak of this God as "transcendent," this wouldn't quite convey the sense of the encounter: It would be better to say that God always actively transcends the attempt to attain to Him, or to represent Him – even to describe the manner in which He transcends these attempts. God always escapes: He is something like light, but even were we to imagine a brilliance that saturated the cosmos, we would be thinking in too restrained a fashion. God is not merely the light, as the phenomenon of apocalyptic dazzlement we experience when staring at the sun, a seeing that engulfs our very

---

[11] *conf.* 7.10.16; on the *regio dissimilitudinis*, see James Wetzel, *Parting Knowledge: Essays after Augustine* (Eugene: Cascade Books, 2013), 38–39.

[12] *conf.* 7.10.16: *Et clamasti de longinquo: "Immo vero ego sum qui sum."*

[13] *conf.* 7.17.23; WSA I/1, 176.

[14] *conf.* 7.17.23; WSA I/1, 177–8.

[15] *conf.* 7.10.16: *Et cum te primum cognovi.*

capacity to see. God is above us, but above us in a manner beyond anything we can comprehend.[16] It is obvious that the image of oil resting lightly on the water, with all the close contact and mutual dependence that requires, is insufficient. Yet even earth and sky cannot adequately describe the way God's existence differs from our own. This is a loftiness secured not simply by relative position or substantial difference, but by absolute priority and asymmetrical dependence. In contrast to the transience of all else that we experience, this God is *incommutabiliter*, unchangeable.[17]

Yet, for all Augustine's emphasis on how God slips through his every imagining of Her, She does not remain utterly unknown. Those who know truth – any truths, even created truths – know Her; above all, She is known in and through our love. While comprehension – getting our arms around God, coming to know Her on all sides in a manner that would be exhaustive and final – is denied, understanding is not. Alongside recognition of God's transcendence comes an awareness of Her as the source of all the good things we encounter in the world. The light, the oil, the air: All these are able to serve as signs of God, because She is their source and origin; "they are real because they are from you," and they are good because they receive their life from the one who is Herself the Good.[18] We come to know of God through these creaturely likenesses, knowing truly, but never finally.[19]

---

[16] Jean-Luc Marion describes revelation as the phenomenon's "saturation of saturation," filling and exceeding all possible horizons of manifestation, at *Being Given: Toward a Phenomenology of Givenness*, trans. Jeffrey L. Kosky (Stanford: Stanford University Press, 2002), 235.

[17] Cf. Roland J. Teske, *To Know God and the Soul: Essays on the Thought of Saint Augustine* (Washington, DC: The Catholic University of America Press, 2008), 131–152; and Michel René Barnes, "The Arians of Book V, and the Genre of De Trinitate," *The Journal of Theological Studies* 44.1 (1993): 185–195.

[18] *conf.* 7.11.17; WSA I/1, 173.

[19] While Augustine does not work it out in nearly the detail that Thomas Aquinas will centuries later, he clearly operates with an account of analogical predication; cf. Gerald Boersma's identification of a "nascent doctrine of analogy with all of its accompanying theological leverage" in Augustine at Gerald P. Boersma, *Augustine's Early Theology of Image* (Oxford: Oxford University Press, 2016), 196. In my own

The created world is able to serve as a sign of God, because each creature exists only by receiving a share in God's own existence:

> His very nature is to be, and so true is this that, when compared with him, all created things are as though they had no being. When not compared with him they do exist, for they derive their being from him, but compared with him they do not exist, because he is true being, unchangeable being, and this can be said of him alone. He is being, as he is also goodness, the good of all good things.[20]

This is why Augustine's prayer to God as *superior summo meo* ("higher than my highest summit") is matched by a prayer to Her as *interior intimo meo* ("more inward than I am to myself") – it is *because* God transcends all things that She may also be known as the Truth within all truths, and loved in loving all our beloveds.

In its most basic outlines, then, this is what Augustine hopes that we will love: a God who is beyond anything that we might finally or exhaustively know, but a God who we encounter intimately as the source of all the beauty, and goodness, and truth we find in our world. Fidelity to this vision of God will channel Augustine's thinking about the One who assumes flesh for the salvation of the world.

∗∗

Augustine will, as we have just seen, occasionally refer to God as Being, or as the Good – *est enim est, sicut bonorum bonum, bonum est.*[21] His most distinctive and revealing name for God, however, is *idipsum* – the Selfsame.[22] The term is found throughout Augustine's

---

understanding of our knowledge of God through created likenesses, I have found most useful David Burrell, *Aquinas: God and Action*, (Scranton, PA: University of Scranton Press, 2008), and David Burrell, *Knowing the Unknowable God: Ibn-Sina, Maimonides, Aquinas* (Notre Dame, IN: University of Notre Dame Press, 1986).

[20] *en.Ps.* 134.4; WSA III/20, 193.

[21] *en.Ps.* 134.4; WSA III/20, 193.

[22] Cf. James Swetnam, "A Note on *in Idipsum* in Augustine," *The Modern Schoolman* 30.4 (1953): 328–331; Jean-Luc Marion, *In the Self's Place: The Approach of St. Augustine,* trans. Jeffrey Kosky (Stanford: Stanford University Press, 2012), Ch. 7;

literary career, and its use as a name for God appears to be original to him.[23] One *locus classicus* for this denomination is found in Augustine's *Enarratio in Psalmum* 121:

> What is *idipsum*? What am I to say, if not *idipsum*? Brothers, if you are able, understand *idipsum*, for whatever else I go on say, I will not have truly said *idipsum*. Even so, let us try through some proximate words and significations to lead our infirm minds to the thought of *idipsum*. What is *idipsum*? That which always is the same way; that which is not now one way, and then another. What, then, is *idipsum*, except that which is? And what is that which is? That which is eternal.[24]

It would be easy to misconstrue the significance of this name. It might initially appear as the ultimate metaphysical principle, the self-identical A = A at the heart of all being that guarantees the ontological order of things. This is not wholly absent from Augustine's thought; he does indeed think that God is true Being, and that the existence of all things depends upon and is given order by participation in God. Yet, taken by itself, such a reading would not be able to explain the way Augustine speaks of *idipsum* here. As a name for God, Augustine presents it here

and Lewis Ayres, *Augustine and the Trinity* (Oxford: Oxford University Press, 2011), 200–208. At 204, Ayres notes that Augustine's "portrayal of *idipsum* as a name of God for himself finds no parallel in his predecessors." See also Matthew Drever's discussion of *idipsum* in the context of the fall of the devil (155–7) and deification (170–9) in Matthew Drever, *Image, Identity, and the Forming of the Augustinian Soul* (Oxford: Oxford University Press, 2013).

[23] Cf. *mor.* 14.24; WSA I/19, 42: "Hence, we ought to love God, a certain triple oneness, Father, Son, and Holy Spirit, and I shall say that God is nothing other than being the Selfsame (*quod nihil aliud dicam esse, nisi idipsum esse*)" (translation amended). See also mid-period texts like *conf.* 9.4.11 and 12.7.7, and later texts like *trin.* 2.18.35. For a discussion of Augustine's use of *idipsum* in the context of his philosophical and theological predecessors, see Ayres, *Augustine and the Trinity*, 204–5.

[24] *en.Ps.* 121.5: *Quid est idipsum? Quomodo dicam, nisi idipsum? Fratres, si potestis, intelligite idipsum. Nam et ego quidquid aliud dixero, non dico idipsum. Conemur tamen quibusdam vicinitatibus verborum et significationum perducere infirmitatem mentis ad cogitandum idipsum. Quid est idipsum? Quod semper eodem modo est; quod non modo aliud, et modo aliud est. Quid est ergo idipsum, nisi, quod est? Quid est quod est? Quod aeternum est.*

as unsurpassable: It points us not to a principle of logic that might easily be comprehended, but to the very incomprehensibility that is proper to God. Whatever Augustine might say, it will not be enough to say *idipsum*; this sounds very far from a principle that provides for a stable ontotheology.[25]

Rather, *idipsum* points us to difference that marks off God as distinct from everything else that is.[26] Everything that is not God exists in a relation of dependence upon Him; a dependence not merely historical, in that God created it, but a persistent dependence in which each thing is preserved in existence solely as it receives its being as divine gift. Creatures do not exist from themselves, but from God – this is what it is for them to be creatures. Because the gift by which God gives creatures to exist constitutes them as likenesses of God, their relation to Him is best described as one of participation.[27]

Because the divine term of this relation of likeness is unknowable, we should not expect to give anything approaching an exhaustive metaphysical account of what this relation *is*. To be able to do that, we would have to give an account of what the act is by which God grants creatures existence; but this would require us to give an account of the unknowable divine life itself. Participation is thus

---

[25] Cf. Marion, *In the Self's Place*, 299–300.

[26] I have in mind here "the Christian distinction" that Robert Sokolowski identifies between God and all that is not God: see Robert Sokolowski, *The God of Faith and Reason: Foundations of Christian Theology*, 2nd ed. (Washington, DC: The Catholic University of America Press, 1995), 1–40; and David Burrell, *Faith and Freedom: An Interfaith Perspective* (Oxford: Blackwell, 2004), 3–19.

[27] Augustine uses the term *participatio* in this sense at, for instance, *trin.* 8.3.5. David Vincent Meconi has written several articles on the christological resonance of participation in Augustine, and indeed his book *The One Christ* is among the recent texts to analyze Augustine's theology of the *totus Christus* most extensively. As this book goes to press, Meconi has recently been credibly accused of sexual abuse of a minor; as a result, he is no longer a member of the Society of Jesus, and has been laicized. In view of these facts, as well as in recognition of the fact that citational practices are not morally neutral, I have omitted reference to these texts.

best spoken of as a "figure," a shorthand for the grammar of our speech about God and the world in relation to God.[28]

What marks God off as distinct from everything else that is is that there is, in the divine life, nothing of participation. God *is* absolutely, without dependence on anything else. Alone among all the things that are said to exist, God requires nothing for the fullness or actualization of the divine life, because She is eternally in Herself the Good by which all good things are good. This is no sheer valorization of self-sufficiency, but rather a marker of how we are to relate to God: God is ever the giver of all good things, the source of all blessing that bestows life without suffering loss. Correspondingly, if God possesses the fullness of all goodness in Herself, then creation can add nothing to Her or make any contribution to the divine life. There is no internal need for creation in God, and so, when we relate to God, we relate to Her always as giver – as one who constitutes us by and meets us with grace.[29] God is the Selfsame, the one who does not participate, but on whom all things depend.

In contrast to names like Being or the Good, or even metaphorical names like the Lion of Judah, the name *idipsum* refers not to any particular quality by which some creature might be more or less like God, but to the very distinctness of God's life. If this name is an unsurpassable one for Augustine, it is because it points us to the singularity of God, the difference that marks God off from all else that is. For all the metaphysical terms that Augustine will use at times to describe creation's likeness to God and to describe God Himself as the source of all creation, it is finally this claim of God's radical distinction from all else that exists that is determinative of his thought: *Thus says the Lord, the King of Israel, and his Redeemer, the Lord of hosts: I am the first and I am the last; besides me there is no god. Who is like me?*

---

[28] So Paul J. Griffiths, *Intellectual Appetite: A Theological Grammar* (Washington, DC: The Catholic University of America Press, 2009), 86–87.

[29] Cf. Sokolowski, *God of Faith and Reason*, 19.

At base, then, *idipsum* is an apophatic term.[30] Where other names of God indicate creaturely likenesses to God, this marks off a fundamental unlikeness, a dissimilarity so thoroughgoing that whatever we may say, we will not truly have said *idipsum*. It points us to the life of God, a life that is utterly distinct from all that exists in dependence upon it. It is a sign that stands against all the affirmations we might offer of God: God exists, but not as we do; God is good, but not as we are; God loves, but in a manner incomprehensible to us. In fact, the distinctness of God's life ensures that there is *no* common term that might be predicated of God in the same way it is predicated of creation: as Augustine would write in the *De trinitate*,

> We should understand God, if we can and as far as we can, to be good without quality, great without quantity, creative without need or necessity, presiding without position, holding all things together without possession, wholly everywhere without place, everlasting without time, without any change in himself making changeable things, and undergoing nothing. Whoever thinks of God like that may not yet be able to discover altogether what he is, but is at least piously on his guard against thinking about him anything that he is not.[31]

The categories Augustine rejects here as inadequate are Aristotle's, yet we may extend the point to any other conceptual categories by which we seek to characterize the divine life, be they Kantian or phenomenological transcendentals, concepts of contemporary analytic metaphysics, patterns of usage of ordinary language philosophy, or the historicized concepts employed and deconstructed by poststructuralist philosophy.[32] These tools are not fit to the task of

---

[30] This apophatic tendency is present in Augustine's thought from a very early date, as at *ord.* 2.18.47: God is the one "of whom no knowledge is in the soul, except the knowledge that it cannot know Him (*cuius nulla scientia est in anima, nisi scire quomodo eum nesciat*)."

[31] *trin.* 5.1.2; WSA I/5, 190.

[32] Cf. Aristotle, *Categories and De Interpretatione*, trans. John Lloyd Ackrill (Oxford: Oxford University Press, 1963), 5.

describing God. Though they may assist us in coming to the partial knowledge of God proper to created intellects, any words or concepts we apply to God will fail to carve reality at the joints, for *this* life is lived in a manner that is in principle beyond our comprehension, and thus beyond the reach of any categories we might apply to it. This is true even of our attribution of ineffability to God: We cannot utter this as a positive predication of the divine life, but can only observe that all our theological statements must fail to describe God adequately.[33]

The fundamental Augustinian affirmation about God's life – or, at any rate, the fundamental affirmation about the divine life within my own reception of Augustine's works – is *si cepisti, non est Deus. Si comprehendere potuisti, aliud pro Deo comprehendisti.* If you have captured it, it is not God. If you have been able to comprehend a thing, you have comprehended something other than God.[34] This is the claim that the identification of God as *idipsum* marks off: God is the Selfsame, the one who does not participate, the uncreated, the one whose life is incomprehensibly other than our own.

***

Taking *idipsum* as a basic description of God's life can function at times to create a certain austerity in our speech about God, a healthy wariness of thinking about Him in a way that He is not. Indeed, many of the claims that broadly Augustinian theology will make about the divine life are rooted in, or at least articulated in light of, this fundamental recognition of God's transcendence and incomprehensibility. Take, for instance, our attribution of will to God. In our experience of the created order, we are accustomed to speaking of ourselves as performing distinct volitional acts: I will to take a walk in the morning, or to pick up the glass of water that lies on the table before me, or resolve that in the afternoon I will reach out to an old friend. Precisely how we understand such volitional acts is

[33] Cf. *doct. Chr.* 1.1.6.
[34] *s.* 52.16.

not important for the moment; what is significant is that these seem to me distinct exercises of my will, marked off from one another by the ends to which they are ordered. It seems to me that even the nonhuman actors I have encountered in the world display an at least analogous pattern of pursuing their desires through distinct exercises of agency: The lion pursues the gazelle, and then lies down for a nap. It seems, too, that my own life is especially bound up with my volitional acts: I am capable of untold numbers of such acts of will, and they have played a significant role in the course my life has taken.

But God's life is not like mine. I know that my acts of willing serve as a creaturely likeness of God's life, for Scripture often speaks of God's will: God wills to create the world, to make covenant with Abraham, wills to redeem the world in Christ, and perhaps wills that I (or you) should sell all we have and give the money to the poor. Yet even as we attribute this willing to God, we must remember that God's life is utterly distinct from our own; we do not, and cannot, know it as it truly is, for the life of God is incomprehensible. This drops, as it were, a veil between our understanding and how it is with God: While we can know that our acts of willing serve as a likeness of God's willing, we cannot pass to the far side of the veil and affirm with any confidence what God's willing is like. (Which, importantly, is not to say that we know nothing about what God wills – just that we don't know *how* She wills.) Does God's life include distinct acts of will, ordered to distinct ends? We cannot say so; such an affirmation would presume that we knew how willing is in the life of God. Neither can we affirm, however, that there is numerically one act in God, ordered to one end. This would, in precisely the same way, presume too much of how it is with God's life. We may speak of there being one act in the divine life, then, but this should not be understood as a positive affirmation about God. It is rather an admission that there are no distinctions we can draw within God's life to describe how She wills. In saying that there is only one act of God's willing, we are thus attributing to God not a lack of plurality, but singularity. We are saying that whatever God's willing is like, it is utterly unique to God Herself; we have no competence to describe how it is in God's life more fully.

Yet we must pursue this line of thinking to another register. We speak of what God is like in many different ways: We speak of God knowing, loving, commanding, and so on; we speak of God as good, beautiful, merciful, compassionate, righteous, jealous. Here again, in our experience of the created order, all these attributions seem quite distinct from one another. To be merciful is quite different in our understanding of it than to be jealous, and knowing is not at all the same as commanding; never mind that the act of issuing a command is evidently a different sort of thing than being beautiful. Yet the logic of God's singularity holds here, as well. Though we know these diverse acts and qualities to be different from one another in the created order, and indeed, though we know that being an act and being a quality are quite distinct sorts of things, we cannot know how any of this is with God. Here again, we can say on the basis of Scripture and the theological tradition that each of these attributes, when found in creation, serves as a likeness of God, teaching us something about Him; but we cannot know how it is with God's mercy, or jealousy, or act of love. We cannot even say enough about God's mercy to distinguish it confidently from God's jealousy, or God's beauty from God's act of command. Each of them shows us something of what God is like, but each of these predications lead us beyond the veil of incomprehensibility back to the life of God – to God Himself. Beyond this veil, we cannot say that God's mercy is distinct from His justice; or, conversely, that His mercy and justice are numerically one in such a way that the intensions of these terms as we understand them would necessarily conflict with one another.[35] We can only say that they lead us back to the Selfsame life of God.

[35] Thus responding to one of the central criticisms raised against divine simplicity within analytic philosophy of religion; see especially Alvin Plantinga, *Does God Have a Nature?* (Milwaukee, WI: Marquette University Press, 1980). For more extensive responses to Plantinga's objections against divine simplicity, see Lawrence Dewan,

The conclusion toward which this line of argument leads is that, if we take philosophical reason as our guide, there are *no* distinctions whatsoever that we may draw conceptually within the life of God. There are no "real distinctions" (to use a vocabulary more Thomist than Augustinian) that reason can justify drawing within the divine life, no distinctions we can draw that we can confidently or even hesitantly say depict how the life of God really is in itself. Whatever affirmations we wish to make of God in light of the creaturely likenesses through which we know Her, we must offer them under the proviso that these predicates apply to the one same life of God about which we can say little more. In itself, the life of God is like a sealed black box to which our predications may point us, about which they may teach us, but into which they are unfit to penetrate.

This is, to my mind, the proper way to understand what is commonly called the "doctrine of divine simplicity." To say that God is simple is not to say that we are able to describe how our many predications of God are unified in the divine life. Were we able to do this, we would be able to know the incomprehensible, to say *idipsum* fully and finally. Affirming God's simplicity is not (or need not be) a positive affirmation at all: It is a confession of the limit beyond which our speech and intellects cannot pass, a recognition that the nonparticipatory manner in which God exists is so different than anything else we have ever known, and so intrinsically beyond the limits of our intellects, that we cannot speak confidently of its interiority at all. Divine simplicity is thus what David Burrell has called a "formal feature" of our speech about God[36] – it is not a positive attribution describing the divine life, but

---

"Saint Thomas, Alvin Plantinga, and the Divine Simplicity," *The Modern Schoolman* 66.2 (1989): 141–151; and Brian Leftow, "Is God an Abstract Object?," *Noûs* 24.4 (1990): 581–598.

[36] Burrell, *God and Action*, 20. Burrell does not emphasize simplicity as an apophatic doctrine quite so fully as I have here, but in either case, it results in the denial of

a limitation we must acknowledge as inherent to any of our speech about God.

While I have attempted to render the teaching that God is simple as modestly as possible, we should not underestimate the extent to which it shapes our reasoning about God. If the life of God is so utterly singular that we are incapable of drawing any distinctions within it, then we are unable to attribute any sort of composition to God. We should not say that God has a body, because to do so we would have to say that God is extended in space, with different parts occupying different locations. We should not say that God inhabits the temporal order alongside us, for that would require that God's life is extended in time, His life composed by one moment, followed by another, followed by another. And this claim extends not only to our customary divisions of time – seconds, minutes, hours – but to the very notion of succession itself. If we can draw no real distinctions in God's life, we cannot distinguish between any before or after in Him. Consequently, we can affirm no possibility of change in God – any change we might want to ascribe to God would depend on exactly the sort of real distinction in God's life that we have had to renounce.

Far from being an attempt to peer into the metaphysics of the divine life, then, the doctrine of divine simplicity is an attempt to safeguard its mystery. We cannot know the *modus sine modo* by which God gives Herself to us, and gives us to love Her; the "way without a way" in which God acts and exists is simply beyond us.[37] Inasmuch as our constant tendency is to trespass across this boundary of theological speech, the refusal to accept any composition or

---

composition in God, and so functions largely the same way within our accounts of divine predication.

[37] The phrase *modus sine modo* comes from the Numidian Bishop Severus, who writes it in *ep.* 109.2 to Augustine as a way of describing the manner in which we are to love God. Kevin Hart speculates that the phrase "may well have been indebted to Augustine in the first place"; Kevin Hart, "The Unbloody Sacrifice," *Archivio di Filosofia* 76.1/2 (2008): 189–197; 195.

real distinction in God keeps us honest. Professing it is an act of intellectual humility, acknowledging that our minds are not capable of ascending to knowledge of God as She is: We must wait for Her to lower Herself to our condition.

***

All that said: Though we cannot know God as He is in Himself, we can learn *of* God through the things that He has made. Were this not the case, we could know nothing about God whatsoever.[38] Yet the very language of Scripture presses against such a radical conclusion. We say, with the Scriptural witness: *The Lord is good.* And we speak of God's goodness in many different ways. We express gratitude (*The Lord has been good to me.*). We recount God's steadfast care in Her dealings with Israel (*The Lord is good; His mercy endures forever.*). We pray for illumination (*You are good and you bring forth good; instruct me in your statutes.*). We express of intimacy and delight in God's presence (*Taste and see that the Lord is good.*).

Utterances like these are the building blocks of Christian speech about God: They are sung in worship; read as appointed lections; preached upon; studied devotionally; meditated upon by contemplatives; studied as a historical record of the development of Israel's religious practice; offered as praise at moments of joy and grief; recontextualized and woven into liturgical speech; and printed on throw pillows or as artwork used to adorn one's walls. These words and other words like them indicate a history of election, faithfulness, sin, forgiveness, and trust. They are probed and explored by theologians and philosophers, tested for their sense and implications, placed into synthetic unity with other Christian speech about God. But these words, both as Scripture and liturgy, constitute the bedrock of both proclamation and theological reflection – of the language used every day in conducting a life of Christian faith, and in the

---

[38] As, for instance, Clement of Alexandria comes close to saying; cf. Andrew Radde-Gallwitz, *Basil of Caesarea, Gregory of Nyssa, and the Transformation of Divine Simplicity* (Oxford: Oxford University Press, 2009), 49–59.

reflexive analysis of that language conducted for the sake of clarifying and extending speech about God.[39]

These statements do not occur within a vacuum, but are intimate with our other practices of speaking of the goodness of things: I say I have had a good day; I call someone a good person; when I have had enough and have been offered more, I decline with a casual "I'm good." The grammatical form of the ways I speak of God as good have more than a little overlap with the ways I speak of other things as good. Within my linguistic practice, there is at least a family resemblance here.[40]

Yet, as I have already argued, the singularity of the divine life requires that we cannot attribute goodness to God in the same way we attribute it to any other thing. When I say that God is good, the most I can say is that the goodness of the things I have encountered in the world serves as a likeness of God's life – their goodness shows us something of God, and draws us into encounter with Him. The derivative goodness of creation teaches us about the goodness of its source, holding the potential to move us toward a goodness hidden in the incomprehensibility of God's life. We do not need to know what God's goodness is like to make this affirmation, only to know that the goodness attributed to creation is also attributed to God as its origin in Scripture and the Church's prayer.

Once we have affirmed that something like goodness is a feature of the divine life, however, a great deal follows. When I call a person good, I am not claiming that she is herself "the good"; were I to do this, I would make her the standard against which all other potentially good things are measured. Instead, I speak of goodness as a quality

---

[39] Cf. George A. Lindbeck, *The Nature of Doctrine: Religion and Theology in a Postliberal Age* (Louisville, KY: Westminster John Knox Press, 1984).

[40] Cf. *en.Ps.* 134.4; WSA III/20, 193: "What more can I say? In creation I discover a good sky, a good sun, and good stars; I regard the good earth and find all things that come to birth upon it to be good and all of them dependent on the earth and rooted there . . . You will find no good thing anywhere that does not depend for its goodness upon him."

that characterizes her: She is one thing, and the goodness she exemplifies is another. Yet, if God's life is utterly incomprehensible, we cannot make even this sort of distinction with respect to God. If we call God good, we must say that God is Herself the Good – the very goodness by which all things are good. This gives some teeth to Augustine's identification of God as *idipsum*: Whereas the goodness of creation is a likeness of God dependent for its existence on God's life, God's goodness is the same as God Herself. To say anything else would be to draw a real distinction in God. Accordingly, if we can call God good on analogy to the things we know in creation, we must say that the divine life is itself the Good by which all things are good. As Augustine writes, "When I turn to God, I think it better to attach no other word but to say simply that he is good. Our Lord Jesus Christ himself, who spoke of *a good man*, also said, *None is good except one, God alone* (Mk 10.18). Did he not thereby prompt us to seek further and distinguish a good which is good by derivation from some other good, from a good that is good of itself?"[41] God is this Good, the Selfsame, the one for whom every attribution made of Her is identical to the incomprehensibility of Her own life.

Even though it is articulated in terms of a denial about God's life, this cultivates in us a very particular understanding of what it is for God to be Good. God is not only an example of goodness, God is the standard by which all attributions of goodness within creation are made.[42] When we say that God is the Good, then, we are not simply saying that God is better than everything else that is, or even that God is merely maximally good – as good as any thing might possibly be. We are, instead, saying that God is definitionally the standard of goodness. The situation is similar to that of Wittgenstein's discussion of the Paris meter: When the measurement "one meter" was normed and secured by an actual platinum and iridium alloy bar kept under

---

[41] *en.Ps.* 134.4; WSA III/20, 193.

[42] Richard Stanley Bluck argues the best way to understand Plato's doctrine of forms within a broadly Wittgensteinian philosophy of language is as standards of predication; see R. S. Bluck, "Forms as Standards," *Phronesis* 2.2 (1957): 115–127.

precise atmospheric and temperature conditions in Paris, it was not contingently the case that this bar was one meter long. What it *meant* to be one meter long was defined as being precisely the same length as this bar.[43] In the same way, God is not the most good as if measured against some external standard; the divine life is *itself* the Good in likeness to which all other things are called good. This means that God's goodness could not possibly grow or diminish, because that incomprehensible divine life is the very standard against which any such judgment might be made.[44] We should regard God, then, as definitionally being the fullness of all Good, in which no good can possibly be lacking, for what it is to be Good is to be exactly as God is.

Goodness is not, of course, the only attribution we make of God on the basis of Scripture and Christian teaching. Yet if each of these predications is truly made of God, each of them can pick out nothing but the Selfsame incomprehensibility of God's life. Each of them must finally have the same referent: "God ... is indeed called in multiple ways great, good, wise, blessed, true, and anything else that seems not to be unworthy of him; but his greatness is identical with his wisdom (he is not great in mass but in might), and his goodness is identical with his wisdom and greatness, and his truth is identical with them all; and with him being blessed is not one thing, and being great or wise or true or good, or just simply being, another."[45] This does not, of course, mean that our understanding of wisdom is exactly the same as our understanding of goodness. As we encounter them in creation, they are quite different attributes, and to say a thing is like God with respect to being

---

[43] Ludwig Wittgenstein, *Philosophical Investigations*, 4th ed., eds. Peter M. S. Hacker and Joachim Schulte, trans. Gertrude Elizabeth Margaret Anscombe, Peter M. S. Hacker and Joachim Schulte (Oxford: Wiley-Blackwell, 2009), 29 (§50).

[44] The easy slide from God's goodness as separable from God, to God's goodness as itself variable, can be observed in respectively in Yujin Nagasawa, *Maximal God: A New Defense of Perfect Being Theism* (Oxford: Oxford University Press, 2017); and Anne Jeffrey, Asha Lancaster-Thomas, and Matyáš Moravec, "Fluctuating Maximal God," *International Journal for Philosophy of Religion* 88.3 (2020): 231–246.

[45] *trin.* 6.7.8; WSA I/5, 211.

wise is accordingly quite different than to say it is like God with respect to being good. But the end to which each of these affirmations points is nothing other than the incomprehensible life of God. Just as attributing goodness to God entails that God is Himself the Good, so also attributing wisdom to God entails that God is Wisdom itself, and because these cannot be distinguished from one another in God's life, the Good and Wisdom both name nothing other than the simplicity of the divine life. That by which creatures are good through participation is the very same as that by which creatures are wise through participation. Since God is the source on which the existence of all things depends, we should finally hold that all the qualities that offer diverse creaturely likenesses of God are transcendently one in God's own life.[46]

To call God the Selfsame, to deny that God is what She is by participation as all other creatures are, thus teaches us to regard God's transcendence in a specific way. It is not that God is utterly unknown to us, but that all we know of God is true of Her in an absolutely unknown manner. She is Wisdom, and Truth, and Goodness, and Beauty – but all this at once, absolutely, each a description of the same incomprehensible life, each somehow definitive of who God is. If we wish to (not quite) say *idipsum*, we must add to our apophatic black box an apophatic explosion of theological terminology, an unknowing that is stunned to silence by the proliferation of speech about God rather than left at a loss for words. Denys Turner has identified this tendency as the sort of apophaticism at work in St. Julian of Norwich.[47] Contrasting her theological style with that of the author of the *Cloud of Unknowing*, who "writes as if the apophatic recognition that God is beyond speech required him to watch his language at every point lest he

---

[46] Cf. *civ.* 11.10; WSA I/7, 12. See also John P. Rosheger, "Augustine and Divine Simplicity," *New Blackfriars* 77.901 (1996): 72–83.

[47] Julian is commemorated on May 8 of the sanctoral calendar of the Episcopal Church. Though she has not been formally canonized by the Roman Catholic Church, one may hope that this sister branch of the Catholic Church will soon come to its senses.

get God wrong,"[48] Julian "gets to the same apophatic place . . . by an excess of affirmation that, as it were, collapses under the weight of its very excessiveness . . . [I]n the matter of talk about God, if every word fails, every word should be tried."[49] In Augustine's texts, we may think here of the incredible diversity of images for God he provides in his sermons and exegetical texts, perhaps above all in the *Enarrationes in Psalmos*.[50] As we will see, this proliferation of sometimes contradictory images is, for Augustine no less than for Julian, a defining feature of the rhetoric of his christological teaching.

The God who is *idipsum* is thus utterly unknowable in Himself, even as He is known in all things. This Selfsame one is source and analogate of worm and windhover; mother and daughter no less than father or son; black and queer not exclusively in the histories by which God takes the part of the marginalized and victims of violence, but as the transcendent creator of those good lives that challenge and contest the violent classifications of our social discourse. This is the God whose unknowable life must, we find in Scripture, often be described in terms all too familiar to our human experience: mercy, jealousy, anger, forgiveness, even repentance. These attributions are not only compatible with God's changelessness; they remind us that God's changelessness itself is of a sort that we cannot conceive. We learn who the unknowable God is (rather than *what* He is) through history: the history of Israel; the history of the Church; above all, the life of Christ; and inseparable from this, our own histories.

---

[48] Denys Turner, *Julian of Norwich, Theologian* (New Haven, CT: Yale University Press, 2011), 24.

[49] Turner, *Julian*, 25. See also Turner's earlier reading of Julian as exemplifying many of the virtues of Meister Eckhart's Neoplatonic theology at Turner, *The Darkness of God*, 159–162.

[50] John Cavadini has noted the substantial continuities between Augustine's preaching and his theoretical texts at "Simplifying Augustine," in *Educating People of Faith: Exploring the History of Jewish and Christian Communities* (Grand Rapids, MI: Wm. B. Eerdmans, 2004): 63–84.

These histories, and the recognition that the God revealed in them is the incomprehensible source of all the diverse goods we find in creation, render our theological speech unruly – they move us to pray in tongues that may be challenging or even scandalous to some, but testify to the one God all the same. To repurpose a characteristically Augustinian insight, "everything that exists is good," and so each thing in creation may speak to us of the God in whom it participates in its very particularity and difference.[51] Each creature may be asked, "Tell me of my God, you are not he, but tell me something of him," and may truly reply "Ze made us."[52]

***

Even at the point where one might expect a lapse in this fundamental apophatic restraint – as Augustine speaks of the inner triunity of the divine life – his emphasis on what is unsayable in God persists. Indeed, one of the key questions animating Augustine's trinitarian theology is how our language of Father, Son, and Holy Spirit can be truly predicated of a God who is unknowable to us in Her simplicity. We know by revelation that the one God is these three; but how are we to accommodate this threeness within our God-talk without positing distinctions within the Lord of just the sort we are trying to avoid – distinctions that propose to map out features of the unknowable life of God using human language?

It is precisely this overreach of theological language that Augustine's trinitarian theology takes care to avoid. Augustine's use of the term *persona* in relation to the Triune Lord is notable precisely in its disavowal of the metaphysical freight we might attach to the category; it is useful for him not because of what we understand *personae* to be within creation, but because we need a term to attach to God's threeness: "when you ask 'Three what?' human speech labors under a great dearth of words. So we say three persons, not in order to say that precisely, but in order not to be

---

[51] *conf.* 7.12.18; WSA I/1, 174.
[52] *conf.* 10.6.9; WSA I/1, 242 (modified).

reduced to silence."[53] Similarly, his justly famous account of relational predication within the Trinity is needed *only because* of his apophatic refusal to predicate accidents of the divine life in a manner that would compromise the unknowability of the divine life. Peter King has argued compellingly that Augustine's account serves principally to demonstrate that relational predicates can be used of one and the same subject of predication.[54] Said differently, they show us how relational predicates can refer to one and the same subject (the unknowable life of God), without constituting Father, Son, and Holy Spirit as separable existents on the "near side" of God's unknowability. These relational predicates can be used truly of God – and they do indeed, as we know by revelation, point to the eternal tripersonality of the divine life. Each use of them, however, points us back to the one who is *Idipsum*, incomprehensible in the otherness of His divine life. We know these three, and we know them together to be the one unknowable God; accordingly, even the threeness of God appears within trinitarian thought as an eternal and ineffable relatedness in God, rather than a mere countability in which the predicate "three" would apply to God in precisely the way it applies to three apples sitting on a kitchen table.

Once we have at our disposal this grammar of relational predication, the key lines of this Augustinian approach to God-talk are clear. All predications made of God should be understood as pointing to the unknowable simplicity of the divine life, considered either in the common distinction of the trinitarian persons from all else that exists, or according to the mutual relations of the

---

[53] *trin.* 5.9.10; WSA I/5, 196.

[54] Peter King, "The Semantics of Augustine's Trinitarian Analysis in De Trinitate 5–7," in *Le De Trinitate de Saint Augustin: Exégèse, logique et noétique*, eds. Emmanuel Bermon and Gerard O'Daly (Paris: Institut d'Études Augustiniennes, 2012): 123–135; 133. King has shown that we have the semantic resources to use inverse reciprocal correlatives in a situation where reference is made to only one object, but he has not done so by locating some feature in God on the far side of the divine life's incomprehensibility. What he has done, following Augustine, is use language to point at that incomprehensible life in three intrinsically interrelated ways.

trinitarian persons within that simple life of God. One predicates according to the distinction of the divine life from all the creation when one calls God, for example, great, good, wise, blessed, and so on, and because any of the triune persons considered in themselves are *idipsum*, predicating Greatness, Goodness, Wisdom, or Blessedness of the Father (or Son, or Spirit) are predications according to the distinction of God's life from creation rather than according to the trinitarian relations. This leads to rejection of accounts holding that the Father is not wise without the Son, or accounts holding that only the three triune persons in relation may be validly considered to be great, good, wise, or blessed.

On the other hand, there is a class of names and predications that are made of one or more of the three persons of the Trinity considered in their relations to the others. Among which: Father, Son, Holy Spirit; Word; Paraclete; Father of our Lord, wisdom of the Father, Spirit of Christ; light from light, True God from True God. More broadly, we can speak of the Father as the source of divinity, the Son and Holy Spirit as the Father's two hands, and so on. There will be some cases that may be difficult to determine on a first pass; it is clear that "begotten" and "spirated" are relative terms, but "unbegotten" seems to be a substantial predicate that does not require an inverse reciprocal correlate.[55] Yet upon closer inspection, we find even "unbegotten" to be a relational predicate: "when the Father is called unbegotten, it is not being stated what he is, but what he is not. And when a relationship is denied it is not denied substance-wise, because the relationship itself is not affirmed substance-wise."[56] Strictly speaking, every divine predication refers either to the divine life of God considered in itself and distinguished from all else that is, or to the three persons in which that divine life eternally consists.

In a sense, then, Augustine does not give us an account of God's life such that we are able to "distinguish" Father, Son, and Holy

---

[55] Precisely the argument of Augustine's opponents in *trin.* 5.6.7.

[56] *trin.* 5.6.7; WSA I/5, 193.

Spirit in the divine Being, formally reconciling simplicity and tri-unity. Each of the divine persons stands on the divine side of the creator/creation divide, and so the subsistence of each person is hidden in the simplicity of God's life. There are no fully comprehensible distinctions we can draw here that can describe the trinitarian persons in a manner proper to their existence – for if we could do so, we would need to say there are three Gods. Even our language of modes of origination or relationships provide mere analogies of the sense in which what it *is* to be God eternally enfolds the relations of Father, Son, and Holy Spirit to one another. Both God's threeness and God's oneness stand on the far side of our apophatic reserve, and so the sense in which these three are one bears the mark of divine unknowability.

It is a theological dead end, then, to argue about whether the threeness or oneness of God is more basic.[57] The incomprehensibility of the divine life is logically prior to both God's oneness and threeness. We must always remember that asking after the Trinity is asking after the mystery of God's own life, and so we should expect a strict limit to our ability to comprehend it. Rather than seeking to render the doctrine of the Trinity coherent with the doctrine of divine simplicity, our more restrained aim should be to undermine claims of its incoherence – and this is precisely what an Augustinian grammar of relational predication offers, showing us how our words can function to render sensible the notion of inverse reciprocal correlative predicates applying to one substance. This Augustinian account has not provided a comprehensive understanding of God's way of being, but has given us enough of a linguistic and conceptual foothold that we can reason about and understand something of God's triunity.

At the same time, we need not career into an epistemically motivated attraction to modalism. While we should renounce any aspiration of comprehending the metaphysics of the Trinity, the

---

[57] On which, see, Michel René Barnes, "De Régnon Reconsidered," and Sarah Coakley, "Re-Thinking Gregory of Nyssa: Introduction – Gender, Trinitarian Analogies, and the Pedagogy of The Song," *Modern Theology* 18.4 (2002): 431–443.

Church holds that God is tripersonal not only in the work of redemption, but even in God's eternal life *in se*. While our attempts properly to distinguish God from creation establish that God's life must lack composition, the doctrine of the Trinity informs us beyond the limits of reason's grasp that this simple life is eternally inwardly related as Father, Son, and Holy Spirit. The doctrine of the Trinity emerges not from our philosophical distinctions, but through reflection on Scripture, and on the councils of the Church. Though we (should) have no metaphysical story to tell of *how* it can be the case that God is both simple and eternally Father, Son, and Holy Spirit, such is the faith of the Church, and should be believed by all Christians. Indeed, it is the faith of the Church that secures the trinitarian relations as relations of origination, undergirding the important pro-Nicene account of the "monarchy" of the Father. Viewed strictly as a grammar of relational predication, this Augustinian account would not require any inward "movement" within the Trinity, and could be viewed merely as logical distinctions.[58] It is the teaching of the Church that leads us to view the triune Being and act of God as always a movement from the Father, through the Son, in the Holy Spirit, and to view the trinitarian relations as always beginning with the Father as *fons deitatis*, who eternally begets the Son and from whom the Spirit proceeds with and through the Son.

---

[58] I have in mind here Linn Marie Tonstad's rejection of the language of modes of origination to describe the trinitarian relations, preferring to speak of them as "asymmetrical exchanges" and "triadic intransitive relations"; see *God and Difference*, 229. While I am in significant agreement with Tonstad's evaluation of the negative effects of using trinitarian relations as a basis for descriptions of sexual difference, the language of modes of origination seems too theologically basic and too integral to God's manner of revealing the mystery of the Trinity *tout court* to be dispensable. Tonstad's attention to the distortive consequences of importing gendered language into the divine life has, however, led me to deemphasize the nuptial imagery of Augustine's doctrine of the *totus Christus*; on which, Kimberly F. Baker, "Augustine on Action, Contemplation, and Their Meeting Point in Christ" (Unpublished Ph.D. Dissertation, University of Notre Dame, 2007), 99–105.

As we evaluate the language of trinitarian theology, trying as rigorously as possible to conform our speech to God's transcendent difference from all else that exists, we are left with what Karen Kilby has recently called an "apophatic trinitarianism." Kilby asks,

> What if we were to suppose that how the three are one, how to relate the divine persons, what the inner relations between the persons are, are all questions which are quite simply beyond us? . . . What answers we may appear to have – answers drawing on notions of processions, relations, *perichoresis* – would be acknowledged as in fact no more than technical ways of articulating our inability to know.[59]

These terms do not tell us *nothing*, but they do not positively tell us what God *is*. Consequently, we should be quite wary of attempts to base ethical accounts of human social relations on the trinitarian relations proper to God's own life.[60] The more we seek to understand what these relations are, they more they slip away from our intellectual grasp until we arrive as always at the simple mystery of God's life. God is, eternally and intrinsically, Father, Son, and Holy Spirit; yet we can only be as confident that we understand this claim as we are that we understand the divine nature itself.

Moreover, we should be wary of accounts that understand the incarnation of the Word through the model of one of the Trinity's three centers of consciousness or agency assuming flesh – for this fundamentally misconceives how the language of agency and act is applied to the triune persons in the first place.[61] In his *sermo 52*, Augustine's guiding question is "Does the Father do anything that

---

[59] Karen Kilby, "Is an Apophatic Trinitarianism Possible?," *International Journal of Systematic Theology* 12.1 (2010): 65–77.

[60] Cf. Kathryn Tanner, *Jesus, Humanity, and the Trinity*, 82: "One should avoid modeling human relations directly on trinitarian ones, because trinitarian relations, say, the co-inherence of trinitarian Persons, simply are not appropriate as they stand for human relations."

[61] This is, of course, frequently how social trinitarians describe the persons of the Trinity. For a critique of the use of Patristic theology by social trinitarians, see Sarah Coakley, "'Persons' in the 'Social' Doctrine of the Trinity: Current Analytic Discussion and

the Son doesn't do, or the Son do anything that the Father doesn't do?" noting also that when God "has brought our efforts to a successful conclusion, we will have to understand that the Holy Spirit too is in no way excluded from the activity of the Father and of the Son."[62]

That Augustine describes this activity of the Father and the Son here with the singular *ab operatione* rather than the plural *ab operationibus* reminds us that this whole discussion takes places under an important proviso: We are speaking of God "as if separable" (*quasi separabile*), when no true separation is possible within the divine life. It is *one* activity that is ascribed to the God who is Father, Son, and Holy Spirit, even at those moments where Christian faith demands our clearest attributions of some divine work within the created order to one person in particular: "It was not indeed the Father, but the Son who suffered; yet the suffering of the Son was the work of both Father and Son. It wasn't the Father who rose again, but the Son; yet the resurrection of the Son was the work of both Father and Son."[63]

This description of the work of Father, Son, and Spirit as one *operatio* rather than three *operationes* raises what may be a lingering ambiguity in the classical trinitarian formulation *opera trinitatis ad extra indivisa sunt* (the works of the Trinity toward that which is not God are indivisible), an ambiguity directly relevant to the description of the Word's act of assuming flesh I will provide in the next chapter: Are these works to be understood as inseparable in the sense that the divine life is "*composed* of distinct actions, performed

---

'Cappadocian' Theology," in *Powers and Submissions: Spirituality, Philosophy, and Gender* (Oxford: Blackwell, 2002), 110–129.

[62] *s.* 52.4: *intelligitur etiam Spiritus sanctus ab operatione Patris et Filii nequaquam discedere*; WSA III/3, 52. Lewis Ayres has written extensively and insightfully on this sermon in his "Remember That You are Catholic (serm. 52.2): Augustine on the Unity of the Triune God," *Journal of Early Christian Studies* 8.1 (2000): 39–82.

[63] *s.* 52.8: *Non est quidem passus Pater, sed Filius: passionem tamen Filii et Pater et Filius operatus est. Non resurrexit Pater, sed Filius: resurrectionem tamen Filii et Pater et Filius operatus est*; WSA III/3, 54.

by distinct agents"?[64] Or is it a mistake to think of three individual if finally inseparable activities in this manner?

Based on the description I have offered of how theological language points us to the divine life, it is clearly a mistake to speak of three individual activities, performed by three distinct agents, composing together the divine life. Describing the actions of the trinitarian persons in this way would locate the threeness of God on the near side of God's incomprehensibility: It would be to say that our concepts of distinctness and relation apply univocally to God. Rejecting this claim is not, of course, to *deny* that distinctness and relation are truly predicated of God's eternal life: This would be to say that the three persons are reducible in the divine life, that we may *speak* of God as Father, Son, and Holy Spirit, but that God's incomprehensibility ultimately leads us to affirm the priority of God's simple life. This option would default in the other direction, denying the revealed truth of God's triunity.

We must affirm God's triunity on the far side of the divine incomprehensibility, holding that God is truly and eternally Father, Son, and Holy Spirit, but is not three in the manner that we customarily understand threeness. God's acts toward that which is not God are inseparable not because they are performed ever-concurrently by three agents, but because the one life of God is always and intrinsically the life of Father, Son, and Holy Spirit together. We may speak of God having one activity, just as we may speak of the one Goodness that is the divine life as

[64] Adonis Vidu offers this framing of the question at "Opera Trinitatis ad Extra and Collective Agency," *European Journal for Philosophy of Religion* 7.3 (2015): 27–47, 34. See also Lewis Ayres' discussions of the inseparable actions of the trinitarian persons at *Nicaea and its Legacy: An Approach to Fourth-Century Trinitarian Theology* (Oxford: Oxford University Press, 2004), 296–300; and *Augustine and the Trinity*, 46–48, where he distinguishes between the doctrine of "common operation," understood as "the argument that all three persons must have the same ontological status because each is described in Scripture as performing the same acts," and the doctrine of "inseparable operations," in which "all three divine persons work in each divine act" (46).

distinguished from all else that exists. So also, we may speak of a distinct activity of the Father, or of the Son, or of the Holy Spirit, just as the Father is Herself the fullness of the Good with reference to Herself (*ad se ipsum*). This activity of the Father *ad se ipsum* just is the activity of the triune Lord in its integral unity, the whole work of God.

Yet the Father only is the Father inasmuch as She is distinguished by reciprocal relation to the Son and the Holy Spirit, and so we may also speak of the distinct activity of the Father in Her relation to the other triune persons. In this sense, the Father is only said to possess a distinct activity in that that activity is distinguished by its relation to the distinct activities of Son and Holy Spirit.[65] One may thus speak of the one activity of God in two ways (as the work of the one God; and as the work of any one of the trinitarian persons, each of whom possesses the fullness of the divine life and so enacts the fullness of the work of the one God), as well as speaking of the distinctive activity of the trinitarian persons in two ways (as the threefold activity of the persons in relation; and again as the work of any one of the trinitarian persons, each of whom possesses the fullness of the divine life and so enacts the fullness of the work of the one God).

When Christians profess that the Son has assumed flesh, or that the Holy Spirit has enabled us to pray truly, we may truly ascribe that action to the person of the Son or the person of the Holy Spirit. Yet since what it is to *be* the Son is to be incomprehensibly related to both Father and Holy Spirit, this act is only understood truly as an activity *of the Son* inasmuch as it is understood to be incomprehensibly inseparable from the activities of the Father and Holy Spirit – which is also to say, inasmuch as it is understood to be an activity of the simple life of the one God. Because God's manner of relating as triune is ineffable, so also the distinction of God's activities according to the persons of Father, Son, and Holy Spirit is ineffable.

[65] This is not to deny the *monarchia* of the Father; but if the Father is to be the source of the *divine* life, then the Father must *eternally* be the source of divinity alongside the *eternal* life of the Son and Holy Spirit.

We may speak of God's life as distinct in eternal relation, and so we can speak of God's acts toward the world as distinct in eternal relation; but we should not be fooled into thinking that we know what we mean when we speak in this way.

It should come as no surprise, then, that the apophatic affirmation already employed to mark off the singularity of God as *idipsum* appears originally in the context of Augustine's trinitarian theology:

> So what are we to say, brothers, about God? For if you have fully grasped what you want to say, it isn't God. If you have been able to comprehend it, you have comprehended something else instead of God. If you think you have been able to comprehend, your thoughts have deceived you. So he isn't this, if this is what you have understood; but if he is this, then you haven't understood it. So what is it you want to say, seeing you haven't been able to understand it?[66]

If Augustine is right – as he seems to me to be – we cannot speak of a oneness more basic than a threeness; we cannot speak of a doctrine *de deo uno* necessarily preceding a doctrine *de deo trino*. It is encountering the triune Lord in the human flesh of Christ that allows us to know more of the simple life of God than any creature could otherwise know. Yet it is reflection on that very incomprehensibility of the divine life, and the lack of any real distinction within it, that rules out any attempt to qualify the divinity of the Son and Spirit as mere θεός against the Father's ὁ θεός, or as merely ὅμοιος or ὁμοιούσιος rather than ὁμοούσιος. God is a simple multiplicity, and a multiple simplicity (*simplex multiplicitas vel multiplex simplicitas*).[67] What was it, beyond that, that we were trying to say?

---

[66] *s.* 52.16: *Quid ergo dicamus, fratres, de Deo? Si enim quod vis dicere, si cepisti, non est Deus: si comprehendere potuisti, aliud pro Deo comprehendisti. Si quasi comprehendere potuisti, cogitatione tua te decepisti. Hoc ergo non est, si comprehendisti: si autem hoc est, non comprehendisti. Quid ergo vis loqui, quod comprehendere non potuisti?*; WSA III/3, 57.

[67] *trin.* 6.4.6.

2 | The Human Life of God

The argument of the previous chapter has left us in what might seem a tenuous christological place: For if this Augustinian picture of God is right, then God does not (in Her divinity) enter into the series of created temporality and undergo Christ's experiences in succession; God is not the sort of being whose thoughts or willings can be mapped in a one-for-one correlation onto Christ's thoughts or willings, for the intellect and will of God are none other than the simplicity of Her life; the persons of the Trinity are not three independent centers of consciousness or agency such that one of them might come to find his divine consciousness within Christ. The mere predication of intellect, or will, or constancy of love to the Trinity significantly underdetermines the shape of Christ's life, for none of these concepts (or any other) truly describe the divine life *in the way* we apply them to God.[1] Within the divine life, we are without a compass, unable to mark off where God's existence ends and Her act begins; where Her Goodness shades into Her Beauty and Truth; unable to locate even a before or an after, the basic temporal categories that structure all our experience of the world.

Yet even as this underdetermination leaves a relatively open christological terrain, we must ask: What might it mean for such a God to become incarnate? How might such a God possibly enter into the course of our world's history, live a human life, grow and speak and

---

[1] Cf. Lawrence Dewan's discussion of the Thomist distinction between the *res significata*, which does indeed truly apply to God in the case of something like Good or Truth, and our *modus significandi*, which predicates goodness to God as a quality distinct from other qualities like goodness and beauty. See Lawrence Dewan, "Saint Thomas, Alvin Plantinga, and the Divine Simplicity," *The Modern Schoolman* 66.2 (1989): 141–151.

suffer and die as one of us? Such questions, as is true of all questions that seek to describe the act that is the Being of the triune Lord, push theological speech beyond its point of defection. One can feel this strain in the rhetorical patterns with which Augustine often begins his sermons on the Nativity:

> *My mouth will speak the praise of the Lord*: that Lord, through whom all things were made, and who was made among all things; who is the revealer of his Father, and the creator of his mother; the Son of God from his Father without mother, son of man from his mother without father; the great Day of the angels, small on the day of man; God the Word before all times, the Word enfleshed at the appropriate time; author of the sun, finished beneath the sun; ordering all ages from the bosom of the Father, hallowing this very day from the womb of his mother; remaining there, proceeding here; maker of heaven and earth, appearing below heaven on earth; ineffably wise, wisely without speech; filling up the world, lying in a manger; ruling over the stars, nursing at the breast; and thus great in the form of God, but finite in the form of the servant, such that the greatness was not diminished by that finitude, nor the finitude suppressed by that greatness.[2]

Augustine struggles for ever more surprising oppositions, seeking to enflame his congregation's hearts with the love of God and draw their minds more deeply into the mystery of the Incarnation. Some of this pattern of speaking is, no doubt, attributable to Augustine's search for a tenor of speech suitably elevated to the festal day.[3] Yet there is also an important guide to his broader christological concerns in this passage. Augustine is seeking a habit of language that reflects the ineffable God's incomprehensible assumption of flesh.

What he settles upon is this vertiginous oscillation between the exaltation of the *forma Dei* and the humility of the *forma servi*.[4]

---

[2] *s.* 187.1. The date and location of the sermon are unclear.

[3] Cf. *doctr. chr.* 4.2.3; WSA I/11, 201.

[4] On the centrality of this formulation in Augustine's christology, see especially Albert Verwilghen, "Le Christ médiateur selon Ph 2, 6–7 dans l'oeuvre de saint

Through these juxtapositions, and through his consistent hermeneutical deployment of the *forma Dei/forma servi* motif, Augustine outlines the guiding principles of his christological reflection: In assuming flesh, both Christ's divinity and humanity remain what they are, without change to either nature; yet the two are truly one in the one life of Christ. The two sides of each opposition – the Word before time enfleshed on a particular day, the God who maintains the sun in its course dying beneath the sun – make clear both the reality of the Incarnation and the preservation of the distinction between divinity and humanity, even in the human life which is God's.[5]

Augustine's language here is meant to be paradoxical; it is meant to emphasize the care with which we must approach even the most foundational questions of christology, and the ineffable mystery at the heart of its central claims.[6] When we speak of the Incarnation,

Augustin," *Augustiniana* 41.1/4 (1991): 469–482; and Lewis Ayres, *Augustine and the Trinity* (Oxford: Oxford University Press, 2011), 142–147. Michael Cameron notes the use of this passage in Manichean thought at *Christ Meets Me Everywhere*, 107, and discusses its particular significance in debate with Fortunatus at 124–129.

[5] Augustine's use of such paradoxical christological statements parallels, in some respects, St. Cyril of Alexandria's claim that the Word "suffers impassibly" in Christ; see Cyril, *Scholia on the Incarnation* 35, and John J. O'Keefe, "Impassible Suffering: Divine Passion and Fifth-Century Christology," *Theological Studies* 58.1 (1997): 39–60; and J. Warren Smith, "Suffering Impassibly: Christ's Passion in Cyril of Alexandria's Soteriology," *Pro Ecclesia* 11.4 (2002): 463–83. Augustine's use of paradoxical constructions, in contrast with Cyril's, much more obviously preserves the distinction of natures even in the context of the Incarnation, in a manner that was to prove quite influential on the Tome of Leo; see John Thomas Newton, Jr., "The Importance of Augustine's Use of the Neoplatonic Doctrine of Hypostatic Union for the Development of Christology," *Augustinian Studies* 2 (1971): 1–16. See also McGuckin, "Did Augustine's Christology Depend on Theodore?," 52 n.38 on the Augustinian roots of Leo's Tome by way of Prosper of Aquitaine; and Brian Daley, "The Giant's Twin Substances: Ambrose and the Christology of Augustine's Contra sermonem Arianorum," in *Augustine: Presbyter Factus Sum*, eds. Joseph T. Lienhard, Earl C. Müller, and Roland J. Teske (New York: Peter Lang, 1993), 477–495, 488.

[6] Brian Daley has noted that "Many of Augustine's allusions to Christ are deliberately phrased, it seems, to bring out the central paradox of Christ's person, as the Christian tradition proclaims it, and to do this by rhetorical means rather than technical terminology"; Brian E. Daley, *God Visible: Patristic Christology Reconsidered* (Oxford: Oxford University Press, 2018), 151. Van Bavel similarly notes from the time of

we speak of an act of the triune Lord. We might say: If you think you have understood this act, it is not the divine act by which the Word assumes flesh. The image Augustine offers to help his congregation understand this mystery, characteristic of his mature christological thought, is that of the expression of an "internal word" in the physical phenomenon of speech.[7] Whatever the merits of the philosophy of language here, the relevant point is that the purely intelligible word takes on what is radically improper to its nature – the movements of lips, tongue, and vocal chords; the air waves that transmit sound; the vibrations of the hearer's eardrums – without undergoing any change in itself. At no point is the inner word transmuted into physical signs, even as it becomes manifest to other intellects by means of such signs. So, too, the Word of God: Augustine consistently portrays the Incarnation as the addition of flesh to the Word, without any change to the divine life itself.[8] Augustine puts the point clearly to his listeners: "When from the world of time [the Word] took flesh, in order to come forth into our time-bound life, it did not in the flesh lose eternity, but rather on the flesh too bestowed immortality."[9]

It is this opposition between God's eternity and our temporality – or again, God's changelessness and our mutability – that presses the

---

Augustine's consecration as bishop on that he favors constructions like *humanitatis divinitatis et divinitas humanitatis* (*en.Ps.* 15.3); cf. Tarsicius J. van Bavel, *Recherches sur la christologie de saint Augustin, l'humain et le divin dans le Christ d'après Saint Augustin*, (Fribourg en Suisse: Editions universitaires, 1954), 15 n.7.

[7] *s.* 187.3; WSA III/6, 28: "the matter itself (*res ipsa quae dicenda est*), before any variety of expression in any language, is so to say naked to the intelligence in the bed-chamber of the mind, and which in order to come out from there is clothed in the voice of the speaker." On Augustine's theology of the *verbum internum* (or the *verbum mentis*) and its Stoic origins, see R. A. Markus, *Signs and Meanings: World and Text in Ancient Christianity* (Liverpool: Liverpool University Press, 1996), 94–101; and Eugene TeSelle, *Augustine the Theologian* (Eugene, OR: Wipf and Stock, 1970), 300–309.

[8] Cf. *s.* 187.3; WSA III/6, 28: "None of you therefore should believe that the Son of God was converted and changed into a son of man; but rather we must believe that while remaining the Son of God he became the son of man, and that the divine substance was not consumed, while the human substance was perfectly assumed."

[9] *s.* 187.4; WSA III/6, 29.

christological challenge of the union of divinity and humanity most forcefully. For how can the Lord who is without any before or after live in the intrinsic temporality of a human life? How can the God who teaches, and loves, and acts, and offers Himself over to sinners in the life of Christ possibly be the God who Augustine describes as dwelling in unchangeable beatitude?

In this chapter, I will take this seeming opposition between God's eternity and our temporality as a lens through which to examine more closely the union of divinity and humanity in Christ. In calling attention to what I take to be one of the points of greatest difficulty in christological reflection, I hope to help us see more clearly what a theologian occupying a broadly Augustinian understanding of God should and should not say about the Incarnation. My aim is not, however, to constrain theological speech: It is to commend the very paradox and opposition that characterizes Augustine's *sermo* 187. The wager of this chapter is that if we first reach clarity on how a timeless God may yet live in history, we will open a register of theological speech every bit as surprising as Augustine's reflections on the Nativity: We will find a christological outlook in which Christ not only lives in the world, but is determined by his relations to it; an outlook in which the world's existence and agency themselves contribute to the identity of Christ, and are drawn unsubstitutably into the work of redemption.[10]

***

In the preceding chapter, I offered a brief argument for God's unchangeability: If we are incapable of drawing any real distinctions in the divine life, then we are incapable of identifying any succession in God. Indeed, the only logical priority or posteriority we can identify in God at all is that of the triune relations: The Son is begotten of the Father; the Holy Spirit proceeds from Father and Son. These cannot, however, be considered relations of succession: Were that the case, it would be true to say "there was when the Son was not" – even if not

---

[10] I draw language of "unsubstitutability" from Frei, *The Identity of Jesus Christ*, 34.

a time, properly, an ontological interval in which the Father is prior to Son and Spirit.[11] The teaching that the divine life is itself the eternal triune relation of Father, Son, and Holy Spirit is meant to deny precisely this possibility. Even the trinitarian relations, then, cannot be understood as introducing succession, or even a real distinction that would be an analogate of temporal succession, in the divine life. There just is no before or after in the life of God.

This denial of changeability in God is, for Augustine, more than just a consequence of the doctrine of divine simplicity: He takes it to mark off one of the key ways that God's life is not like our own. For the creation, the fact that we exist by participation in God is the basis of our capacity for change. We not only participate in God, but can participate more or less fully, turning toward God in grateful reception of our existence or turning away from Her in sin. We can come to participate in God differently, exemplifying some quality that we previously did not. Perhaps I grow from an infant into a toddler, and learn to speak; perhaps I study under a master woodworker, and learn eventually how to produce woodcuts myself. In each case, this new skill allows me to reflect the goodness of God differently than I had previously been able to do. Both before and after, I am one who bears a likeness to God, but now, the likeness I display to God has changed: I am able to speak, analogously to the way God speaks to Moses on Sinai; I am able to draw a new form out of the woodblock, analogous to God's creation and ordering of the cosmos. Because every quality that I might possibly exemplify points back to its source in the divine life, it is right to say that *every* change I might possibly undergo allows me to serve differently as an image-bearer of God.[12]

---

[11] In the language favored by Alexandrian theologians at the outbreak of the trinitarian controversy, there is no διάστημα – "interval," whether conceived as temporal or not – between the existence of Father and Son. See Rowan Williams, *Arius: Heresy and Tradition*, revised edition (Grand Rapids, MI: Wm. B. Eerdmans, 2001), 155.

[12] This is true even of privative changes: for the sinner, as the sinner she is, holds the potential to signify God precisely in her forgiveness and redemption. The only exception would be an annihilative change.

God is not like that. God does not receive His goodness through dependence on anything else, for He is the Selfsame, the one who is Himself the source of all the goods any creature might possibly exemplify. This is why unchangeability is one of the predications of God that Augustine most frequently employs to describe the unsurpassable blessedness of the divine life.[13] As James F. Anderson has put it, "Augustine's *mutabilitas* functions as a kind of potency in the sense of an existential limitation, whereas his *immutabilitas* is simply 'act,' or as he himself often puts it, '*vere esse.*' To be 'immutable' is to be incapable of not-being; to be 'mutable' is to be able not to be."[14] The fact that you and I are in the condition of being capable of being made into saints entails that we are not yet saints; this is a good that our lives presently lack. Similarly, the fact that we are presently alive, changeable, and finite means that someday, we will both die – we will come to lack the good of life. The claim that God is unchangeable is intimately tied to the claim that God is the source of all goodness. As Augustine writes at *De trinitate* 5.10.11, God "is not great with a greatness which he is not himself, as though God were to participate in it to be great; otherwise this greatness would be greater than God. But there is nothing greater than God. So he is great with a greatness by which he is himself this same greatness."[15] If God is Himself the Good, there can be no quality that He did not previously possess but later comes to exemplify, for that would mean that God at one point lacked this goodness. By the same token, He is not able to lose any goodness, because His life is identical to that Good.[16]

Consider the implications of God's unchangeability for how we think of God's knowledge of creation. It would seem to be a good of

---

[13] See, for instance, *Io.ev.tr.* 1.8, and *trin.* 5.2.3.

[14] James F. Anderson, *St. Augustine and Being: A Metaphysical Essay* (Hague: Martinus Nijhoff, 1965), 17.

[15] *trin.* 5.10.11; WSA I/5, 196.

[16] Rowan Williams has drawn out the importance of the unchangeability of God's goodness for moral theology, in response to Kathleen Sands' description of divine goodness as "various, mobile and vulnerable": "Say that the Good is, indeed, properly conceived as 'various, mobile and vulnerable': this might mean that the Good is

the divine life that She know all there is to know, that She be omniscient. If there is any knowledge that She lacks but later learns – say (as an open theist might) that God learns what act I choose to perform as I perform it – then Her knowledge has changed; and if we can draw no real distinction in the divine life between God's knowledge and other attributes, this entails that the divine life and the Good that God is has changed. The same conclusion results from claiming that there is indeterminacy in God's knowledge of creation: Say that God knows all the things I *might* do, but does not know what I *actually* do. If God does not possess this knowledge in full determinacy from all eternity, the same conclusion results: There is change in the divine life itself. For Augustine, then, we can come to reject this conclusion from two different trajectories: Based on his understanding of the divine goodness, any lack of knowledge in God or possibility of change in God's knowledge itself would suggest that God is not Herself the Good.

Similar considerations apply to our understanding of God's will and act. If God does not change, then God should not be conceived of as willing something at one time, and something else at another: "Whatever he wills, he wills once only and all together and eternally, not in repetitive fashion, nor this today and that tomorrow, nor willing later what he did not will previously, nor going back later on what he wanted earlier."[17] If we cannot draw any real

different for different created subjects, to the extent that what is good for one subject is necessarily and permanently at odds with what is good for another; that the Good genuinely differs from circumstance to circumstance, without any 'grammar' of continuity; that the Good of or for certain subjects might simply and finally fail or prove impossible of realization"; *On Augustine*, 99.

[17] *conf.* 12.15.18; WSA I/1, 321–2. See also *conf.* 7.4.6 and 11.10.12, and the interesting exchange in David Bentley Hart, "The Hidden and the Manifest: Metaphysics after Nicaea," in *Orthodox Readings of Augustine*, eds. George E. Demacopoulos and Aristotle Papanikolaou (Crestwood, NY: St. Vladimir's Seminary Press, 2008), 191–226; and David Bradshaw, "Augustine the Metaphysician," in *Orthodox Readings of Augustine*, eds. George E. Demacopoulos and Aristotle Papanikolaou (Crestwood, NY: St. Vladimir's Seminary Press, 2008), 227–252, on the question of whether Augustine believes that God's eternal will includes all historical particulars, or if it is merely the faculty of divine will which is simple and eternal. As will be apparent, I side

distinction in God, we should not claim that God's will is something other than the divine life itself.[18] Even a distinction between what God is and what He does would suggest that our categories of existence and action are fit to be applied to the mystery of God's way of being.

Neither can God's life be subdivided into different moments of time. When Augustine stretches to describe the difference between our own temporal existence and God's eternity, he imagines the flow of time gathered together, an everlasting "Today" that encompasses past, present, and future.[19] While I think it fair to say that Augustine never reaches a settled position on just what time is and how it relates to the life of God,[20] Augustine does, from the time of his earliest writings, maintain a central emphasis on the presence of all things to God's eternity: "To God . . . nothing is absent, and hence nothing is either past or future, but everything is present to God."[21]

with Bradshaw on this issue, and cite also Katherin Rogers' observation that "Augustine says repeatedly that God foreknows the particular sins his individual creatures will commit," paralleling Augustine's statement in *conf.* 11.31.41 that "As you knew heaven and earth in the beginning, without the slightest modification in your knowledge, so too you made heaven and earth in the beginning without any distention in your activity" (WSA I/1, 311); Katherin A. Rogers, "St. Augustine on Time and Eternity," *American Catholic Philosophical Quarterly* 70.2 (1996): 207–223, 209.

[18] Cf. *conf.* 12.15.18; and *conf.* 12.28.38; WSA I/1, 336: "Your will is identical with yourself, and you made all things by no change of will whatsoever, without the emergence of any volition which had not previously been present."

[19] *conf.* 11.13.16, WSA I/1 295: "your years stand all at once, because they are stable (*Anni tui omnes simul stant, quoniam stant*): there is no pushing out of vanishing years by those that are coming on, because with you none are transient. In our case, our years will be complete only when there are none left. Your years are a single day, and this day of yours is not a daily recurrence, but a simple 'Today,' because your Today does not give way to tomorrow, nor follow yesterday. Your Today is eternity."

[20] As a careful study has recently argued, there are in fact "at least *nine* distinct views on the nature of time" in Augustine's thought; Jason W. Carter, "St. Augustine on Time, Time Numbers, and Enduring Objects," *Vivarium* 49.4 (2011): 301–323, 302.

[21] *div. qu.* 17; WSA I/12, 37. It is important to note, however, that this does not suggest for Augustine the eternity of creation itself, cf. *conf.* 11.7.9. For two recent accounts of how affirmation of God's atemporality is compatible with real metaphysical change in the created order, see Paul Helm's essay "The Two Standpoints," in Helm, *Eternal*

Where does this all leave us? First, it means that the act of God, both in its willing and in its performance, must be identified with the one simple life of God itself. Accordingly, there can be no real distinction in God between what we describe as the diverse actions of God: creation; incarnation; divine decrees (if you are of such a persuasion); or whatever other distinctions you are hoping to draw between God's actions in eternity or in relation to the world. Whether we are speaking of God's intra-triune relations or speaking of the activity of God directed to the created order, all that God does is to be identified with the simplicity of the divine life. This is not to say that we cannot *speak* of these acts differently. We may distinguish between God's acts of, *inter alia*, creation and incarnation because the one act of God produces diverse effects in the created order, first bringing it into existence and later uniting created flesh to the Second Person of the Trinity. We should understand what we are doing when we talk about diverse acts of creation or incarnation on the model of how we distinguish between the attributes of God: It is one thing for us to call God good, and another for us to call God true, because we know goodness and truth to be separate attributes of things in the created order. But as we trace our way back from these created effects to the simple life of God in which it exists by participation, we should say that our distinction between what it is to be good and what it is to be true is not reflective of any ultimate distinction in the divine life. So also with all the acts of God: All that God does, God is from all eternity.

Second, then: When we think of the act by which God brings the world into being, we should understand the whole course of history, from its beginning to its ultimate eschatological glorification, as included within the one act by which God gives creation existence. This act founds each moment of created history in all its particulars: every hair on every head; the fall of each sparrow; each quantum

God: A Study of God without Time, 2nd ed. (Oxford: Oxford University Press, 2010), 251–269; and Brian Leftow, "Presentism, Atemporality, and Time's Way," *Faith and Philosophy* 35.2 (2018): 173–194.

state and superposition. As Paul Helm has written, "in creation God brings into being (timelessly) the whole temporal matrix. He knows (timelessly) all about it. In his mind all events are brought together, but they are not brought together at a time, but timelessly. God is time-free."[22] If there were any indeterminacy in God's one creative will, there would be succession in God – for instance, what was previously an indeterminate range of possibilities being rendered determinate by some free act of a creature. And if we distinguish between what is included in God's creative will (say, the will to create free agents) and what is not eternally included in God's free will (the particular choices that free agents will make), we have imposed a division within the incomprehensibility of the divine life. The one timeless act of God's life is irreducibly prior to the existence of creation, and is determinate from all eternity; and so we should hold that all the determinate particulars of created history are included within the creative act of God.

Third, and in a point that will bear christological fruit in later chapters: Augustine identifies the Word of God as being particularly implicated in the ordering of created times. At *conf.* 11.8.10, for instance, he writes that "Everything which begins to exist and then ceases to exist does so at the due time for its beginning and cessation decreed in that eternal Reason where nothing begins or comes to an end. This eternal Reason is your Word, who is the Beginning in that he also speaks to us."[23] This accords with a general theme of Augustine's work on the order of creation, by which the Word as the wisdom (*sapientia*) of God is the one who creates each thing in the proper limits of its nature (often summed up as their "measure, weight, and number"), and sets them in their relations to one

---

[22] Helm, *Eternal God*, 27.

[23] *conf.* 11.8.10; WSA I/1, 291. See also *conf.* 11.7.9; WSA I/1, 291: "Thus in that Word who is coeternal with yourself you speak all that you speak simultaneously and eternally, and whatever you say shall be comes into being. Your creative act is in no way different from your speaking. Yet things which you create by speaking do not all come to be simultaneously, nor are they eternal."

another.[24] This understanding of the Word as the *sapientia* of God, ordering each creature from its beginning to its eschatological completion, will play an increasingly important role in developing the implications of Augustine's christology.[25]

When we try to imagine God's timeless relation to created history, then, the best we can do (as ever) is to think toward God from the familiar phenomena of our temporal experience. As Katherin Rogers suggests, "The temporal phenomenon with which we are familiar which is most like eternity is the present, durationless, instant . . . The analogy points out that eternity may be present to all time as the present instant is to all space."[26] We should conceive of God's life as properly timeless – timeless not in being on one end of a "temporal/non-temporal" distinction, but timeless in that our experience of time simply does not apply to the divine life. This, too, is a basically apophatic category, rather than a claim that God's life is static. We should not think that the analogy to a present instant offers us any firm understanding of how the timeless God relates to the created order. Reflecting on how God's eternal knowledge of creation might be compared to the difference between praying through a psalm and holding the whole psalm in mind at once, Augustine quickly adds, "far be it from us to suppose that you, the creator of the universe, creator of souls and bodies, know all things future and past in this fashion! Perish the thought! Far, far more wonderful is your mode of knowing, and far more mysterious."[27] While reflection on God's timelessness may be useful in clearing away misconceptions about the divine life that constrain it by

---

[24] See William J. Roche, "Measure, Number, and Weight in St. Augustine," *The New Scholasticism* 15.4 (1941): 350–376.

[25] As developed in greater detail in chapters eight and ten of Rowan Williams, *On Augustine*.

[26] Katherin A. Rogers, "Eternity Has No Duration," *Religious Studies* 30.1 (1994): 1–16, 15.

[27] *conf.* 11.31.41; WSA I/1, 311. James Wetzel emphasizes in this passage that "Augustine has here refused himself the consolation of an analogy. He will not let those brief times when he feels at one with his knowing shape his expectation of the divine intelligence"; James Wetzel, *Augustine: A Guide for the Perplexed* (London: T&T Clark, 2010), 125.

attributing to it the same limitations of our own historical experience, we must never think this allows us to occupy the standpoint of eternity – to know as God knows.

***

This account of God's relation to created temporality will, I suspect, be deeply unsatisfying to many. While I have no illusions of being able to assuage all these worries, let me address three particular concerns about this approach in the interest of clarifying my own position. These worries are: first, about the freedom of God; second, about the freedom of creatures; and third and finally, about God's responsibility for sin.

First, then, the position I have outlined is wholly compatible with ascribing freedom to God's creative will.[28] Augustine comments at *civ.* 5.10 that "we certainly do not make the life of God and the foreknowledge of God subject to necessity if we say that it is necessary for God to live eternally and to foreknow all things, just as his power is not diminished when we say that he cannot die or that he cannot be deceived. And this is not possible because, if it were possible, he would actually have less power."[29] If we were to say that God did not always possess the will to create the world and become incarnate in Christ, we would have to say that this volition arose in Her; but this would be to attribute mutability to God.

Similarly, if God did not know from all eternity that She would create the world and become incarnate within it, we would have to say God attained this knowledge at some point. Here we might say with Augustine that if this were possible, God would be diminished. To attribute freedom to God is to say that God is under no constraint or compulsion to create, and especially that creation adds

---

[28] For more sustained arguments in favor of this claim, see Lynne Rudder Baker, "Why Christians Should Not Be Libertarians: An Augustinian Challenge," *Faith and Philosophy* 20.4 (2003): 460–478; and Jesse Couenhoven, "Augustine's Rejection of the Free-Will Defence: An Overview of the Late Augustine's Theodicy," *Religious Studies* 43.3 (2007): 279–298.

[29] WSA I/6, 156–157.

nothing to God.[30] Nevertheless, God is always who God is; the character of God's Goodness is established from all eternity. God would not be less good had God not chosen to create, for this would imply some lack in God that is fulfilled through creation; or again, if we understood creation as some sort of mechanical emanation from God, God could not be God without creating. The eternity of God's will to create only comes to appear problematic or like the constraint of necessity if we view the Being of God as more basic than God's will, such that God's will is constrained by what is essential to God's existence. Or again, the eternity of this will only appears like naked voluntarism if we view the will of God as more basic than God's Being, such that this will is construed as an unmotivated choice between alternative possibilities in which God assigns content to God's Being. Yet throughout, I have been concerned to maintain the incomprehensibility of the divine life as a boundary that profoundly disorients our conceptual categories. If neither God's Being nor will are considered logically prior to the other, we need not fear that the eternity of God's Being constrains God's will into a necessary creation, nor worry that the ontological basicality of God's will voluntaristically determines God's Being in unmotivated fashion. Consequently, no threat of creation's necessity arises, even as we claim that God was never without the will to create and become incarnate.

Second, the understanding of creaturely agency I propose can best be understood through Kathryn Tanner's now-standard account of the "non-competitive" relation between divine and creaturely freedom.[31] Tanner writes, "God does not give on the same plane of being and activity as creatures, as one among other givers

---

[30] Sokolowski, *God of Faith and Reason: Foundations of Christian Theology*, 2nd ed. (Washington, DC: The Catholic University of America Press, 1995), 8–10.

[31] Tanner's move from the language of a "non-contrastive" relation in *God and Creation* to that of "non-competitive" in later works seems to be a terminological innovation only; cf. Kathryn Tanner, *God and Creation in Christian Theology: Tyranny or Empowerment?* (Minneapolis, MN: Fortress Press, 1998).

and therefore God is not in potential competition (or cooperation) with them."[32] The crucial point to note for the time being is that not only does God not compete with creaturely action contingently – Ze does not even compete *potentially*. If it were possible under any circumstances for God's act to be in competition with our own, it would indicate that they operated on the same plane, that God could (if only potentially) elbow our freedom out of the picture by exercising Her own agency. If God's agency is simply on another plane than our own, however, God may be perfectly free in willing, and we may similarly be perfectly free, without there being any conflict or competition: "The glorification of God does not come at the expense of creatures."[33]

This noncompetitive relation does not serve to quarantine off God's agency from the created order, but rather "suggests an extreme of divine involvement with the world – a divine involvement in the form of a productive agency extending to everything that is in an equally direct manner."[34] Because all creaturely agency and causality are founded upon the act of God, there is nothing that exists that is distant from God's action upon it; God's action must be understood as "immediate and universally extensive."[35] Neither does it negate the possibility of co-agential activity performed by both God and creation.[36] God's agency does not close off our freedom – it founds it. Even if all the works we will ever perform are known and included in their determinate particularity within God's creative will, God still creates us as agents who are free to will and act as we wish. God's agency, because it is not on the same plane as our own, places no constraint upon created agency.

---

[32] Tanner, *Jesus, Humanity, and the Trinity*, 3.

[33] Tanner, *Jesus, Humanity, and the Trinity*, 2.

[34] Tanner, *God and Creation*, 46.

[35] Tanner, *God and Creation*, 47.

[36] Tanner, *God and Creation*, 93: "Where created causes are operative, it is improper to claim that God's work is separately sufficient for a created effect to the exclusion of created causes. Such a statement is not well formed since God's creative intention includes in the instance the founding of created causes."

Though divine timelessness does not figure largely into her account, Tanner's resultant picture is very close to the Augustinian one I have offered: "Christian talk of God's creative agency [must] be worked out in a genuinely radical way: God must be directly productive of everything that is in every aspect of its existence."[37] There is nothing that exists, in any of its particulars, that does not exist as God wills it to be. All that is, to the extent that it is, is the gift of God, and exists precisely as God wills it. As a result, we must understand the simple creative act of God as the one act in which God wills the entire course of created history, from beginning to end. "The divine will is radically transcendent, in other words, but necessarily efficacious: What God wills has to happen."[38]

This affirmation, third and finally, raises the question of God's responsibility for sin. Tanner leaves the question aside;[39] Augustine, for better or worse, goes somewhat further. In a letter written at the end of his life, he says of God:

> Of course nothing happens unless he himself does it or permits that it be done, and since he willingly does it and willingly permits it, absolutely nothing happens if he does not will it. Yet it is true to say that whatever is displeasing to him is done contrary to his will. Still, he permits evils to happen because he is powerful enough to produce good, which is his, out of evils, which are not his.[40]

Importantly, Augustine affirms here a true sense in which the whole course of created history, inclusive of all the horrors sin wreaks on the world, is included within God's eternal will, with a priority to any created willing (sinful or otherwise). To put this in the starkest

---

[37] Tanner, *God and Creation*, 47.

[38] Tanner, *God and Creation*, 73.

[39] In her most precise account of the noncompetitive/noncontrastive relation between God and the created order, Tanner notes: "Questions of sin and evil are left out of account in what follows; the intelligibility of evil if a theologian follows our rules is a further question not addressed in this work"; *God and Creation*, 174 n.12.

[40] *ep.* 2*.8; WSA II/4, 237. Wetzel discusses this passage at James Wetzel, *Augustine and the Limits of Virtue* (Cambridge: Cambridge University Press, 1992), 209–210.

possible terms, God brings into being a created history that includes sinful acts – a somewhat stronger statement than saying God brings into being a world knowing that there will be sin. We are pushed to this stronger formulation by two considerations: First, God brings the whole course of created history timelessly into being, and so there is no moment of that history that comes into being earlier than another with respect to God's life. Second, God not only "foreknows" what created agents will do, but knows what they will do as She brings them into being. Said differently, God's knowledge is itself creative. But if this is right, then God brings created agents into being knowing unquestionably that they will sin.

Does this not straightforwardly make God the author of sin? Not quite. For as Tanner observes, "it is axiomatic that God creates only what is good," and this is no less true for Augustine.[41] The appropriate question to ask is thus: What is the good that God wills in creating the creaturely agent who sins? There are two answers to this question.

First, God wills the existence of the creaturely agent *qua* creaturely agent. Things exist by participation in God's life, and to the extent that they exist, they are good. For there to be any creature, whether sinful or no, it must exist solely by participation in God – and so there is some sense in which it is good, a claim that can be made of even the most vitiated creaturely agents. Furthermore, in willing it to exist, God wills it to exist *as* good. This is to say that God gives the creaturely agent all the agency it needs to will the good. If it goes on to sin, it is not as a result of the deficiency of God's gift, but as a result of a deficiency in its use of the agency God gives it. God wills the good, but the creature uses the true freedom that God grants it to sin.

Yet there is still a problem: God still brings a creature into existence knowing that it will do evil. What can be the good in *that*? Second, then, God wills the good purpose that will be accomplished through and in spite of the sinful history that the creature

---

[41] Tanner, *God and Creation*, 174 n.12.

wills. This is to say: The history of redemption is a history in which God wills the good of creation in spite of creaturely sin, and accomplishes that purpose perfectly.

This is bound to be an unsatisfying answer, and quite rightfully so. In fact, I wish to say that it is less an answer, and more a refusal of the present possibility of answering this question.[42] Though this response bears the superficial features of resolving a conceptual difficulty, it is far from a theodicy. It draws together a formal claim – that God can will only the good in creation – with a refusal to identify any conceivable good as the good that God wills in creating a history inclusive of creaturely sin. It says that, at present, there is no good we can possibly imagine that would account for the tragedy, the despair, the meaningless death we see all around us. It refuses to do anything that would mitigate the enormity of the world's sin, and refuses to place responsibility for this suffering anywhere but on the shoulders of God's permission that there should be a sinful creation.

Yet theology *may* ask after God's righteousness in bringing this world into being. It is too easy, to my mind, to dismiss all such questions as "modern" attempts to justify God rationally, rather than relating to God in faith.[43] If theology is faith seeking understanding, faith may validly ask how the overwhelming suffering and evil we encounter in the world is compossible with the goodness of God. The lament of God's suffering people is fundamentally an

---

[42] I have been influenced on this point by Rowan Williams' response to the work of Marilyn McCord Adams, "Redeeming Sorrows: Marilyn McCord Adams and the Defeat of Evil," in *Wrestling with Angels: Conversations in Modern Theology*, ed. Mike Higton (London: SCM Press, 2007), 255–274. See also Denys Turner's discussions of Julian's refusal to deny either a strong sense of God's providence or that God does bear responsibility for sin throughout his *Julian of Norwich: Theologian*.

[43] As, for example, Stanley Hauerwas and John Swinton threaten to do in their respective rejections of theodicy as a strictly modern problem; see Stanley Hauerwas, *God, Medicine, and Suffering* (Grand Rapids, MI: Wm. B. Eerdmans, 1990), and John Swinton, *Raging with Compassion: Pastoral Responses to the Problem of Evil* (Grand Rapids, MI: Wm. B. Eerdmans, 2007).

expression of this faith, and the hope that God will intervene powerfully in history on the side of the oppressed – not least through sending Her Body the Church to bind the wounds of the suffering. Yet if God has created us with the capacity to contemplate Her, and has enabled us to discern both God's goodness and the damage that sin has wrought upon the world, then faith may hope to know how this world is one that a good God might have made. Lament deserves a response, and it should grieve us, and serve as a check on our triumphalism, that Christian theology does not have one to give.

In saying that God wills some good purpose in willing this devastated history, my aim is not to foreclose the question of God's justice; quite the opposite. To say that God permits a sinful creation is to lay a charge at God's feet: Will He answer to it? Even the recognition of God's own suffering in the flesh of Christ can serve as no easy resolution here. The Body of Christ believes in faith, not by sight, that this broken cosmos can be the creation of a good God. In that light, responding that God wills some good in the course our broken cosmos follows can only be a profession of faith, a hope expressed that at the last day, what we have experienced here will be known as a happy fall. Until that day, the question remains painfully open.

***

God is thus unchangeable, timeless, eternally bringing the whole course of created history into existence with full determinacy. How can such a God become incarnate?[44] As can be seen with particular

---

[44] For defenses of the compatibility of God's timelessness and incarnation, see Douglas Blount, "On the Incarnation of a Timeless God," in "On the Incarnation of a Timeless God," in *God and Time: Essays on the Divine Nature*, eds. Gregory E. Ganssle and David M. Woodruff (Oxford: Oxford University Press, 2002), 236–248; Brian Leftow, "A Timeless God Incarnate," in *The Incarnation*, eds. Stephen T. Davis, Daniel Kendall, and Gerald O'Collins (Oxford: Oxford University Press, 2004), 273–299; Eleonore Stump, "Aqunas's Metaphysics of the Incarnation," in *The Incarnation*, eds. Stephen T. Davis, Daniel Kendall, and Gerald O'Collins (Oxford:

clarity in the writings of his last several decades,[45] Augustine emphasizes that the Incarnation effects a change not in God, but in humanity: "The man, of course, was added to God; God did not withdraw from himself."[46] The act of incarnation should thus be considered from two sides, both as an act of the triune Lord and in the human flesh that God assumes.

Considered as an act of God, we should view the Incarnation as an act of the simple and timeless divine life. More properly, we should view it as a created effect of the proper activity of the Son, indivisible in the simplicity of the divine life from the activity of the Father and Holy Spirit. Augustine is clear even in his earliest writings that the assumption of flesh is an act properly attributable to the person of the Second Person of the Trinity, the Wisdom of God.[47] We should therefore hold that the act by which the Word assumes flesh is itself the divine life of the Son – the act which is Her Being, eternally and inseparably related in the simplicity of the divine life to the Father and the Holy Spirit. Though the act of assuming flesh is not the *only* work properly attributed to the Son within the created order – the whole life of Christ is a created effect of the Son – considered as a divine act, one cannot draw distinctions between the act of assuming flesh and any other act within the divine Son's eternal life. Accordingly, we must also hold that the Incarnation is included within the Son's life from all eternity: "in the Wisdom of God, there was timelessly contained the time in which that Wisdom was to appear in the flesh. So while without any

---

Oxford University Press, 2004), 197–218; Jonathan Hill, "Incarnation, Timelessness, and Exaltation," *Faith and Philosophy* 29.1 (2012): 3–29; and Timothy Pawl, *In Defense of Conciliar Christology: A Philosophical Essay* (Oxford: Oxford University Press, 2016), 187–209.

[45] Particularly important christological sources here are *epistula* 137 to Volusanius (411–2); *epistula* 187 (417), also known as the little treatise *De praesentia dei*; *Contra sermonem Arrianorum* (419); and *Conlatio cum Maximino Arrianorum episcopo* (427–8).

[46] *ep.* 137.3.10; WSA II/2, 218.

[47] Cf. *Gn. adv. Man.* 2.24.37, and van Bavel's remarks at *Recherches*, 6–7.

beginning of time *in the beginning was the Word and the Word was with God and the Word was God* (Jn 1:1), without any time there was in the Word the time at which the Word would become flesh and dwell among us (Jn 1:14) ... The whole series of all times is time-lessly contained in God's eternal wisdom."[48]

A similar thing must be said of each moment of Christ's life, inasmuch as it is considered an act of the Second Person of the Trinity. Because the Son only exists as a trinitarian person in Her mutual relations to Father and Holy Spirit, Christ's divine agency is inseparably related to the agency of the Father and Holy Spirit. Yet because all this is eternally included in the simplicity of the divine life, it cannot be described as a change in God's life. In this way, predicating "being enfleshed" to the Word is akin to predicating "being the Creator" or "being the Lord of Israel" to God or "speaking over the waters of Jesus' baptism" to the Father, which are true not because of any change in God, but because of changes in the created order.[49] Throughout his christological reflections, Augustine will clearly demarcate what should and should not properly be ascribed to the divine life of the Son, even in the context of Christ's incarnate flesh.[50] This is not to say that things like suffering and death cannot *truly* be attributed to the divine Son; only that they must be ascribed to the Son in virtue of something else – namely, his human flesh.[51]

---

[48] *trin.* 2.5.9; WSA I/5, 103.

[49] Cf. *trin.* 5.16.17.

[50] Cf. *ep.* 187.3.9; WSA II/3, 235: "when we call Christ the Son of God we do not exclude the man, nor when we call the same Christ the Son of Man do we exclude God. For as man he was on earth, not in heaven where he is now, when he said, *No one goes up into heaven except him who has come down from heaven, the Son of Man who is in heaven* (Jn 3.13); though as the Son of God he was in heaven, as the Son of Man he was still on earth and had not yet ascended into heaven. Similarly, as the Son of God, he is the Lord of glory, but as the Son of Man he was crucified ... And for this reason the Son of Man as God was in heaven, and the Son of God as man was crucified on earth ... in accord with the immutability of God he had never left paradise because he is always everywhere."

[51] Augustine clearly affirms the *communicatio idiomatum* at *c.s.Arrian.* 8.6; WSA I/18, 146. As van Bavel notes, "Saint Augustine always begins his expositions with the

Second, then, the Incarnation may be considered as a created effect of God's act, which creates the human flesh of Christ and unites it to the person of the Word. Again consistently throughout his work, Augustine stresses against the Apollinarians that the human flesh assumed by the word is a "complete man" (*homo perfectus*), consisting of both soul and body.[52] While Augustine employs language in his earlier writings that suggest that a human *person* is assumed by the Word, he fairly quickly recognizes the potential danger of this terminology; speaking in this way suggests that there is a human person, Jesus, who exists independently of the Word and who is subsequently assumed, rather than affirming that the Word's humanity exists only in union with the Second Person of the Trinity.[53] By the time of his later writings, Augustine clearly guards against this misconception, writing, "Nor was he assumed in such a way that he was first created and then assumed; rather he was created in being assumed (*nec sic assumptus est ut prius creatus post assumeretur, sed ut ipsa assumptione crearetur*)."[54] From the year 411 on, we find Augustine adopting Tertullian's

distinction between the two natures ... It is justifiable to speak of God as crucified, because the Incarnation is the mystery of God made human and of humanity becoming God ... The unity of subject – a unity which permits distinction, but not separation – is the basis of the communication of attributes"; *Recherches*, 58.

[52] *div. qu.* 80.3; on the Incarnation as perfection of Christ's humanity, see van Bavel, *Recherches*, 53.

[53] Herman Diepen, "L' 'Assumptus Homo' patristique," *Revue Thomiste* 71 (1963): 225–245.

[54] *c.s.Arrian.* 8.6; WSA I/18, 145. See also the important reading of this *c.s.Arrian.* at Brian Daley, "Giant's Twin Substances." Daley notes, "What is new here is [Augustine's] explicit, metaphysically precise reflection on the continuing, functional completeness of Christ's human nature, within the unity of a single subject, as a way of showing the continuity between the New Testament evidence and the faith of Nicaea" (480). This emphasis on the persistence of two natures in Christ should complement and qualify Babcock's emphasis on an "identity-action" schema, which at times decenters attention to the qualities proper to each nature in Christ, and puts more distance than I think warranted between the christologies of Augustine and the *Tome* of Leo; see William Babcock, "The Christ of the Exchange: A Study in the Christology of Augustine's *Enarrationes in Psalmos*" (Unpublished, Ph.D. dissertation, Yale University, 1972), 241–275, and Daley, "Giant's Twin Substances," 488.

description of Christ as "one person in the two natures (*Unam . . . personam in utraque natura*), that is, God's and man's."[55] In sum, for the mature Augustine, "the one person who is Christ is the Word and man, but man is soul and flesh; hence, Christ is Word, soul, and flesh. Therefore, we should understand that he has two substances, namely, divine and human, with the human substance composed of soul and flesh."[56]

All this goes some distance toward helping us understand the constitution of Christ's humanity, and shows that Augustine anticipates a great deal of the terminology of later Chalcedonian (and indeed, dyothelite) christology.[57] Yet it does little to tell us precisely

[55] *c.s.Arrian.* 7.6; WSA I/18, 145. The earliest explicit use of the formula *una persona* to describe the union of divinity and humanity in Christ comes in 411/412, with the letter to Volusanius (Daley, *God Visible*, 155); see ep. 137.3.9; WSA II/2, 217: "now a mediator has appeared between God and human beings so that, uniting both natures in the unity of his person, he may raise up the ordinary to the extraordinary and temper the extraordinary to the ordinary." Hubertus Drobner has charted Augustine's evolving use of the language of "person" in his *Person-exegese und Christologie bei Augustinus: zur Herkunft der Formel "Una Persona"* (Leiden: Brill, 1986); on these initial uses, see 241–249.

[56] *c.s.Arrian.* 9.7; WSA I/18, 147. Augustine's emphasis on Christ's persistent substances motivates the argument first proffered by August Dorner, and later taken up by Harnack, TeSelle, and McWilliam, that Augustine's christology is either implicitly or explicitly Antiochene in character; see August Dorner, *Augustinus. Sein theologisches System und seine religionsphilosophie Anschauung* (Berlin: Wilhelm Hertz, 1873), 87–107; Adolf von Harnack, *History of Dogma*, Vol. 5, trans. Neil Buchanan (Boston: Little, Brown and Co., 1905), 125–134; Eugene TeSelle, *Augustine the Theologian*, 153–6; Joanne McWilliam Dewart, "The Influence of Theodore of Mopsuestia on Augustine's Letter 187," *Augustinian Studies* 10 (1979): 113–132. Against an Antiochene reading of Augustine, however, see McGuckin, "Did Augustine's Christology Depend on Theodore?," and Rowan Douglas Williams, "Augustine's Christology: Its Spirituality and Rhetoric," in *In the Shadow of the Incarnation: Essays in Honor of Brian E. Daley, S.J.* (Notre Dame, IN: University of Notre Dame Press, 2008), 176–189, 185–186.

[57] Augustine's anticipation of later pro-Chalcedonian dyothelitism has been noted by Brian Daley at "Making a Human Will Divine: Augustine and Maximus on Christ and Salvation," in *Orthodox Readings of Augustine*, eds. George E. Demacopoulos and Aristotle Papanikolaou (Crestwood, NY: St. Vladimir's Seminary Press, 2008), 101–126; and Han-Luen Kantzer Komline, "The Second Adam in Gethsemane: Augustine on the Human Will of Christ," *Revue d'études augustiniennes et patristiques* 58 (2012): 41–56. Komline notes that Augustine's dyothelitism "has been largely neglected in scholarship on

how the timeless Word can be united to human flesh like our own. To approach this question, we require some account of how God is present to the created order more broadly. In *epistula* 187 (the *De praesentia dei*) Augustine offers the analogy of God being like the health of a body, which is present everywhere in it, yet is not itself material.[58] In our common practice, we can speak of the health of a body as a whole, but we can also speak of the health of different parts of a person's body ("Her heart is fine, but her kidneys are ill."). We are able to speak of immaterial realities as obtaining in various degrees, even in material objects; and so perhaps, Augustine reasons, we may speak also of God's presence in creation in varying degrees, of some places being more saturated with the presence of God than others.[59] Yet one important difference between God's presence and the body's health is that whether or not health is present at all depends upon whether the body is functioning properly. By contrast, "if God is received less (*si minus capitur*) by one to whom he is present, he is not therefore himself less."[60]

Understanding how God is present to the created order actually requires us to distinguish between three senses of presence. On the one hand, God is identically and essentially present to the whole created order, just as, in Rogers' analogy, the whole of space is understood to be present to the present moment of time. On the other hand, there is a sense in which God is present and active within the creature to the extent that the creature is capable of receiving God. The analogy Augustine uses here is that of a sightless eye: The light shines on the eye in the same way that it would if the eye were healthy, but the eye cannot receive the light.[61]

---

the history of doctrine"; Han-Luen Kantzer Komline, *Augustine on the Will: A Theological Account* (Oxford: Oxford University Press, 2020), 278.

[58] *ep.* 187.4.12–3; WSA II/3, 236.

[59] *ep.* 187.6.18; WSA II/3, 238–9.

[60] *ep.* 187.6.18; WSA II/3, 239.

[61] *ep.* 187.5.17. Augustine is interestingly modern in this moment, viewing light as flooding into the eyes instead of viewing the eye as emitting a ray that extends outwards to the object of sight. See also *Io.ev.tr.* 39.8 for a parallel use of this metaphor.

In like manner, then, we may say that "God is everywhere by the presence of his divinity but not everywhere through the indwelling of grace"; and this latter is to be identified with "the grace of his love" (*gratia dilectionis*).[62] How, then, should we understand the Word of God to be present in the flesh of Christ?

First, the Word is present in the flesh of Christ with the same omnipresence with which She is present to everything in the created order. The Word remains present both to the flesh of Christ in the tomb, and to the soul of Christ in Hell;[63] this is very likely the reason why Augustine always describes the Resurrection as a return of Christ's *soul* to his body, rather than as a return of the *Word* to the body.[64]

Second, the Word is present to Christ's flesh by His *gratia dilectionis*, to the extent that Christ's human flesh is able to receive it – which is to say, perfectly, as fully as any human could possibly receive the presence of God. The gratuity of the Word's presence in Christ, and the Holy Spirit's role as the "unction" that creates in Christ's human flesh the capacity to receive God's presence perfectly, is a predominant theme in the christological texts of the anti-Pelagian period.[65] It is the Spirit's gracious act sanctifying the flesh of Christ that ensures there can be no conflict between his human and divine wills, for though Christ possesses a true and complete human will, the Spirit renders it perfectly receptive to the will of the

---

[62] *ep.* 187.5.16; WSA II/3, 237. This reference to grace makes the ultimate contrast of this view with the Pelagians clear: this capacity to receive God is *created in* humans by the very same activity that they then receive; as Augustine writes, "those in whom he dwells possess him in accordance with their different capacities, some more, others less, and he himself makes them a most beloved temple for himself by the grace of his goodness" (*ep.* 187.6.19; WSA II/3, 239).

[63] *ep.* 187.3.7.

[64] Van Bavel, *Recherches*, 71; van Bavel points to *Io.ev.tr.* 47.10–3, *ep.* 164.7.20, and *civ.* 17.18.2 as examples.

[65] See, for instance, *corrept.* 11.30–32; *praed. sanct.* 15.31. Brian Daley has identified this new emphasis on the grace of the incarnation as resulting from his encounter with the Pelagians at "A Humble Mediator," 108–110.

Word.[66] We should consider also in this context Augustine's frequent descriptions of the human soul of Christ as the intermediary between the Word and the material body of Christ: An ensouled body is much more capable of receiving the gratuitous presence of Christ than a corpse. Consequently, we should not make the mistake of thinking that the distinction between omnipresence and gratuitous presence maps neatly onto a distinction between God's presence to material creation and God's presence to immaterial realities like souls and the angels.[67] To summarize this second sense, the Word is present to Christ as fully as possible, for the human flesh of Christ receives the Word's presence as perfectly as possible.

Yet there is a final indispensable sense in which the Word is present in and to Christ, in a manner qualitatively distinct from anything else in the created order.[68] In the years after 411, Augustine consistently expresses this through the description of the Word and humanity of Christ as *una persona*.[69] As he writes in 415, for instance, "just as in any man – apart from the one who was assumed in a singular manner – soul and body are one person, so in Christ the Word and the man are one person."[70] Augustine leaves unasked the question of whether this *una persona* is to be directly identified with the person of the Word, as in later christology.[71] Yet it is

---

[66] *c.s.Arrian.* 18.9. The most complete account of Augustine's account of the will is Komline, *Augustine on the Will*; for the christological dimensions, see especially pages 277–330.

[67] Even in light of Augustine's intimations that the Word remains present to Christ's body in the tomb, then, it would be a mistake to conclude that the Resurrection effects no change in the Word's presence to Christ's material body.

[68] *ep.* 187.13.40; WSA II/3, 249: "of no saint could or can or will it be able to be said, *And the Word became flesh* (Jn 1.14) ... That assumption, then, is singular, nor can it in any way be shared by some human saints, no matter how outstanding in wisdom and holiness."

[69] Drobner, *Person-exegese*, 241–249. Drobner prefers the date 411 for these first uses, and identifies *s.* 186 alongside *ep.* 137.

[70] *ep.* 169.2.8; WSA II/3, 110

[71] Bruce McCormack argues for the presence of a consistent ambiguity in the Chalcedonian tradition: at times, emphasizing the single subject of the Logos; at other

difficult to see how, within the limits of his doctrine of God, he could say anything otherwise: The Word is eternally a person, one of the three triune persons; and there can be no change in the Word by the addition of human nature, such that this eternally existent person would be altered to accommodate Christ's humanity within

times, speaking of the divine-human Christ as the single subject of christological attribution; see Bruce Lindley McCormack, *The Humility of the Eternal Son: Reformed Kenoticism and the Repair of Chalcedon* (Cambridge: Cambridge University Press, 2021). His worry here is offered in service of his larger christological project, which is one of the most ambitious and insightful christological proposals offered in recent decades. He is exemplary in his attempt to make the historicity of Christ matter within the work of redemption, and our understanding of the eternal Word; indeed, rather than a "divine identity" christology, it would be more appropriate to describe him as offering a "human identity" logology, in which the human history of the man Jesus comes to be definitive of the Word's eternal life, on account of the Son's hypostatic identity as wholly receptive both to the Father and to Christ. McCormack's account deserves more detailed consideration than I am able to offer here, engagement that will be made even more fruitful as the remaining volumes of his trilogy are published, but to anticipate my response: McCormack is right to say, of classical Chalcedonianism and my own project, that "Jesus of Nazareth contributes nothing to the constitution of the 'person'" of the Word (31). Yet the real source of his worry seems to be the way that this undermines the significance of Christ's humanity within the work of redemption: "it is necessary to deny to Jesus any spontaneous, self-activating agency" (31). Accordingly, "Jesus was supposed to be 'fully human' – having a mind, will, and energy of operation entirely his own. And yet he played no role whatsoever in defining the Christological subject – an exercise in taking back with one hand what had just been given with the other" (32). Yet, I submit, this problem only arises because of an assumption that I and the Chalcedonian fathers do not share: namely, that "If one is firmly committed to dyothelitism, then one simply has to make one of the wills active and the other receptive if anything approximating a single-subject Christology is to be achieved" (63). But a noncompetitive account of divine and human agency allows precisely for the full activity of both the Word and Christ's humanity, while also ruling out what I see as category mistakes in relating Christ's divinity and humanity such that we might desire the Word to be "the affective subject of human sufferings" (47). On my account, then, the humanity of Christ *is* fully human in the sense McCormack desires, and plays a *critical* role in defining the christological subject – as does his extended Body; and yet, this requires no duality of subjects, only an appropriately conceptualized relation of divine and creaturely agency. Nevertheless, McCormack has set the high-water mark for contemporary christological proposals, and his sustained and creative theological dialogue with Barth has served as a salutary model in my own engagement with Augustine.

a newly constituted *persona*. For Augustine, unless the trinitarian *persona* and the christological *una persona* are wholly equivocal, the *una persona* must be the person of the Word.[72]

Accordingly, the personal existence of Christ is the person of the Word. We must acknowledge that the identification of the Word as Christ's person limits our ability to describe precisely how the union of divinity and humanity can be understood. If Christ is one person with the divine Word, then this person is incomprehensible, for the incomprehensible action of the Word is the principle of the unity of this one person. We can, therefore, only hope to understand this union on its human side.

At this third level, then, God's presence in Christ points to the particular foundation of Christ's existence in the will and act of the Word. The will to create and assume the human flesh of Christ is present in God from all eternity as an act of the Word, in union with the Father and Holy Spirit; the content of this eternal will and act is that this human flesh should *be* the Word's own humanity. This human flesh does not exist apart from its union with the Word; it has no proper existence of its own, considered as separated from the Word (as Augustine clearly affirms).[73] If we are asked what marks off God's presence in the flesh of Christ from all else that is, this is what we should answer: This flesh is the Word's own flesh; this flesh *is God*. Because the relation between Word and humanity is noncompetitive in Christ (as in creation as a whole), there is no

---

[72] Cf. Daley, "A Humble Mediator," 102: "although he does not put it in these terms – Augustine clearly understands the Logos to be the active subject of the Incarnation, the personal center which shapes and gives identity to Jesus the man."

[73] This latter is the error of the repentant Gallican monk Leporius, who Augustine tells us was "afraid that the divinity would be believed to have been changed in the man or corrupted by uniting with the man. This was a pious fear but a careless error. He piously saw that the divinity could not be changed, but he carelessly presumed that the Son of Man could be separated from the Son of God so that the one would not be the other and so that one would be Christ and the other would not be or that there would be two Christs" (*ep.* 219.3 [written 418]; WSA II/4, 70–1). Brian Daley helpfully discusses this incident at *God Visible*, 156–158.

difficulty in ascribing a humanity to Christ complete in soul and body, possessing memory, intellect, will, the capacity to touch and be touched. This humanity truly is the humanity of the Son of God, and so whatever he experiences – joy and delight alongside fear and pain – is truly the human experience of the Word of God.

Yet while these are truly the *experiences* of the Word, they are *experienced* by the Word in the same way we experience them – humanly.[74] They are not experienced divinely – at least if we take

[74] Cf. Babcock, "Christ of the Exchange," 338–339: "The themes of the *homo assumptus* and of *Deus latens*, in qualifying and specifying the sense in which Christ is to be identified as God, also indicate how the humanity functions as the instrument of the Word's participation in our world and condition. The manhood equips him, as it were, with the qualities and attributes of this world – the weakness, mutability and death of which he is not capable in himself. It hides those qualities and attributes of the Word as God, especially his divine power, which would have made the events and happenings of his human life impossible; and, in doing so, it points us toward that final moment when we shall see Christ as he is." This thematic – of Christ's humanity as truly the humanity of the Word, and thus revelatory of the Word and redemptive precisely in its human limitations – corrects another tendency Babcock identifies in Augustine's christology: "The problem, then, is not so much a reduced emphasis on the humanity of Christ as it is the unremitting hegemony, as Otto Scheel calls it, of the divine Word in determining all that the human Christ thinks and feels and does. No room is left, in Augustine's view, for a humanity which acts or reacts in a purely human way. All the normal patterns of human thought and feeling are suspended; and Christ's human life is made totally subordinate to its function as the Word's instrument for making himself present to us and providing an example for us. It has no independent status, no independent development, no independent, purely human significance" (333). Babcock's point is well taken; Augustine does, at many points in his thought, make precisely the error I have attributed to "divine identity" christologies. Yet – especially in moments like his exegesis of the Cry of Dereliction, or in his identification of the Church's sufferings as his own in appearing to Saul – I believe Augustine gives us resources for moving beyond this impasse (Babcock comes close to this recognition as well at 108). The problem is not, I argue, with the structure of Augustine's christology itself, but in an insufficiently carried-through apophaticism with respect to what our predication of, e.g., knowledge to the Word entails for our understanding of that same Word's human knowing in Christ. Augustine's christology permits us to see that it is precisely *through* Christ's human limitations that his humanity is most fully instrumental in revealing the Word. That said, Babcock's interpretation seems to me at moments of his writing (341–342, for instance) to over-literalize Augustine's attributions of hunger to the Word in His

"experienced" here to mean something like "undergone succes-
sively in the flowing course of time" – for the divine Word in Her
simple eternal life remains timelessly unchangeable.[75] The moments
that comprise Christ's experiences are known by the Word divinely
in the manner proper to divinity; which is to say: eternally, causa-
tively, incomprehensibly, in a presence more intimate to these
historical moments than they are to themselves, and yet transcend-
ing them absolutely in the timelessness of the divine life. To say
anything else would be to say that the divine Word changes in the
Incarnation, that the Word loses Herself in becoming flesh. It is,
rather, right to say that the human flesh of Christ *opens* the Word to
temporal experience. From all eternity, the Word wills that these
temporal experiences should be Her own, by undergoing them in
Her human flesh.

***

Let me pause, briefly, to pull together several of the argumentative
threads that will be significant moving forward.

As we approach Augustine's account of the Incarnation, we find,
first, a resolutely apophatic account of theological language that is
carried consistently through his doctrine of God, his account of the

divinity; certainly, Christ's hunger is the Word's hunger, but the Word is only capable
of hungering *in His humanity*. Babcock himself recognizes this (see 343), but – because
he is assuming the correspondence of divine and human experience more than
I believe Augustine did – believes that the Word's instrumentalization of Christ's
humanity requires that Christ's hunger be located, in a diminished or theologically
interpreted form, in the Word's divinity as well. Babcock presents Augustine's
"pattern of exchange" in the Incarnation as a qualified realism; where he chooses to
emphasize the realism of ascribing Christ's experiences to the Word, I wish to
emphasize the significant qualifications that the Word's immutability and
transcendent unknowability maintain within even the realistic ascriptions of
Augustine's christology (on which, see Babcock, 51–52; 98–99).

[75] Cf. *ep.* 219.3; WSA II/4, 71: after Leporius "recognized that the Word of God, that is, the
only begotten Son of God had become man in such a way that neither was changed
into the other, but that, with each remaining in its own substance, God endured
human sufferings in the man in such a way that he retained in himself his divinity
unimpaired."

trinitarian persons, and accordingly, his understanding of what it might mean for the Second Person of the Trinity to assume flesh. Resolutely, I maintain, but not *absolutely* apophatic; the point is not that God is wholly unknown to us, but that God is *incomprehensible*. This means that any theological description of the divine life is consigned, from the start, to insufficiency; and not merely wrong in some particulars that might later be ironed out through a process of theological purgation, but *constitutively* insufficient. Human language, human knowledge, are incapable of knowing the divine life as it is, for the only knowledge of God adequate to the divine life is the divine knowing that simply *is* that life. This apophatic reserve is not infringed upon in reflection upon the Incarnation. The Word is unchanged in assuming flesh; the Word lives, freely and eternally, in the beatitude and simplicity of the divine life – ever timeless, ever transcendent, according to the action proper to the divine nature from before the foundation of the world. Though the Incarnation tells us that the timelessness of the divine life is not all that must be said about the life of the Word, it does not (at least on an Augustinian account) suggest that this transcendence of the created order is abrogated. Rather, the mystery of the Incarnation is only properly understood insofar as this distinction between God and creation is *maintained*, precisely as some part of creation is identified as ingredient to the Word's own life.

Second, and proceeding from this account of the divine life's transcendence of the created order, we find in Augustine an insistence that all times – all the developments creatures undergo, all the relations to other creatures into which they enter by means of time – are ordered by and to the Word. Not, that is, ordered by the divine life without further specification, but ordered by that life's Second Person, who becomes incarnate within time. When we contemplate creation's potential to reveal the Word; when we inquire after what parts of creaturely temporality may come to be revelatory of Christ, or to be employed by Christ for the salvation of the world; when we wonder what parts of created history may be significant in defining the human course of Christ's life, the answers are – in principle, at least – unbounded. *Each moment* of created history should be considered at least potentially relevant to articulating the person and work of Christ within christology, for *each moment* of created history – from first to last, with full specificity – is ordered from all eternity by the Word. Whether or not we end up saying that each moment of history does in fact bear some redemptive significance is a separate question, to be considered more extensively in the subsequent paragraphs.

Third, the human Jesus Christ is, uniquely within the created order, identified with the eternal Word – indeed, is identified *as* the eternal Word. This goes well beyond (though is not less than) a coincidence of divine and creaturely agencies or ends, a mere alignment – even if a perfect one – of two different ontological planes. The Word is present in Christ by Her universal presence in which all things exist by participation in the divine nature, present by an unmerited grace perfecting Christ's loves – but present too, in a manner not reducible to either of these first two modes of presence, through the personal identity of this human life with the life of the Word. Jesus of Nazareth *is* the Word: From all eternity (for there can be no shadow of change in the Word's divine life), the Word wills to be and is this human in time. When we encounter this one in history, we meet the Second Person of the Trinity – not, it must be said, directly in the unknowability of Her divinity, but mediately, through the creaturely effect that She has brought into being as Her own. Precisely in view of the apophatic reserve noted earlier, we cannot specify *how* this human life is the Word's, any more than we can describe the eternal generation of Her person. All we can say is that, from all eternity, the Word wills that this life should be *Her own*, that She should *be Jesus*, without the activity proper to either of Christ's natures being compromised or confused.

The confluence of these points serves, as I have suggested, to habituate us out of certain pictures of imagining the relation of divinity and humanity in Christ. Very obviously, it cautions against mythological construals of the divine life: kenotic pictures in which the Word must limit the exercise of divinity in order to inhabit the bounds of Christ's human life; overworked epic tellings of the relations of the trinitarian persons, in which the events of Christ's life are blown into a history within God; pictures in which the Word is thought to "accompany" Jesus in time, living the life of Jesus "in real time," as it were: experiencing divinely what Jesus experiences humanly alongside his experiencing, willing divinely in a series of volitions (willing first to call the disciples, then later to heal a paralytic, still later to turn his face toward Jerusalem) parallel to the series of Jesus' human willings. By the lights of the Augustinian christology I am articulating, all these pictures fundamentally confuse the proper relation of the Word's timeless life and His historical human life.

Yet these three emphases lead us to question also a picture that is much less obviously mistaken: a picture in which our predication of knowing, or loving, or willing, or mercy to God are taken to constrain the field of christological possibility. We might say, for instance, "Well, of course Jesus knows *that*, because the Word is omniscient"; or we might say, "Jesus is angry at these sinners because *God* is angry at them"; or that, "Jesus wills to offer himself as a sacrifice for the sin of the world because the Son wills it." In each case, the predication of some quality or activity to God is taken as a sufficient explanation for the appearance of some parallel quality in the life of Jesus; but this sort of thinking trades on a conceptual slippage that is ruled out by the apophatic emphasis I have maintained earlier. *Of course* we can talk about the Word's knowledge, or anger, or will – but it is not at all clear how these attributions to the Word's divine life should be translated into the creaturely plane of activity proper to the Word's human life. We can and should attribute the will to redeem the world through the Cross to the Word – but this should not, or should at least not *obviously*, be taken as a sufficient explanation for why the Word wills this sacrifice in Her humanity. Other, creaturely causes may in fact be necessary to account for why Jesus desired this self-offering, even given the fact that the Word who he is wills this same from all eternity. Indeed, it may be the case that Jesus *could not* have willed the redemption of the world absent the creaturely influences upon him of his mother, his teachers, his friends.

A straightforward deduction from what we predicate of the Word in eternity to the shape of Christ's human life forecloses this christological possibility prematurely, through an overestimation of our concepts' ability to gain purchase on the divine life. The Word's eternal knowing, or willing, or love certainly ground the Word's historical knowing, and willing, and love in Jesus; but the *major dissimilitudo* that obtains even between the Word's two natures should make us wary of assuming that the character of the Word's divine life offers a direct and sufficient explanation of the shape of that Word's human life. The Augustinian picture I have offered instead suggests that, precisely for the sake of understanding the humanity assumed into union with the Word, it is necessary to remain clear-eyed about the persistent (though inseparable) distinction between the same Word's lives in the divine and creaturely plane, so as to account for the full scope of Word's action in assuming flesh. So Augustine: "Christ did not manifest himself to us on earth; what he manifested was his flesh."[76]

We might put it this way: When we think of the Word's life within the creaturely plane of existence – the plane of temporal succession; of the unfolding stream of lived experience; of responsive relation; of desire for the world's yet-to-be-realized salvation, or anger at His heard-hearted auditors, or heartbreak at the persistent consequences of sin, or delighted approval of the faithfulness of His followers – all there is, exhaustively, is the human life of Christ. My aim is not to banish the Word from time: The Word timelessly knows all things within created history; the Word wills, from all eternity, to dispense blessings to particular creatures; the Word is timelessly and

---

[76] *en.Ps.* 37.11; WSA III/16, 154. This epistemic interval between the vision of Christ's flesh and the vision of his incomprehensible divinity persists even in his *Parousia*; see Babcock, "Christ of the Exchange," 206–209.

sovereignly able to bring about particular effects, even miraculous effects, within time; indeed, the Word is more present to each moment of time, and each creature within it, than they are to themselves. Yet, even so: When we meet the Word of God within our creaturely plane of existence, we have to do with His humanity, and with His divinity only inasmuch as this humanity is His. The Word is not made temporal in the Incarnation, except (and the exception is what makes all the difference) in His humanity; He is not, in His divinity, responsive to the succession of times and the events that unfold therein. It is a mistake, then, to imagine that at each moment of Christ's human life, the Word looks around, reflects on what the situation requires, makes a decision, and communicates that decision to Christ's humanity so that his human volition can will the same thing in response. No: When we speak of the life of the Word in time, we are speaking of a human life like any other human life, excepting the presence of sin. In time, Christ perceives, desires, deliberates, and wills just as any human might.[77]

[77] In putting it this way, I thus take the side of St. Thomas Aquinas' attribution of *liberum arbitrium* and *electio* to Christ, rather than St. Maximus the Confessor's denial of *gnomic* will in him; see ST III.18.4ad1. As Ian McFarland notes, for Maximus "*gnome* is a feature of the will only when willing hypostatized under the conditions of ignorance and doubt. Since Christ's human will is, by virtue of its enhypostatization by the Second Person of the Trinity, fully deified, it is permanently oriented to God in a way that precludes any need for deliberation"; Ian A. McFarland, "'Willing is Not Choosing,': Some Anthropological Implications of Dyothelite Christology," *International Journal of Systematic Theology* 9.1 (2007): 11–12. Similarly, Blowers writes that after Maximus' early attribution of *gnome* to Christ, by the time of his later writings, "*gnômê* now specifically evoked the fallen mode or disposition of the will in which hesitation about worthy ends had to be unlearned, as it were, in the quest for virtue"; Blowers, *Maximus the Confessor*, 164–165. The crux of my dissent is not, then, located in a differing understanding of the will, but in my different assessment of the necessary deification of Christ's intellect in the course of his ministry. As I will argue more extensively in Chapter 5, I hold ignorance and even error in Christ's human intellect to be perfectly compatible with his humanity existing solely in hypostatic union with the Word, if this ignorance or error is part of the *forma servi* and ordered to the end of humanity's redemption. Christ has *liberum arbitrium* and *electio*, and thus may be rightly said to deliberate and choose, as Thomas believed – though

My aim in emphasizing this is not to drive a wedge between Christ's divinity and humanity; these natures are truly united in His one person. On the contrary, by emphasizing the distinction between the divine and human activities of this one person, my hope is only to bring into clearer focus the full scope of what it means for the human Jesus Christ to be the Word of God. The life of this one person need not be understood as a bare parallelism of something like a divine personality being translated into a human one. The life of the Word is more capacious than that, unknowably so. Plausibly, at least, we might hold that the life of the Word is *so* capacious that this divine Person's life within our creaturely order might depend upon, and come to include, the lives of *other* creatures – that to be the human life of God, the shape of the Word's human life might be constituted in part by the relations it bears *to* the created order. Because the human life of Christ is noncompetitively related to the divine life of the Word, we can hold that the course of Christ's human life is affected by, shaped by, and responsive to his environment and the people around him, all without undermining the claim that this human life truly is the life of God.[78]

Thomas, in common with Maximus, held to the necessary deification of Christ's intellect. See especially Peter Totleben, "Thomas Aquinas and Maximus the Confessor on Free Choice in Christ," Academia.edu, www.academia.edu/35580907/Thomas_Aq uinas_and_Maximus_the_Confessor_on_Free_Choice_in_Christ. See also J. David Moser, "The Flesh of the Logos, *Instrumentum divinitatis*: Retrieving an Ancient Christological Doctrine," *International Journal of Systematic Theology* 23.3 (2021): 313–332; which notes that on Thomas' account Christ "can judge between alternatives just like we do" (325). It is worth noting that, even in the unquestioned victory of Maximus' theology at the Sixth Ecumenical Council, the Council did not see fit to enshrine the denial of *gnomic* will to Christ in its definition of faith; cf. Heinrich Denzinger, *Compendium of Creeds, Definitions, and Declarations on Matters of Faith and Morals*, 43rd ed., eds. Peter Hünermann, Peter Hünermann, Helmut Hoping, Heinrich Denzinger, Robert L. Fastiggi, and Anne Englund Nash. (San Francisco, CA: Ignatius, 2012), 550–560.

[78] This extends even to the microbial level; see Norman Wirzba's theological assessment of the "soil-bound" character of human life at *This Sacred Life: Humanity's Place in a Wounded World* (Cambridge: Cambridge University Press, 2021), 73–75. Indeed, Rebecca Copeland expands the circle still farther, considering the Incarnation's

Clearly distinguishing Christ's divine and human activities (even in their inseparable union in Him) holds open the possibility of a full-throated endorsement of the world's contribution to the redemptive shape of Christ's life, without projecting the categories of relation or history into the divine life. It serves to emphasize that it is *vere Deus* who has become incarnate. Not some aspect of God closer to the created order, not God in an obscure more temporal sense. It is the true God, the one who has dwelt in eternity from before the foundation of the world and who is present to me *interior intimo meo* who assumes flesh and lives a human life, without losing anything of Her eternity.

The only way to account for this reality is by love, the eternal Love that God is. The true God has not willed to remain apart from us; the true God has the possibility of making human flesh His own, living alongside us by taking on our nature. God's will to be with us has been God's will from before we were made – and the Love by which God takes on our nature is, in the simplicity of the divine life, the very Love by which God loves Himself as Father, Son, and Holy Spirit, the very Love by which God draws this world into being and providentially orders its unfolding.

Far from depersonalizing God, rendering God a frigidly transcendent other, this Augustinian outlook is precisely calibrated to produce the bracing contrasts we see in Augustine's christological preaching. The Incarnation scrambles what might otherwise have been a clear priority of spirit over matter, both doubling down on a broadly Neoplatonic picture of the transcendent God in whom all things participate, and taking this picture out at the knees. God is

significance for inanimate material bodies, vegetative material bodies, "irrational" and "rational" animal bodies; see Rebecca L. Copeland, *Created Being: Expanding Creedal Christology* (Waco, TX: Baylor University Press, 2020), chapter 3. I affirm Copeland's intention to see the Incarnation as affecting and particularizing God's presence to the fullness of created being, even if I do not share her conviction that this is best accomplished by positing one *ousia* in which all created being shares, rather than individuated natures.

not just – and therefore not really – the placid and distant One from which all derives. The Incarnation teaches us that the One is also a baby gurgling at his mother's breast, injuring himself in his father's workshop, sharing a meal with a disreputable woman. The Incarnation demands we recognize God's presence to us in incomprehensible selfsameness, but also God burping at the table next to us after drinking a glass of sheep's milk.

Without losing anything of its incomprehensibility or eternity, the life of Christ shows us that the transcendent One is Herself Love, a Love that crosses the distinction between creator and creature by taking human flesh to Herself. In the flesh of Christ, the true God is truly our neighbor.

Part II | The Incarnation of the Word

3 | The Work of Incarnation

What is this flesh that the Word assumes? What is the humanity that God unites to Her own life?

The answers to these questions may seem straightforward, if still mysterious: From all eternity, the Word wills to assume human nature; having taken upon Himself our nature, this nature is hypostatized in the one life of Jesus Christ, born of Mary, crucified under Pontius Pilate, who dies, is buried, descends into Hell, and is raised on the third day. He is *vere Deus*, and *vere homo*, like us in all things excepting sin. The Incarnation should not be reduced to the historical emergence of a new possibility of relation with God from within human nature; it must not be diminished into a mere symbol; it is as far from a universal possibility of human personhood as one might get. The Incarnation is the true *sacramentum*, the ineffable mystery by which the incomprehensible God lives among us, as one of us. In the Word's assumption of flesh, we meet the Second Person of the Trinity in all the concrete particularity of a human life. We learn that eternity has a name, and it is Emmanuel: God with us.[1]

This is the central affirmation of Christian faith, as taught by the Fathers and Mothers of the Church and authoritatively defined by the ecumenical councils. And yet, by the lights of Augustine's christology, it is not a complete description of who Christ is. While, as we saw in the last chapter, Augustine is quite happy to speak of Christ as a union of God and humanity, and even in his later work to speak of the union of divine and human natures in

---

[1] Augustine speaks of "eternity's name" at *s.* 7.7.

one person, one of the most distinctive features of his christology is the theology of the *totus Christus* – the whole Christ.

The doctrine of the *totus Christus* appears with some regularity, even predictability, in his christological reflection. One can trust that a discussion of the whole Christ is close to hand when Augustine invokes a few choice passages of Scripture: *Saul, Saul, why are you persecuting me? My God, My God, why have you forsaken me? When did we see you hungry, Lord, and feed you?* The first suggests that, even after his ascent into heaven, Christ's Body remains extended in the world in the lives of the faithful; To wound one of those whose lives are enfolded in Christ's own by baptism is to wound the Lord himself.[2] The second presents such an intractable exegetical problem that it points to a mystical unity that *must* obtain between Christ and the Church: How could God Herself utter these words if She were not speaking in our own voice? How could She speak in our voice if our lives were not truly united to Her own?[3] The third suggests that this is not an individual matter, but that Christ is found – and one is found in Christ – through meeting him in the poor.[4]

The theology of the *totus Christus* appears most prominently, in Augustine's thought, as an exegetical necessity. So, for instance, at *en.Ps.* 37.6, Augustine considers the words, *There is no peace in my bones in the face of my sins.* The problem, however, is that this is

---

[2] Augustine's references to both Acts 9.4 and Psalm 22.1 (reckoned Ps. 21 in the *Vetus Latina* and the Vulgate; also Matthew 27.46) are legion. For a few characteristic examples, including several examples in which both texts appear together in the same homily, see: (on Acts 9.4) *en.Ps.* 30.ii.3, 32.ii.2, 37.6, 44.20, 54.3, 67.36, 86.5, 90.ii.5, 103. iii.7, 108.28, 122.1, 138.2, 140.7, 148.17; (on Ps. 22.1) 21.ii.3, 37.6, 58.i.2, 70.i.12, 87.14, 90.ii.1, 140.5–6.

[3] So *en.Ps.* 70.i.12; WSA III/17, 423: "Christ made the words his own inasmuch as he spoke in our name: not from his own power and majesty, not from what he was, he who made us, but from what he had become for our sake."

[4] Tarsicius van Bavel notes the importance of Acts 9.4 and Matthew 25.36–41 at "The Concept of the 'Whole Christ'," 268, while Cameron notes the importance of the Cry of Dereliction at *Christ Meets Me Everywhere*, 197–207. Kimberly Baker similarly identifies the *totus Christus* as a doctrine developed under exegetical pressure at "Augustine on Action," 71–77.

A psalm for David himself, for a remembrance of the Sabbath.[5] Within Augustine's exegetical practice, this is a clear sign that the speaker of this psalm is Christ himself, as is true of the Psalms generally for Augustine.[6] But how can these words acknowledging one's own sin be attributed validly to Christ?[7] Characteristically, Augustine tells us that we must read this passage in light of the whole Christ:

> The need to make sense of this forces us to recognize that "Christ" here is the full Christ, the whole Christ; that is, Christ, Head and Body (*plenum et totum Christum, id est caput et corpus*) ... Now we are quite certain that Christ was sinless and free from all faults, so we might begin to think that these psalm-words are not his. Yet it would be very difficult, indeed wrong-headed, to maintain that the earlier psalm [i.e., Ps. 21] does not belong to Christ, when it describes his passion so plainly that it might almost be reading from the gospel ... Let us hear them as one (*Sic audiamus tamquam unum*), but let us listen to the Head as Head, and the Body as Body. The *personae* are not separated, but in dignity they are distinct, for the Head saves and the Body is saved. May the Head dispense mercy, and the Body bemoan its misery. The role of the Head is to purge away sins, the Body's to confess them. Wherever scripture does not indicate when the Body is speaking, when the Head, we hear them speak with one single voice. We have to distinguish as we listen, but the voice is one.[8]

---

[5] *en.Ps.* 37.2; WSA III/16, 146.

[6] Jason Byassee, *Praise Seeking Understanding: Reading the Psalms with Augustine* (Grand Rapids, MI: Wm. B. Eerdmans, 2007), 73.

[7] See Baker's discussion of this point at "Augustine on Action," 82, connecting Christ's appropriation of the sins of humanity to his taking on the sufferings of the poor in exegesis of Matthew 25.

[8] *en.Ps.* 37.6; WSA III/16, 150–1 (modified). This exegetical strategy appears almost from the beginning of the *Enarrationes in Psalmos*; see *en.Ps.* 3.9, among the earliest series of these homilies preached. Though, as Michael Cameron notes at *Christ Meets Me Everywhere* 336n.94, it is at *en.Ps.* 17.2 that we find the earliest known usage of the phrase *totus Christus*.

The emphasis of this and other similar passages falls on that of the speaker: Certainly the words are Christ's, but he speaks in the voice of his Body, all those who have been united to him by the Holy Spirit. "The key to the image [of the *totus Christus*]," Babcock notes, "is an extended sense of the first person pronoun, already evident in the language of Scripture, which permits us to say that Christ is involved in the sufferings of his followers, even though he is not physically present."[9] Because of this union – indeed, to display the reality of this union – Christ is able to take on their words. By making our union with him visible, Christ helps us see that our lives are clothed in his, turning our hearts back to him through his purifying mediation of God's grace. While Augustine speaks of *personae* in this text, suggesting it is a fundamentally rhetorical or linguistic category, the increasing emphasis of his thought is to speak of Christ as *unitas persona* – one person.[10] As Rowan Williams has written, "Augustine ... leaves us to work out how the single speaking subject who is the eternal Word can 'personate' human nature, give it voice, enact its conditions and reshape them, without in any way whatsoever ceasing to be what it eternally and 'necessarily' is, the pure agency of God subsisting as Son."[11] Some of the most successful studies of Augustine's christology have focused precisely on the rhetorical aspects of this union, examining how the true union of divinity and humanity in the Head makes possible his assumption of the words of his Body.[12]

---

[9] William Babcock, "The Christ of the Exchange: A Study in the Christology of Augustine's Enarrationes in Psalmos" (Unpublished, Ph.D. dissertation, Yale University, 1972), 326.

[10] As Rowan Williams has written, "Augustine regularly uses the word *persona* to denote 'what there is one of' in Christ ... Augustine understands *persona* as pointing to the source of what is said and done in Christ and also to the role of human subject which Christ enacts ... [As] his thought matures, it is clear that he has come to see *persona* as always designating the ultimate source of communication and of action in general"; *Christ the Heart of Creation* (London: Bloomsbury Continuum, 2018), 71.

[11] Williams, *Christ the Heart of Creation*, 74.

[12] In addition to Drobner, *Person-exegese* and Cameron, *Christ Meets Me Everywhere*, I have especially in mind Michael Fiedrowicz, *Psalmus Vox Totius Christi Studien Zu*

Augustine's most searching discussion of the *totus Christus* is undoubtedly found in his *sermo* 341, discovered in its fullest version by François Dolbeau only in 1990.[13] This version, likely preached in Carthage on December 12, 417[14] and presently known as *sermo Dolbeau* 22 or as *s.* 341 augmented, will be the focus of our attention. In it, Augustine tells his listeners:

> Christ is named in three ways, whether he is being proclaimed in the law and the prophets, or in the letters of the apostles, or through our confidence about his deeds, which we know about from the gospel. One way is: as God and according to that divine nature which is coequal and coeternal with the Father before he assumed flesh. The next way is: how, after assuming flesh, he is now understood from our reading to be God who is at the same time man, and man who is at the same time God, according to that pre-eminence which is peculiar to him and in which he is not to be equated with other human beings, but is the mediator and head of the Church. The third way is: when he is preached to believers and offered for their approval to the wise as in some manner or other the whole Christ in fullness of the Church, that is, as head and body, according to the fullness of a certain *perfect man* (Eph 4.13), the man in whom we are each of us members.[15]

We have already discussed at length the first two ways in which Christ is known – as eternal Word and in the union of human flesh with that Word – and Augustine's treatment in this sermon rehearses many of the points we have seen him make elsewhere. The Word is present fully in both glorious unity with the Father and

---

Augustins Enarrationes in Psalmos (Freiburg: Herder, 1997), and Rowan Williams, "Augustine and the Psalms," *Interpretation* 58.1 (2004): 17–27.

[13] *Vingt-six sermons au peuple d'Afrique*, ed. François Dolbeau (Paris: Institut d'études augustiniennes, 1996).

[14] WSA III/11, 305n.1. What Hill calls a "truncated" version of the sermon, published by the Maurists as *s.* 341, may be found in translation in WSA III/10.

[15] *s. Dolbeau* 22.2; WSA III/11, 283–4 (modified).

in the humility of Mary's womb, without any possibility of division;[16] the Word's existence both in glory and in life of Christ is compared to a spoken word undivided in spite of being heard by multiple listeners;[17] any suggestion of inferiority to the Father given in Christ's human life (the "second way") is to be referred to the human nature he has assumed in the *forma servi*, rather than to the glory proper to the Son's divine nature.[18] Here, we have to do with the third way we can name Christ: as Head and Body, Christ and the Church in its eschatological fullness (*plenitudo*).[19]

Later in the sermon, as Augustine turns to consider this *tertium modum*, he will strengthen his language beyond that of fullness, speaking of Head and Body together as "complete" (*integer*). He is aware of the risks of speaking in this manner, cautioning:

> Not that he isn't complete without the body, but that he was prepared to be complete with us as well, though even without us he is always complete, not only insofar as he is the Word, the only-begotten Son equal to the Father, but also in the very man whom he took on, and with whom he is both God and man together.[20]

What sort of completeness is being affirmed here, and what incompleteness rejected?

Clearly, Augustine is concerned to guard against any implication that Christ is not truly or fully human without his union to the heavenly Church: "Christ is one with his body because he graciously

---

[16] s. *Dolbeau* 22.8.

[17] s. *Dolbeau* 22.9.

[18] s. *Dolbeau* 22.13–15.

[19] Augustine makes clear that the Body of Christ at issue in the *totus Christus* is not only the Church as presently constituted, but the "heavenly Church," the whole complement of those who will be redeemed from Abel to the end of history (s. *Dolbeau* 22.19).

[20] s. *Dolbeau* 22.19: *non quia sine corpore non est integer, sed quia et nobiscum integer esse dignatus est, qui et sine nobis semper est integer, non solum in eo quod Verbum est unigenitus Filius aequalis Patri, sed et in ipso homine quem suscepit et cum quo simul Deus et homo est*; WSA III/11, 298.

consents to be, not because he has to be."[21] There is no deficiency in the Word's union with human flesh that must be filled up through Christ's relation to the redeemed; the divine will to take on humanity lacks nothing, and is perfectly sufficient to bring about God's life in time. This is a completeness of person, a metaphysical completeness. However we understand divine and human natures, the Son's effectual will to become incarnate ensures by itself that Christ will be perfect in both, as whole in his humanity as any human could be.

In what sense, then, should we understand the Word willing *nobiscum integer esse* – to be complete *with* us? Is this a "completeness" that is added to Christ's metaphysical completeness? Or should we rather take this to be a description of *what it is* for Christ to be metaphysically complete, a description of the *manner* in which the Word has willed to be complete in His humanity? Or is the *totus Christus*, in the words of one recent interpreter, "a theological metaphor, [which] does not imply anything concrete about the 'metaphysical biology' of the Incarnate or risen Christ"? In Dominic Keech's judgment, "Augustine does not state explicitly that speaking of the *totus Christus*, head and body, is a theological-literary device, but his point is clear."[22] This is precisely the point of ambiguity in Augustine's thought. In what sense may we truly say with Augustine that every Christian "not unfittingly carries the person of Christ (*non incongrue sustinet personam Christi*)"?[23]

While Augustine's language is incredibly suggestive on these points, a full account of how the Church "completes Christ" requires, in my judgment, systematic resources beyond Augustine's own texts. This is the task in which we have been engaging; this is the task we will continue to pursue, in continuity with but extending the

[21] *s. Dolbeau* 22.19; WSA III/11, 299.
[22] Keech, *Anti-Pelagian Christology*, 180. Compare to Williams' more realistic (if still mystical) sense of the Church's union with Christ at *Christ the Heart of Creation*, 75: "As Augustine insists in, for example, his *enarratio* on Psalm 142, Christ cannot be separated from the Body he has chosen; we cannot, so to speak, *add* the Body to Christ, any more than we can add Jesus to the Word."
[23] *Gn. adv. Man.* 2.25.38; translation from Cameron, *Christ Meets Me Everywhere*, 60.

particularities of Augustine's christological insights. While Christ is truly God and truly human solely by the Word's act of assuming flesh, the Word has chosen to be complete *with us* – *integer nobiscum*. It would be a mistake to think that this will to be complete with us (Augustine's third sense) makes no difference to the life and identity of the human Jesus Christ (Augustine's second sense). The Word's assumptive act ensures that there can be no deficiency in Christ's humanity that needs to be filled up, but Christ is not the human that he is without his relations to the Body.

The central task of this work is to articulate the christological significance of this distinction – to see what difference Christ's willing to be complete with us makes for Christian reflections on the Incarnation and on God's redemptive work. Augustine himself moves us closer to understanding this claim: It is not enough to say that we cannot understand our own lives apart from Christ's; we must also say that we cannot understand Christ's life apart from our own. Knowing Christ is as much an endpoint as it is a beginning. And from our beginnings, we may yet come to know the End which is without end.

At this point, we will be best served by turning back – back to the questions with which this chapter began, and further still.

***

How have I become the person that I am? It is not, of course, clear to me just who I am; I do not mean to imply any fixity or settledness in the identity, or self, or self-representation presupposed by this question. I am quite happy to admit that even in asking it, I am asking for a narrative that fashions for me a picture of myself, a narrative that is bound to be provisional, selective, and distortive in its avoidance of a truth of my life that my wounded eyes cannot yet bear.

Even so. I act in the world; I know parts of it, I speak and listen, I deliberate and judge, I desire things within it – and I seem to do all this in a manner particularly my own. What's more, I am conscious at times that my experience of all these aspects of life changes: I become aware of having misunderstood something, I learn a new word, I find that I no longer enjoy the music I once did. How have I come to this unstable moment between who I have been and who I will be, this present constellation of experiences and desires that is no less singular for all its transience?

My aim here is not a philosophical cartography of the self; I have no desire to enumerate the steps by which self-consciousness dawns in us, whether in the language of philosophy or of developmental psychology. Nor do I wish to provide a descriptive account of the soul and its operations. These tasks may be useful at times; or, at any rate, they may be stimulating diversions. My purpose here is rather to recognize the inescapable materiality (which is also to say sociality) of our lives. Particular accounts of these features of human life might be (and have been) given in the vocabulary of a theology or anthropology of relation, or of the other-in-the-same at the heart of subjectivity, or of the mutual participation or chiasmus of I in you and you in me. Each of these formulations might do quite nicely, depending on the ends one pursues in giving such an account.[24]

For the moment, I am concerned only with the bodily reality of my dependence on others for existence and survival in its barest and most untheorized form. Our bodies come into being only as they are drawn from the flesh of our parents; as they develop, they require months of dependence on the circulatory system, digestive system, renal system, and uterus of our mothers before they have any possibility of sustaining our lives in the world. Once we are born, we possess little facility with perceiving or moving within our surroundings for years, and are utterly reliant on others to provide us sustenance, shelter, and protection from predators. The survival of new human life is, in a very literal way, impossible without the

---

[24] I have drawn these examples from, respectively, Catherine Keller, *Cloud of the Impossible: Negative Theology and Planetary Entanglement* (New York: Columbia University Press, 2015); Emmanuel Lévinas, *Otherwise than Being: or, Beyond Essence*, trans. Alphonso Lingis (Dordrecht: Springer Science and Business Media, 1991); and Graham Ward, *Christ and Culture* (Oxford: Blackwell, 2008).

presence of other people (or in very remarkable cases, other animals) around us, providing for us, inducting us into the bodily practices of sociality. In some cases, adequate provision of food and shelter is inadequate, and survival requires extensive use of culturally specific knowledge and technological arts: ventilators that assist a newborn in breathing, understandings of bacterial infections, hospital procedure that establishes certain spaces as neonatal intensive care units. The contingency of our lives is only underlined by the fact that virtually all human persons who have lived have done so without the availability of this knowledge and technology. While our biological dependence on things outside us can be seen with particular clarity in the case of newborns, it does not end with our births; we have only to consider the central role that bacterial ecosystems within our bodies play in our digestive and immune systems to see that the very continuance of our lives is made possible through our relations to that which we are not.

The case of a parent (or caretaker) and child offers a particularly poignant example of the interweaving of our lives with others, but it points to our deeper implication within a causal order marked by unpredictability and contingency. Our lives unfold within this network of confluences of an unimaginable number of events and in response to them, events which establish the very conditions in which our lives take place. Never mind the incomprehensible number of microphysical processes at play in the cosmological origins and development of the universe, all necessary for at least one of one sun's satellites to produce life at all. Our lives are decisively shaped by events occurring outside the agency of any finite creature: the rainstorm that causes me to stay inside and read a book that will change the way I think about a friendship; the landslide that extinguishes the life of the brilliant nine-year-old who might have pioneered a new agricultural method for feeding impoverished communities; the diminished fish stocks that force me to move away from my parents' home and way of life to find employment in an urban center.

The point is not, of course, that we are simply subject to the vicissitudes of a natural order unshaped by human agency – no one living through this time of rapid climate change can afford to believe that the processes of nature are unresponsive to our agency – or that our lives are unknowingly determined by these events. The point is rather that the fields in which our lives are lived out are not entirely, or even mostly, under our control. The world in which we learn and exercise our agency, the world which we come to understand with the concepts we are given and develop, impinges on us – it constrains and enables the ways in which we are able to exercise agency, it provides for us and pushes back on us.

Likely even more important than the simple physical constraints of our bodies (though, as we have seen, inextricable from them) are the social realities of our lives. The newborn does not stay thus forever, and from the moment of her birth she is plunged into a world that is inescapably structured by the lives of others. Here again, philosophical accounts abound of the constitutive openness to others and the world that informs our sense of ourselves as capable of loving and being loved, as agents able to effect changes in the world, and as speakers able to represent the world to one another.[25] Here again, my point is a basic one: In all our actions, in all the concepts we employ to make sense of the world, in our very sense of ourselves *as* selves, we are dependent on others and the world we share with them. As Rowan Williams writes, both the language we learn from other speakers and the "friction" with which the world pushes back on and corrects our language use are integrally related to our ability to view our lives as a unified whole in which we are able to exercise agency within the world.[26]

---

[25] Three compelling accounts of these phenomena may be found in, respectively: Jean-Luc Marion, *The Erotic Phenomenon*, trans. Stephen E. Lewis (Chicago, IL: University of Chicago Press, 2007); John McDowell, *Mind and World* (Cambridge, MA: Harvard University Press, 1996); and Rowan Williams, *The Edge of Words: God and the Habits of Language* (London: Bloomsbury, 2014).

[26] Williams, *The Edge of Words*, 44.

And, as Williams notes in discussing language's "riskiness, its unstable connection with what it engages with,"[27] we are also able to lie to one another: Using the language we have learned from others, we are able to describe the world falsely to them. These false descriptions can come to pattern our social relations, the concepts we use to describe others, and even the narratives that others adopt to make sense of their own lives. For better or worse, we come to understand ourselves only alongside others, and with the language they give us and we extend. My view of the goals and aspirations available to me, of the value and dignity society does or does not afford my body, of my perception of my body as unthreateningly normative or menacingly aberrant (or then again, in some spaces, menacingly normatizing) – all this is worked out in a complex negotiation between the narratives and past experiences that have shaped my understanding of who I am on the one hand, and the narratives, ways of thinking, and social orderings of those around me on the other. Our lives are at all points an interplay of what Stephen Mulhall has identified as "inheritance" and "originality" – the ways that we are indebted to others in our ability to understand the world and act within it, and the distinctive ways that we freely draw upon this inheritance: changing it, extending it, and recipro-cally influencing the way others think and act in the process.[28]

There is virtually no part of our lives that is untouched by cultural formation; but neither should we underestimate the extent to which our bodies – our biological capacities – enable and channel these social possibilities. We are drawn into particular forms of life that may involve driving automobiles to large air-conditioned spaces wherein we will coordinate the shipping of goods across the world, using our vocal cords and the electronic devices we have manufac-tured to communicate with partners across the world in several different languages we have been taught through formalized

---

[27] Williams, *The Edge of Words*, 44.
[28] Stephen Mulhall, *Inheritance and Originality: Wittgenstein, Heidegger, Kierkegaard* (Oxford: Oxford University Press, 2001).

educational practices; or, very differently, we may awake each day in the same remote village in which we were born, humming to ourselves songs passed from parent to child over many generations as we go to fetch water from a well dug miles away. In each of these cases, our bodies make us available for the interdependent relations that mark us as members of particular ethnicity or culture, that teach us the habits and customs of a (or, often, several different) social groups, that render us capable of speaking particular languages, making certain sorts of art, learning particular ways the world is. Our flesh is the site, too, of more intimate relations to one another: We learn and are able to express, pleasure or displeasure on our faces or with our limbs, to signal relaxation or tense anxiety; we exchange embraces to comfort one another in our sorrow or pain; we offer touches that communicate desire and love.

If our lives are built substantially out of the relations of dependence we bear to the world and those in it, it is also the case that we are often broken by these relations. Our flesh makes us susceptible to the bodily wounds that we suffer through the course of our lives, a vulnerability that is no less important in giving our lives their shape. Just as our agency is enabled by the cultural formation we undergo, so also it is constrained: Even as children, we will be punished corporally for engaging in certain sorts of proscribed action, though what precisely counts as taboo can be as contingent as whether we greet one another with a handshake or a bow. We will be corrected and reproved when we do not follow local conventions, punished with labor or confinement. We will find that we are excluded from certain paths of action solely by virtue of our bodies, told that there are certain people we ought not touch, that there are certain careers for which we are not fit, that there are certain social spaces where we are not welcome. In dramatic (though not uncommon) cases, we will find our bodies treated by others as objects – bought and sold, used to gratify another's desire with little or no consideration of my own, valued solely for its capacity to produce for another's profit. And our flesh is literally vulnerable: vulnerable to weather and hunger, able to be restrained physically by others, susceptible to corruption by disease, easily damaged through accident or malice. We tire from overexertion, we bleed when we are cut. Vulnerability shapes our lives no less than our interdependence, and in fact, these two categories shade into one another. The vulnerability of my parents causes me to grow up an orphan, or the course of my life is changed by a spinal cord injury suffered while playing sports. I am abducted and tortured by a madman, a trauma that leaves scars both physical and psychological. I suffer violence at the hands of one I trust, or lose a child in the midst of war. These, no less than the meals we share with friends or the embraces we receive from family, constitute the fabric of our lives. To live as vulnerable in this world is, very often, to live with tragedy and injustice. It is, finally, to live in a body that will die, losing all bodily availability to those we love and all the worldly goods that we love.

Even after I die, my life will continue to have effects radiating outward through causal chains, and through the agency of others whose agency I have shaped. What distinguishes the shape of my life from the mere effects of my life is that, while my flesh lives, I am in responsive relation to the world – my life makes an active difference to the world, at a level even broader than (though inclusive of) my exercise of agency to make a difference within the world intentionally.

This is the flesh that we are: formed biologically in and through natural processes stretching billions of years into the cosmic past; formed socially through the material and linguistic relations we bear to those around us; exposed to others and the surrounding world both for intimacy and violence. And, if the Word has joined Herself to humanity in Jesus Christ, *this* is the very flesh She has assumed.

***

To press further, it will be useful to clarify a few key terms. Several will be concepts traditionally employed within the tradition of conciliar christology – which is to say, the christological tradition represented by the teaching of the seven ecumenical councils of the

Church – both contemporary to Augustine's time and in the centuries after his death; several will be my own.[29]

First, human nature. Affirmation of the claim that there is such a thing as human nature seems required by the language of Chalcedon and III Constantinople, if one takes these conciliar statements to be theologically authoritative. Within the Augustinian tradition, a thing exists only by receiving its being as God's gift. This reception of life from God is often described as a thing's "participation" in God's own life, a dependence-relation that also entails some likeness between the participant and that in which it participates. God is the source and perfection of all created goodnesses; the goodness of any creature can never serve as a perfect image of the divine Good (as, for example, the Word is the perfect image of the Father's Good), but can only ever reflect God's originary Goodness. Each individual creature reflects God's goodness in a manner unique to it, as the individual existent it is; but it also exhibits a likeness to God proper to the *sort* of creature it is. That is to say, every creature of that sort exhibits a likeness to God in a common way, necessarily in virtue of being that sort of creature. We may thus describe a nature as a "mode" or "manner" of creaturely participation in God's life, a manner in which all creatures of that sort will consistently reflect God's Goodness. Abstract natures or forms thus find their origin and proper subsistence in the simple life of God, as "divine ideas"; and one such nature is human nature, according to which some creatures participate "humanwise" in the simple life of God. We need not give an overly metaphysically freighted definition of what participating in God humanwise requires, but we may take the conciliar christological definitions as a starting point. At a minimum, we should say that possession of human nature entails that one is "composed of rational soul and body (ἐκ ψυχῆς λογικῆς καὶ σώματος)" (Chalcedon; Denzinger 301), and that as a result of the Word's

---

[29] The rhetoric of "conciliar christology" has been significant within recent analytic theology and analytic philosophy of religion; see Timothy Pawl, *In Defense of Conciliar Christology: A Philosophical Essay* (Oxford: Oxford University Press, 2016), 1.

assumption of flesh, Christ possesses "two natural volitions or wills and two natural actions (δύο φυσικὰς θελήσεις ἤτοι θελήματα αὐτῷ, καὶ δύο φυσικὰς ἐνεργείας)" (III Constantinople; Denzinger 556), a divine and a human one, thus suggesting that being human entails having a natural volition (or will) and an action proper to that nature. A second term is that of a human person. We can take Boethius' loose definition of a person as an "individual substance of a rational nature" as a guide.[30] What is relevant for my purposes here is the qualification of a person as an *individual* substance – or, in the terminology of later theology, as a distinct subsistence or *suppositum* (subject) of existence. Put in the terms I have preferred, to be a human person is to be a created subsistence or subject participating humanwise in the simple life of God. Being a human person thus entails, by the light of conciliar definition, that one has a rational soul and body, a will, and the "proper act" of human nature. Very importantly, attributions of human personhood need not rest upon consciousness or a philosophical understanding of the "self," with the ability to perform intentional actions by free will (this should be distinguished from having a soul with a natural volition or will, which does not entail the actuality of consciousness or volitional ability in any individual person), with a certain measure of intelligence or certain capacities to feel pain – all of which would function to exclude the profoundly mentally disabled from being identified as human persons. In practice, human capacities vary immensely; but being a human person is about the sort of thing one *is*, about what God has made one. Even in light of the preceding recognition of our interconnectedness, personhood as such is "relational" only in that our existences depend upon our relation to God.[31] It is through this relation that each human person, simply in virtue of their humanness, is a bearer of the image of God.

---

[30] *Persona est rationalis naturae individua substantia (Liber de Persona et Duabus Naturis 3).*

[31] We are still persons apart from our relations to one another. Harriet A. Harris has convincingly shown the metaphysical problems that arise from accounts that take

According to the Chalcedonian christological tradition, Christ is said to have a human nature, but not to be a human person – for if he were a human person, he would be so in addition to his divine personhood in the person of the Word. Thus, there would be two persons in Christ, the "two sons" that Nestorius' critics held inevitably resulted from his teachings. The centuries subsequent to the Fourth Ecumenical Council sought to bring further metaphysical clarity to the constitution of Christ's person both in defense of Chalcedon and in opposition to it, centering upon the relation between nature and person.[32] Within Chalcedonian christology, a key conceptual advance is offered by what Johannes Zachhuber has described as Leontius of Jerusalem's philosophy of the hypostasis and his "insubsistence Christology," the understanding of Christ's humanity as a universal nature that exists only in the hypostasis of the Son.[33] This insubsistence christology is taken up by St. John of Damascus and wedded to Leontius of Byzantium's philosophical terminology of the *enhypostatos*,[34] enabling the Damascene's affirmation that Christ's humanity exists only *enhypostatically*.[35]

personhood itself as relational at "Should We Say That Personhood Is Relational?," *Scottish Journal of Theology* 51.2 (1998): 214–234.

[32] Johannes Zachhuber has offered the most philosophically perspicacious reading of post-Chalcedonian christology; see his *The Rise of Christian Theology and the End of Ancient Metaphysics: Patristic Philosophy from the Cappadocian Fathers to John of Damascus* (Oxford: Oxford University Press, 2020). See also the foundation work undertaken by Brian Daley at "A Richer Union: Leontius of Byzantium and the Relationship of Human and Divine in Christ," *Studia Patristica* 24 (1993): 239–265; and *Leontius of Byzantium: Complete Works* (Oxford: Oxford University Press, 2017); as well as Uwe M. Lang, "Anhypostatos-Enhypostatos: Church Fathers, Protestant Orthodoxy and Karl Barth," *Journal of Theological Studies* 49 (1998): 630–657.

[33] Zachhuber, *Rise of Christian Theology*, 262–269.

[34] Zachhuber, *Rise of Christian Theology*, 225.

[35] Zachhuber, *Rise of Christian Theology*, 292. Richard Cross continues mapping the history of Latin thinking on the existence of person and nature at *The Metaphysics of the Incarnation* (Oxford: Oxford University Press, 2002), charting the rise and arguing in favor of the analogy of an accident's inherence in a substance for the nature of the dependence of Christ's human nature upon his divine person. While my apophatic

Within contemporary christology, this byzantine history of christological development has been taken up into varied theological idioms. For Barthians, Christ's human nature is held to be *anhypostatic* (it has no individual *hypostasis*/subsistence and is not a *suppositum* apart from its union with the Word) and *enhypostatic* (it is hypostatized and subsists only in its union with the Son of God).[36] In the language preferred by Thomists, there is no distinct human subsistence (*suppositum*) or *esse* in Christ; the Word is the existent subject to which all affirmations of Christ's person ultimately refer.[37] On either account, Christ is not a human person; he is a divine person who subsists in divine and human natures.

The Late Antique development of the technical terminology of Christ's person undoubtedly reflects the apologetic pressures placed upon Chalcedonian christology by miaphysite christology, on the one hand, and the so-called Nestorian christology of the Church of the East, on the other. Yet such attempts to define more precisely the constitution of Christ's person – both in post-Chalcedonian attempts to re-found classical metaphysics on the concept of *hypostasis* (as in Leontius of Jerusalem and, arguably, John of Damascus) or in contemporary proposals to safeguard the unity of Christ's person by emphasizing the mixture or even identity of divinity and

emphasis cautions against some aspects of the metaphysical speculation Cross traces in the later Middle Ages, my approach stands in greatest continuity with that of Bonaventure; see *The Metaphysics of the Incarnation*, 78–81 and 208–209.

[36] See Bruce L. McCormack, *Karl Barth's Critically Realistic Dialectical Theology: Its Genesis and Development 1909–1936* (Oxford: Clarendon Press, 1995), 327; Paul Dafydd Jones, *The Humanity of Christ: Christology in Karl Barth's Church Dogmatics* (London: T&T Clark, 2008), 17–26, and 50–52; and most recently, James P. Haley, *The Humanity of Christ: The Significance of the Anhypostasis and Enhypostasis in Karl Barth's Christology* (Eugene, OR: Pickwick, 2017).

[37] See Thomas Aquinas' discussion of the Word as the sole *suppositum* of Christ at *ST* III.2.2, as well as Rowan Williams, *Christ the Heart of Creation*, 12–35. I leave aside the question of *esse secundarium* in the *De unione*; see Cross, *The Metaphysics of the Incarnation*, 62–64; and Roger W. Nutt, "Thomas Aquinas on Christ's Unity: Revisiting the *De Unione* Debate," *Harvard Theological Review* 114.4 (2021): 491–507.

humanity in Christ[38] – presume a greater confidence than is warranted in our conceptual grasp of the terms "nature" or "hypostasis" and their mutual relation as applied to a divine person. The divine person of the Word is and remains incomprehensible even in union with the human nature encountered in Christ's flesh. We can give no final account of *how* humanity subsists in the Word – any more than we can render the Word's eternal generation by the Father sayable – because the Word's hypostasis exceeds the remit of our philosophical concepts. We may deny particular claims within the creaturely sphere (that Christ's humanity has an independent subsistence, that Christ is a human person), but we should prescind from attempting to render more precisely how the human nature of the divine person we meet in Jesus Christ can be hypostatized in his unknowable divinity. He meets us with a humanity as real as our own, but a divine personhood that is incomprehensible to us even as it enfolds and is inseparable from our common nature.

Better, then, to abide by a metaphysically chastened Wittgensteinian grammar grounded in the language of the Councils that is nevertheless realist with respect to the existence of natures. In response to the question "Who is Jesus Christ?" it will at times make sense to reply, "That man over there, writing in the dust." At other times, and always when speaking strictly about the union of divinity and humanity in *una persona*, the same question will require the response "The Word of God." It will *never* be appropriate to speak of the human Jesus Christ as existing separately from or possessing a personhood in union with but distinct from that of the Word, for he *is* the Word. At times it will make sense to make predications of Christ's humanity ("In his humanity, Jesus was hungry and tired and slept"), but only within a grammatical

---

[38] Christopher A. Beeley, "Christological Non-Competition and the Return to Chalcedon: A Response to Rowan Williams and Ian McFarland," *Modern Theology* 38.3 (2022): 592–617; Jordan Daniel Wood, *The Wholy Mystery of Christ: Creation as Incarnation in Maximus Confessor* (South Bend, IN: University of Notre Dame Press, 2022).

structure affirming that this humanity is the humanity of the Word, and that all these predications may validly be ascribed to the Word; for this humanity is Her own. Ruled out of court are any locutions in which we might be tempted to say things like "This suffering is the suffering of Christ's humanity, but *not* the Word's." Such a locution (mis)attributes the suffering to a person – it seeks to answer the "Who?" question. By contrast, saying "Christ suffers in his human nature, not in his divine nature" describes the *locus* of the Word's suffering, answering the "How?" question of the one divine person who has assumed flesh. Such an account resists the metaphysical closure afforded by some post-Chalcedonian christ-ology, precisely by retaining a lively sense of the apophatic in both the discussion of Christ's person and in predications made of the *una persona*. Christ's humanity is the humanity of God, and precisely as such, it opens contemplation directly into the mystery of God's incomprehensibility.

Yet this grammar also directs us to a wider field of christological inquiry, frequently obscured by an over-focus on the metaphysical constitution of Christ's person. Consider the question of whether the very same person Jesus the Messiah could have been born of one other than Mary of Nazareth. According to one seminal account within analytic modal metaphysics, I am essentially the child of my parents. There is no possible world in which I exist but am not the child of my parents, for there is no "me" that could conceivably be born of different people.[39] What it is for me to be "me" is for me to be a particular union of soul and body that marks me off as a unique subsistence of human nature. My personhood rests upon a soul created by God being joined to a particular body, what we know to be a particular sperm and egg carrying genetic material of two irreplaceable parents. Yet if Christ is a divine person rather than a human one, the same cannot be said of him. If it could, it would

---

[39] Saul Kripke, *Naming and Necessity* (Cambridge, MA: Harvard University Press, 1980), 110–111.

mean that the Word assumes some particular subsistence of human nature, that his personhood is dependent upon some particular flesh produced by some particular parent or parents. But Christ's personhood is wholly the personhood of the Word: There is no distinct subsistence of human nature that is assumed, but rather human nature itself, hypostatized by its union to the person of the Word.[40] Consequently, we should hold that the person of Christ is not even essentially the child of Mary, but rather that the very same person of the Word might – considered strictly as being within the power of the Second Person of the Trinity to will – have been born of a different mother (and indeed, even without a virginal conception), in a different place, at any point in human history.

While such a statement seems demanded by the logic of conciliar christology, I do not mean to hold it forth as a serious christological possibility. Alongside clarifying the implications of the claim that Christ is not a human person, I wish to show that if we take the metaphysical completeness of Christ's person as our sole christological data point, it very swiftly takes us away from anything recognizable as the concrete life through which God has revealed Himself in history. We should say with Augustine that Christ is complete without us in both divinity and humanity – but this affirmation is in itself very far from the actual life of the savior, born of Mary, proclaiming the coming of the Kingdom of God on the shores of Galilee, crucified beyond the city walls and raised on the third day. Claims of this sort cannot be accounted for by Christ's metaphysical completeness alone. They require Christ's relation to the world around him. They are claims made about how Christ has willed to be complete *with* us.

The third term, then, is the "shape of one's life."[41] As the above example (as well as the broader discussion of our interdependence

---

[40] Thomas Aquinas, *ST* III.4.3.

[41] For the language of the "shape" of a life, I am indebted to Kathryn Tanner; see, for instance, *Jesus, Humanity, and the Trinity*, 20, where Tanner describes "the shape of Jesus' whole human life" as "the out-working of God's own trinitarian life."

above) shows, much of what I think of as "me" is not provided by my bare metaphysical constitution or self-experience. The shape of my life is my life as it is lived in relations of interdependence: the physical, biological, and social histories that have conditioned my environment, and that I will in turn influence through my action within them; the relations I bear to those around me, the people who teach me to speak a particular language, the friends who play a role in fashioning my moral and aesthetic judgments, the relationships that will last through the course of my life allowing for unmatched depths of intimacy and responsibility; and the events that turn the course of my life, the decisions I make that ramify through the rest of my days, the accident or chance encounter that forever reconfigures the possibilities of my life.[42] Apart from these concrete histories, relationships, and events, I may still be a person, but I am not *me*. The shape of my life, inclusive of my own exercise of agency in my course of living it, is inseparable from my becoming not *a* person, but *the* person who will one day stand before the judgment seat of God bearing a determinate history and an unsubstitutable way of existing. The shape of my life is what makes my being the person that I am distinct from other ways my life might have gone, what makes me recognizable to myself as myself. Because my life is not yet complete, and because so much of my life remains hidden to me even now, it is not yet apparent what the shape of my life will be; yet from the standpoint of God's eternity, the shape of my life is complete and defined, as is the role I play in defining the shapes of others' lives.

***

[42] Cf. Hans Frei, *Identity of Jesus Christ*, 138: "The identity of Jesus . . . is not given simply in his inner intention, in a kind of story behind the story. It is given, rather, in the enactment of his intentions. But even to say that much is not enough. Rather, his identity is given in the mysterious coincidence of his intentional action with circumstances, partly initiated by him, partly devolving upon him. The latter kind of occurrence also, in part, shapes his identity within the story."

How, then, does Christ's life receive its shape? This might, at first blush, appear a puzzling question. Surely Christ is the Son of God, whose human life is the expression in time of the eternal life that He receives in His eternal generation by the Father? While this is undoubtedly a foundational principle of orthodox christology, it has tended to result in systematic descriptions of Christ's life in which the divine life overshadows the contribution that the world makes to the unfolding of Christ's human life. So for instance, in spite of all Barth's laudable attention to the particularity of Christ's humanity, Graham Ward may justly observe that for Barth,

> The work of Christ cannot be characterized in terms of the ordinary human operations of that world – its politics, economics, social and cultural milieu, his friends, his family, his enemies, his admirers. Christ becomes the perfect expression of Cartesian subjectivity: autonomous, self-determining, self-defining, the atomized subject of a number of distinct properties or predicates; as Barth himself puts it, the "epistemological principle." Christ becomes either the absolute subject or the absolute object: he "who is the subject and object of the basic act of God, the subject and object of the consummating act of God that reveals that basis" . . . [D]espite the matrix of relations in which the New Testament situates Jesus Christ, Barth's Jesus Christ is not a social animal; he is an other, an alien, a "pure act[s] of [the] divine grace" of God.[43]

Restated in the terms I have preferred here, Ward's critique is that the shape of Christ's human life is in Barth's thought determined wholly by the eternal life of the Son. As both the subject and object of God's divine decision, the one overriding fact of Christ's life is God's act of election, a redemptive will that so thoroughly defines Christ's life that the world is rendered an accessory to this revelatory self-communication. There is little room for consideration of how the culture, the context, the natural environment, the particular

---

[43] *Christ and Culture*, 12; citing Barth, *CD* IV/1, 50.

people and decisions and events constituting the world in which Christ lived might make an unsubstitutable contribution to the human life in which God is revealed, shaping Christ's body and human agency. This is a characteristic temptation of proposals that hew most closely to the formulations of classical christology, and Ward's critique could be applied with the relevant revisions in conceptual framework to many contemporary Thomist and Balthasarian positions.[44]

By contrast, and in response to this historically dominant christological tradition, many thinkers have opted to emphasize the human becoming and relationality of Christ. For these varied theological streams, Christ's life receives its shape through his implication in the contingencies of creaturely becoming – but more than that, God's revelation in Christ in the midst of creaturely becoming reveals God's own reciprocal relationship to the world, and God's own becoming alongside the world. So, for instance, process theologians have emphasized Christ's growth and human development;[45] Latin American liberation theology has brought to light the revolutionary nature of Christ's proclamation of the Reign of God by situating him fully within his social context;[46] proponents of "deep incarnation" have called attention to Christ's implication in the great sweep of cosmic history, inclusive of microphysical processes occurring in Christ's body reaching down even to the quantum level and the evolutionary development of his human flesh.[47] In general, those theologies most attentive to what I have

---

[44] See, for instance, Thomas Joseph White's very impressive *The Incarnate Lord: A Thomistic Study in Christology* (Washington, DC: Catholic University of America Press, 2015).

[45] John B. Cobb, Jr., *Christ in a Pluralistic Age* (Eugene, OR: Wipf and Stock, 1998), particularly Chapter 8.

[46] Sobrino, *Jesus the Liberator*, Chapter 3; Jon Sobrino, "Jesus' Approach as a Paradigm for Mission," in *Jesus of Galilee: Contextual Christology for the 21st Century*, ed. Robert Lassalle-Klein (Maryknoll, NY: Orbis Books, 2011), 85–98.

[47] See, *inter alia*, Niels Henrik Gregersen, "Deep Incarnation: Why Evolutionary Continuity Matters in Christology," *Toronto Journal of Theology* 26.2 (2010): 173–188;

called the shape of Christ's life have been those which have revealed the abiding significance of the Incarnation for contemporary theological understandings of the significance of race, gender, sexuality, disability, class, and the particularity of Israel's calling within God's redemptive work.[48] Yet these theologies have frequently determined that recovering this full-blooded sense of Christ's social existence and its liberatory potential requires substantially modifying or reinterpreting the claims of conciliar christology.[49]

The promise of an Augustinian theology of the *totus Christus* is its potential to hold together both the classical understanding of God's relationship to the created order with a real sense of the unsubstitutable place of created agency and causality within the life of Christ.[50] Attention to the "whole Christ" enables a christological outlook that forces no decision between the transcendence of God and the priority of the Word's assumptive act, on the one hand, and the true implication of Christ's human life and identity in creaturely becoming, on the other.

Elizabeth A. Johnson, *Creation and the Cross: The Mercy of God for a Planet in Peril* (Maryknoll, NY: Orbis Books, 2018); Denis Edwards, *Deep Incarnation: God's Redemptive Suffering with Creatures* (Maryknoll, NY: Orbis Books, 2019); and Rebecca L. Copeland, *Created Being: Expanding Creedal Christology* (Waco, TX: Baylor University Press, 2020).

[48] Mayra Rivera's recent *Poetics of the Flesh* has synthesized a great deal of ancient and contemporary theological and philosophical reflections on the importance of relationality to human flesh.

[49] See, among many possible examples, Cobb, *Christ in a Pluralistic Age*, 163–164; and Sobrino, *Christ the Liberator*, 222–224. The deep incarnation movement's theological revisionism has generally tended to be motivated by concerns to reconstruct theology in light of modern science, but has also stressed the need to give up the teaching of God's impassibility so as to underline Her identification with the suffering of human and non-human creatures on the Cross; see Edwards, *Deep Incarnation*, 113–117.

[50] I am, of course, far from the first to have identified or attempted to resolve this impasse. Troy A. Stefano has traced the way that christology since the time of Schleiermacher has returned again and again to what he calls the "elliptical problem," the question of how properly to relate the historical or (using Pannenberg's categories) "quantitative" dimension of christology and the eschatological or "vertical" dimension; Stefano, "Christology after Schleiermacher," 363.

If, then, we ask how Christ's life receives its shape – how he becomes the person that he is, rather than a human *simpliciter* – we require a distinction between two further terms: fourth, the Word's "act of incarnation," and fifth, what we might call the "work of incarnation."

In speaking of the *act* of incarnation, I refer to the eternal act of the simple life of God, by which the Second Person of the Trinity wills to assume human nature into unity with Her hypostatic life. This act depends on no precondition or contribution from the side of creation, and is entirely sufficient to bring about the Son's assumption of flesh. This act requires nothing from the created order for its completion, for as the act of God, the act of incarnation is the very divine life, utterly perfect and eternally complete in itself prior to the existence of the created order. Considered in itself, this act stands on the far side of the divine incomprehensibility, pointing us only to the *sui generis* and unknowable life of God. This means that, again considered in itself as but one name for the simple triune life of God, we lack any criteria by which we might mark off the act of incarnation from the act of creation as two distinct acts within the divine life. They cannot be two acts, for they are two names for the simple triune activity which is the life of God.

The only distinction that may be drawn between them is according to the category of relation, in light of the revelation of God's life as triune, and so we may affirm that the act of incarnation is properly ascribed to the Son in eternal and inseparable relation to Father and Spirit, while creation is taken to be an indivisible act of the whole Trinity as it grants life to all that is not God. While it is true that we often speak of God's acts as distinguished from one another by the effects that they bring about in the created order – in this case, the act of creation bringing about the effect of calling the world into being, and the act of incarnation bringing about the effect of uniting human nature to the Son – we attempt to peer too deeply into the mystery of God's incomprehensibility if we think we can know of anything in the divine life that answers to this diversity of effects. Here as always, God is *idipsum* in the simple life of Father, Son, and Holy Spirit.

When I speak of the *work* of incarnation, however, I refer to God's will to live a particular human life in the human nature He has assumed – the life of Jesus Christ, conceived by the Holy Ghost and born of Mary; who preached and healed and exorcized demons in Galilee; who suffered under Pontius Pilate, was crucified, died, and buried; who was raised on the third day, and ascended into heaven. In contrast to the act of incarnation, which has to do with the Word's will to assume flesh, the work of incarnation has to do with the Word's will to occupy a particular place within God's providential ordering of created history. Where the act of incarnation speaks of the Word's will to assume human nature, the work of incarnation speaks of the Word's will to assume the particular shape of Christ's life that we find described in the Gospels and the theological tradition of the Church.

With slightly more philosophical rigor, we might say: The act of incarnation names the domain of created effects that are conditionally necessary given the Word's will to assume human flesh into hypostatic union, while the work of incarnation names the domain of created effects given the Word's will to assume flesh that might have been otherwise without metaphysical change to the constitution of Christ's person. Both the act and work of incarnation are thus seen to be grounded in the one eternal will of the Word who is the simple triune Lord.

The distinction between the act and work of incarnation is suggested by the affirmation that Christ's humanity has no existence independent of the Word: It is not a particular subsistence of human nature that is assumed by the Word, but human nature itself; but if it is a *true* human nature that is hypostatized by the Word, Jesus' humanity must be capable of entering into the many different sorts of relationships – spatiotemporal, environmental, affective, linguistic, and so on – that are proper to human life.[51]

---

[51] This is not, of course, to say that we can be overly confident about *which* relations are proper to human nature based on empirical observation. For instance, empirical observation would plausibly lead us to believe that it is proper to human nature that each human person should be in a relation of sinning against every other human

While the Word eternally wills to assume human nature in Christ, the act of incarnation is a relatively barren metaphysical thesis if it is not viewed in its inward relation to God's providential ordering of creation.[52] The Word assumes not only the nature of humanity, but in hypostatizing it within creation, wills the whole shape of Christ's life. Though he exists only because the Word has assumed human nature, not only the nature but *this particular human life* is united to the Word – for Jesus Christ *is* the Second Person of the Trinity.[53]

To guard against misprision, however, let me be clear: In distinguishing the act of incarnation from the work of incarnation, I do not intend to suggest that there is any indeterminacy in the Word's will to assume flesh, or to suggest that the Incarnation is a process that is progressively realized throughout Christ's history. The Incarnation is as full and entire at the first moment of Christ's conception as it remains today, as Christ's ascended body sits at the right hand of the Father. Still less do I mean to propose a "two stage" incarnation, according to which (on one construal) the Word assumes first an abstract nature, and subsequently a concrete one. The distinction between the act of incarnation and the work of

---

person they encounter – but this is not something I would wish to ascribe to Christ. Nevertheless, I think we are on fairly firm ground in saying that there are at least *some* relations that all human essentially bear to other things in the created order, and that whatever those are, Christ must exemplify them in the humanity hypostatized by the Word.

[52] It is clear that, at least by the end of his life, Augustine understands both the Word's will to assume flesh and the particular bestowals of grace according to which sinful humans are renovated and drawn back to God as two aspects of one and the same providential order of history. These concerns come together in Augustine's discussions of Christ as himself predestined, as at *praed. sanct.* 15.30–1.

[53] Cf. Kathryn Tanner, *Jesus, Humanity, and the Trinity*, 54: "It is the particularity of Jesus' humanity, its specific shape or mode, that comes to include us. We are not included in Christ's life simply because the humanity assumed by the Son in Christ is common, shared by Christ and every other human being. It is this particular person – and not the humanity of Christ *per se* – that has universal efficacy, in so far as everyone else is drawn to it, united to Christ's own life. Jesus' own life, in its particular shape as a human version of the Son's, includes us by continuing in the form of a life with us, a life, that is, in which we are made to participate by the Holy Spirit."

incarnation is properly drawn solely within the created effects of the eternal act of God: The act of incarnation unites human nature to the person of the Word, while the work of incarnation is a function of the providence of God, considered in its ordering toward Christ as the one in whom all things hold together. It is in virtue of the act of incarnation that the Word is human, but it is in virtue of the work of incarnation – the specific order of God's providence in relation to Christ – that his humanity is *thus and so*, that his humanity bears *these particularities* and *these relations to other creatures*. Where the act of incarnation includes only the nature of humanity as its creaturely *terminus*, the work of incarnation includes not only Christ's humanity as *terminus*, but the existence and agency of all those creatures which God wills to use to give definition to Christ's human particularity.

Because God's act is simple and eternal, we cannot draw any real distinction between these acts in the divine life; both are acts of the Word in inseparable operation with the Father and Spirit. Indeed, the Word who assumes flesh is none other than the Wisdom according to which all creation is ordered in this particular way, *toward* this one.[54] From all eternity, the Word wills not only to take on human flesh, but to live a particular human life within the providential order of history; and these wills are one will. Accordingly, we can speak not only of God willing to assume human nature, but willing to assume the shape of Christ's life – willing to assume the relations that Christ bears throughout his human life to the rest of the created order.

Where the distinction between the act of incarnation and the work of incarnation becomes analytically useful is in noting that, while the act of incarnation is wholly and completely an act of the

---

[54] Recall Augustine's words at *trin.* 2.5.9; WSA I/5, 103: "in the Wisdom of God, there was timelessly contained the time in which that Wisdom was to appear in the flesh. So while without any beginning of time *in the beginning was the Word and the Word was with God and the Word was God* (Jn 1:1), without any time there was in the Word the time at which the Word would become flesh and dwell among us (Jn 1:14) . . . The whole series of all times is timelessly contained in God's eternal wisdom."

Son, the *work* of incarnation is the human activity of the Son in its relations to the created order. As the will of the Son, the work of incarnation is founded upon the eternal act of God. Yet included within the Word's will to assume the particular shape of Christ's life is the existence, causality, and agency of the created order. In assuming the shape of Christ's life, the Word wills, for instance, that She should attend a wedding at Cana and miraculously convert water into wine. Yet for this to be included in the shape of Christ's life, it cannot depend upon Christ's existence and activity alone. For this to be an event of the human life that the Word eternally wills to lead, a dizzying array of creaturely considerations must be included in the Word's will, everything from geological and environmental processes that allow for habitation in towns in the northern Levant, to the evolutionary history of grapevines and the technical history of fermentation, to social orders and religious practices that render sensible and meaningful the rituals of marriage and feasting, to particular kinship relations and local customs that would result in Jesus and Mary being invited to this wedding, to the particular agencies of the two persons and their families (and all the likely uneven distribution of power in the exercise of those agencies) in bringing about the betrothal and marriage. For the shape of Christ's life to be what it is, all these many aspects of the created order must be included within the work of incarnation.

The work of incarnation cannot, therefore, be the act of the Word alone. The act of the Word is logically prior to – and is indeed the presupposition of – the whole work of incarnation, but the shape of Christ's life itself requires the existence and the agency of the created order. In being used to give Christ's life its shape, the world is drawn *into* the work of incarnation. It is used by the Word to make Christ the person that he is, in all his concrete particularity. He is not who he is, and does not accomplish the redemption of the world, apart from the relations he bears to it. In willing the creation and providential order of the world, God wills that creation should hold together in such a way that, as the Word wills to be born into time, the world should bring about *this* particular human life. It is as if the Word sculpts the shape of Christ's life from the relations he bears to the created order, using its existence and agency as a tool. Christ is intrinsically and essentially the person of the Word, an identity secured by the act of incarnation. To be the crucified and resurrected Messiah of Israel, however, to be the son of Mary, to be the one who brings good news to the poor and oppressed and who proclaims release to the captives, to be the one at whose feet every knee shall bow – in short, to be Jesus the Christ, who is worshipped as the result of the redemptive acts he performs in Jerusalem two thousand years ago – his life is inextricable from his relations to the world. Christ's identity as the Redeemer includes the existence and agency of the world, and is impossible apart from it.

***

It is in this sense, I argue, that we should understand how the Word wills Her life to be complete with us. It might have been complete with us otherwise; but for Christ's life to be what it is, for him to be who *he* is rather than one we might relate to quite differently than we do, the existence and agency of the world occupies an unsubstitutable place within the work of incarnation.

The work of incarnation thus offers us a framework within which we can make sense of even Augustine's most shocking statements about the *totus Christus*. This is not to say that he would have put matters in the way I have here; yet I think this theology of the work of incarnation constitutes a valid extension of the theological trajectory Augustine begins, filling in many of the details that remain hazy in his own discussions of the whole Christ. Jesus can speak with our words, he can be considered one person with his Body the heavenly city, because our lives are essential to the shape of his own. He is not who he is without us, and we are most truly who we are only in him.

To anticipate the conclusions of future chapters, it is the whole shape of Christ's life which is the redemptive sign by which God draws the hearts of sinful humanity back to Himself. Consequently, the existence and agency of the created world not only give Christ's life its shape, but are used by God to accomplish the work of redemption itself. These very relations that help shape Christ's human life are made signs pointing to his flesh, signs that God uses to direct our hearts to Him. And as we will see, because every creature is a sign that by its very existence points to Christ's flesh, the work of incarnation has a cosmic scope: The whole order of creation redemptively points to this one human life, and so this whole order is included within the Word's will to live as Jesus Christ. His identity as the Redeemer is completed in the lives of those joined to him by the Holy Spirit, as their lives come to serve as signs of his own, and as his very human loves reanimate their sinful hearts. The shape of Christ's life is only achieved as the redemption of all those joined to him is made perfect: Because he has willed to be complete *with* us, as a human in relation to the world, he is not fully who he is unless and until we are fully who he wills us to be, children reconciled to God.

Precisely as the act of the Word who works inseparably from Father and Spirit, the work of incarnation is a fundamentally trinitarian act. In the inseparable unity of the divine life, the Word assumes flesh not alone, but as sent by the Father into a fallen creation, to reveal the invisible God to the world and draw our hearts back to Her. Or again, the Word assumes flesh not alone, but in a manner that itself joins with the Father in the procession of the Spirit. The Word's act of incarnation is, in the triune simplicity of the divine life, the very same as the act-in-relation by which the Word spirates the Holy Ghost alongside the Father. There is no distinction in God's life between an "immanent" and an "economic" life: The eternal act that produces temporal effects (the parting of the Red Sea, for instance, or the Word's living a human life) is the very same as the eternal act by which Father, Son, and Holy Spirit are one God in mutual relation. The Word's assumption of human flesh is thus, in the divine life, indistinguishable from the Word's spiration of the Holy Ghost – the Spirit is breathed by the Father and Son *with the very will* to include our lives in the lives of God. Were this not the case, the will of the Father and Son would be indeterminate within the divine life until the spiration of the Holy Spirit. If, however, the Father wills the whole will of God changelessly from all eternity and as the origin of this will in the Son and Holy Spirit, then their persons are intrinsically ordered to these trinitarian missions. This is not to say that the missions are necessary to God, only that they are part of the divine will from all eternity.[55] This requires us to affirm that these missions are contained within the will of the Father, changelessly and with full determinacy, logically prior to the begetting of the Son and their mutual spiration of the Holy Ghost.

The *totus Christus* thus serves as an image in time of the divine life of a Word who is inseparable from the Father and the Spirit. As the Word's life is, from all eternity, bound up in the relations of begottenness and co-spiration, so also the historical particularity of Christ's humanity is bound up in the lives of those united to him by the Spirit. Christ breathes into them his own human life, that this breath may return to him and, empowered by the Spirit, extend his life and complete his redemptive work. As the life of Christ and the Spirit's dwelling in his Body reflect their eternal processions, these divine persons reflect their mutual indwelling historically as they together draw our humanity back to the Father through our union with Christ's humanity. In the work of incarnation, we find our humanity always already included within Christ's own in the Word's eternal will to assume flesh, just as the Word and Spirit are one in the simplicity of the divine life. We are truly Christ, and made ever more so by the work of the Holy Ghost.

---

[55] On how this the will of God may be fully determinate from all eternity and identical to the simplicity of the divine life, without thereby being necessary to God, see Joseph E. Lenow, "Shoring Up Divine Simplicity against Modal Collapse: A Powers Account," *Religious Studies* 57.1 (2021): 10–29. My argument there is framed specifically apologetically, in categories native to analytic philosophy of religion; for a parallel account articulated through the resources of classical Thomism, see Jared Michelson's excellent essay "Thomistic Divine Simplicity and its Analytic Detractors: Can One Affirm Divine Aseity and Goodness without Simplicity?," *Heythrop Journal* 63.6 (2022): 1140–1162.

4 | A Historical Icon

Theological attention to the work of incarnation suggests that Jesus' human life is given shape, in significant part, through his relations to the world: his physical environment, his sociocultural context, the individuals he encounters, and (as I will argue in subsequent chapters) all the lives that are redeemed through incorporation in his Body. This is not just a point about theological schemas – it pertains to Jesus in his historical actuality. Just as, in excess of our theological claims *about* Jesus, there is some fact of the matter about his existing roughly two thousand years ago in Roman Judea, there is also some fact of the matter about the details of his life: Was he born in Bethlehem, or Nazareth? Did he spend several years of his life in Egypt, or not? Did – or how did – his discussions with local rabbis as a youth, or the cultural particularities of Galilee's Lake Region, or his encounters with the vulnerable and marginalized in the course of his ministry shape his understanding of the mission he had been given by the Father, and even his sense of intimacy with the Father?

These are properly historical questions: They concern historical existents and past events, and at least some of the answers we might give to these questions are true or false in virtue of how it was with these existents and events. In principle, these questions are permissive of scientific-historical investigation, using study of Christian and non-Christian texts, archaeological remains and material culture, and analysis of ancient social and cultural patterns to produce a reconstruction of Christ's life that may dispose us toward some answers to these questions rather than others. This is precisely the scholarly trajectory that "historical Jesus" research has pursued since at least D. F. Strauss' *The Life of Jesus*,[1] often in ways that have proved both generative and challenging for christological reflection.

In this chapter, I continue and extend the work of systematic theologians like Wolfhart Pannenberg and Jon Sobrino who have taken historical Jesus research as a resource for systematic theology. Indeed, Sobrino has appealed to explicitly Augustinian language, writing that "it is the historical Jesus who is the key providing access to the total Christ."[2] Rather than attempting to provide a complete reconstruction of Christ's life, however, my purpose here will be to render more clearly the implications of attending to the work of incarnation. How, concretely, might the life of Christ have received its shape through his relations to the world?

We should keep two points of caution in mind in our use of this historical scholarship. The first and obvious point is that such reconstructions are generally only effective in communicating to us historical probabilities. We can admit frankly that the answers to many questions about the influence of the world on Christ's human life are unknown to us, and that no level of historical study, however rigorous, will yield definitive answers to them.

More importantly, we should remember that historical study, as presently constituted, is a scientific enterprise: It depends upon observational experience, and reasons probabilistically on the basis of a presumption of causal regularity. Because we do not commonly see humans walking on top of the waves, or encounter paralytics healed at a touch, the historian *qua* historian rightly attributes a vanishingly small probability to the thesis that these miraculous events took place, and does not customarily include them in historical reconstruction of past events. Even supposing

---

[1] David Friedrich Strauss, *The Life of Jesus, Critically Examined*, 3 vols., trans. George Elliot (London: Chapman Brothers, 1846[1835–6]).

[2] Jon Sobrino, *Christology at the Crossroads*, trans. John Drury (Maryknoll, NY: Orbis Books, 1978), 352.

(as I do) that historical study generally does a good job of accurately reporting past events, we should note that the method comes at least very close to excluding the possibility of the miraculous. Historical improbabilities may be included in reconstructions of the past through a preponderance of evidence, but that which violates all our experiences of the regular functioning of natural law seems excluded in principle by the historical method.[3]

The upshot is that how we hold our historical reconstructions matters a great deal. On the one hand, we can have an epistemically modest understanding of what historical reconstructions are: They are something like the outputs of an algorithm; we make certain judgments about how the world works at both the physical and social level based on observational experience, apply those judgments to the evidence we have about the past on the basis of an expectation of causal regularity, and what results is a picture of what is most probable based on the way that we initially set up this procedure of reasoning. (The functioning of such a metaphorical algorithm would, of course, build in all kinds of culturally conditioned judgments – importantly, sexist ones, or racist ones, or colonialist ones – and would produce outputs distorted to reflect precisely these judgments. I have no interest in maintaining an account of historical reasoning as neutral or innocent.) If, as seems unquestionably the case, the observable world is generally a causally regular place, then these pictures will in most circumstances present a roughly accurate representation of the past. Even if we think that the world does *not* always unfold as our everyday

---

[3] See, classically, the chapter "Of Miracles," in David Hume, *An Enquiry Concerning Human Understanding: A Critical Edition*, ed. Tom L. Beauchamp (Oxford: Oxford University Press, 2000), 83–99. Where Hume understands miracle as absolute violation of natural law, Augustine tends to view miracles as an epistemic category: They are works of God that are surprising, even unanticipatable, based on what we know of the regular operation of the natural world, but they are not to be understood as the special entry of divine power into a natural order otherwise closed to it. It is interesting to consider what, if any, circumstances might lead a historian to include the miraculous in her historical reconstructions.

experience would suggest – if sins can be forgiven, if bodies rise from the dead – these pictures can nevertheless prove quite valuable, bringing to light and emphasizing features of past events that might otherwise have gone unacknowledged.

On the other hand, some historians might make a stronger judgment: that our procedures for creating these historical constructions are the uniquely best method for determining what happened in the past, and that these reconstructions should be privileged over all other possible sources of knowledge of past occurrences. If one held to this judgment, one would likely conclude that later New Testament traditions, historical christological developments, and medieval or contemporary mystical encounters with Christ cannot plausibly be thought to provide knowledge of the historical life of Christ. Such sources are, of course, almost wholly useless for the project of scientific history, and rightly so: It operates from the presumption of observability and repeatability, and we do not generally learn of historical events through mystical revelations.

But why should the theologian accept these constraints of scientific history unless she has smuggled in normative convictions about the way the world is, and about what it is possible for God to do within it? Do we doubt that the Holy Spirit can reveal historical truths of Christ's concrete human life in later New Testament texts, or Church councils, or mystical experience? To the extent that the scientific historian's account is guided by acknowledged or unacknowledged normative commitments, the theologian has no obligation to accept them. On my account, then, scientific-historical reconstructions can help fill out our picture of the historical Christ, rather than serving as their determinative focus. Historical-critical readings are resources for the theologian, but so are, *inter alia*, narrative, intertextual, literary, typological, and allegorical readings.[4]

---

[4] Paul DeHart's *Unspeakable Cults*, published in the late stages of revising this book, is in many ways the contemporary christological project closest to my own – but it is precisely in our relative estimations of the utility of historical methodology that we depart from one another. I fully agree that DeHart's christological essay unfolds wholly

In this chapter, then, my aim is not to provide a "reconstruction" of Christ's life according to scientific-historical methodology. Rather, I hope to direct our attention to the historical particularity of Christ, and thereby to his true humanity. As Augustine notes at *trin.* 8.4.7:

> Even the fleshly face of the Lord (*Nam et ipsius facies Dominicae carnis*) is pictured with infinite variety by countless imaginations, though whatever it was like he certainly only had one. Nor as regards the faith we have in the Lord Jesus Christ is it in the least relevant to salvation what our imaginations picture him like, which is probably quite different from the reality. What does matter is that we think of him specifically as a man.[5]

The passage cuts several ways. On the one hand, it is clear that Augustine believes we shouldn't place much redemptive weight on the specifics of how we imagine Jesus' life – wise counsel,

---

within the bounds of noncompetitive christology, and offers an extraordinarily provocative and thought-provoking reconfiguration of historical teaching about Christ. Where I seek to present a fairly classical picture of Christ's person and work that is reconstituted in potentially surprising ways, DeHart's project is quite intentionally experimental – he seeks to show us the far edges of the theological terrain that he and I both hope to open, without necessarily committing himself to every conclusion he argues is possible or christologically permissible (63). While I affirm DeHart's attention to what I have called Christ's historicity, we differ in our evaluation of the place of historicism: DeHart believes that "historical consciousness" – narrowly construed as the sort of critical historical scholarship exemplified for him by Jonathan Z. Smith – "is a precious gift of the modern age whose delicate critical mechanics are easily and routinely thrown out of balance by Christian apologetic bias, whether unconscious or open" (2–3). I agree that such scholarship can be incredibly productive for theologians to engage; but too often, in my judgment, it assumes unstated and unargued-for normative commitments from which the theologian may properly dissent; for more rigorous argument of this claim, see Tyler Roberts, *Encountering Religion: Responsibility and Criticism after Secularism* (New York: Columbia University Press, 2013); and William Wood, *Analytic Theology and the Academic Study of Religion* (Oxford: Oxford University Press, 2021), 193–286. I am less impressed by this construal of "historical consciousness" than DeHart, and thus my christological proposal reaches a very different endpoint even as we travel by similar means.

[5] *trin.* 8.4.7; WSA I/5, 246 (modified).

considering how frequently historical reconstructions of Christ's life change in often dramatic ways. It is through "general and specific notions" – for instance, of what it is to be a human, or what it is to be a mother or martyr – that we are able to love Jesus, or Mary, or Paul, in spite of the fact that we have never seen them.[6] Yet the point remains: "when we believe some material or physical facts we read or hear about but have not seen, *we cannot help* our imaginations fabricating something with the shape and outline of bodies as it may occur to our thoughts."[7]

The question, then, is whether these imaginings play any role in enabling our love of these heroes of the faith. At least in this passage, Augustine seems to think they do not: Since our historical imaginings are likely false, they do not truly connect us to these ancient figures. Perhaps the most that can be said for them is that the process of producing these imaginings is necessary if we are to love Jesus or Mary or Paul as humans that have determinate historical qualities. They are epiphenomenal to the life of faith.

Yet there is another possibility open to us of relating to these historical imaginings, what we might call an iconic approach to them. As St. Theodore the Studite would write hundreds of years after Augustine, the fact that the Word has been circumscribed in human flesh makes the Word susceptible to representation: "If Adam the first man is circumscribed by His form, then Christ the second Adam, as He is both God and man, can equally be portrayed in his bodily form."[8] Even if the iconographer is unskilled, the fact that the icon resembles its prototype – that it is an icon *of* Christ or Mary or Paul – makes it worthy of veneration, and useful within the life of faith.[9] There may thus be many details that are historically inaccurate in any depiction of Christ – the

---

[6] *trin.* 8.5.8; WSA I/5, 247.

[7] *trin.* 8.4.7; WSA I/5, 246 (emphasis added).

[8] St. Theodore the Studite, *On the Holy Icons*, trans. Catharine P. Roth (Crestwood, NY: St. Vladimir's Seminary Press, 2001), 101–102.

[9] St. Theodore the Studite, *On the Holy Icons*, 104.

length of his hair, whether or not he had a beard, his skin tone – yet they are nonetheless depictions of *him*, exhibiting what Natalie Carnes has described as a "prosoponic likeness" to him.[10]

We may, similarly, consider our historical reconstructions of Christ literary icons. Augustine's words of caution are worth remembering: Our faith should not rest on these images; we should expect them to be wrong in many respects. Yet though they risk misleading one about the details of Christ's life in Roman Judea, the prosoponic likeness they offer, born of our attempts to consider Christ in his concrete historical particularity, may nevertheless serve to direct our hearts and minds to him. Whether they *in fact* do so has much less to do with the details of the reconstructions than it does with the affective constellation of the one using them.

In this spirit, this chapter draws – admittedly selectively – on canonical depictions of Christ, and contemporary historical scholarship on his life. I make no claim that it is a final or definitive icon of Christ's historicity: My account here has benefited from other such historical icons of Christ extending from the ancient world to the present day. My hope is that it might inspire other such images of Christ that are more self-conscious in their appeal to the work of incarnation. In general, I have selected those sources that I judge to be most fruitful in allowing us to think through the implications of the theology of the work of incarnation.

Rather than attempting to provide an overview or narrative construction of Christ's life, I have organized my discussion around moments of Christ's life that are especially effective in drawing attention to the way his life receives its shape through his relations to the world. My examples here seek to draw attention to several spheres in which Christ's receptivity to the world is especially important in giving shape to his human particularity. These are, in the order with which I will treat them and with some shading

---

[10] Natalie Carnes, *Image and Presence: A Christological Reflection on Iconoclasm and Iconophilia* (Stanford, CA: Stanford University Press, 2018), 128.

between these categories in the individual sections of this chapter: (1) Christ's relation to the nonhuman world; (2) Christ's location within the context of Roman Palestine; (3) Christ's spiritual and intellectual formation within Second Temple Judaism; and (4) the significance of Jesus' religious upbringing for his messianic consciousness.

I should confess at the outset that the theses of this and the next chapter are especially speculative. My hope is to expand our sense of how we might understand the work of incarnation. The conclusions I reach here seem to me wholly compatible with the christological statements of the ecumenical councils; but that is a claim properly adjudicated by the Church.

***

When the time came for their purification according to the purification according to the law of Moses, they brought him up to Jerusalem to present him to the Lord (as it is written in the law of the Lord, "Every firstborn male shall be designated as holy to the Lord"), and they offered a sacrifice according to what is stated in the law of the Lord, "a pair of turtledoves or two young pigeons." (Luke 2.22-4)

This first moment, Jesus' presentation in the Temple in accordance with the Mosaic law, serves a twofold purpose in our account of the work of incarnation. First, it reminds us that, within God's providential ordering of creation, Christ's life and redemptive significance unfold within the whole history of God's relations with Israel.[11] Second, it allows us to see the way that God's history with Israel and Christ's life in particular are bound up in relation to the nonhuman world: namely, the two turtledoves, which serve as the sacrifice that mediate Christ's inclusion into the covenant.

---

[11] Andrés García Serrano has argued that the Presentation in the Temple offers a proleptic summary of the major themes of Luke's Gospel and the Acts of the Apostles; see García Serrano, *The Presentation in the Temple: The Narrative Function of Lk 2:22–39 in Luke-Acts* (Rome: Gregorian & Biblical Press, 2012), 359–366.

This sacrifice takes place because of, and is rendered symbolically intelligible within, the history of Israel's reception of the Law after its liberation from slavery in Egypt. Luke points to two texts from the Hebrew Bible as rationale for the sacrifice. The first, a loose rendition of Exodus 13.2, claims the firstborn of Israel as holy to the Lord. The command to sanctify the firstborn is given in the midst of the passage out of Egypt, and in the context of Israel's perennial observance of the Passover (cf. Ex. 13.13–5). The infant Jesus is brought to the Temple as one whose life has been redeemed by God through the covenant – one who is, by virtue of the righteousness of God, preserved from the death meted out to the firstborn of Egypt. All firstborn children are sanctified to the Lord, but this male child has been preserved from the death God deals to the nations.

The second referenced text from the Old Testament (Lev. 12.8) directs the sacrifice of two turtledoves or two pigeons, "one for a burnt offering and the other for a sin offering." Here, the priest makes atonement on behalf of mother who has given birth, restoring her ritual purity. The mother is commanded to bring "a lamb in its first year for a burnt offering, and a pigeon or a turtledove for a sin offering" (Lev. 12.6); she is only permitted to offer two pigeons or doves "if she cannot afford a sheep" (Lev. 12.8). This sacrifice is thus dense with christological significance: The sacrifice on Christ's behalf is the sacrifice of the poor; it is both a burnt offering signaling covenantal faithfulness, and a sin offering marking a failure of law-observance and absolution; it is substitutionary, as the dove is offered in place of a lamb. More generally, the blood of sacrifice itself indicates that life comes only from and is properly offered in response to God.[12]

But consider the doves: Their lives, no less precious to God than any sparrow, are integral to the cultic act by which Mary and Joseph fulfill their and their son's covenant obligations as members of the people of Israel. In a real way, their deaths mediate Christ's inclusion within the people of God; they minister to Christ no less surely than

---

[12] Ephraim Radner, *Leviticus* (Grand Rapids, MI: Brazos Press, 2008), 125.

do the wild beasts of Mark's Gospel who meet Jesus in the wilderness. Without the deaths of these animals, Christ's observance of each jot and tittle of the law would be imperfect. Their lives and deaths are integral to Christ's performance of the law, and thus integral to the redemptive significance of Christ's life. The death of these birds occurs just days after Jesus' birth, structurally the same narrative location as the murder of the Holy Innocents in Matthew's Gospel. Each slaughter echoes and amplifies the other, just as each points back to the death Pharaoh deals to the children of Israel, and the death of Egypt's children from which the Lord preserves Israel's firstborn.

The victims themselves are ζεῦγος τρυγόνων ἢ δύο νοσσοὺς περιστερῶν – two turtledoves or two young doves, in Luke as well as in the Septuagint's Leviticus. The περιστερά of these passages is matched by the dove (περιστερά) of Genesis 8, whose arrival signi-fies the moment that the annihilating waters begin to recede. The beloved one is called περιστερά throughout the Song of Solomon, while the Book of Common Prayer (1662) beseeches, "O deliver not the soul of thy turtle-dove unto the multitude of the enemies: and forget not the congregation of the poor for ever" (Ps. 74.20).

It is significant that the manner in which these doves are able so richly to signify Christ's work depends upon very particular features of the form of life proper to doves. Doves are able to fly, to light out from the bow of a ship, take a sprig of olive in their beaks; they often return to their place of origin. If environmental conditions allow, they can sustain a large population in a small geographic space, and may thus be inexpensively captured for sacrificial use. Blood courses through their bodies, blood that can be spilled on the stone altar. If exposed to fire, they are utterly consumed. These are not facts about the flesh of the Son of God; they are facts about the flesh of doves. Yet this moment of the Son's human life in the Jerusalem Temple only reveals the salvation of the Lord in its relation to the flesh of doves, and in relation to the common lives that humans and doves have shared within God's history of redemption, stretching through the primeval history of Noah through the routine sacrifices offered by Israel's poor.

The invisible God is made visible in the flesh of Christ, but not without the flesh of doves – alongside numerous other creatures: The animals that the second Adam learns to name as a toddler; the fishes he caught and ate on the shores of Galilee; the lilies of the field; the cursed fig tree; the vines that fill the stone jars at Cana, and the cup in the upper room. Jesus frequently makes use of his environment as he draws human hearts to himself.

Yet it is not only a matter of signs: The nonhuman creation is itself given an unsubstitutable role within the work of incarnation. Christ's human flesh, as drawn from Mary's flesh, receives its form through an extended evolutionary history.[13] The deaths of these two doves can be seen, then, as a synecdoche of the deaths of all the nonhuman animals through which God works to give rise to the human form in time. The possibility of Christ's redemptive death itself depends upon the deaths of these other creatures. Their lives, too, give Christ's life its shape; they too are drawn into the work of incarnation.

And, perhaps, it does not go too far to find in the moment of Christ's baptism a recognition of their mediatory work. As he begins his revelatory public ministry, the Holy Spirit appears in the form of the creature that had been sacrificed for the sake of his inclusion within Israel's covenant. As it descends, the Spirit bears the weight of Abraham's election and a history of faithful sacrifice; as it rests upon him, the Temple is built again on its true cornerstone.

***

Now after John was arrested, Jesus came to Galilee, proclaiming the good news of God, and saying, "The time is fulfilled, and the kingdom of God has come near; repent, and believe in the good news." As Jesus passed along the Sea of Galilee, he saw Simon and his brother Andrew

---

[13] Niels Henrik Gregersen, "*Cur deus caro*: Jesus and the Cosmos Story," *Theology and Science* 11.4 (2013): 370–393, 388.

casting a net into the sea – for they were fishermen. And Jesus said to them, "Follow me and I will make you fish for people." And immediately they left their nets and followed him. As he went a little farther, he saw James son of Zebedee and his brother John, who were in their boat mending the nets. Immediately he called them; and they left their father Zebedee in the boat with the hired men, and followed him. They went to Capernaum; and when the sabbath came, he entered the synagogue and taught. (Mark 1.14–21)

This second moment calls attention to the specificity of the environment, both natural and social, that Christ inhabited. There are obvious details of Christ's teaching that reflect the circumstances of his life: most evidently, the Aramaic dialect he spoke, or the regionally specific flora, fauna, and political and military structures that appear within his sayings and parables. Yet the Gospel witnesses also suggest less apparent environmental and social effects upon Christ: This passage tells us that Jesus *came* to Galilee, presumably from Nazareth; that his ministry takes place in significant part in the region surrounding the Sea of Galilee; and that Capernaum seems to have been an important center, even the "headquarters,"[14] of Jesus' Galilean period. How might these local contexts have affected Jesus' proclamation of the Kingdom of God?

The region of Lower Galilee containing Nazareth was described by Josephus as an especially fertile area.[15] It is likely, then, that Nazareth was a farming community: Seán Freyne argues that its inhabitants "were not just mere subsistence farmers, but like all colonizers in the Mediterranean as elsewhere, worked the land

---

[14] As Eric M. Meyers refers to Capernaum at "The Cultural Setting of Galilee: The Case of Regionalism and Early Judaism," *Aufstieg und Niedergang der römischen Welt* 19.1 (1979): 686–702, 698. See also the compilation of scholarly affirmations of Capernaum's importance at Rene Alexander Baergen, "Re-Placing the Galilean Jesus: Local Geography, Mark, Miracle, and the Quest for Jesus of Capernaum" (Unpublished Ph.D. dissertation, Toronto School of Theology, 2013), 19–22.

[15] Josephus, *The Jewish Wars*, 3.43; see also Freyne's discussion at *Jesus, a Jewish Galilean: A New Reading of the Jesus Story* (London: T&T Clark International, 2004), 38–39.

intensively, participated in the redistributive system and were able to support a relatively comfortable lifestyle."[16] Their crops would likely have been sold in the nearby urban center of Sepphoris, a little more than an hour's walk away from Nazareth. The village's close proximity to Sepphoris leads Eric Meyers to describe Jesus as "growing up along one of the busiest trade routes of ancient Palestine at the very administrative centers of the Roman provincial government."[17] Though trade seems to have been an important part of the local economy, this should not lead us to overestimate the cosmopolitanism of Jesus' upbringing. Archaeological evidence shows that the population of Galilee in Jesus' day was overwhelmingly Jewish.[18]

Jesus' childhood would have been marked by significant sociopolitical upheaval in the region. Near the time of his birth, the death of Herod the Great in 4 BC occasioned a popular uprising throughout Galilee.[19] In the aftermath of this insurrection, the Roman army destroyed Sepphoris and enslaved its population.[20] This encounter with the power of Rome cast a long shadow over the area. While the Roman army was not regularly stationed in Galilee, they traveled

---

[16] Freyne, *Jesus, a Jewish Galilean*, 44.

[17] Meyers, "The Cultural Setting of Galilee," 698.

[18] Mark A. Chancey, *The Myth of a Gentile Galilee: The Population of Galilee and New Testament Studies* (Cambridge: Cambridge University Press, 2002), 167–170. Galilee had been settled by a Judean population during the Hasmonean period; see Mark A. Chancey, "The Ethnicities of Galileans," in *Galilee in the Late Second Temple and Mishnaic Periods*, Vol. 1, eds. David A. Fiensy and James Riley Strange (Minneapolis, MN: Fortress Press, 2014): 112–128.

[19] This was the revolt of Judas son of Hezekiah; see Thomas Scott Caulley, "Notable Galilean Persons," in *Galilee in the Late Second Temple and Mishnaic Periods*, Vol. 1, eds. David A. Fiensy and James Riley Strange (Minneapolis, MN: Fortress Press, 2014): 151–166, 152–153. It is unclear whether this Judas is the same as Judas the Galilean (d. 6 AD); Richard A. Horsley argues that they are separate figures at "Social Movements in Galilee," in *Galilee in the Late Second Temple and Mishnaic Periods*, Vol. 1, eds. David A. Fiensy and James Riley Strange (Minneapolis, MN: Fortress Press, 2014): 167–174, 170.

[20] Richard A. Horsley, *Galilee: History, Politics, People* (Norcross, GA: Trinity Press International, 1995), 62, referencing Josephus, *The Jewish Wars* 2.68.

often enough through the region that its inhabitants "would have had daily reminders of Rome nevertheless,"[21] as the army continued to cross through Lower Galilee *en route* to other locales.[22]

During Jesus' childhood, Herod Antipas resolved to rebuild Sepphoris as "Autocratis," the "imperial city."[23] Subsequently, he founded in the same region the entirely new city of Tiberias, intended as "a 'royal' city and another center of Roman political-cultural influence."[24] Freyne notes that both these building projects "inevitably put extra pressure on the traditional way of life of the peasant landowners,"[25] while James Crossley observes that the "labour and materials [for these projects] had to come from somewhere and so people would have faced the possibility of dislocation."[26] While there is reason to think that Lower Galilee was economically productive, Agnes Choi argues that the agricultural system depended upon a tenancy system in which the landowners lived comfortable lives in the cities, while the rural farmworkers remained poor.[27] Choi concludes that the agricultural distribution process "was structured in such a way that the rural population, specifically tenants and small farmers, bore the brunt of transportation costs. In short, in economic interactions between the urban and rural populations of Lower Galilee, the rural population was at a distinct disadvantage."[28] Evidence also suggests that Lower

---

[21] Mark A. Chancey, *Greco-Roman Culture and the Galilee of Jesus* (Cambridge: Cambridge University Press, 2005), 229.

[22] Baergen, "Re-Placing the Galilean Jesus," 183.

[23] Horsley, *Galilee*, 65.

[24] Horsley, *Galilee*, 65.

[25] Freyne, *Jesus, a Galilean Jew*, 45.

[26] James Crossley, *Jesus and the Chaos of History: Redirecting the Life of the Historical Jesus* (Oxford: Oxford University Press, 2015), 23. See also James Crossley, *Why Christianity Happened: A Sociohistorical Account of Christian Origins (26–50 CE)* (Louisville, KY: Westminster John Knox Press, 2006), 46–47.

[27] Agnes Choi, "Urban-Rural Interaction," in *Galilee in the Late Second Temple and Mishnaic Periods*, Vol. 1, ed. David A. Fiensy and James Riley Strange (Minneapolis, MN: Fortress Press, 2014): 297–311, 306.

[28] Choi, "Urban-Rural Interaction," 309. See also Douglas E. Oakman, "Late Second Temple Galilee: Socio-Archaeology and Dimensions of Exploitation in First-Century

Galilee's high susceptibility to malaria exacerbated urban-rural tensions: Deaths in the rural areas led to an unstable working population, and the even higher mortality rates of low-lying cities led to a constant drain of rural populations as people sought economic opportunities in the cities, replacing the higher number of people who had died in the urban centers.[29] Josephus records that at the time of the Jewish uprising of 66–70 AD, the people of Galilee themselves pillaged Sepphoris, as a result of the "ill will" they bore to the city as a result of its complicity with Rome.[30] We may tentatively conclude, then, that the Galilee of Jesus day was politically and economically fraught, as several royal urbanization projects caused tensions with and adversely affected neighboring rural communities like Nazareth.

As Rene Baergen has convincingly argued, however, Nazareth and Lower Galilee are not the only or even the most significant regions we must consider when contextualizing Jesus' ministry: It is Capernaum that is Jesus' "own town," according to Matthew 9.1. The Lake Region containing Capernaum is a distinct geographical, climatological, and cultural region in first-century Galilee.[31] While the Lake Region is fertile in common with Lower Galilee, its rocky basalt makes agriculture immeasurably more difficult.[32] As might be expected, the Sea of Galilee served as an important feature of daily life and economic activity, including fishing and trade with the

Palestine," in *Galilee in the Late Second Temple and Mishnaic Periods*, Vol. 1, eds. David A. Fiensy and James Riley Strange (Minneapolis, MN: Fortress Press, 2014): 346–356.

[29] Jonathan L. Reed, "Mortality, Morbidity, and Economics in Jesus' Galilee," in *Galilee in the Late Second Temple and Mishnaic Periods*, Vol.1, eds. David A. Fiensy and James Riley Strange (Minneapolis, MN: Fortress Press, 2014): 242–252.

[30] Josephus, *The Life of Flavius Josephus* 67; see also Crossley, *Jesus and the Chaos of History*, 23. Josephus, *Life* 8 also says that "the Galileans had resolved to plunder [Sepphoris], on account of the friendship they had with the Romans."

[31] Baergen, "Re-Placing the Galilean Jesus," 42–45.

[32] Baergen, "Re-Placing the Galilean Jesus," 38; citing Jonathan L. Reed, *Archaeology and the Galilean Jesus: A Re-Examination of the Evidence* (Norcross, GA: Trinity Press International, 2000), 144.

other villages and cities dotting the lake shore. Mark Chancey observes that

> In the border areas of Galilee, in contrast to the interior, daily contact with inhabitants from the villages and cities surrounding the region can be assumed ... Consider the area around the Sea of Galilee. A thirty-minute walk from Capernaum brought one into what was during the time of Jesus Philip's tetrarchy. The population did not instantly and dramatically change the moment one crossed the border – witness the lack of clear evidence for paganism at Bethsaida – but nonetheless, when one crossed the Jordan, one was, in effect, entering into predominantly gentile territory ... Travel by boat was also a possibility, of course, as the trips of both Jesus and Josephus illustrate. On the sea, fishermen, merchants, and travelers from both sides of the water would have sailed past each other, and often. Contact was virtually assured by the relatively small size of the lake.[33]

Jesus was not alone in relocating from the village of Nazareth to the larger center of Capernaum: in part because of the growth of nearby Tiberias, the population "more than doubled" between 50 BC and AD.[34] This expansion seems to have played a part in the importance of fishing in the Lake Region: As Baergen argues, "the fishing 'industry' of the first century CE had more to do with a land base insufficient in quality and quantity to support the region's immediate population, which was evidently growing, than it did with the fish market."[35] The relatively hot and humid climate of the lakeshore, 200 meters below sea level, suggests frequent seasonal

---

[33] Chancey, *Myth of a Gentile Galilee*, 164. Baergen, citing this passage, helpfully observes that Chancey, along with a great deal of contemporary historical Jesus scholarship, often notes the distinctiveness of the Lake Region, but fails to incorporate it into its reconstructions of the historical Jesus; see Baergen, "Re-Placing the Galilean Jesus," 45–53.

[34] Baergen, "Re-Placing the Galilean Jesus," 62.

[35] Baergen, "Re-Placing the Galilean Jesus," 72.

outbreaks of malaria, likely reflected in the stories of Jesus healing fevers in Capernaum.[36]

What does such a picture of first-century Galilee contribute to our account of the work of incarnation? We must acknowledge that many particularities of Christ's life are lost to us – personal or family experiences, formative chance encounters or events, and the like. Yet this glimpse of Jesus' context does help us make sense of some of the most important features of his ministry.

Chief among these is the relation between the economic system of Lower Galilee and Jesus' proclamation of the Kingdom of God. James Crossley has observed, for instance, that Jesus' public teaching frequently employs "ideas about the stark opposition of wealth and poverty, God and mammon . . . the recurring theme of debt . . . concern for those without food, clothing, drink, and community . . . opposition to wealth, fine clothing, and eating well . . . and the theme of stark difference between rich and poor."[37] All of this accords quite well with a picture of a region unsettled by "the social upheavals in Galilee, with the rebuilding of Sepphoris and the building of Tiberias."[38] If there was indeed tension between the imperial urban centers, on the one hand, and the smaller settlements like Nazareth and Capernaum, on the other, it also might account for the fact that the Gospels never record Jesus as visiting or preaching in Sepphoris or Tiberias.[39] Jesus' message was directed especially to those who had been left out of the growth in wealth that Herod Antipas oversaw; it was directed to those who bore the brunt of Roman control, without reaping any of the benefits. This economic focus is inseparable from the healing ministry of Christ, as widespread sickness and fever rent social bonds not only through

---

[36] Baergen, "Re-Placing the Galilean Jesus," 67–68; citing Mt 8.14–5; Mk 1.29–31; Lk 4.38–9; and Jn 4.46–54.

[37] Crossley, *Jesus and the Chaos of History*, 70.

[38] Crossley, *Jesus and the Chaos of History*, 70.

[39] Though it is worth recalling that, according to the tradition, Saints Joachim and Anne were residents of Sepphoris.

death, but through a constant population drain from the villages to the cities.

The proclamation of the Kingdom was thus, as Latin American liberation theology has consistently emphasized, a message to the poor. It is their lives especially who give Christ's life its shape; it is their suffering that figures most prominently in his understanding of the divine work that has drawn near, and their tears which are dearest to him. It is the particular suffering of this people that is drawn most intimately into the work of incarnation, as Christ's preaching of the Kingdom is offered in response to it. In response to their conquest by the Romans, Christ teaches that God Herself will be enthroned in Israel. In response to the recognition that Israel itself (in the person of Antipas) has come to exploit Israel, Christ promises that the son of David will rule justly. As the people suffer from illness and death, Jesus shows them that the power of God's Kingdom is close at hand through healings and exorcisms. All of these point to a fundamental transformation of the political and social conditions that oppressed these people.

We should note too that the context of Jesus' ministry exposes him to people beyond Israel. Capernaum's cultural location at the interstices of Jewish Galilee and the tetrarchy of Philip opens the possibility that regular encounters with Gentiles led Jesus to an expansive vision of the Kingdom that included those outside the people of the covenant. As we will see in the next chapter, there is reason to think that such encounters played a role in expanding Jesus' own sense of the scope of his message.

In sum: Jesus' message of the Kingdom is not detachable from the lives of the poor, the marginalized, the sick, and the unclean to whom he preached: This too is the work of incarnation. Within this work of incarnation, God has providentially ordained that *these* social factors, *this* political context, the particular cultural situations of Galilee and Capernaum, are the creaturely forces that shape Christ into the one who can proclaim the coming of the Kingdom of God. His context provides him not only the language and metaphors he will employ to describe the Kingdom, but also contributes to *Christ's own* ability to imagine and understand humanly what his Kingdom is like. The particularity of this message, spoken at this particular time to these particular people, is itself christologically significant: Following Christ today requires no less definite an analysis of who is vulnerable in our society.

***

One sabbath he was going through the grainfields; and as they made their way his disciples began to pluck heads of grain. The Pharisees said to him, "Look, why are they doing what is not lawful on the sabbath?" And he said to them, "Have you never read what David did when he and his companions were hungry and in need of food? He entered the house of God, when Abiathar was high priest, and ate the bread of the Presence, which it is not lawful for any but the priests to eat, and he gave some to his companions." Then he said to them, "The sabbath was made for humankind, and not humankind for the sabbath; so the Son of Man is lord even of the sabbath." (Mark 2.23–8)

This moment of Christ's life raises for us especially the question of his relation to the religious practice of the Jewish people, both in the question of his observance of the Law, and in the question of how he understood the title "Son of Man" and his own messianic role.

The incident recounted here might seem a narrative of a familiar type: Jesus' prophetic signs of the coming of God's kingdom brings him into conflict with the Jewish authorities; he proposes a new and deeper spiritual sense of Israel's law, freeing his disciples from its rigorous outward observance; Jesus is portrayed, likely by later followers who are not themselves Torah-observant, as claiming a messianic prerogative to reinterpret the law in a manner that differentiates the nascent Christian movement from the religion of Israel.

Such readings presume a picture of Christ's ministry that is defined by his novelty within the context of first-century Judaism. As James Crossley has noted, Jesus is viewed as the archetypal

"Great Man" who stands apart from and transforms his world through applying his own genius, and is presupposed by the historian to be "*different from* the world around him" – the primary index of which, Crossley notes, has been the depiction of Jesus as "Jewish . . . but not *that* Jewish."[40] This tendency reaches its methodological zenith in the formulation of the "criterion of dissimilarity," according to which departure from expectations of the Judaism of Jesus' day is held to be a mark of a saying or incident's authenticity.[41] Even thinkers who wish to emphasize Jesus' Jewish apocalypticism "will regularly construct or assume a construction of what constituted Jewish identity in some way, or at least present Jesus as doing something new and unparalleled either generally or on some specific (and often crucial) issue, typically involving the Torah and/or the Temple."[42] This passage from Mark's Gospel, for instance, is frequently taken as an indication of Jesus' own departure from traditional sabbath-observance.[43]

Increasingly, however, this and other instances of Jesus' supposed transgression of his society's standards of Torah-observance are being read in accordance with the Judaism of his day. Géza Vermes cites Rabbis Simeon ben Menasiah and Jonathan ben Joseph, two Tannaitic near-contemporaries of Jesus, as offering teachings that closely parallel Jesus' statement that the Sabbath is made for humanity rather than humanity for the Sabbath.[44]

---

[40] Crossley, *Jesus and the Chaos of History*, 18. The problem is not, of course, restricted to historical reconstructions of Christ's life: Within the realm of systematic theology, Linn Marie Tonstad (following Katherina von Kellenbach, et al.) has identified regular reference of Jesus' exceptionalism against his Jewish background as an anti-Jewish trope within theologies aiming at inclusivism; see Linn Marie Tonstad, "The Limits of Inclusion: Queer Theology and its Others," *Theology and Sexuality* 21.1 (2015): 1–19; 3.

[41] Crossley discusses the "criterion of dissimilarity" at *Jesus and the Chaos of History*, 35–9.

[42] Crossley, *Jesus and the Chaos of History*, 4.

[43] Géza Vermes, *The Religion of Jesus the Jew* (Minneapolis, MN: Fortress Press, 1993), 21–24.

[44] Vermes, *The Religion of Jesus the Jew*, 24.

Crossley summarizes an extensive body of scholarship on Mark by commenting that "the Sabbath disputes in Mark 2 and 3 show no indication of any biblical Sabbath law being undermined, and ... both these purity and Sabbath disputes echo what is known about early Jewish Sabbath disputes over the specifics of interpretation."[45] Daniel Boyarin offers an attractively fine-grained suggestion that many of the disputes between Jesus and groups of Pharisees and Sadducees can best be understood as "a conservative reaction against some radical innovations in the Law stemming from the Pharisees and Scribes of Judaism."[46]

The Pharisees seem to have been the dominant school of Jewish practice in the Galilee of Jesus' day, as attested in the archaeological record by the rising prevalence of stone vessels that were understood as immune from becoming unclean.[47] This despite the fact that the heart of the proto-rabbinic movement was in Judea. While it is unwise to think that Galilean Torah-observance differed markedly from Judean practice, there is evidence of very limited divergences. Martin Goodman concludes that, while there is little evidence for a meaningfully distinct Galilean halakhic tradition, there is some reason to think that Galileans (like many rural Judeans) would not have been as strict in their halakhic observance as the urban Pharisees.[48] Seán Freyne finds more evidence for the

[45] Crossley, *Jesus and the Chaos of History*, 30; see also the many sources Crossley cites at *Jesus and the Chaos of History*, 182 n.104.

[46] Daniel Boyarin, *The Jewish Gospels: The Story of the Jewish Christ* (New York: The New Press, 2012), 104.

[47] Roland Deines, "Religious Practices and Religious Movements in Galilee: 100 BCE-200 BCE," in *Galilee in the Late Second Temple and Mishnaic Periods*, Vol. 1, eds. David A. Fiensy and James Riley Strange (Minneapolis, MN: Fortress Press, 2014): 78–111.

[48] Martin Goodman, "Galilean Judaism and Judaean Judaism," in *The Cambridge History of Judaism, Vol. 3: The Early Roman Period*, eds. William Horbury, William David Davies, and John Sturdy (Cambridge: Cambridge University Press, 1999): 596–617, 606–607. Lawrence H. Schiffman, however, rejects any difference in Galilean practice, arguing that rabbinic materials generally present Galileans as being even *more* strict in their observance; see "Was There a Galilean Halakhah?", in *The Galilee*

possible distinctness of Galilean Torah-observance, noting that in the Gospel of John Jesus is accused of "being a member of the Galilean *'am haaretz*, that is, one who not only does not follow Pharasaic *halakhah* with regard to purity, but who is ignorant of Torah and is therefore accursed (Jn 7.15, 49). Such a characterization of Galileans generally does raise the general question of how and how well the Torah and Torah-observance were disseminated among the Galilean populace in Jesus' day."[49]

Boyarin, following the work of Yair Furstenberg,[50] goes further, arguing that Jesus' practices of Torah-observance here and in passages like Mark 7 represent a Galilean observance that differed from the Pharisaic and Scribal communities centered in Jerusalem. If such a view is correct, the dispute is improperly understood if viewed as one between traditional Jewish observance and the messianic freedom of Jesus' followers. Instead, it reflects Jesus' own religious formation:

> His context was the Palestinian Judaism of the north of Palestine (Galilee) in the first century and its religious practices ideas, and controversies, including controversies with Jewish teachers from other places, such as Jerusalem ... Jesus speaks from the position of a traditional Galilean Jew, one whose community and traditional practices are being criticized and interfered with from outside, that is, from Jerusalem, by the Judeans.[51]

It is quite possible, then, to view Jesus as remaining wholly within the constraints of Torah-observance throughout his ministry; all we

---

in Late Antiquity, ed. Lee I. Levine (New York: The Jewish Theological Seminary of America, 1992): 143–156.

[49] Seán Freyne, "Jesus in Context: Galilee and Gospel," in *Jesus of Galilee: Contextual Christology for the 21st Century*, ed. Robert Lasalle-Klein (Maryknoll, NY: Orbis Books, 2011), 17–38, 33.

[50] Yair Furstenberg, "Defilement Penetrating the Body: A New Understanding of Contamination in Mark 7.15," *New Testament Studies* 54 (2008): 176–200.

[51] Boyarin, *The Jewish Gospels*, 125.

need to do is recognize that Torah-observance itself was far more diverse in first-century Judaism than we might have anticipated.

Against explicitly or implicitly anti-Jewish readings of Jesus' ministry that abstract his teaching and practice from the religious life of Israel, attention to the work of incarnation gives us a richly Jewish Jesus.[52] He is one who learns about the God of Israel at the feet of his rabbis. Indeed, not only does he learn of the God of Abraham through his religious practice: We can imagine him learning a regionally specific way of practicing his devotion to the Lord, in a manner that ramifies through his teaching in the Galilean countryside. Jesus' teaching ministry does not constitute a break with Judaism, but an expression of it. It is the view of God learned through Jesus' own very traditional Jewish practice that enables him to proclaim the coming of the Kingdom; and perhaps, it is this same Jewish tradition that helps him come to know his own messianic purpose.[53]

***

Jesus' reference to the Son of Man in Mark 2 raises the questions: Did Jesus understand "Son of Man" to be a messianic title? Did he consider himself the messiah, and if he did, what might he have meant in claiming this role?

---

[52] The dire consequences of forgetting the Jewish particularity of Christ's flesh have been forcefully argued by, among others, Eugene F. Rogers Jr., *Sexuality and the Christian Body: Their Way into the Triune God* (Oxford: Blackwell Publishers, 1999); J. Kameron Carter, *Race: A Theological Account* (Oxford: Oxford University Press, 2008); and Willie James Jennings, *The Christian Imagination: Theology and the Origins of Race* (New Haven, CT: Yale University Press, 2011).

[53] While I have emphasized the Jewishness of Jesus' teaching and practice, DeHart stimulatingly considers an alternative historical icon: Jesus as Magician; *Unspeakable Cults*, Chapter 3. My aim here is parallel to his; producing such a historical icon gives us an account in which we can imagine Jesus' own sense of his ministry as deeply conditioned by those around him. In DeHart's words, "divinization can be seen as a cultural dynamic that Jesus himself might well have participated in, providing terms for his own self-understanding as well as for the acceptance and deeper exploration of that self-understanding in his cult" (91).

There is, of course, a long tradition within historical Jesus scholarship of holding that Jesus himself made no messianic claims.[54] Yet historians find it increasingly plausible that Jesus himself claimed a messianic vocation. Dale Allison has pointed to extensive testimony from the Gospels and from early Christian writings that Jesus' early followers not only proclaimed him to be the messiah, but held this proclamation to be part of the content of Jesus' own teaching.[55] Such sayings have frequently been excluded from reconstructions of Jesus' life as embellishments, but the turn against criterialism in historical Jesus research has provoked a reevaluation of their historical veracity.[56] Rather than turning to criteria that would exclude a messianic claim as departing too far from the Jewish practice of his day, Allison has concluded that "we are more likely to find the historical Jesus in the repeating patterns that run throughout the tradition than in the individual sayings and stories."[57]

The widespread communal memory of Jesus having claimed messianic kingship, recorded in the Gospels, offers evidence (Allison holds) that he did teach his followers of his own importance within the Kingdom of God. It would be especially puzzling for Jesus' followers to believe he was messiah only *after* he had been executed and his body had disappeared; the most convincing explanation of the proclamation of Jesus as messiah after his death is that he made this claim before crucifixion.[58] Allison thus

---

[54] J. C. O'Neill provides an overview of this history in Chapter 1 of *Who Did Jesus Think He Was?* (Leiden: E.J. Brill, 1995).

[55] Dale C. Allison, Jr., *Constructing Jesus: Memory, Imagination, and History* (Grand Rapids, MI: Baker Academic, 2010), 227–230.

[56] See, for instance, Gerd Theissen and Dagmar Winter, *The Quest for the Plausible Jesus: The Question of Criteria*, trans. M. Eugene Boring (Louisville, KY: Westminster John Knox Press, 2002); Rafael Rodríguez, "Authenticating Criteria: The Use and Misuse of a Critical Method," *Journal for the Study of the Historical Jesus* 7 (2009): 152–167; *Jesus, Criteria, and the Demise of Authenticity*, ed. Chris Keith and Anthony Le Donne (London: T&T Clark, 2012).

[57] Allison, *Constructing Jesus*, 23.

[58] Allison, *Constructing Jesus*, 240–244, against Rudolf Bultmann's position in *Theology of the New Testament* II (New York: Charles Scribner's, 1955), 26.

concludes, "when [Jesus] looked into the future, he saw thrones, including one for himself."[59] He is far from alone in this estimation. Crossley holds that "The earliest teaching in Jesus' name does seem to have envisaged him as having a prime position in the impending kingdom of God, as did the developing Christology in his name."[60]

The claim that Jesus took himself to be messiah, and even a divine figure, is further supported by setting his ministry within the Judaism of his day. While Peter Schäfer is reticent to speak of Jesus' self-understanding, he does note that "There can be little doubt that pre-Christian Judaisms developed ideas that helped pave the way to a 'binitarian' theology – cases in point are speculations about Logos and Wisdom, certain angelic figures, Adam as the original *makro-anthropos*, and other exalted human figures."[61] Perhaps the paradigmatic instance in Jesus' immediate context is the late first-century BC Similitudes of *1 Enoch*, which culminates in the revelation that the visionary "Enoch himself is the Son of Man, the chosen, the embodiment of righteousness . . . whose just rule will mean never-ending bliss for the people of Israel."[62]

On the basis of such sources, Allison and Boyarin hold that it is entirely plausible that Jesus believed himself to be a divine figure. Both accounts hinge on Jesus' seeming self-ascription of the title "Son of Man."[63] Noting the strangeness of the phrase ὁ υἱὸς τοῦ

---

[59] Allison, *Constructing Jesus*, 303.

[60] Crossley, *Jesus and the Chaos of History*, 64.

[61] Peter Schäfer, *The Jewish Jesus: How Judaism and Christianity Shaped Each Other* (Princeton, NJ: Princeton University Press, 2012), 141. On the broader subject of divine figures in Second Temple Judaism, see also Larry W. Hurtado, *One God, One Lord: Early Christian Devotion and Ancient Jewish Monotheism*, 3rd ed. (Edinburgh: T&T Clark, 1998), 53–96.

[62] Schäfer, *The Jewish Jesus*, 77. Boyarin also appeals to the Similitudes as a source of Jesus messianic self-understanding at *The Jewish Gospels*, 71–95.

[63] Allison presents considerations in favor of interpreting the third-person statement about the Son of Man as a self-ascription at *Constructing Jesus*, 295–6, but Allison is less confident than Vermes; cf. Geza Vermes, "The Son of Man Debate Revisited (1960–2010)," *Journal of Jewish Studies* 61.2 (2010): 193–206. A more extensive telling of the history of interpretation of this term extending into the ancient world is found at

ἀνθρώπου in Greek, Allison follows a great deal of contemporary scholarship in registering the presence of an underlying Aramaism, thus suggesting that the phrase goes back to Jesus himself (or at least to the memory of his disciples).[64] Canvassing the messianic theology of the first century, Allison proposes that if Jesus indeed referred to himself as Son of Man, he may have had in mind the notion of a heavenly twin with whom he is eschatologically identified.[65]

Boyarin's account is still more sweeping. Reading Jesus' seeming self-description as "Son of Man" in light of the vision of the Ancient of Days reported in Daniel 7,[66] Boyarin contends that the Son of Man should clearly be considered a divine figure, citing J.A. Emerton's remark that: "The act of coming with clouds suggests a theophany of [YHWH] himself. If Dan. vii.13 does not refer to a divine being, then it is the only exception out of about seventy passages in the O[ld] T[estament]."[67]

Further evidence of this position is the presence of two thrones in heaven in Daniel's vision, and the presence of both an "old god" in the Ancient of Days and a "young god," the warrior-deity who accomplishes the redemption of Israel.[68] Boyarin takes this apocalyptic imagery to point to a more ancient stratum of Israelite belief underlying Daniel 7, "one in which . . . the 'El-like sky god of justice and the younger rider on the clouds, storm god of war, have not

---

Delbert Royce Burkett, *The Son of Man Debate: A History and Evaluation* (Cambridge: Cambridge University Press, 1999).

[64] Allison, *Constructing Jesus*, 293; more extensively, see Burkett, *The Son of Man Debate*.

[65] Allison, *Constructing Jesus*, 300–303.

[66] While Vermes wisely cautions against interpreting the locution "son of man" exclusively through Daniel 7 (see *The Jewish Jesus*, 177–191, and especially the useful table correlating the "son of man" passages to Daniel's vision at 179), it is arguably too strict a criterion to hold that a passage must explicitly reference Daniel in order to be informed by it; see Allison's argument at *Constructing Jesus*, 294 n.306.

[67] John Adney Emerton, "The Origin of the Son of Man Imagery," *Journal of Theological Studies* 9 (1958): 231–232; cited at Boyarin, *The Jewish Jesus*, 40.

[68] Boyarin, *The Jewish Gospels*, 50.

really been merged as they are for most of the Bible."[69] This theology reflects the "tense and unstable monotheism" produced by drawing together the diverse religious cults devoted to 'El and YHWH in ancient Canaan.[70] On this basis, Boyarin argues there are "two legacies left us by Daniel 7: It is the ultimate source of 'Son of Man' terminology for a heavenly Redeemer figure, and it is also the best evidence we have for the continuation of a very ancient binitarian Israelite theology deep into the Second Temple period."[71] Perhaps most controversially, Boyarin proposes that this Ancient Near Eastern religious context helps account for the christological claims of early Christianity: "I submit that it is possible to understand the Gospel only if both Jesus and the Jews around him held to a high Christology whereby the claim to Messiahship was also a claim to being a divine man."[72]

It is, of course, worth remembering that attribution of messianic consciousness to Jesus is quite controversial in the literature. Even so, taking seriously the claims of, *inter alia*, Allison, Crossley, and Boyarin opens us to the theological possibility that Jesus was indeed one who claimed to be the messiah of Israel, and understood this messianic claim, as in the *Similitudes of Enoch*, as conferring a divine status upon him. It is otherwise difficult to explain how, so soon after his crucifixion and proclaimed resurrection, his followers attributed to him "the form of God" and "equality with God" (Phil. 2.6), or why the first generation of Jewish Christians worshipped Jesus alongside the God of Israel, baptizing in his name and singing that at this same name "every knee should bend, in heaven and on earth and under the earth, and

---

[69] Boyarin, *The Jewish Gospels*, 46.

[70] Boyarin, *The Jewish Gospels*, 49.

[71] Boyarin, *The Jewish Gospels*, 52.

[72] Boyarin, *The Jewish Gospels*, 55. Boyarin's conclusions parallel those of the "Early High Christology" school of contemporary New Testament studies; see Andrew Chester, "High Christology: Whence, When, and Why?", *Early Christianity* 2.1 (2011): 22–50.

every tongue should confess that Jesus Christ is Lord, to the glory of God the Father" (Phil. 2.10–1).[73]

If Allison, Crossley, Boyarin, et al. are correct, there is reason to think that Jesus' messianic consciousness is *itself* indebted to his religious formation. This possibility is only historically viable because there were *already* currents of Jewish thought that could imagine a ruler over Israel alongside the God of Sarah and Abraham.[74] It is possible to imagine, then, that Jesus' human self-understanding as Messiah – even his self-understanding as God – was learned at the feet of others. We may, historically at least, imagine that Jesus humanly *came to know* he was Messiah and God in moments of prayer alongside his family, in conversations with his rabbi, in observing the desperation of his Galilean compatriots and the hopes of his neighbors that God's reign might extend across the earth. This, too, is the work of incarnation: God bringing it about that His human life should be lived at *this* time, among *these* people, who would shape his life into that of the divine-human redeemer He willed to be.

But how do these historical possibilities sit with christological claims that Jesus *is* the divine Son of God – that he is, from all eternity, identical to the one who is Himself the Good, the True, the Beautiful, incomprehensible *vere Deus* in inseparable relation to the Father and Spirit? How can Christ learn – in a manner that really contributes to his human self-understanding – what he already knows as God? How can any answer to this question avoid introducing a distinction between the divinity and humanity of Christ that would compromise the reality of the Incarnation?

---

[73] Cf. Hurtado, *One God, One Lord*, 105–108.

[74] Cf. Matthew V. Novenson, *Christ among the Messiahs: Christ Language in Paul and Messiah Language in Ancient Judaism* (New York: Oxford University Press, 2012), 34–64, and Matthew V. Novenson, *The Grammar of Messianism: An Ancient Jewish Political Idiom and Its Users* (New York: Oxford University Press, 2017), 187–216.

5 | Christ among Us

In the last chapter, we considered the work of incarnation through the environmental, social, and political forces which likely affected Christ's life. Yet this discussion, especially when set alongside the claims of classical christology, raises a number of substantive christological questions about the relation of divinity and humanity in Christ's life. Can we really imagine Jesus learning about the God of Israel from his parents and rabbis if he is himself the all-knowing Word of God? Can Jesus be humanly ignorant without inevitably lapsing into disordered love of the world? If Jesus exercises his human agency in deeply sinful social contexts, does he incur any guilt or responsibility for social sin?

As is likely clear by now, I do not seek simply to restate Augustine's answers to these questions, or to respond as he might have responded. Rather, I take Augustine's thought to provide a matrix of christological concerns within which such questions *might* be answered, in ways that both accord with or dissent from Augustine's own understanding of the relations between the Word and the operations of Christ's soul. The answers we provide to these questions set the bounds for how thoroughly we can understand Christ's human life to be responsive to the world's existence and agency. To ground our theology of the work of incarnation, it will be necessary to address them with some precision.

***

In the story from Mark 2 quoted above, as the disciples are accosted for picking heads of grain on the Sabbath, there is a detail never mentioned by Augustine and rarely commented upon within the patristic period: At the time of the incident Jesus recounts, Abiathar is *not* high priest. When David breaks into the Temple granaries in 1 Samuel 21.1– 9, the high priest is Ahimelech; Abiathar, his son, is nowhere mentioned in the story.[1] The problematic nature of the phrase ἐπὶ Ἀβιάθαρ ἀρχιερέως ("when Abiathar was high priest") accounts for its omission from the parallel sayings in Matthew (12.4) and Luke (6.4), as well as the absence of the phrase in the majority of pre-Byzantine manuscript families of Mark.[2] Contemporary exegetes do not hesitate to identify Jesus' words as an error.[3]

Those few patristic commentators who address the incongruity are forced into rather tenuous exegetical positions: Chrysostom speculates that Ahimelech actually had two names, one of which was Abiathar; Jerome suggests that the fault lies with the evangelist, rather than the Lord.[4] Even these solutions resolve the problem for the theological interpreter only superficially: One must still account for why God providentially disposed created history such that Scripture should represent Christ as misremembering who was high priest.[5] The plain sense of Mark 2 indicates that Jesus himself was mistaken about who was high priest. It remains to be seen what spiritual sense might be signified by the Gospel's depiction of Christ as forgetting.

This quiet moment of Mark's Gospel – perhaps even more than Christ's statement that not even the Son knows the day or hour of Her return, which so exercised patristic exegetes – raises for us the christological question of the relation between Christ's divine and human intellects. Is it christologically conceivable that the incarnate

---

[1] He first appears at 1 Sam 22.20.

[2] John William Wenham, "Mark 2²⁶," *The Journal of Theological Studies* 1.2 (1950): 156.

[3] See Francis J. Moloney, *The Gospel of Mark: A Commentary* (Peabody, MA: Hendrickson, 2002), 69; and Morna D. Hooker, *The Gospel According to Saint Mark* (London: A&C Black, 1991), 103.

[4] Craig A. Evans, "Patristic Interpretations of Mark 2:26 'When Abiathar Was High Priest'," *Vigiliae Christianae* 40.2 (1986): 183–186, 184–185.

[5] See Simon Francis Gaine's discussion of this problem at *Did the Saviour See the Father? Christ, Salvation and the Vision of God* (London: T&T Clark, 2015), 130–131.

Word should have made such a mistake, misremembering Abiathar for Ahimelech? Should theology regard Christ as lacking ignorance or error not only according to his divinity, but according to his humanity? Most basically, what are the necessary implications of union with the Word for Christ's human intellect?

Responses to these questions, as well as related discussions of Christ's possession of the beatific vision, have been quite varied in both premodern and modern theological discourse (though it should be noted that, as in so many areas of theology, the thought of Thomas Aquinas has exerted a significant influence upon much later reflection).[6] Discussions of the necessary implications of union with the Word for Christ's human nature must keep in mind two central christological principles.

First: Christ is by nature what we hope to be by grace. The human flesh of Christ is, from its very foundation, brought into being in union with the Word. Christ's humanity does not, as the Thomist tradition will say, exist as its own distinct *suppositum* – its own subject or attributive ground.[7] Say that my arm is scarred. On at least one plausible account of the metaphysical implications of our speech, it is a different thing to say that my arm is scarred than it is to say that *I* am scarred. It is true that my arm is the part of me that is scarred, but my arm properly exists as a part of me, rather than as

---

[6] Raymond Moloney provides an overview of the range of outlooks on Christ's knowledge or ignorance at Raymond Moloney, *The Knowledge of Christ* (London: Continuum, 1999), 41–68. Jeremy Wilkins provides a useful survey of the present *status quaestionis* on Christ's beatific knowledge at "Love and Knowledge of God in the Human Life of Christ," *Pro Ecclesia* 21.1 (2012): 77–99; see especially 83–84 on the development of this discussion since Rahner.

[7] See Thomas Aquinas, *ST* 3.2.2–3; 3.17–19. Rowan Williams and Aaron Riches have each quite usefully explicated the theology of a sole *suppositum* in the incarnate Word, rendering especially clear that the identification of Christ's humanity as a *secondarium esse* is wholly compatible with, and even demanded by, an appropriate recognition of the metaphysical non-competition of divine and creaturely being. See Rowan Williams, *Christ the Heart of Creation* (London: Bloomsbury Continuum, 2018), 12–40 (see especially 27–30); Aaron Riches, *Ecce Homo: On the Divine Unity of Christ* (Grand Rapids, MI: Wm. B. Eerdmans, 2016), 185, 222–224.

a subject in its own right. I am the subject of the predication "scarredness" in a truer way than my arm is, for it is ingredient to my manner of existing to be the bearer of such predicates, whether predicates I actually possess or only potentially possess.[8]

In a more explicitly theological key, I exist as the created term of the act by which God grants me life. I am called into existence from the *nihil* precisely as the recipient of God's gracious gift of existence; what it means for me to "participate" in God is for me to be the one who is called into being *as* recipient of this gift. The same cannot, so this picture supposes, be said for my arm: It is called into being as *I* receive the gift of existence. But, it should be noted, it is not any activity on my part that accounts for this difference – any response I can offer is necessarily "too late" to the call by which I am brought into being.[9] The marmot, or the stone, or the lepton, or whatever fundamental existents there are, are no less called into existence as recipients of God's life than I am, and they are similarly the proper subjects of many predicates, each (again, at least plausibly) a distinct *suppositum*.

To deny this of Christ's human nature is to say that the only *suppositum* in Christ is that of the Word: He is the proper subject of all Christ's human attributes, in a manner analogous to my being the proper subject of all my arm's attributes. This includes all Christ's physical qualities, as well as his intellective and volitional acts. But more basically, it requires that there is no properly independent human existence of Christ: His nature does not subsist apart from the Word (it is *anhypostatic*), but rather exists only as it is fully united to the Word (it is *enhypostatic*). When we speak of Christ's human flesh, then, we speak of human flesh that is utterly and intrinsically united to his divine nature. To think of it without being so united is not to perform a bit of metaphysical surgery,

---

[8] Cf. Cross' analysis of Aquinas' "concrete part-concrete whole" christology; *The Metaphysics of the Incarnation*, (Oxford: Oxford University Press, 2002), Chapter 2.

[9] See Jean-Louis Chrétien, *The Call and the Response*, trans. Anne A. Davenport (New York: Fordham University Press, 2004), 17–19.

separating out the human from the divine; it is rather to imagine a distinct *suppositum* entirely, since all that is particular to Christ's humanity exists only as the humanity of the Word.

Christ, then, is by nature what we hope to be by grace: As we hope to be united to God eschatologically by the work of redemption, Christ is by the very constitution of his human existence. If the redeemed state of humanity is perfect in love, perfect in wisdom, incorruptible, lacking the ignorance and weakness that accompany our vitiated state, then so must Christ properly be. There is thus significant theoretical pressure to affirm that Christ's human intellect is a perfected human intellect, and this perfection deeply shapes the logic of Thomist positions on Christ's human intellect: According to Thomas, Christ not only possesses the gratuitous nonconceptual knowledge of the beatific vision and the similarly gratuitous conceptualized infused knowledge, he also possesses a perfected active intellect that enables him perfectly to learn from his sensible experience.[10] While this does allow Thomas to affirm that Christ acquired knowledge from the world, his mode of learning is more distant from our experience than we might suppose. In the course of denying that Christ learns from any human, for instance, Thomas writes that "as words formed by a man are signs of his intellectual knowledge; so are creatures, formed by God signs of His wisdom ... Hence, just as it is better to be taught by God than by man, so it is better to receive our knowledge from sensible creatures and not by man's teaching."[11] If Christ ever knew that Ahimelech was high priest when David ate the bread of the Presence, it is not because Christ learned it from any person or text, but because he was able to reason backward from the sensible objects of his experience, "go[ing] on to understand effects from causes, and causes from effects, like from like, contrary from contrary. Therefore Christ, though He did not experience all things, came to the knowledge of all things from what He did experience."[12]

[10] *ST* III.12.1.
[11] *ST* III.12.4ad.2.
[12] *ST* III.12.3ad.2.

There is, of course, no necessity that all theological approaches should understand the intellect and its perfection according to these Aristotelian categories; indeed, I am quite skeptical of the epistemic confidence with which, *inter alia*, many Thomisms believe they can discern the metaphysical structure of the world. Yet Thomas serves as one expertly developed instance of this first principle: However we understand the subjects of our predications, or however we understand the intellect and its perfection, we should affirm that Christ's humanity possesses no subsistent existence independent of its assumption by the Word, and that whatever we understand the eschatological perfection of the human intellect to be, such perfection is proper to Christ's humanity in virtue of its hypostatic union with the Word.

Second: The humanity of Christ manifests in time the Word's divine life in eternity. As we will see, Augustine believes Christ is both *via* and *patria*, *scientia* and *sapientia*, the one whose life is a redemptive sign drawing us back to God, the focus of desire that teaches us to love the God who we can now know only in faith and hope.[13] The life of Christ reveals to us the life of God, the character of love that defines both the blessedness of Father, Son, and Holy Spirit and God's dealings with creation.

Yet what is significant for my purposes here is *how* this triune life is revealed in Christ's humanity: temporally – not in the integral simplicity of God's eternity, but scattered across created spacetime. No individual moment of time is capable of manifesting the whole

---

[13] On the role of faith as animating this journey toward Christ who is the Truth, see Basil Studer, "Loving Christ According to Origen and Augustine," in *In the Shadow of the Incarnation: Essays on Jesus Christ in the Early Church in Honor of Brian E, Daley, S. J.*, trans. Peter W. Martens (Notre Dame, IN: University of Notre Dame Press, 2008), 149–75, 158–164. Sarah Stewart-Kroeker is right to warn against a too-simple association of *via* with Christ's humanity and *patria* with his divinity to which Studer at times falls prey; though Christ reveals and mediates in his humanity, this mediation can only occur because his is the humanity of the Word, in the unity of his one person. See Sarah Stewart-Kroeker, *Pilgrimage as Moral and Aesthetic Formation in Augustine's Thought* (Oxford: Oxford University Press, 2017), 64–70.

of God's eternal life; this is what the triune persons do, the Son and Spirit each a perfect image of the Father's substance. But more than that, no individual moment of Christ's life can manifest the whole of God's eternal life as fully as it can be manifested within the created order – for it is Christ himself, constitutively temporal in his humanity, who is the image of the invisible God. We should expect any individual moment or period of his life truly to reveal something of the life of God, but also to be marked by a temporality improper to God in Herself.

One notable example, well-established in christological discourse, concerns Christ's fleshly corruptibility. By the lights of our first principle, fleshly corruptibility is wholly improper to Christ's humanity. His flesh is fully united to the Word by nature, as we hope to be by grace. There is no place for death or decay in the flesh assumed by Life itself. Yet it is one of the central claims of Christian faith that Christ was scourged, crucified, and died. How are we to reconcile these seemingly contradictory claims? Augustine answers that Christ's fleshly corruptibility should be understood as a work of divine power. At *en.Ps.* 86.5, for instance, he notes that Christ

> suffered what it was appointed to him to suffer, and he did so of his own volition, not under any necessity flowing from sin . . . Who is this, who departs from life in the way that Christ went forth from his body? Who ever could? He alone who had first said, *I have the power to lay down my life, and I have the power to take it up again. No one takes it away from me; but I lay it down of my own accord, and I take it up again* (Jn 10.18,17). He laid it down when he willed, and took it up when he willed; no one took it away, no one wrested it from him.[14]

In the terms I have proposed, the moments of Christ's suffering and death manifest the life of God differently – we might say, with a different modulation – than do the moments of the Transfiguration or following the Resurrection. Christ's glorified flesh reveals the full

---

[14] WSA III/18, 250–251.

incorruptibility of human nature united to God, while Christ's lacerated and bleeding flesh reveals the mercy of God, and His power to lay aside the glory proper to the divine life in uniting Himself to the condition of sinful humanity. These moments, properly interpreted, serve as no challenge to the claim that Christ's flesh places before us an image both of the eternal life of the Word, and of a human life joined wholly to God.

We can be still more precise in understanding how the temporal life of Christ manifests God's eternity. Paul Griffiths has recently offered a distinction between "occasionalist" and "generic" variants of Christ's vulnerability to damage.[15] Both variants begin from the presumption that Christ's flesh is by nature what we hope to become by grace, and so both variants in common understand all damage suffered by Christ's flesh to be permitted by an act of divine will. Rather than taking our experience of human frailty as the standard for what is "truly" human, Griffiths makes *Christ's* humanity normative, revealing to us what our human flesh should, and *Deo volente* will, be like.

On an occasionalist account, each instance of fleshly vulnerability encountered in the narratives of Scripture – the cleaving of flesh from flesh in Christ's circumcision, the pangs of hunger, the lash that tears across his back – has been specifically permitted to damage Christ's flesh by an act of divine will, to both a redemptive and revelatory end. Absent such permission, Christ's flesh remains impervious to damage from others or his environment, and so we should regard him as immune to harm from, for instance, viruses, wild animals, falls, storms, or even the decay that accompanies aging. While Griffiths takes stories like Jesus' pacific disposition in the boat on stormy seas as evidence that Christ's flesh was immune to damage he did not permit, the Scriptural evidence he adduces is not, I think, so convincing as he hopes. For instance, if Christ is unperturbed by the storm raging outside the boat because he is invulnerable to environmental harm, why does he chastise the disciples for their own fear – surely they aren't similarly

---

[15] Paul J. Griffiths, *Christian Flesh* (Stanford, CA: Stanford University Press, 2018), 35–41.

invulnerable? But if the point of the story is rather that the disciples should be faithful even in the midst of the fearsome storm, then Griffiths' reading of why Christ is unafraid is harder to substantiate. So also, doesn't Christ's exchange with Satan in the wilderness presuppose that if he hurled himself off the pinnacle of the Temple and was *not* caught by angels, his body would indeed be damaged by the fall?

Rather than the occasionalist view, then, I prefer Griffiths' "generic" variant of Christ's fleshly vulnerability. According to this view,

> It isn't that Jesus gives case-by-case providential permission – permission for damage by this fast, that whip, those nails – but rather that the consent to incarnation carried with it permission for any and all such things to damage Jesus' flesh, just as they would any human flesh, *post lapsum*. Such a permission, were it to have belonged to the incarnation, would have meant that Jesus' flesh would have been damaged from time to time by viruses, falls, fights, and so on, as human flesh ordinarily is. This view makes Jesus' flesh less like Superman's, and more like ours; this also makes it easier, perhaps, for latter-day Christians to identify with Jesus, and to understand their own quotidian fleshly sufferings as imitative of and participatory in his.[16]

Though Christ's flesh is properly incorruptible by virtue of his human nature's union with the Word, in a work of power ordered to the redemption of creation the Word opens his flesh to damage. This permission does not require a series of intentional acts on Christ's part unfolding serially throughout his life, but is given in the very act by which the Word assumes flesh, and presumably concludes at the glorification of Christ's flesh in the Resurrection.

This discussion of Christ's fleshly vulnerability may serve as a model for parallel (though in some respects, quite different) discussions of Christ's ignorance and potential for error. On this account, we should state first that Christ's human intellect exists only as it is united to the *suppositum* of the Word, and thus is wholly

---

[16] Griffiths, *Christian Flesh*, 39.

deified. As the divine Word, Christ possesses the fullness of the divine knowledge that is identical to the divine life itself, and his human intellect has been perfectly assumed into unity with his divine nature. Second, we should affirm that the life of Christ is the manifestation of the Word's life in eternity, and so we should expect that the Word's divine omniscience will be revealed in Christ's human intellect. Because Christ's life shows us in time who God is in eternity, the perfection of his divine knowledge and his deified intellect must be revealed in his human life. Third, however, we should not expect that this omniscience will be revealed identically at each moment of Christ's life. Though there might be theological considerations that lead us to the view that Christ humanly possessed knowledge of all things from the time of his infancy,[17] there may also be theological considerations that lead us to view the manifestation of the divine omniscience as quite varied across Christ's life. Just as the lifeless corpse on Golgotha does not undermine the revelation of Christ's incorruptibility on the Mount of the Transfiguration, neither does Christ's substitution of Abiathar for Ahimelech undermine the revelation of his divine knowledge as he talks to the woman at the well. Fourth, any such ignorance or error attributed to Christ should be regarded as an act of divine power ordered to the end of redemption, as the Word assumes the condition of sinful humanity, in spite of its impropriety to the state of deified humanity.

---

[17] It unclear whether Augustine at all stages of his thought attributed this sort of knowledge to Christ; see *div. qu.* 75's interpretation of Luke 2.52. Nevertheless, *div. qu.* 65 and especially *c. Max.* 2.9 both suggest that Augustine believed Christ to possess the vision of the Father in his earthly life, and as Gaine argues at *Did the Saviour See the Father?*, 54–59, the implication of Augustine's texts is that this vision of the Father precludes Christ's human ignorance. By contrast, my account agrees with McFarland that the hypostatic union does not require any particular superiority in Christ (apart from moral perfection), but rather "within a Chalcedonian framework the *perfection* of Jesus' humanity connotes chiefly its *ordinariness*"; Ian A. McFarland, *The Word Made Flesh: A Theology of the Incarnation* (Louisville, KY: Westminster John Knox Press, 2019), 129.

Fifth and finally, one may propose occasionalist or generic variants of Christ's intellectual defectibility. On an occasionalist account, specific facts might be hidden from Christ's human intellect by an act of divine will – for instance, the day and hour of the Son's return. On a generic account, Christ's human intellect possesses no innate knowledge of the created order or of his own divinity – if he has not learned something, he does not humanly know it. Christ would thus rightly be said to be ignorant of a great many truths about the created order according to his humanity, even as he is properly said to be omniscient according to his divinity. Such an account also has the benefit of emphasizing the work of the Holy Spirit within Christ's life. Scripture offers a great many instances of Christ knowing more than any other human might reasonably be expected to know: He sees Nathaniel under the fig tree, he knows his betrayer, he is able to discern that the Kingdom of God is at hand. He even – if we trust the Scriptural record – knew that he was the Word of God: *Before Abraham was, I am.*

A significant benefit of an account in which the Son wills by an act of divine power to assume generic human ignorance and error is its consonance with the Scriptural witness. In the affirmations that Christ grew in wisdom as well as stature, in his confession that even he does not know the day and hour of his return, even in such seemingly trivial matters as the substitution of Abiathar for Ahimelech (though stronger christological claims have been made on the basis of less Scriptural evidence than this), Scripture with some consistency presents Christ as lacking conceptual knowledge of all things during the course of his precrucifixion ministry. In reaching this conclusion, I follow especially Charles Gore's conclusion that patristic exegetes affirming the absence of ignorance of Christ's human soul "have at best but taken particular texts and explained them away in the light of an *a priori* assumption as to the effect of the Godhead on the manhood."[18] So also, I follow Gore and

---

[18] Charles Gore, *Dissertations on Subjects Connected with the Incarnation* (London: John Murray, 1895), 202; but see also the evidence of what seems at least openness to the confession of ignorance in Christ's human soul Gore finds in SS. Athanasius

his younger colleague Frank Weston, sometime Bishop of Zanzibar, in their discomfort in departing from such a clear late-patristic teaching, and in emphasizing that Christ's human ignorance requires no change at all in the divine attributes of the Word, merely in the exercise of these attributes in Christ's life.[19] In contrast to the more radical of the German and Scottish kenoticists, their Anglo-Catholic theologies hope to hold together both the possibility of ignorance in Christ's human intellect and all the classical affirmations of conciliar orthodoxy (though they accomplish this imperfectly).

The principal theoretical benefit of this account, to my mind, is that it provides for a robust account of the work of incarnation. This theology resists the myth of a human life lived alone, unmarked by the relations it bears to others. The human life of God can encompass ignorance and error not because these are qualities proper to our nature, but so that God can include our agency in Her own redemptive life. Just as God wills to hunger so that She may nurse at Her mother's breast, God wills to learn at the feet of those She has come to save.

**

We may raise an Augustinian objection to this generic ignorance of Christ's human nature: As Tarsicius van Bavel has noted, even though some of his peers were open to such an opinion, "the Bishop of Hippo never makes recourse, in a realist sense, to the formula: Christ is ignorant according to his human nature,"[20] and this even though he formally distinguishes between the uncreated Wisdom of the Word and the human intellect of Christ that participates in it.[21] While

---

(*Orationes adversus Arianos* 3.43–8; 51–56), Nazianzen (*Oratio* 30.15–6), and Basil (ep. 236.2) at *Dissertations*, 122–129.

[19] Marilyn McCord Adams has drawn on Gore's and Weston's thought in exemplary fashion at *Christ and Horrors* (Cambridge: Cambridge University Press, 2006), Chapter 3.

[20] Tarsicius J. van Bavel, *Recherches sur la christologie de saint Augustin, l'humain et le divin dans le Christ d'après Saint Augustin,* (Fribourg en Suisse: Editions universitaires, 1954), 159.

[21] van Bavel, *Recherches*, 148, citing *en.Ps.* 118.23.1.

Augustine commonly denies what Dubarle calls "moral ignorance" of Christ,[22] there are clear instances as at *en.Ps.* 63.10 where Augustine concludes directly from Christ's divinity to the absence of ignorance in him.[23] Augustine's principal motivation for denying ignorance in Christ seems to have to do with his moral psychology: As Robert Dodaro notes, "When Augustine uses the term 'ignorance' in the context of original sin, he refers to an incapacity to know oneself, others, and God with utter moral clarity. Ignorance therefore prevents the soul from seeing itself in relation to the highest good, or understanding completely the motivations behind its own moral choices."[24]

If, the argument goes, Christ lacked perfect knowledge of himself, others, and the Good, he could not be perfect in his love of the creatures he encountered. Ignorance of his own desires might lead to self-deception in Christ, leading him unwittingly to love the creation improperly. Ignorance of the world might lead him to misjudge the goodness of some creature, loving it falsely or in a manner inappropriate to it, and thus imperfectly as a sign of the divine life in which it participates. Ignorance of his own divine goodness would introduce a systematic defect in his love of creation, as mistaken knowledge of the standard by which all finite goodnesses are judged would leave him unable to judge their goodness properly and love them as he should in view of their goodness. In each case, some species of ignorance seems to leave Christ susceptible to, or even lead him necessarily into, sin.

The question, then, is this: Can Christ perfectly love what he does not perfectly know? Or, more precisely: Can Christ perfectly love with his human affections what he does not perfectly know with his

---

[22] André-Marie Dubarle, "La conaissance humaine du Christ d'aprés Saint Augustin," *Ephemerides Theologicae Lovanienses* 18 (1941): 5–25.

[23] *en.Ps.* 63.10; WSA III/17, 253: "God saw them all the time, and Christ too saw them, for Christ is God"; cited at van Bavel, *Recherches*, 161. See also *div.qu.* 65, WSA I/12, 102, where Augustine refers to "the Lord, who committed no sin and was ignorant of nothing."

[24] Robert Dodaro, *Christ and the Just Society in the Thought of Augustine* (Cambridge: Cambridge University Press, 2004), 28.

human intellect? We might think that the former requires the latter, for if one does not perfectly know the endpoint toward which our desire moves us, how can we love it with the richness and depth that is deserved?

At this point, however, we must remember: *This human is a divine person.* Christ does, necessarily, perfectly know each creature, for each creature only exists through his generative knowledge of it. Christ does, necessarily, perfectly love each creature, for Love is his very nature. Christ enters into the world with human affections ordered perfectly by the love of God, for his human flesh has been assumed wholly into unity with the Son.[25] While he may bear in his flesh some of the characteristic effects of sin – paradigmatically, fleshly corruptibility; possibly by extension, intellectual ignorance – there can be no possibility of sin in him, for God is the light in whom there can be no darkness.

We may grant the claim that perfect love requires perfect knowledge, for the two are ultimately identical in the simple life of God; loving as God loves requires knowing even as we are known. Within human life, however, these attributes are necessarily diverse, though intellection and love are always bound together in any affective movement of the soul. Rather than holding that Christ's perfect human love of the world springs from his judgments of the goodness of each thing in view of his perfect knowledge of it, we may hold that his love springs directly from his human soul's union to

---

[25] In this respect, I intend to preserve the core conviction of Augustine's teaching on Christ's impeccability; see Han-Luen Kantzer Komline, *Augustine on the Will: A Theological Account* (Oxford: Oxford University Press, 2020), 400–401. I surrender only the claim that the hypostatic union necessitates the perfection of Christ's human intellect at each moment of his life, but this is perfectly compatible with the claim that it is *grace* – the grace of incarnation, and the gracious operation of the Holy Spirit dwelling within Christ – that renders his human will incapable of sinning. In allowing an interval between the deification of his intellect and this grace in his will, I am doubling down on the description of Christ's human perfection as the effect of unmerited grace, and proposing in Christ's moral psychology an echo of the way love outstrips knowledge in the sanctification of his Body the Church.

the Love that is his divine nature. Adapting Dodaro's phrasing above, we may say that whether or not he is able to understand completely the motivations behind his moral choices, he is nevertheless capable of moral perfection in virtue of his soul's union to the Word.[26] His humanly perfected loves are rooted in his divine love, which is itself identical to his perfect divine knowledge; there remains a connection here between knowledge and love in Christ's person. Yet his perfect human affections do not depend upon the intellect's reference to an external standard of goodness according to which a judgment may be formed about the value of our love's objects. Christ's perfect human love of creation is thus not a contingent feature of his human life or dependent upon his historical experience, but a necessary feature of his divine-human personhood.

While Christ may bear the weakness of our intellect just as he bears the corruptibility of our flesh without sin, his loves must be perfect, or God Himself would be guilty of sin. When Christ encounters something in the world, his soul responds to it in perfect love – even if he lacks perfect knowledge in his human intellect of what he encounters, or lacks self-knowledge of his motivations for loving the creature as he does. Where such ignorance might lead another into misshapen loves, the perfection of Christ's loves is never imperiled, for they spring naturally from a deified heart. To anticipate one of the conclusions of the later chapters of this study: It should not surprise us that, in Christ as well as in the redeemed, love outstrips knowledge.

Christ's loves are thus importantly distinct within the work of incarnation: While the world may contribute to the particularities of his affective constitution in presenting him with created goods to love – giving him, perhaps, a special delight in olives, rather than a love of corn tortillas and *pico de gallo* – the quality of his loves is

---

[26] Cf. McFarland, *The Word Made Flesh*, 94: "For [Christ's] earthly actions to be a reliable index of divinity . . . it is not necessary that he be deified in every respect, but only in his will, as the source of those actions."

perfect as a consequence of his human soul's union with his divine nature. We might also say that, while his encounters with the world cannot contribute any higher perfection to his loves, they *can* (if we allow for limitation in Christ's human intellect) allow him to understand his loves more fully. As I have suggested, Christ learns at the feet of the world that the one he knows as Father is the God of the covenant with Abraham; he learns from Simeon, Anna, and John that the Kingdom of God is at hand. Though these experiences do not perfect his loves, we may entertain the possibility that they frame his human understanding of his affections: He comes to know through these experiences why his love for God leads him to a piety so often opposed to that of the Pharisees, or comes to see that the prostitutes, tax-collectors, and lepers he loves in such shocking fashion are entering into God's presence ahead of the conventionally pious. It is Christ's love for the world that enables him to live a perfect and redemptive life, but his knowledge of God's work that enables him to proclaim the good news of salvation to others.

***

It is comforting – comforting to me, at least – to imagine the Jesus I have sketched out: to imagine him subject to the same gaps of knowledge, misrememberings, and casual misunderstandings that characterize our own lives; and yet, for all that, drawing throughout his life from an untinctured and ever-flowing well of perfect charity. He is a Lord who lives not merely beside us, but among us; whose human life is irreducibly marked by those with whom it is shared.

It is all too easy to see those marks, and rather more difficult to see the face of the Lord, in the seventh chapter of Mark's Gospel:

> *He could not escape notice, but a woman whose little daughter had an unclean spirit immediately heard about him, and she came and bowed down at his feet. Now the woman was a Gentile, of Syrophoenician origin. She begged him to cast the demon out of her daughter. He said to her, "Let the children be fed first, for it is not fair to take the children's*

food and throw it to the dogs." But she answered him, "Sir, even the dogs under the table eat the children's crumbs." Then he said to her, "For saying that, you may go – the demon has left your daughter." So she went home, found the child lying on the bed, and the demon gone.

The discomfort I (and, I suspect, you) feel in reading this passage should be acknowledged as a distinctly modern one: Augustine, who generally prefers to comment on Matthew's version of this narrative (Mt 15.21–8), explains that "she was knocking loudly; and he was pretending to ignore her, not in order to refuse her a kindness, but in order to inflame her desire."[27] It's not merely this woman who is a dog, it is all the idolatrous gentiles represented in her: "if she had gone away at these words it would mean she had come up as a dog and gone off as a dog; but by knocking she was turned from a dog into a human being."[28] Augustine is not wholly insensible to the troubling nature of Jesus' words, however, acknowledging them as *veluti convicium* – seeming abuse.

Modern interpreters have tended to emphasize the scandal of Jesus' words to this woman. Elizabeth Struthers Malbon regards it as a story in which the "Markan Jesus is shown as learning from a Gentile woman about inclusive community," imagining Jesus telling this woman "What you say brings me up short."[29] Did Jesus lack this knowledge before his encounter with the Syrophoenician woman? Delores Aleixandre renders the situation even more vividly, imagining the woman's perspective as Jesus calls her a dog: "I didn't dare raise my eyes to his face as I heard him say what I had basically feared he would ... In despair, I thought my words had shattered against the impenetrable wall built between

---

[27] *s.* 77.1; WSA III/3, 317. Pablo Alonso, has examined Augustine's interpretation of the Markan passage and its Matthean parallel in the broader context of Patristic readings of the passage at "La Mujer Sirofenica en la Interpretación Patrística," *Estudios Ecclesiásticos* 80.314 (1995): 455–483.

[28] *s.* 77.10; WSA III/3, 322.

[29] Elizabeth Struthers Malbon, *Hearing Mark: A Listener's Guide* (Harrisburg, PA: Trinity Press International, 2002), 47.

that Jew and me, but not even that wounded or humiliated me, because the memory of [my daughter's] suffering left no room for any other feelings."[30] Does the fact that this woman recognizes a tone in Jesus' voice that lets her know the conversation is not over save Jesus from the effect that his words have had on this worried mother in Aleixandre's presentation of this interaction?[31] Jewish scholar Joseph Klausner is more definitive in his judgment: "If any other Jewish teacher of the time had said such a thing Christians would never have forgiven Judaism for it."[32]

The more carefully one looks at this passage, the more Jesus' words appear enmeshed in the social concerns of first-century Palestine. Joel Marcus, rejecting attempts to lessen the scandal of Jesus' words, writes that "we must accept that [Mark] 7:27 as spoken by the historical Jesus was meant as a refusal, probably because he viewed his mission as limited to Israel."[33] Ranjini Wickramaratne Rebera thus finds in Jesus' initial response a "rejection of the Syrophoenician woman based on her race and ethnicity," noting, "She and her daughter are portrayed as being unclean."[34] Postcolonial exegetes have consistently seen this episode as an instance of Jesus' ethnocentric outlook being challenged and overcome through the clever subversion of this anguished woman, even as they worry about how the story has been used by colonial powers to cultivate submissive responses in the face of

---

[30] Dolores Aleixandre, "Jesus and the Syrophoenician Woman: A Tale from the Margins," *Concilium: Frontier Violations*, eds. Felix Wilfred and Oscar Beozzo 2 (1999): 73–79, 76.

[31] Joel Marcus cites F. V. Filson and I. Hassler as proponents of the view that Jesus gave some nonverbal sign that he did not intend his insult seriously; Joel Marcus, *Mark 1–8, Vol. 27 of The Anchor Bible* (New York: Doubleday, 1999), 468.

[32] Joseph Klausner, *Jesus of Nazareth: His Life, Times, and Teaching* (New York: Macmillan, 1929), 294; cited by Joel Marcus at *Mark 1–8*, 468.

[33] Marcus, *Mark 1–8*, 468.

[34] Ranjini Wickramaratne Rebera, "The Syrophoenician Woman: A South Asian Feminist Perspective," in *A Feminist Companion to Mark*, eds. Amy-Jill Levine with Marianne Blickenstaff (Sheffield: Sheffield Academic Press, 2001): 101–110, 103.

insult and to foster anti-Jewish sentiment.[35] To issues of ethnic identity, we may add class as a factor complicating Jesus' interaction with the Syrophoenician woman. Sharon Ringe, expanding on the scholarship of Gerd Thiessen, has called attention to the fact that Mark's narrative is set in Tyre, a wealthy and predominantly Gentile city in a poor and predominantly Jewish countryside.[36] Jesus may thus have considered the Syrophoenician woman "part of a group in that region whose policies and lifestyle would have been a source of suffering for her mostly poorer, rural, Jewish neighbors."[37] Finally, we must attend to the deeply patriarchal social context within which this interaction occurs. As Hisako Kinukawa has perceptively written,

> This woman has been accustomed since birth to being subjugated and looked down upon; she has shouldered all sorts of grief and sacrificed herself for the honor of men. Having been taught to remain silent, hidden, and obedient all through her life, she only hears from Jesus what she is used to hearing. His response would not upset her. On the contrary, she must be well aware that merely her appearing there is defiling and goes against the accepted custom.[38]

---

[35] Kwok Pui-Lan, *Discovering the Bible in the Non-Biblical World* (Eugene, OR: Wipf and Stock, 2003), 71–83; Surekha Nelavala, "Smart Syrophoenician Woman: A Dalit Reading of Mark 7:24–31," *The Expository Times* 118.2 (2006): 64–69; and Zhang Jing, "Beyond What She Said: On the Syrophoenician Woman," *Chinese Theological Review* 20 (2007): 102–136. On the Matthean parallel, see especially Musa W. Dube, *Postcolonial Feminist Interpretation of the Bible* (St. Louis, MO: Chalice Press, 2000), 127–201.

[36] Sharon H. Ringe, "A Gentile Woman's Story, Revisited: Rereading Mark 7.24–31," in *A Feminist Companion to Mark*, eds. Amy-Jill Levine with Marianne Blickenstaff (Sheffield: Sheffield Academic Press, 2001): 79–100; 84ff.

[37] Ringe, "A Gentile Woman's Story, Revisited," 86.

[38] Hisako Kinukawa, *Women and Jesus in Mark: A Japanese Feminist Perspective* (Maryknoll, NY: Orbis Books, 1994), 58. See also Sharon H. Ringe's original essay emphasizing the gender dynamics at play in the Syrophoenician woman's interactions with Jesus, "A Gentile Woman's Story," in *Feminist Interpretations of the Bible*, ed. Letty M. Russell (Philadelphia, PA: Westminster Press, 1985), 65–72. See also Kelly Brown Douglas, *The Black Christ* (Maryknoll, NY: Orbis Books, 1994), 91.

Each of these exegetical emphases calls attention to the social and interpersonal world within which the Word of God lives Her human life, and so each of these outlooks adds flesh to the bones of our theology of the work of incarnation. Yet, singly and collectively, they raise a troubling question: If Jesus receives the shape of his life through his relations to the world, can the human life of God remain untouched by patriarchy, or ethnocentrism, or colonialism, or class resentments? If his human agency is exercised within the midst of unjust social structures, is he too guilty of social sin? Marilyn McCord Adams is characteristically clear-eyed and theologically bold in recognizing the possible christological implications of relational anthropologies: "we do not need to take on a commitment to Christ's utter human sinlessness. We are free instead to admit that Jesus had to outgrow parochial racism under the tutelage of the Canaanite/ Syrophoenician woman . . . and to acknowledge that He might have been harsh with His blood relatives!"[39] I am not prepared to go so far as Adams; the Scriptural witness unequivocally claims that Christ is like us in every way, excepting sin. Even so, the story of the Syrophoenician woman, and Adams' response to it, force the question of Christ's participation in social sin.

While the literature on social sin and its relation to sinful social structures is extensive, there is no single understanding of these categories accepted by all those who use them.[40] Broadly, we may observe that the analysis of the concept of social sin has been developed with particular clarity among Roman Catholic ethicists, and that within that tradition two trajectories may be observed: a discourse

---

[39] Adams, *Christ and Horrors*, 79.

[40] Standard reference points for these accounts include Mark O'Keefe, *What Are They Saying about Social Sin?* (New York: St. Meinrad Archabbey, 1990); José Ignacio González Faus, "Sin," in *Mysterium Liberationis: Fundamental Concepts of Liberation Theology*, eds. Ignacio Ellacuría and Jon Sobrino (Maryknoll, NY: Orbis, 1993): 532–542; and Kenneth R. Himes, "Social Sin and the Role of the Individual," and "Human Failing: The Meanings and Metaphors of Sin," in *Moral Theology: New Directions and Fundamental Issues: A Festschrift for James P. Hanigan*, ed. James Keating (New York: Paulist Press, 2004): 145–161.

emerging principally from Latin American liberation theology that emphasizes the social formation of moral agency and the inescapability of social sin, and a magisterial tradition that tends to focus more on the foundation of social sin in the agency of the individual.[41] Yet in view of the lack of a shared vocabulary in theologies of social sin, it will be worthwhile to state clearly how I am using the key terms of this discussion. While I make no claim that terms I will employ and the manner in which I will use them are the sole or even only helpful way to approach them, I do believe they are useful both in clarifying the relation of individual agency and social context in discussions of social sin, and broadly in line with the use of these terms throughout the Christian theological tradition.

To begin with, by "an evil," I mean to speak of a created good that has been corrupted as a consequence of sin.[42] These two defining features are necessary and sufficient to establish any evil as such: first, that it is the good creature of God, brought into being solely by God's good pleasure; and second, that it is not as good as it should be, a condition at which it has arrived through some part of the creation turning away from the God who is the source of its existence. This is not, of course, to say that every evil has been so corrupted as a result of its *own* turning away from God; indeed, some evils have no agency at all, and thus no self-directed possibility of turning away from God. But every evil is a good thing that has been corrupted through some creature or other sundering the relationship by which it draws life from the Triune Lord.

Second, and a bit more obliquely: A sin is that which can be forgiven through the life, death, and resurrection of Christ. This formulation

[41] See Hormis Mynatty, "The Concept of Social Sin," *Louvain Studies* 16 (1991): 3–26; Margaret Pfeil, "Doctrinal Implications of Magisterial Use of the Language of Social Sin," *Louvain Studies* 27 (2002): 132–152; and more recently Kristin E. Heyer, "Social Sin and Immigration: Good Fences Make Bad Neighbors," *Theological Studies* 71.2 (2010): 410–436.

[42] This is, of course, to be distinguished from evil as such, which is simply the absence of the good, that which is not willed by God. My nominalizing "evil" in this context serves to clarify below how we might appropriately speak of "structural evils."

intentionally deemphasizes the ontological structure of sin within the realms of the doctrine of God and moral anthropology; if we wished to offer a definition of sin framed in terms more natural to these discourses, a contemporary Augustinian might say to the former that a sin is a creaturely action that draws the one performing it away from the God who is the source of its existence and closer to the nothingness from which it was created, and to the latter that a sin is an action proceeding from a love improperly ordered to the only true *telos* of our affections. Yet by defining sin in soteriological mode as "that which is susceptible to divine forgiveness," two key aims are accomplished: First, a definition of sin is provided that is likely agreeable to a broader audience than the inescapably amative terms preferred by Augustinian moral anthropology; second and more importantly, sin is defined in such a way that the proper *subject* of sin is clearly identified. On this account, sin is not simply a nebulous entity that exists somewhere out in world (as it sometimes appears to be in discussions of social sin), but it is something – in all individual instances – *of which* one is guilty, and *for which* one may be forgiven. Sin is properly attributed, then, only to one for whom a possibility of reconciled fellowship with God has been opened through the redemptive work of Christ.

Each of these two central terms may be further specified in light of contemporary moral theology's emphasis on the communal effects of humanity's fall. To speak of structural evil is to speak of the corruption of some good – namely, the good of human society. Daniel Finn has defined social structures as "systems of human relations among social positions," where social position incorporates a wide range of factors inclusive of race, gender, sexual orientation, gender identity, class, age, abledness, and so on.[43] Kristin Heyer has argued that social structures should be considered "both consequential and causal in nature" as they relate to individual

---

[43] Daniel K. Finn, "What Is a Sinful Social Structure?", *Theological Studies* 77.1 (2016): 136–164, 145.

moral responsibility.[44] In speaking of social structures as a consequence of the exercise of moral agency, we acknowledge that social structures depend upon and are thus reflective of human volition. At one level, this observation is quite banal: no humans, no human social structures. More complicatedly, we may affirm with Heyer and Finn that human social structures, both in the production of the multifarious social positions that human persons might possibly inhabit (for there is nothing obvious or necessary about the possible social positions that are enabled by human community) and in the relations that obtain between those social positions, are marked by the agency of those who establish them.

Structural evil, then, simply describes the corruption to a greater or lesser degree both of the social positions that are rendered inhabitable by any particular system of human relation, and of how those social positions are related to one another as a consequence of sin. Any configuration of human relationship but the perfect society of the Kingdom of God will contain some measure of structural evil, as the sinful exercise of moral agency necessarily compromises the patterns of social existence that are described by the phrase "social structure." Yet, analogous to Augustine's identification of "the two loves" in *City of God* 14.48, a further distinction is possible: Just as Augustine postulates two cities founded on two loves, the love of God to the contempt of self, and the love of self to the contempt of God (and leaving aside for the moment the adequacy of such an eschatological politics), we may distinguish between social orders that tend to move the people who inhabit them to greater sinfulness on the one hand, and social

---

[44] Heyer, "Social Sin and Immigration," 425. Heyer draws the categories of consequence and cause from Cardinal Ratzinger's "Instruction on Certain Aspects of the 'Theology of Liberation,'" (1984): www.vatican.va/roman_curia/congregations/cfaith/docu ments/rc_con_cfaithdoc_19840806_theology-liberation_en.html: 15. It should be noted, however, that Ratzinger and the Congregation for the Doctrine of the Faith were arguing for a primarily consequential understanding of social structures, rather than Heyer's balancing of both consequence and cause.

orders that tend to move their inhabitants to greater virtue on the other – what Daniel Daly identifies as a "structure of vice."[45] Both may (and in fact, will) contain structural evil, and thus be validly described as a "sinful social structure," but in order to register as a structure of vice, it is necessary that a social order should tend to form the moral habits of those who dwell within them in the direction of intensifying wickedness – adapting Heyer's vocabulary, exerting a vicious causative moral force. This is not to be confused with a species of social determinism, however: Such a vicious tendency may in some instances be successfully resisted, even if it is endemic to a sinful social order.

Because a social structure is itself a system of relations between social positions, and thus constituted by a set of habits of human relations, a sinful social structure will result in an at least ostensibly stable domination of marginalized individuals and groups. Accordingly, structural evil, as a characteristic of sinful social structures, tends to fall unevenly on the shoulders of those who come to occupy marginalized social positions and thus consistently are made the objects of social violence. Finn speaks of sinful social structures as characterized by "restrictions, enablements, and incentives . . . [that] encourage morally evil actions."[46] Precisely because the good that has been corrupted is a good of human society, and thus of habits of human interaction and the institutions generated by them, these restrictions, enablements, and incentives will, when marked by structural evil, result in habitual and intensifying harms falling upon marginalized populations. These effects cannot be attributed to the agency of any individual person, or even to the intention of all these moral agents considered collectively: The social structure, precisely as the confluence of the exercise of moral agency of individuals in more-or-less stable patterns, produces unpredictable recursive effects in shaping our moral action beyond what any or all of the participants

---

[45] Daniel J. Daly, "Structures of Virtue and Vice," *New Blackfriars* 92.1039 (2011): 341–357, 354–357.

[46] Finn, "What Is a Sinful Social Structure?", 155.

in that system had intended. Such habitual harms are a persistent feature not only of structures of vice in the sense specified above, but of any fallen social order exhibiting structural evil.

What, then, of "social sin"? On this account, social sin is sin in the true theological sense – that is, it is something that imperils one's soul, and is susceptible to forgiveness through Christ's redemptive work. We are born into, and thus come to participate more or less fully in these sinful social structures in ways we both recognize and fail to recognize – even the white abolitionist bears at least traces of racial prejudice (likely much more than traces), seen clearly a century after his death but hidden from him at the time. As we act in accordance with this socially implicated disordering of our desires, our action, precisely as *sinful* action, serves further to derange our common life.[47] As we become active participants in these sinful patterns of social action – as our exercises of agency are reflective of the sinful structures in which we are implicated, and come to contribute to their further disordering – we individually become guilty, even as infants, of these social sins and require forgiveness for them. Though the operation of these social forces upon us is not strictly mechanical, the disordered status of our desires at our entry into the world leaves us helpless to avoid the effects of this sinful social distortion entirely. We are, then, inevitably guilty of the social sins into which we are born.

What distinguishes social sin as such from merely personal sins is that one must be forgiven not simply for the actions one has performed, but for one's causal role in the social structure's corruption. Recall that structural evil is not simply the sum of the harm caused by sinful actions, but is understood to produce harm *in excess* of the individual actions. Living as an African-American

---

[47] This is not to say that this further disordering can *only* compound some particular social sin; it would be puzzling to say that, in all cases, the action of the abolitionist further compounds the sin of racism. The exercise of agency within some systems can mitigate a particular communal sin, even as it introduces other new distortions into the social world.

within a society characterized by pervasive white supremacy does not merely expose one to a series of unconnected instances of racialized violence: The very inescapability of this racialized violence generates dehumanization and marginalization that can be neither disconnected from the actions of other individuals, nor reduced to it. By inhabiting and acting from the standpoint of whiteness within a white supremacist society (a subject position intrinsically marked by structural evil, rather than a mere description of skin tone), one's agency functions to maintain and compound the structural evil of that vicious social order.[48] In this way, one's action has become ingredient to the excessive harm produced by the structure of vice considered as a whole.

In this respect, social sin functions something like the amplification of a waveform. Imagine a solitary wave, extending through space; now imagine a second wave occupying the same space. If the two waves are out of phase – if the peaks of the first wave fall at the troughs of the other – the interaction of the two waves will cancel one another out; but if the peaks and troughs of both waves are aligned, the waves will amplify one another, leading together to much deeper peaks and troughs than either wave might have reached alone. In similar fashion, the consistent and socially pervasive exercise of agency in a manner that consistently harms some marginalized group produces culture-wide harms far in excess of what any individual desired or believed herself to be accomplishing; the "moral troughs" that a society reaches extend far deeper than the wickedness that could be attained through the solitary action of any individual. Yet by contributing to this structural evil, one has become a constituent cause of the end harm – and this is what renders one guilty of, and requiring forgiveness for, a social sin.

By its very nature, a social sin is a guilt borne by multiple persons, for it is a guilt that accrues as a result not of mere individual action,

---

[48] Jesse Couenhoven offers a particularly insightful analysis of structural sins within an Augustinian framework, taking sexism as an example; see *Stricken by Sin, Cured by Christ*, 198–213.

but of collective interaction. One is guilty, strictly speaking, of one's causal role in bringing about a structural evil. In most cases, of course, this is not the *de novo* creation of a structure of vice; the white supremacy, and the patriarchy, and the heterosexism of our society (*inter alia*) precede the birth of any reading these words. Yet as sinful actors within a sinful social structure, each of us has exerted a continued causal force in deepening the structural evils of our social order. Not merely the continued maintenance, but the plasticity and novelty of our society's particular configuration of structural evil – different today than it was yesterday, and will be tomorrow – is causally dependent upon the continued action of sinful persons within it. Though our social order may not be on an unrelenting march to perdition, the constitutive sinful action of sinful persons within our sinful social order succeeds in uncovering fresh hells of structural evil. This – the generation of new configurations of structural evil – is the sin we (can) perform only together, and thus the distinctively social sin for which we require forgiveness.

Here we find the meeting point of individual agency and social context, and a guilt for sin that accrues at only this point. Alongside Julie Hanlon Rubio's argument that the language of social sin requires a supplementary emphasis on cooperation with evil,[49] this account suggests that our moral reflection should focus specifically upon the *novelty* of the structural evil that our action interposes within our social relations. As I come to understand more deeply my own complicity in social sin, I may ask: How does my participation in these structural evils differ from that of others? How do the particularities of my context, or the unique features of the social position I inhabit, inflect the way I contribute to structural evil, and thus bear the guilt of social sin? It may be that these sites at which my own agency comes to bear on the extension and adaptation of sinful social structures are the points at which I may make

[49] Julie Hanlon Rubio, *Hope for Common Ground: Mediating the Personal and the Political in a Divided Church* (Washington, DC: Georgetown University Press, 2016), 42.

the most direct contribution to undoing them. In most cases, this will likely push one toward a sustained and local attempt to counteract the effects of structural sin, rather than the safety of commitment to general principles of justice or the catharsis of public declarations on matters quite distant from one's daily life – again, following Rubio, cultivating an attention to "the seemingly innocent things we do every day."[50] Here is where we must commit to undoing structural evil most consistently, for here is where our guilt for social sin is most acute.

***

So, then, what are we to say of Christ's participation in these sinful social structures? Is he, after all, guilty of social sin? We need not – and I would argue, guided by Scripture and the theological tradition, should not – say so.[51]

It seems indisputable that Christ lived and acted within a profoundly unjust social context deeply marked by sin. We should be wary of overstating this point; Judith Plaskow rightly critiques the way that analysis of Jesus' social context often functions in anti-Jewish fashion by contrasting his moral rectitude to the supposedly regressive priestly and Pharisaical backdrop of his ministry.[52] Without implying, then, that Jesus' social context is one that is uniquely or even remarkably oppressive situated within the context of Roman Palestine and the broader Ancient Near East, we may nevertheless observe that Christ's life unfolds within a society deeply marked by what we would identify today as patriarchy, economic injustice, ableism, and imperialism. If merely living and acting within a patriarchal order is sufficient to render one guilty of social sin, then Christ is unquestionably so guilty and thus requires

---

[50] Rubio, *Hope for Common Ground*, 42.

[51] Augustine explicitly denies that Christ might have had any impulse of evil will at *corrept.* 11.30.

[52] Judith Plaskow, "Feminist Anti-Judaism and the Christian God," in *The Strength of Her Witness: Jesus Christ in the Global Voices of Women* (Maryknoll, NY: Orbis Books, 2018), 86–99.

God's forgiveness. The clear Scriptural and conciliar teaching that Jesus lives an absolutely innocent life is, if held to be authoritative, sufficient to show that this cannot be the correct understanding of social sin.

While Christ unquestionably lives and exercises moral agency within sinful social structures, there is no insuperable argument in favor of the claim that he does so in a manner that is causative of the *sinfulness* of that social structure. Put simply, Christ does not further the corruption of the social good: He does not clearly inhabit a subject position intrinsically constituted as sinful, and does not clearly act in a manner that creates or reconfigures the structural evil of his society. Consider, for example, Rosemary Radford Ruether's description of Christ's "*kenosis* of patriarchy": "the Word of God does not validate the existing social and religious hierarchy but speaks on behalf of the marginalized and despised groups of society. Jesus proclaims an iconoclastic reversal of the system of religious status: The last shall be first and the first last."[53] In contrast to our sinful participation in our own sinful social orders, Christ acts in perfect accordance with the goodness of the God who he is: His actions are just, and the desires from which they proceed are perfectly holy, the natural desirings of a human soul united to his own divine life. There is no susceptibility of his desires to malformation, and there is no exercise of his agency that of itself produces a further sinful derangement of the social order. All this is perfectly compatible with the account of social sin offered above, and compatible too with the recognition that the sinless Christ acts within a sinful social order. While Christ's agency is exercised within a social context defined by sin, Christian theology may affirm that he does not participate in these patterns of action in such a way that he requires forgiveness for social sins. To say otherwise would be to say that God Himself can sin, and that sinful

---

[53] Rosemary Radford Ruether, *Sexism and God-Talk: Toward a Feminist Theology* (Boston, MA: Beacon Press, 1993), 136–137.

humanity can be redeemed by the self-offering of a sinful life. Here, piety should fear to tread.

But can we honestly read this narrative in Mark's Gospel, in knowledge of the many harms inflicted upon women and those perceived as cultural outsiders throughout history, and say that there is no trace of violence in Jesus' words? This would, in my judgment, be a mistake. Attention to the work of incarnation reveals to us that considering Christ's exercise of agency solely as a consequence of his divine-human constitution gives an incomplete picture of his moral action. As the divine-human person he is, his agency is always exercised in relation to the world around him, inextricable from the social context he inhabits. Christ's humility in the Incarnation extends even as far as his moral action in the world: He hands himself over to the moral landscape we have created, taking a place within the sinful patterns of social action that we have established.

This discussion opens for us a new avenue for interpreting the encounter with the Syrophoenician woman and similar Scriptural narratives. We need not take these stories to require the conclusion that Christ is guilty of social sins like patriarchy and ethnocentrism. Yet neither must we close our eyes to the recognition that encountering Jesus may have been a source of deep pain for this unnamed woman. The fact that Christ's participation in our sinful social world does not direct his desires away from God does not leave his actions totally unmarked by the consequences of sin. Even as he is wholly without sin at every point of his participation in our moral world, he acts in relation to those who *have* been deeply and grievously wounded by the sin of others, and who dwell within particular social positions and patterns of relations between those positions – as, crucially, does Christ. Instead, we may see in these stories a narrative identification with the victims of structural evil, for the purpose of showing that *even sinless action*, when performed within a sinful social context, may cause harm.

It is essential to this narrative that the Syrophoenician woman has lived her entire life in a social world that subjected and subjects women, and especially women of marginalized ethnic or racial identity, to systematic violence. It is significant that she is a Gentile in a border-region where she would often have encountered Jews, with all the possibilities for hybridized identities (how, in Matthew's Gospel, does she know to call Jesus "Son of David"?), transformative encounters across difference, and inter-group tensions and hostilities that so often characterize these cultural meeting places. It is inescapable that – sinless or no – Jesus is a man in a social world that assiduously guarded and guards men's social superiority, and that Jesus was a member of a religious culture that was at best different than her own and at worst threateningly alien. Neither she, nor Christ, enter this interaction on a socially neutral field: The deck is stacked against her, even before we pull our focus out to take in the other Jewish men who are party to it.[54]

Let us take Mark's Gospel at its word: Jesus really does respond to the woman's desperate plea by telling her it is not fair to take the children's food and throw it to the dogs. Let us even presume a very charitable reading of Jesus' behavior. As Kenneth Bailey has summarized the version of the episode found in Matthew's Gospel in terms that seek to preserve Jesus from any blame (even as his reading depends on what seems a troublingly anti-Jewish judgment of the disciples),

> Jesus is irritated by the disciples' attitudes regarding women and Gentiles. The woman's love for her daughter and her confidence in him impress Jesus. He decides to use the occasion to help her and challenge the deeply rooted prejudices in the hearts of his disciples. In the process he gives the woman a chance to expose the depths of her courage and faith.[55]

Even were we to grant the adequacy of this reading (and I think we should not), Jesus' behavior occurs within a broader social history

---

[54] Matthew's Gospel includes them as explicit actors in the episode, as they implore Jesus, "Send her away, for she keeps shouting after us" (15.23).

[55] Kenneth E. Bailey, *Jesus through Middle Eastern Eyes: Cultural Studies in the Gospels* (Downers Grove, IL: IVP Academic, 2008), 222.

of the degradation of women, and a society that in many cases demands that women should abase themselves in order to receive mercy from powerful men. Can Jesus' words here, whether offered as a test of the woman's faith or as an opportunity for her to display that faith to the world, entirely escape the intersubjective harm of social patterns that regularly humiliate and dismiss women's desperate pleas for aid? At least one possible version of this scenario, and not an unlikely one, imagines this woman saying whatever she needs to for her daughter to be healed, even leaving with faith in a Lord who could recognize her faith and would speak powerful words of mercy to her – but leaving, too, wounded by yet one more interaction in which she had to prove she was not a dog.

This narrative thus issues us a word of caution: While it cannot, to my mind, overthrow the teaching of Christ's sinlessness, it does press us to recognize that even sinless action exercised in a fallen world may cause harm. Jesus' words and actions are not wholly his own: They are spoken and performed in a world that is already damaged by sin, and are directed to those who already bear histories of suffering and trauma.

The comparison to Christ's cry of dereliction is an instructive one. Here, as there, we are confronted with a picture of Jesus that seems impossible to reconcile with the perfect love and beatitude proper to the incarnate Son of God. How can the Son experience abandonment by the Father? How can God's perfect love be seen in the words Christ speaks to this victim of a patriarchal order? As in the Cry of Dereliction, Christ's words to the Syrophoenician woman are theologically baffling apart from the recognition that the Word has truly entered into union with the condition of sinful humanity, in a way that marks the possibilities of his own human experience. Here again, this reality is not uncomplicated: Just as we may hold that Christ truly experiences doubt and fear on the Cross by virtue of his union to the godforsaken state of sinful humanity, we may hold also that there is an analogue to social sin in Christ without holding that he himself participates and extends, and thus bears the guilt of, social sin.

The best way of reconciling Christ's sinlessness with the words he speaks to this suffering woman is to regard them as a revelation of the fact that *even his* actions, properly ordered to God, may yet further the harms that the world Jesus inhabits has already inflicted on the vulnerable. Our reaction to the story is precisely the theological point. It shakes us to perceive the sinless one as speaking in a way that degrades the Syrophoenician woman – even as it undoubtedly shook many to gaze up at the face of their Lord and find there a likeness to an abusive husband, or to a member of the crowd that had burned one's home in the midst of ethnic strife.

I spoke in the last chapter of our historical imaginings of Jesus as icons of his particular human life. We can note here a corollary to the historical teaching on the representability of the face of Christ: If the Word has assumed a particular human face, this means that Christ's likeness is already weighted with the histories of pain and suffering that we bear, drawing our minds not only to the eternal God but to the concrete human faces that have harmed us in the past. As he moves through the world, as he acts within it, Christ is not innocent of these likenesses, or of the privilege that his particular body and socially located agency afford him.

The story of the Syrophoenician woman, and the words he speaks to her, render this conclusion inescapable; indeed, on my interpretation, this revelation is the story's whole point. Certainly, Jesus loves this woman with the perfect love of the one who created her; yet in their interaction, he makes clear that their ability to meet one another as fellow humans is inevitably conditioned by the violence that defines all fallen human community. Though he is sinless, they meet in a fallen world, and on its terms. In Jesus' words to the woman, he clearly reflects his culture's dismissal of women like these.[56] If it is not (as it cannot be) his own sin at issue, we must conclude that it is *our*

---

[56] Although she seems to me to come too close to admitting sin to Christ, Kelly Brown Douglas' words are instructive here: She notes that the story moves from a presentation of Jesus as "controlled by the biases of his society" to one in which "Jesus realizes how he had succumbed to the privileges of being Jewish and male in

violence reflected back at us, a violence that conditions even this woman's expectations and fears as she goes to meet her redeemer. Christ is innocent, yet encountering him still opens this woman to harm as a result of the sinful order of her social world. This story is remarkable only in that it makes scandalously clear a dynamic potentially at play for all who meet Christ.[57]

And the point can be broadened: The Gospels bear clear witness that Christ is implicated in the death-dealing endemic to a fallen creation. He is clearly portrayed, at multiple points in the Scriptural narratives, as engaging in practices of predation: fishing, and eating fish. I would not characterize these instances of predation as sinful, but this is precisely the point: Christ exists in a world that is fallen; Christ is raised within a society that assumes practices of fishing and eating to be customary, and gives no indication even of discomfort with the custom; and his actions participate in this death-dealing, even though they are situated within a life that accomplishes the redemption of the world and brings about an end to the groaning of creation, where death shall be no more. The moral valence of Christ's carnivorousness is of course quite different than that of his encounter with the Syrophoenician woman, but suggests to us a possibility in which his sinlessness is not exclusive of his participation in death-dealing and harm.

Yet if we cannot avoid the social violence on display in Mark 7, neither should we miss the narrative movement it effects. While Christ's relation to the Syrophoenician woman is mediated at the

---

that particular society. With that apparent realization, Jesus rejects the validity of those privileges by helping the woman"; Kelly Brown Douglas, *The Black Christ*, 91.

[57] M. Shawn Copeland raises a similar point in relation to Jesus' use of slavery as a metaphor in Mark 12.1–11 (The Parable of the Wicked Tenants), noting that Jesus' parable's pedagogical force trades on his society's assumption that while violence is legitimately inflicted upon enslaved bodies, it is a new level of depravity when the vineyard owner's son is killed. Copeland quite reasonably concludes that enslaved African-Americans would have seen themselves in the slaves sent to do the master's bidding – and thus, in those whose suffering the logic of Jesus' parable values less. See M. Shawn Copeland, *Knowing Christ Crucified: The Witness of African-American Religious Experience* (Maryknoll, NY: Orbis Books, 2018), 51–52.

story's opening by the fallen social world, it culminates in a genuine encounter between them that tends to healing and restoration. We should recall Ruether's description of the "kenosis of patriarchy," as Christ abandons the social script that he had been given for interactions between Jewish men and Gentile women. But more importantly, and as the feminist and postcolonial interpreters cited above have recognized, the story becomes one in which this woman's agency comes to expand his own sense of the scope of his earthly mission. Through this woman's agency, Christ comes humanly to understand himself as sent both to Gentiles and Jews. In this respect, he humanly learns his own divine will from this woman, no less surely than he learns of the God of Israel at the feet of the rabbis.

And this is true not only for Christ himself: Pablo Alonso has argued that "the evangelist seeks to help the readers of his narrative tackle problems of inclusion arising in the early Christian community through reminders of the historical attitude of Jesus. Mark challenges Christians to change their minds just as Jesus did and attacks narrow assumptions about 'who may share in God's salvation.'"[58] In setting this example for the Church, Christ has given his Body the resources to challenge the discriminatory patterns of their own life. This redemptive work is accomplished as the Syrophoenician woman's agency affects Christ's own, her determination and creativity directing him to an even more capacious sense of restoration than he had previously understood.

If we are attentive, we may even find in Jesus' later teaching echoes of this encounter. Luke's Gospel does not record this episode with a Syrophoenician (or, as Matthew would have it, Canaanite) woman. It does, however, repeat the constellation of images she gives Jesus: When Jesus tells the story of Lazarus and the rich man in Luke 16, Lazarus – the beloved of God, whom the rich man

---

[58] Pablo Alonso, "The Woman Who Changed Jesus: Text and Context," in *Jesus of Galilee: Contextual Christology for the 21st Century*, ed. Robert Lassalle-Klein (Maryknoll, NY: Orbis Books, 2011), 121–134, 126.

initially overlooks – is described as one waiting for crumbs to fall from the rich man's table, as one who finds himself in the place of the dogs. Does it go too far to wonder if the Syrophoenician woman's words have lingered with him, if they have given him the grist for his parable?[59]

We find that Jesus becomes who he is, the Redeemer, in part through this woman's influence upon him, drawing her existence and agency into the divine work that he has willed from all eternity through the mediation of his human life. If we are not saved without Christ, it is also true to say that the redemption of the world is not accomplished apart from the agency of this Gentile woman.

***

At this point, let me respond head-on to a challenge that I suspect has occurred to many readers over the preceding two chapters. In the course of this argument, I have speculated about Christ learning of the God of Israel from the Jewish leaders of his time, have suggested that he may at times have been humanly ignorant on matters small and large (Abiathar's high priesthood, the day and hour of the return of the Son of Man), and even that interaction with the Syrophoenician woman may have shaped his understanding of the scope of his earthly ministry. But how can these theses be affirmed, without surrendering the central claims of conciliar christology? How can the Word be omniscient while Christ displays human ignorance, without positing two conflicting subjects of intellection in Christ? Is this not straightforward Nestorianism?

It is not. While these claims would likely not have been affirmed by any of the Church Fathers and Mothers – certainly not by Augustine – they are entirely compatible with the christological teachings authoritatively defined by the seven ecumenical councils. In advancing these theses, I intend no modification of or departure from conciliar christology whatsoever. Rather, I hope to show that the logical space of theological positions compatible with conciliar

---

[59] I am grateful for this suggestion to conversation with Rhody Walker-Lenow.

christology is considerably roomier than we might have expected.[60] The belief that such positions are incompatible with conciliar christology is, in fact, rooted in theological error.

To demonstrate this error, let me point to an argument recently advanced by Thomas Joseph White, O.P. in favor of the view that Christ enjoyed both the beatific vision and the beatitude of infused conceptual knowledge of his own divinity at every moment of his earthly life. White argues,

> The human actions of Jesus are actions of one person who is divine, and what the Son wills humanly is expressive of his personal identity. However, this person, the Son of God, possesses a divine will, and it is impossible for the Son of God to act personally in such a way that his divine will should be absent from his personal action. The Word incarnate, then, must be humanly conscious of his own divine will in all his actions, so that his human actions are indicative of his personal, divine willing as God ... If the Son is going to adequately manifest the mystery of the Holy Trinity in his human decisions and choices, then he must be humanly aware of what the Father who sent him wills and of what he wills with the Holy Spirit, so that he can express this in his human actions and choices. He can only do this because he is conscious in his human decisions of the divine will that he shares with the Father and the Holy Spirit.[61]

White finds support for his argument in the work of Herman Diepen, who notes, "There is certainly a human consciousness in Christ, but not the consciousness of a human self, either metaphysical or psychological ... To say that the humanity knows, acts, is

---

[60] In this, I aim to carry on much as Sarah Coakley does in taking up Rahner's understanding of conciliar christology as a "horizon" of theological reflection; see Sarah Coakley, "What Does Chalcedon Solve and What Does It Not?," in *The Incarnation*, eds. Stephen T. Davis, Daniel Kendall, and Gerald O'Collins (Oxford: Oxford University Presss, 2002), 143–163.

[61] Thomas Joseph White, *The Incarnate Lord: A Thomistic Study in Christology* (Washington, DC: Catholic University of America Press, 2015), 254–255.

aware, these are different expressions which are certainly improper, because it is always the Word to whom these acts belong."[62] On this basis, White argues, "there is not an autonomous 'personality' in the humanity of Jesus, other than that of the Son."[63]

In a parallel discussion of Christ's human consciousness, White appeals to the work of Bernard Lonergan, S.J.[64] Lonergan begins his discussion of Christ's consciousness by arguing that it is appropriate analogically to ascribe consciousness to God, "not because God engages in self-reflection but because God understands, judges, wills, and chooses."[65] He goes on to argue that consciousness is not only properly ascribed to the divine nature as such, but to the trinitarian persons in their mutual relations to one another.[66] As Christ becomes humanly conscious of himself, then, he must become conscious of himself as the person that he is – namely, a divine person united to a human nature.[67] In Lonergan's formulation, "through a consciousness that is truly and properly human, a divine person is conscious of a divine person."[68] At root, Lonergan's argument claims that since the Word is the one who is the ontological subject of Christ's human acts of cognition, Christ must become conscious of a divine person united to human nature. This recognition must accompany the first moment of his human consciousness in becoming conscious of himself. If it did not, he

---

[62] Herman Diepen, "La psychologie humaine du Christ selon saint Thomas d'Aquin," *Revue Thomiste* 50 (1950): 82–118, 531–532. Cited and translated by Thomas Joseph White at *The Incarnate Lord*, 249.

[63] White, *The Incarnate Lord*, 249.

[64] Thomas Joseph White, "Dyothelitism and the Human Consciousness of Jesus," *Pro Ecclesia* 17.4 (2008): 396–422, 413–418.

[65] Bernard Lonergan, *The Collected Works of Bernard Lonergan, v. 7: The Ontological and Psychological Constitution of Christ*, trans. Michael G. Shields (Toronto, OH: University of Toronto Press, 2002), 195.

[66] Lonergan, *The Ontological and Psychological Constitution of Christ*, 201.

[67] See Assertions 1 and 2 at Lonergan, *The Ontological and Psychological Constitution of Christ*, 203–204, and the explanation and defenses of these assertions in subsequent pages.

[68] Lonergan, *The Ontological and Psychological Constitution of Christ*, 211.

would mistakenly become conscious of himself as a subject other than that of the divine Word:

> Through consciousness one becomes aware not only of operations but also the identity of the subject, that is, the subject as self-identical; and although in other human beings this self-identical subject, aware of self on the side of the subject and under the formality of the experienced, is merely human, in the case of Christ the man the self-identical subject, manifest to himself on the side of the subject and under the formality of the experienced, is a divine person.[69]

Consciousness of himself as a divine person must therefore accompany all Christ's conscious acts.

How might we respond to this argumentative trajectory? Lonergan, in my judgment, offers the strongest challenge to my position, so let me respond to his argument first. On his account, consciousness is a prediscursive feature of human experience, a "preliminary unstructured awareness of oneself and one's acts."[70] Yet consciousness is preeminently consciousness *of one's own personhood.*[71] Accordingly, in being conscious of himself in his human intellective acts, Lonergan believes that Christ must be conscious of himself as a divine person acting in a human nature – this is what it means for him to be conscious of himself *as* himself. Even accepting for the sake of argument Lonergan's account of consciousness as including awareness of personhood, we may ask: Where is the necessity here? For the Lonerganain, it is true enough that inasmuch as Christ is *perfectly* conscious of himself as himself, he must be conscious of a divine person acting in the human nature She has assumed. But why should it be inconceivable that, for

---

[69] Lonergan, *The Ontological and Psychological Constitution of Christ*, 239.

[70] Lonergan, *The Ontological and Psychological Constitution of Christ*, 165.

[71] Cf. Lonergan: "consciousness has to do especially with the person, since it is the person *who* is conscious, and it is the person, principally, *of whom* a person is conscious"; *The Ontological and Psychological Constitution of Christ*, 245.

redemptive ends, Christ should *not* be perfectly conscious of his personhood for at least some period of his life? Granting for the moment that Christ possesses a "divine consciousness" that is not kenotically emptied, why should his added human consciousness necessarily know himself as both human and divine, if we conceive of the self-limitation of his human intellect as an act of divine power?[72] This would not be an independent operation of Christ's human consciousness, but a description of the manner in which Christ's divinity wills to act in and through his human consciousness.

More critically of Lonergan, we may ask whether it truly is appropriate to ascribe consciousness to God, even in the modified sense of consciousness Lonergan employs. White, for one, is reticent to do so.[73] Yet if this thesis is rejected, the conclusion may be safely rejected as well: If "consciousness" is not a divine attribute, then the only consciousness that should be ascribed to Christ is a human one. Though Christ certainly knows His own nature divinely, and may know his divine personhood humanly as well, this knowledge need not be held to be intrinsic to Christ's every human intellective act.

Finally, even if one wished to accept both Lonergan's account of consciousness and his ascription of consciousness to God, one might reject that the conjunction of these claims leads to the sort of consciousness of divine-personhood-in-human-act that Lonergan believes characterizes Christ's conscious experience. For what could a prediscursive consciousness of this sort possibly be like? For Lonergan's argument to succeed, this consciousness must be prereflective – "unstructured," in the term he prefers. What sort of unstructured awareness proper to the act of human nature might possibly include – as something like an apperceptive feature of consciousness – a distinction between divine personhood, human

---

[72] Cf. Lonergan, *The Ontological and Psychological Constitution of Christ*, 223.
[73] White, "Dyothelitism and the Human Consciousness of Jesus," 415 n.43.

act, and the proper relation between them? Yet if such knowledge requires discursive rather than prediscursive reasoning, then we may legitimately ask about the conditions under which Christ receives the categories that help him attain to this awareness of divine-human personhood. While Lonergan thus presents a subtle and thoughtful discussion of Christ's consciousness, his conclusions depend on controversial premises, and thus cannot command the assent of all those who wish to remain faithful to conciliar orthodoxy.

The Diepen-White version of this argument is on still shakier ground, for it assumes that, on pain of Nestorianism, the content of the divine knowledge and will are mirrored in the Word's human knowledge and will. If the Word knows His will as received wholly from the Father, then Jesus must know his will as received wholly from the Father; if the Word eternally wills the salvation of the world, then Jesus must, at each moment of his life, will the salvation of the world.

Yet this theological conclusion seems to me deeply mistaken when approached in light of the *maior dissimilitudo* (greater dissimilarity) that obtains within any likeness between God and creation. It rests upon a key presupposition: that the Word's divine willing and knowledge of His willing are the sort of thing that might straightforwardly be translated into a human life. The Word's eternal knowledge of His personhood is the same sort of thing (analogically) as Christ's human knowledge, such that if the Word eternally knows Himself to proceed from the Father, then Christ must know himself as a divine person that proceeds from the Father as well. This is clear in White's denial of "autonomous personality" to Christ: What would make his personality "autonomous" would be having intellective or volitional acts that differ in content from the Word's eternal divine act. If the Word wills something with a will He knows to have been received from the Father, the incarnate Word must humanly will the same thing in full human knowledge that this will has been received from the Father.

But why should we think that the Word's divine knowing and willing are the sort of thing that exhibit a one-to-one correspondence to Christ's human intellective and volitional acts? Recognition of the analogical *maior dissimilitudo* certainly gives us reason to think that, while intellect and willing may certainly be validly ascribed to God, we have a looser conceptual grasp on this connection than we imagine. As I have discussed above, the Word is not "inside" Jesus, controlling his actions one by one; in Jesus, the Word adds to Himself a human nature, while retaining the eternity proper to Her nature. The Word's knowledge and will are properly eternal, wholly timeless in the simplicity of the divine life – there can be no real distinction within the Word's intellective and volitional act, for there is in the Word only the triunely related act of the divine life. As we meet this eternal act in temporal likeness in that same Word's human life, we have no reason to think that the Word's providential self-limiting of Her human intellect is incompatible with Her divine life in its unknowable simplicity. God's life is other; unknowably so, and thus not exclusive in principle of human intellectual limits or even error ordered to God's purpose of redemption.

Just as the vulnerability of Christ's flesh does not undermine Christian belief that his flesh is properly incorruptible through its union to the Word, so also his human intellect might be limited without undermining the truth of that intellect's union with the Word. The fact that the perfection of all knowledge is proper to the Word's divine life in a way that fleshly incorruptibility is not cannot be a decisive refutation, for life unalloyed by death *is* a feature proper to the Word's divine nature – yet She may still grant death temporary power over Her flesh. In like manner, we may say that the Word is eternally perfect in knowledge – and yet, it may suit the good purposes of God for the Word's humanity to err, for the Word's humanity to lack knowledge, for the Word's humanity to learn. This is not to change a classical attribution of omniscience to the Word; only to affirm that one possibility of the Word making Herself known and *actually living* in history is to live an intellectually fallible human life. It only seems necessary to deny this claim if one has assumed a linear correlation between the Word's divine knowledge and Christ's human knowledge, such that the Word divinely knowing all things would necessitate Christ humanly knowing all things at all moments of his life.

Yet even the claim that the Word knows all things while Christ may err does not suggest two independent subjects, or two independent "personalities," in the one person of Christ. It would be completely wrong to state that Christ has an "autonomous personality" in his human nature, separate from the personality of the Word. Rather, if "personality" is a category defined by consistency of character across diverse actions – if it is an intrinsically historical category – it is better to say that the only personality in Christ is a human one. The Word does not have a divine personality of Her own that might be opposed to Christ's. Whatever it is like to be the divine Son of God, it is not something that a human might experience, and which might thus constrain our sense of the possibilities of Christ's human experience.[74] And so, when we imagine what it "feels like" to be Jesus, we should (or at least can) imagine an entirely human experience. This is not Nestorianism, or the suggestion of an independent human subject in Christ – just one more recognition of the scandal that often accompanies the Word's will to live a human life.

---

[74] Whatever sense we can make of the category of "divine experience," it must be distinguished from human experience by a qualitative difference far more thoroughgoing than the difference between human and any other creaturely experience; cf. Rowan Williams, "Negative Theology: Some Misunderstandings," *Modern Theology* (Early View, March 6, 2023), https://doi.org/10.1111/moth.12852, p. 4. As Thomas Nagel has noted, even the experience of bats wildly exceeds our imaginative capacity. See Thomas Nagel, "What Is It Like to Be a Bat?," *The Philosophical Review* 83.4 (1974): 435–450.

6 | The Regime of Signs

To this point, my account has focused predominantly on the conditions and implications of the Word's assumption of flesh.[1] This is not, as has likely become apparent by now, quite the same as what christology has traditionally called a focus on the "person" of Christ. While the early chapters of this study do indeed discuss questions that might fall under this rubric – how we should speak of the divine nature, how the act of incarnation is identical to the eternal act of the Word within the triune life of God, how the divine and human natures are related in Christ – we have also considered how Christ's life receives its shape only through his relations to the world around him, his environment and the human and nonhuman creatures that share it. Though he is a divine person from all eternity, this divine person is only the human he is in and through these relations. If we are to think of Christ as a divine-*human* person not only in his metaphysical constitution, but in his historical particularity, discussions of the person of Christ must necessarily shade into questions of his work.

---

[1] The title of this chapter is a rather loose rendering of Augustine's *dispensatio similitudinum* as a description of the present age at *trin.* 1.8.16, rendered by Hill at WSA I/5, 76 as: "It is *when he cancels all sovereignty and all authority and all power* that the Son will reveal the Father, that is, when there is no more need for the regime of symbols [*dispensatio similitudinum*] administered by the angelic sovereignties and authorities and powers." Gerald Boersma has noted that, for Augustine, creaturely *similitudines* can be described alongside Christ as images of God through the key concept of *aequalitas*: Christ is an image equal to the Father, while creaturely likenesses (which also exhibit unlikeness to God) can be described as images unequal to the Father; *Augustine's Early Theology of Image*, 200–202, 260–261, interpreting *div.qu.* 74.

In service of this end, we have looked at the Scriptural witness to consider how Christ's human identity might have grown and changed in response to the world around him – his landscape, the built environment, the animal populations of Galilee, the social and cultural forces that may have shaped his religious and political outlook, and even his own messianic self-knowledge. Attention to this Scriptural record has raised challenging questions for christology about the possibility of ignorance in Christ, and about our Lord's implication in sinful social structures. Even if these speculations are, as I have argued, wholly compatible with the claims of conciliar christology, they have carried us beyond the bounds of what the Church Fathers and Mothers generally affirmed – certainly beyond the limits of what Augustine was prepared to say of Christ. Nevertheless, these perspectives, leading us to a Christ who – not out of any natural necessity but by the fitting disposition of grace – wills to be who he is only *with* the natural environment of Galilee, only *with* a Jewish community that longed for a new divine Kingdom and could imagine a deified Messiah, only *with* the religious insiders and outsiders that helped him discover his holy purpose and see its capaciousness, all seem to me a licit extension of the Augustinian teaching that the broadest conception of Christ's personhood, the *totus Christus*, is one that includes both Head and Body, Christ and the City of God. Only a Christ this deeply bound to humanity can make room for the lives of all the redeemed in his own human life; only a Christ whose sinless life is entwined with the life of sinful humanity can truly cry in the voice of his Body, *My God, my God, why have you forsaken me?*

The remaining chapters of this book thus turn to Christ's work of redemption. The work of redemption is finally inseparable from the work of incarnation: If the work of incarnation describes the Word's assumption of the shape of Christ's life, moving into the determinate particularity of human life, the work of redemption traces the opposite movement, as our lives are included by grace within Christ's humanity. This chapter and the next keep the focus

on Christ's historical life and ministry, with this chapter considering how Christ's life comes to serve as a redemptive sign and created
manifestation of the triune Lord, and the next chapter focusing on
the consummation of Christ's redemptive work on the Cross. The
final three chapters expand the focus to the Body which is the
selfsame Christ, describing the life of the Church as an extension
of the Incarnation.

The question of this chapter is a fairly direct one: Granted that
the Word has assumed human flesh and that through his relations
to the world his life assumes a definite shape, how is his human life
redemptive? How does *this* life come to matter for our own? In
answering these questions, I hew fairly closely to the arguments
Augustine offers in books 4 and 13 of the *De trinitate*. While my own
systematic account will develop his insights in here in ways he likely
would not have, it will be useful to have the outlines of this
Augustinian story of redemption in mind as we seek to understand
more fully the work of incarnation.

***

Midway through book four of the *De trinitate*, Augustine summarizes the condition of sinful humanity: "we were incapable of grasp-
ing eternal things, and weighted down by the accumulated dirt of
our sins, which we had collected by our love of temporal things, and
which had become almost a natural growth on our mortal stock; so
we needed purifying."[2] As a result of sin, we have lost the ability to
know and rest in God; rather than persisting in the stability of
contemplating His eternity, we are fixed on the realm of temporal
things. Augustine's language is fluid here: While he will speak at
times of our loves weighing us down and hindering our ascent to
God, he also describes us as blown from changeable thing to
changeable thing, like dust swept away in the wind.[3] This is revealing: It is the ever-shifting novelty of our desires that keeps us

---

[2] *trin.* 4.18.24; WSA I/5, 169.
[3] *en.Ps.* 1.4.

anchored to this world, presenting us a created simulacrum of inexhaustible goodness that transfixes our loves precisely by refusing to offer any love as final. This is the restlessness of *divertissement*, a ceaseless parade of half-loves that distract us from the emptiness at their heart. By Pascal's reckoning, "men are not able to cure death, misery, or ignorance, so they are well-advised, if they want to be happy, not to think of these things."[4] In this condition, it is possible for us to catch only the occasional glimpse of God, leaving our knowledge of Him indistinct and confused.

What we need, then, are *visa congrua peregrinationi* – "sights suited to our wandering state, to admonish us that what we seek is not here, and that we must turn back from the things around us to where our whole being springs from."[5] Because our minds are trained on temporal things, only temporal things "like those we were already bound to in a servile adaptation" can effect the purification we require to hold our minds on eternal things.[6] God must meet us where we are already looking – and this is precisely what She does in Christ.[7] Augustine tells us, "I am struggling to return from this *far country* (Lk 15:13) by the road he has made in the humanity of the divinity of his only Son (*per viam quam stravit humanitate divinitatis unigeniti sui*); and changeable though I am, I breathe in his truth the more deeply, the more clearly I perceive there is nothing changeable about it."[8] There is something in this mutable flesh that draws us into contact with the eternal, "carrying

---

[4] Blaise Pascal, *Penseés*, 124, in Pascal, *Œuvres Completes* II, ed. Michel Le Guern (Paris: Gallimard, 2000), 583. Compare *trin.* 4.1.2. On the Augustinian roots of Pascal's understanding of disordered love and *divertissement*, see William Wood, *Blaise Pascal on Duplicity, Sin, and the Fall: The Secret Instinct* (Oxford: Oxford University Press, 2013), 20–26, 42–47.

[5] *trin.* 4.1.2; WSA I/5, 153.

[6] *trin.* 4.18.24; WSA I/5, 169.

[7] Adam Ployd notes the christocentric basis of Augustine's account of our redeemed intellection at *Augustine, the Trinity, and the Church: A Reading of the Anti-Donatist Sermons* (Oxford: Oxford University Press, 2015), 79–80.

[8] *trin.* 4.1.1; WSA I/5, 153.

us over to his eternity (*ad aeternitatem ipsius traiceremur*)."[9] He comes "to capture our faith and draw it to himself, and by means of it to lead us on to his truth."[10] Christ opens a pathway back to the Father that had previously been closed to us, giving us a fixed point in this shifting world by which we are oriented back to God.

The argument of the early books of the *De trinitate* unfolds against the backdrop of Latin theology's controversy over the Trinity. As Michel René Barnes has convincingly argued, Augustine is consistently on guard against the claim that "the Son's character as revealer – or the Son's 'noetic visibility' – constitutes the Son's inferiority to the Father."[11] In the view of some Latin Homoians, and even Ante-Nicene Fathers,[12] the Son's visibility is taken to be proper to His existence, in contrast to the invisibility characteristic of the Father's life.[13] If the Son does not possess the same essential invisibility as the Father, the conclusion that His existence is only "like" that of the Father, and that He is thus a lower grade of divinity, seems unavoidable.[14] The Father's invisibility is beyond question for both Pro-Nicene and Homoian Christians, grounded in both Scriptural evidence[15] and what they judged to

---

[9] *trin.* 4.18.24.

[10] *trin.* 4.18.24; WSA I/5, 170.

[11] Michel René Barnes, "The Visible Christ and the Invisible Trinity: Mt. 5:8 in Augustine's Trinitarian Theology of 400," *Modern Theology* 19.3 (2003): 329–355; 330.

[12] Brian Daley notes that St. Irenaeus calls the Word "the visible of the invisible God"; *God Visible*, 161. See also Kari Kloos, *Christ, Creation, and the Vision of God: Augustine's Transformation of Early Christian Theophany Interpretation* (Brill: Leiden, 2011) on Augustine's relation to earlier discussions of the Old Testament manifestations of God.

[13] Cf. *trin.* 2.9.15, where Augustine writes that his opponents "say that the Son is visible not merely in the flesh which he took of the virgin, but even before that in himself. For it is he, they say, who showed himself visibly to the fathers" (WSA I/5, 107).

[14] Hence Augustine's explicit affirmation in *trin.* 4.19.26; WSA I/5, 171, that the Son "could not even be seen, as he is in his equality with the Father, even after he had been sent."

[15] Augustine at *trin.* 2.8.14 offers 1 Tim 1.17 and 1 Tim 6.15 as examples.

be sound philosophical reasoning.[16] The inevitable conclusion for Augustine is that the Son too possesses the same invisibility that characterizes the life of the Father.

To view this polemical orientation of the *De trinitate*'s early books as merely a quirk of history would be to miss a significant point: Even when we speak of the Son revealing the Father – or, by extension, the Spirit – each of the trinitarian persons remains essentially hidden to us. As Barnes writes,

> The Son *is not* a revelation of the divine in any direct, available-to-the-senses, way; the Son *is not* divinity-insofar-as-it-may-be-perceived; the Son, as divine, *is not* the occasion of human faith (the Son, as human, is). The divinity of the Son is, until the eschaton, unseen and unseeable, although it can be symbolized or signified by some created artifact, just as the divinity of the Father and Holy Spirit can be, and is.[17]

The Son remains noetically invisible – which is to say, unknowable – *even in the context of the Incarnation.* When we speak of the Son's manifestation of the Father, then, we must remember that the sole point of divine visibility is the *humanity* of Christ. Barnes again is helpfully lucid:

> The most important fact about the identity of Jesus of Nazareth cannot be known, for it is not available to any kind of sight, material or noetic. Obviously this is true for those who live "now" (an era which includes both Augustine and ourselves), since Jesus the Son of God is not available to be seen. More importantly, this was true for those who lived when Jesus was available to be seen: all that could be seen was the human, Jesus of Nazareth.[18]

---

[16] See especially Part III of Rowan Williams, *Arius: Heresy and Tradition*, revised ed. (Grand Rapids, MI: Wm. B. Eerdmans, 2001).

[17] Barnes, "The Visible Christ," 335.

[18] Barnes, "The Visible Christ," 343.

Put simply, Jesus is all there is to be seen in the Word's temporal life. If we wish to look for the Second Person of the Trinity in history, it is a human face that we seek. This is not to deny that God is truly known to us in the life of Jesus, only to mark off the limits of that knowledge: Before the beatific vision, knowledge of God in Herself is impossible to us. In the present dispensation, we always come to know God through the mediation of created things, being directed to God through the humble things that She has made.

It is thus on account of his *humanity* that Jesus is the mediator between God and humanity. As Augustine writes at *De civitate dei* 11.2, "it is as man that he is the mediator, and it is as man, too, that he is the way ... there is only one way that is fully proof against all errors, in that he is himself both God and man: the goal as God, the way as man."[19] It is in his humanity that Christ opens to us a path back to God, for it is in his humanity alone that God becomes visible within creation.[20]

Similarly, it is in his humanity that Christ serves as the center of the whole regime of created signs (*dispensatio similitudinum*) that God has ordered within the economy of salvation. All creation, but particularly those *similitudines* that God has given within Scripture, testifies to the human flesh of Christ which the power of God raises from the dead. Beginning with the Old Testament theophanies, Augustine tells us that "all the sacred and mysterious things that were shown to our fathers by angelic miracles, or that they

---

[19] *civ.* 11.2; WSA I/7, 3. See also *civ.* 9.15.

[20] On the theme of Christ as mediator, see Brian E. Daley, *God Visible: Patristic Christology Reconsidered* (Oxford: Oxford University Press, 2018), 158–164. The invisibility of the divinity of Christ is a pronounced emphasis of Ian A. McFarland, *The Word Made Flesh: A Theology of the Incarnation* (Louisville, KY: Westminster John Knox Press, 2019); see, e.g., the two theses on page 8. DeHart similarly emphasizes the invisibility of the Son in the Incarnation: "if God truly speaks the eternal Word into the flesh of history and culture, the divine presence as such (eternal, omnipotent, infinite) simply cannot be directly visible in any historical phenomenon"; *Unspeakable Cults: An Essay in Christology* (Waco, TX: Baylor University Press, 2021), 164–165.

themselves performed, were likenesses (*similitudines*) of him, so that all creation might in some fashion utter the one who was to come (*ut omnis creatura factis quodam modo loqueretur unum futurum*) and be the savior of all who needed to be restored from death."[21] This is, as Michael Cameron has noted, the presupposition of all Augustine's Scriptural exegesis: "As I make my way and gasp in that sweat coming from our human condemnation, Christ meets and refreshes me everywhere in those books, in those scriptures, whether openly or in a hidden manner."[22] It is this conviction that underlies an exegetical practice for which the dimensions of Noah's ark are a likeness of the proportions of Christ's human body;[23] for which Christ is the rich mountain of Isaiah 2.2 and the cheese that feeds his people;[24] and for which he appears as the hen that makes herself weak protecting her chicks, in contrast to the swallows, sparrows, and storks that fly away and abandon them.[25] Yet it is not the case that only Scriptural images serve this role. As Augustine affirms, *omnis creatura* testify to this mediator: We find, for instance, that the winter solstice is a sign of Christ's birth, as the longest night of the year gives way to increasing light after the Incarnation.[26] In some way, all things rightly serve as signs of the Word's human flesh.

It is, above all, in revealing himself as Son of the Father that Christ is the mediator between God and humanity.[27] Christ teaches

---

[21] *trin.* 4.7.11; WSA I/5, 160.

[22] *c.Faust.* 12.27; WSA I/20, 143. Michael Cameron, *Christ Meets Me Everywhere: Augustine's Early Figurative Exegesis* (Oxford: Oxford University Press, 2012), 11.

[23] *civ.* 15.26.

[24] *en.Ps.* 67.22.

[25] *en.Ps.* 90.i.5.

[26] *s.* 190.1.

[27] Cf. Brian E. Daley, *God Visible: Patristic Christology Reconsidered* (Oxford: Oxford University Press, 2018), 161: "For Augustine, it is this first mission, the sending of the Son in human form to be mediator between God and created minds, that reveals to us the eternal relationship, the unity in distinction, of Father and Son: The Son is sent, *can* be sent from the heart of God and can bring God directly to us, because he *is* God;

us of God's own inner life, granting us a knowledge of God's eternal life that exceeds anything to which our minds might ascend by their own strength.[28] It is through this human life of the Word that we come to know of the relation of the trinitarian persons:

> There you have what the Son of God has been sent for; indeed there you have what it is for the Son of God to have been sent. Everything that has taken place in time, in appearances which have shown forth from eternity and carry us back to eternity, has been designed to elicit the faith we must be purified by in order to contemplate the truth, has either been testimony to this mission or have been the actual mission of the Son of God.[29]

In contrast to the Old Testament theophanies that show us God but not the persons of the Trinity,[30] this mission of the Son reveals to us the trinitarian relations that simply are the divine life. The Son is sent into the world and manifested in created signs because it is proper to the Son's life to proceed from the Father; His existence is itself a sending.[31] This is not to say, however, that the Son's mission in the world is identical to the Son's begottenness, in such a way that the obedience of Christ in the *forma servi* would be proper to his divinity. Rather, the work of redemption he is sent to enact historically testifies to the originary and coeternal begottenness of the Son from the Father.[32] It is the humility of assuming this mortal flesh and rendering God's love manifest to us that distinguishes Christ from the false mediators of pagan philosophy and

---

yet, as one sent, he is also now seen to be God begotten as a 'person' within the divine Mystery, the Son *distinct* from the Father."

[28] Cf. *trin.* 1.1.1.

[29] *trin.* 4.19.25; WSA I/5, 171 (modified).

[30] Cf. *trin.* 2.17.32; WSA I/5, 120 (modified): "All these visions . . . were produced through the changeable creation subject to the changeless God, and they did not manifest God as he is in himself, but in a significatory manner as times and circumstances required."

[31] *trin.* 4.20.28.

[32] *trin.* 4.20.27.

cultus.[33] And, as we will see, it is in his self-offering that he draws our hearts back to the eternal God.

***

Let me pause, at this point, to offer several observations in light of Augustine's discussion so far. Attention to Augustine's christology here in *De trinitate* 4 allows us to draw into focus several features of my broader emphasis on the Word's work of incarnation.

First, and perhaps most importantly for my project, it is essential to note that what is redemptive on Augustine's account is the *whole shape* of Christ's life. It is not merely his sacrificial death, all his actions taken collectively, or even all Scriptural likenesses of him that serve as a redemptive sign drawing our hearts back to God. It is, rather, the concrete particularity of his human life in his relation to *omnis creatura* – all things. As Augustine writes of the Book of Genesis at *Contra Faustum* 12.8, "Everything that we read there, when it is considered clearly and piece by piece, foretells Christ and the Church."[34] While applying first and foremost to the Scriptural witness, the clearest signs by which God manifests Herself to us, the principle applies more broadly to all created signs: All things testify to the humanity of Christ.

Indeed, if my account of God's providential ordering of created history is correct, all these relations to Christ's human life are *intended and included in* the Word's assumption of flesh; the ordering of all created signs to the humanity of Christ *is itself* included within the work of incarnation.[35] It is not coincidence or happenstance that the dimensions of Noah's ark, or the hen, or the winter

---

[33] *civ.* 9.15. Christopher Beeley has usefully discussed the continuity between Augustine's theology of Christ's mediation in *trin.* 4 and *civ.* 9–10 at *The Unity of Christ: Continuity and Conflict in Patristic Tradition* (New Haven, CT: Yale University Press, 2012), 246–255.

[34] *c.Faust.* 12.8; WSA I/20, 130; cited by Paula Fredriksen at *Augustine and the Jews: A Christian Defense of Jews and Judaism* (New Haven, CT: Yale University Press, 2010), 263.

[35] Augustine ties the revelation of Christ to the whole providential order of creation from a very early date in his thought: See *vera rel.* 24.45.

solstice serve as signs of Christ: This is precisely how God has willed to draw all persons back to Herself. Christ is the center of the regime of signs, the one created sign to which all likenesses ultimately refer. When we refer to the work of incarnation, then, it is not sufficient to restrict our scope to those persons and things that contribute to the course of his human life – the people he encounters, the soil on which he walks, and so on. The work of incarnation includes also the Word's assuming a particular place within the semiotic order of creation. In his concrete humanity, he is the type of the Binding of Isaac; in the historical events of the Crucifixion, he is the analogate of all grapes trodden by all vintners in all winepresses throughout all history.[36] These are the signs which, by turning our minds and hearts to the human face of Jesus, carry us back to things eternal. These are the very signs by which the Word has chosen to work our redemption. And so these signs, in their relation to the human flesh of Christ, are included within the work of incarnation; in assuming human nature for the redemption of the world, the Word wills precisely that these signs should point to Her incarnate life in precisely the way they do.

Secondly, this semiotic ordering of all things to Christ's human flesh is *itself* part of the Son's mission – it shows us who the Son is in eternity. Namely, it shows us that the Son is the one through whom all things have been made, and of whom all things are likenesses. After discussing how all things in creation have either testified to the mission of the Son or have been that mission itself (namely, the assumed human flesh), Augustine continues, "Some testimonies foretold that he was going to come, some testified that he had come. It was only fitting that when he through whom every creature was made became a creature himself, all creation should bear

---

[36] Cf. Is. 63.3. So Augustine at *en.Ps.* 8.2: "The divine Word can also be understood as a grape. Even the Lord has been described as a cluster of grapes, which those who were sent on ahead by the people of Israel brought from the land of promise, hanging on a stick like a victim of crucifixion. Therefore when the divine Word takes over the sound of the human voice in order to speak and reach the ears of his hearers, the content of the Word is encased like wine within the sound of the voice which, in turn, is like grapeskins."

witness to him."[37] In manifesting the Word to creation, Christ also manifests the dependence of all creation upon the Word. The regime of signs is itself the revelation of the participation of all things in the Word, and the providential ordering of all things by the *Sapientia* – the Wisdom – of God.[38] All things exist and are providentially ordered within created history through their participation in the Word. When the Word becomes manifest in history in the human flesh of Christ, this participation *itself* becomes manifest. It is no longer sufficient that all things should serve as likenesses of the Word in His divine nature; each thing must also offer a likeness of the human life in which that Word is revealed.

Consequently, we must understand the work of incarnation as extending far beyond the historical particularity of Christ's life, encompassing all his relations to every creature that ever has or ever will exist. In the particularity of this human flesh, the work of incarnation is properly universal. Each creature testifies to the mission of the Son, and so each creature may point us to Her: not only the doves sacrificed in the temple, but all those animals that lived and died as part of the evolutionary history of Christ's human nature; not only the Syrophoenician woman, but each woman whose faith and love show us the face of Christ; not only his shattered body on the Cross, but all those victims of oppression whose bodies are subjected to humiliation and political violence. There you have what the Son of God has been sent for; indeed, there you have what it is for the Son of God to have been sent.

***

---

[37] *trin.* 4.19.25; WSA I/5, 171.

[38] Cf. *trin.* 4.20.27: "The Son of course is the Father's Word, which is also called his Wisdom"; and *doct. chr.* 1.11.12; WSA I/11, 111: of Wisdom, "She is present everywhere, indeed, to inner eyes that are healthy and pure; but to those whose inner eyes are weak and unclean, she was prepared to be seen by their eyes of flesh as well." On the importance of this trinitarian name, see Rowan Williams, *On Augustine*, Chapter 7, where he writes that "the unifying principle of Augustine's mature Christology is the understanding of Christ as *sapientia*" (142).

In his humanity, then, Christ is the mediator between God and humanity, revealing the Father to us alongside the Holy Spirit.[39] But how does this revelation purify (*purgat*) us, as Augustine consistently emphasizes? In *De trinitate* 4, the answer is at best skeletal. At the heart of his account there is the relation between participation (*participatio*) and illumination (*illuminatio*). Participation, as I have discussed it so far, principally refers to the creation's relation of dependence upon and likeness to God. What it is for a creature to be the sort of thing it is, is for it to participate in God in the manner that God gives it to exist. This is true not only of our constitution as creatures, but of the specific likenesses we bear to God. If I am like God in that I am able to know the world, my intellect serves as a likeness of God as it participates in Him – "Our enlightenment is to participate in the Word, that is, in that *life which is the light of men* (Jn 1.4)."[40] My intellect serves most truly as a likeness of God – it participates in Him most fully – when it knows the world truly, and ultimately, when it contemplates as fully as it is able the divine nature itself. Yet this is only possible by the grace of God's self-offering, shedding the light of His own presence upon the soul and calling us to loving contemplation of the Truth of the divine life.[41] To the extent we receive this knowledge through our intellects' participation in God, our minds are illuminated by God's own knowledge of the world.[42]

---

[39] Augustine discusses the revelatory work of the Holy Spirit and their common source in the Father at *trin.* 4.20.29–4.21.31. Only the Son reveals the eternal life of God in Her own person: As Augustine writes of the Spirit's revelation of God, "these visible manifestations were not coupled with him into one person, like the flesh the Word became" (*trin.* 4.21.30; WSA I/5, 175).

[40] *trin.* 4.2.4; WSA I/5, 154–155. For an early discussion of truths about creation being a likeness to God, see *vera rel.* 36.66.

[41] Williams, *On Augustine*, 180–181.

[42] So Lydia Schumacher, *Divine Illumination: The History and Future of Augustine's Theory of Knowledge* (Oxford: Wiley-Blackwell, 2011), 65: "the illumination of Christ does not bear on cognition in any way that undermines the autonomy or integrity of the intellect but in a way that reinstates it, at least for the intellect that stokes rather than extinguishes His light through a decision to work with faith in Him. On

Yet, as Augustine notes in *De trinitate* 4.2.4, our minds are *prorsus inhabile* for this sort of contemplation – utterly incapable. The possibility of a mind perfectly receiving knowledge of the world and of God through the gift of illumination has been foreclosed to us as a result of sin. Our intellects have been darkened, and our knowledge of God and the world has become distorted and unreliable. What is needed, then, is a different sort of participation, a redemptive participation in our own sinful condition, and this is precisely what the Word's assumption of human flesh effects.[43] Augustine speaks of Christ's healing our dissimilarity from God's holiness as a result of sin through "a kind of curative accord or symmetry,"[44] resolving our discordance into "a harmony of salvation (*concinat ad salutem*)."[45]

At one level, this harmony of salvation seems to refer to the whole regime of signs. All things point to Christ's participation in our human condition, all things refer us to the one in whom God is revealed.[46] More narrowly, however, it is the humility and sacrifice

Augustine's account, all that comes to the intellect from the outside is the power to be renewed on the inside; this is the power to illumine the divine being that is received through divine illumination – the power to know like God and thus know God ... unless God gives the capacity to know Him and it is used to the end of knowing Him, there is no such thing as knowing or knowledge at all." Augustine's writings on illumination are especially knotty; in addition to Schumacher's book, see Gerard O'Daly, *Augustine's Philosophy of Mind* (London: Gerald Duckworth, 1987), 199–207; and Robert Dodaro, "Light in the Thought of St. Augustine," in *Light from Light: Scientists and Theologians in Dialogue*, ed. Gerald O'Collins and Mary Ann Meyers (Grand Rapids, MI: Wm B. Eerdmans, 2012), 195–207.

43 Cf. *trin.* 4.2.4; WSA I/5, 155: "he applied the similarity of his humanity to take away the dissimilarity of our iniquity, and becoming a partaker (*particeps*) of our mortality he made us partakers (*participes*) of his divinity." Jonathan D. Teubner has carefully examined the sense of *participatio* at issue in *trin.* 4 at Jonathan D. Teubner, *Prayer after Augustine: A Study in the Development of the Latin Tradition* (Oxford: Oxford University Press, 2018), 97–103. My account differs from his principally in emphasizing the relation of this account in *trin.* 4 to Augustine's broader discussions of creation's existence by participation in God.

44 *trin.* 4.3.6; WSA I/5, 157.

45 *trin.* 4.3.5; WSA I/5, 155.

46 This seems to be one implication of the long section in *trin.* 4 where Augustine discusses Christ's "single" matching our "double" (*trin.* 4.3.5). *Trin.* 4.4.7–4.6.10 go on

of Christ that draws us into this healing symmetry. The Cross is the tonic note of Christ's "single," the root tone that allows our lives to be set in their proper harmonic interval through relation to his: "being clothed with mortal flesh, in that alone he died and in that alone he rose again; and so in that alone he harmonized with each part of us by becoming in that flesh the sacrament for the inner man and the model for the outer one."[47] Pride of place is given in *De trinitate* 4 to the language of *exemplum, sacramentum,* and *sacrificium*:[48] in both his death and resurrection, the great mystery of Christ's sacrifice serves as sacrament of the inner human and model for the outer.

For the outer human, Christ's death teaches that we need not fear the sufferings that others may inflict on our flesh. And if Christ's willing acceptance of death serves as an *exemplum* for us, then so too is his resurrection a model of our own: In the disciples "being shown the complete integrity of his flesh" through being able to touch the risen body of Christ (cf. Lk 24.39, Jn 20.28), they receive "a demonstration of what he had said elsewhere to encourage them, *Not a hair of your heads will perish* (Lk 21.28)."[49]

For the inner human, it is the sacrament of Christ's humble self-offering that is primary, though Augustine is under no illusions about the difficulty involved in tearing ourselves away from the worldly things to which we have attached ourselves through sinful desire. He tells us, "By the crucifixion of the inner man is to be

at great length about not only the harmony of Christ's body, but about the many numbers contained in Scripture and indeed mathematical relations themselves, all of which he believes have something to teach us about Christ.

[47] *trin.* 4.3.6; WSA I/5, 156.

[48] As Basil Studer notes, the pairing of the terms *sacramentum* and *exemplum* is relatively rare in Augustine's thought outside the *De trinitate*; "Sacramentum et Exemplum chez saint Augustin," *Recherches Augustiniennes* 10 (1975): 87–141, 101.

[49] *trin.* 4.3.6; WSA I/5, 157. Robert Dodaro notes that the exemplarity of Christ's crucifixion itself centers for the most part on assuaging our fear of death and suffering at "Christus iustus and Fear of Death in Augustine's Dispute with Pelagius," in *Signum pietatis: Festgabe für Cornelius P. Mayer OSA zum 60 Geburtstag*, ed. A. Zumkeller (Würzburg, 1989), 341–361.

understood the sorrows of repentance and a kind of salutary torment of self-discipline, a kind of death to erase the death of ungodliness in which God does not leave us," and this is complemented by an understanding of the Resurrection as a "sacrament of our inner resurrection" in which we learn to seek eternal things by means of Christ's flesh.[50]

In each case, then, Christ's death as *sacramentum* of the inner human and *exemplum* of the outer has a twofold purpose, both teaching us about our present condition and calling us to a new one.[51] Augustine's description of our present state places us squarely within a series of contrasts between the present age and the age to come. We cannot yet see God, but we have been given sights to trust in faith. We have not yet suffered the death which we owe as a result of sin, yet we find life already being renewed in us. It is a movement from the old to the new that we find ourselves within, and critically, Augustine understands the union of divine and human natures in Christ as the key presupposition of the redemptive efficacy of these signs.[52]

Yet much remains underdetermined here. How, precisely, does Augustine understand faith, and how does trusting in these signs heal us of the effects of sin? If our problem is that we are unable to know God or the things of the world truly, how can God's presenting these signs to us occasion our redemption? Perhaps most pressingly of all, how can *any* created sign succeed in pointing us to a God who remains invisible?

***

---

[50] *trin.* 4.3.6; WSA I/5, 156.

[51] Cf. Studer "*Sacramentum et Exemplum*," 102 (trans. mine): "The sacrament of the inner man refers to the fact that in baptism man dies to sin and recalls at the same time of the obligation to take up a new life. Likewise, the example of the inner man invites one to rise above the fear of bodily death and announces at the same time the resurrection of the body. Sacrament and example are thus both signs which demonstrate and oblige."

[52] Cf. Teubner, *Prayer after Augustine*, 101–102.

These are precisely the questions that motivate Augustine's later discussions in *De trinitate*. "Faith," he writes at the beginning of that book, "is needed by which to believe what cannot be seen."[53] Inasmuch as it is an act of belief, faith involves both the intellect and will, as the intellect entertains a thought and the will assents to belief in it.[54] But how can any created intellectual object or any act of will directed toward it lead us back to God?

To answer this question, it will be necessary to look briefly at the account of the intentionality of our knowing – put differently, the relation between knowing and loving – that Augustine offers in *De trinitate* 11 and 12.

In our intentional perception, the will is that which directs our eyes to certain objects, focusing our attention and struggling to make out details in what we see with greater precision. In at least the voluntary acts of perception through which the will directs sight to perceive some object in the world, "Perhaps we can say that sight is the end and resting place of the will" – the will desires knowledge of something in the world, and sight is the vehicle by which the soul is united to the object of the will's desire.[55]

Yet this process can quickly become more complicated: "the will to see the window has as its end the sight of the window; the will to see passers-by through the window is another will joined onto this one, and again its end is the sight of passers-by."[56] If I wish to see the people walking by outside, I know I must look through the window; yet it is the window to which I turn my eyes, not to the passers-by who may or may not even be outside. Nevertheless, in this process, the window becomes epistemically (as well as, to a greater or lesser

---

[53] *trin.* 13.1.2; WSA I/5, 343.

[54] *praed.sanct.* 2.5; WSA I/26, 151: "although certain thoughts fly quickly, even most swiftly, before the will to believe, and the will follows so soon afterward that it accompanies it as if it were united to it, it is, nonetheless, necessary that thought precedes everything which we believe. In fact, the very act of believing is nothing other than to think with assent."

[55] *trin.* 11.6.10; WSA I/5, 311.

[56] *trin.* 11.6.10; WSA I/5, 312.

degree, physically) transparent to me; in many cases, I am not even conscious of perceiving the window, only of perceiving the objects I desire to see through it. In such cases, the window figures in my sight as a sort of weigh-station, simply passing my vision on to its eventual objects. Yet the window's transparency is not the only model that Augustine provides for how a thing may direct our will to another end. Sometimes, the will simply touches on the object lightly, like a foot rests on a patch of soil in order to launch itself toward another end. More intimately, Augustine allows that our will may delight in a thing, and in its very delight be referred on to a still greater end.[57]

Yet it is the will – the soul's activity of desiring – that directs our sight from one object to the next. If I desire to see the tree through the window, under normal circumstances I am able to do so. But this desire can be subtly derailed; if the window is so dirty as to be a distraction, the window itself can fill the horizon of my sight, drawing my attention to itself and derailing my intent to look at the tree. I can become mired in the ground I was walking upon, or so delight in an object of my affections that it fills the horizon of my desire, not directing me to any other greater end. Augustine imagines a chain of loves in which the will may (or may fail to) be referred from one to the next:

> Now all wills or wishes are straight, and all the ones linked with them too, if the one to which they are all referred is good; but if that is bent then they are all bent. And thus a sequence of straight wishes or wills is a ladder for those who would climb to happiness, to be negotiated by definite steps; but a skein of bent and twisted wishes or wills is a rope to bind anyone who acts so, and have him *cast into outer darkness* (Mt 8.12).[58]

---

[57] *trin.* 11.6.10; WSA I/5, 312: "If however something pleases the will in such a way that it rests in it with a certain delight, and yet is not the thing it is tending toward but is also referred to something else, it should be thought of not as the home country of a citizen but as refreshment, or even a night's lodging for a traveler."

[58] *trin.* 11.6.10; WSA I/5, 312.

Accordingly, the way that we love temporal things stands in continuity with our love of eternal things. Just as, in perceiving the dirty window, I can be distracted from my desire to see the people walking outside and settle on the window itself as the object of my attention, so also attachment to worldly things can prevent us from rising through the *similitudines* of finite creation to contemplation of the God who is their source. The ascent to God is propelled or hindered by the cooperation of our intellect and will. The will, encompassing both intentionality and desire, directs our intellects to bodily things: "If it does this well, it does it in order to refer them to the highest good as their end; if badly, in order to enjoy them as goods of a sort it can take its ease in with an illusory happiness."[59]

This transitory satisfaction is all that is presently possible for us. Because we love the things of the world wrongly, we are confined to knowledge of the temporal objects of our experience, or fragmentary glimpses of the eternal realities underlying them in, for instance, meditation on mathematical truths or in brief moments of illumination like that described at *Confessions* 7.17.23 – nothing like the stable contemplation that would allow us to persist in beatific knowledge of God.[60]

On the basis of this account of the defection of our intellect as a result of a sinful will, Augustine draws a distinction between two types of knowledge. The first, that which is almost entirely impossible for us in the condition of sin, is the *contemplatio rebus aeternorum* that Augustine calls *sapientia*, or wisdom. The sort of knowledge proper to our present state is *scientia*, the "action by which we make good use of temporal things" (*actio qua bene utimur temporalibus rebus*).[61] This is the knowledge that we attain through faith in the temporal signs God has given us – which is to say, knowledge consequent upon an act of the will that has been formed

---

[59] *trin.* 12.12.17; WSA I/5, 331–332.
[60] Cf. Luigi Gioia, *The Theological Epistemology of Augustine's De Trinitate* (Oxford: Oxford University Press, 2008), 224.
[61] *trin.* 12.14.22; WSA I/5, 334.

and enlivened by the Spirit's work – and which gives us the object of assent that the will moves toward.[62] As we assent to the truth of what God has taught us in these signs, our wills gradually begin to climb the ladder back to the contemplation of eternal things. Our wills move first in belief, and as we believe in what God has done, so we are taught to long for the one who has accomplished these things but remains invisible to us now. Yet, to anticipate the account of the reformation of our wills I will give in Chapter 8, even these signs are not sufficient in themselves to draw our hearts back to God. Knowledge of the Word's acts in the life of Christ must be matched by the Holy Spirit's presence enlivening our affections, as we find that the work of God presented to us in external signs is the same activity present within us and purifying our affections.[63]

That both *scientia* and *sapientia* can be considered species of a broader sense of "knowledge" is seen in Augustine's quotation of 1 Corinthians 13.12 immediately after introducing the distinction: "Now I know in part, but then I shall know even as I am known."[64] This is clear enough with respect to our eschatological contemplation of God – whatever we go on to say about what it means to see God, our hope is that we will see Her face to face. Inasmuch as our *scientia* of temporal things is direct knowledge, it is knowledge of the created signs, not of God. In coming to know these created signs, however, we are able to make use of them because they point beyond themselves and back to God; our direct knowledge of these signs enables our belief in the God still invisible.

---

[62] Cf. Han-Luen Kantzer Komline, *Augustine on the Will: A Theological Account* (Oxford: Oxford University Press, 2020), 181: "God must intervene to connect the human agent with the good, that is, with God, first epistemologically and then volitionally. Without God forging these connections, which have been severed by the fall, the objective reality of the good itself will not be enough to draw a person to it."

[63] Cf. Teubner, *Prayer after Augustine*, 102: "Christ's single divine agency harmoniously animates the needlessly complex (because temporally enacted) movement from *homo interior* to *homo exterior*." See also the discussion of the Holy Spirit's work in *trin.* 13 at pp. 103–107.

[64] *trin.* 12.14.22; WSA I/5, 334.

Here again, we see the importance of faith, for some of the most important signs established within the temporal order to point us to God cannot themselves be directly known, but only believed. I can only believe that Deborah was judge over Israel, or that Solomon built the temple from the cedars of Lebanon, for these signs are not present to me. Nevertheless, to the extent that I am conscious of my belief in these realities, the presence of faith in me comes to serve as an object of direct knowledge, similarly focusing our affections. As Augustine writes, "every man sees [it] to be in his heart if he believes, or not to be there if he does not believe."[65] Comparatively rarer (if perhaps still abundant) are the signs of God that I am both able to discern and know directly: the icon on the church wall; the face of my neighbor; the chanted psalm; perhaps paradigmatically, the conse-crated eucharistic host; and most intimately, the faith created in my heart by the Holy Spirit.[66]

To summarize, as our wills are reformed by the Spirit's work, we come to know and love the signs God has given us to direct us to Him; as we come to recognize the signs of God's self-communication, we are given the opportunity to assent to what God teaches us in faith. This faith must be distinguished from the sight that we hope for in the eschaton, but it creates in us the true knowledge of *scientia* even in the absence of *sapientia*. Nevertheless, this knowledge offers us an object of assent that may begin referring our affections back along the long way to God. As we come to desire God by the power of the Spirit, we come to know more of who God is; and as we come to know more of who God is and how God has worked – even if this knowledge is only in faith – our desire for God may grow recursively.

The central importance of Christ's life as a redemptive sign is that he is both the object of *scientia* and *sapientia* – though we cannot

---

[65] *trin.* 13.1.3; WSA I/5, 343.
[66] Karmen MacKendrick offers a helpful discussion of the conversion of knowledge of the sign to love of the sign's referent using the category of the "seductiveness" of signs; see MacKendrick, *Divine Enticements: Theological Seductions* (New York: Fordham University Press, 2013).

now know him with the intimacy of contemplation, in knowing and loving him as the object of faith, we have to do with none other than the one we will adore in eternity. Christ is for Augustine the clearest and most complete image of who God is possible within the created order, offering us a focal point for our desires. If we wish to love God, we are told to love this one, to trust in him and long for his presence within us; and we are taught to believe that, by turning our loves to this one point in history, all our other loves will slowly come to be ordered around him, and so properly ordered to God. The more we turn our desires to this one, the more we find him lovable, and inexhaustibly so; he is the one created thing that we stand in no risk of loving inordinately, because he is to be loved absolutely. In the humility of the Incarnation and Crucifixion, the Word gives us signs teaching us that the man Jesus is to be loved as God; and throughout the Christian life, we find that the more we love him, the more our deepened knowledge of him calls forth an even greater measure of love from us.

Christ is, in the words Goulven Madec draws from Augustine, both *la patrie et la voie* – the homeland toward which we journey, and the way that leads there.[67] In our weakened condition, it is the significatory effects of Christ's life to which we must cling; Augustine reminds us that "all these things that the Word made flesh did and suffered for us in time and space belong, according to the distinction we have undertaken to illustrate, to knowledge (*scientia*) and not to wisdom (*sapientia*)."[68] All the moments of Christ's life – his birth in a stable, his first tentative steps, his teaching at the temple, through to the devastation of the Cross and the bewildering event of Resurrection – all this has been for the purpose of turning our eyes heavenward, giving us the end toward which we can direct our desire in the confidence that our loves will carry our minds back to God. In meditating upon his acts

[67] Goulven Madec, *Le Christ de Saint Augustin: La Patrie et la Voie, nouvelle édition* (Paris: Descleé, 2001).

[68] *trin.* 13.19.24; WSA I/5, 362.

recorded in Scripture, we come to know in faith truths that are not yet manifest in sight, because they are hidden with the invisible Word: the triune life of God, as the man Jesus relates to Father and Holy Spirit through the course of his life; the true union of both divine and human natures in the one person of Christ; the duality of his divine and human wills in his one incarnate life; even, as the Seventh Ecumenical Council declared, the representability of his flesh, the shocking fact of God being able to be depicted without idolatry. All these are truths held in faith, known as *scientia* in order that we might come to know God and desire Him more.

What stands on the other side of this course, as our faith is converted to sight? Augustine's answer is decisive:

> Our knowledge therefore is Christ, and our wisdom is the same Christ (*scientia ergo nostra Christus est, sapientia quoque nostra idem Christus est*). It is he who plants faith in us about temporal things, he who presents us with the truth about eternal things. Through him we go straight toward him, through knowledge toward wisdom, without ever turning aside from one and the same Christ, *in whom are hidden all the treasures of wisdom and knowledge* (Col. 2.3).[69]

By now, it will be apparent the extent to which this conclusion depends upon the personal unity of divine and human natures in Christ – only if the sign of Christ's flesh is in unity with the person of the Word can we truly say that the same one is both knowledge and wisdom. At the heart of Augustine's piety is the sense that Christ can be trusted to draw us back to God: that he dwells within us as the inner teacher, enabling us to see any truth that we can glimpse in this world; that he has disposed all things in such a way that they point from the constitution of their being to God, if only we can learn to see it; and that, when all these signs have served their purpose and we behold the face of God, Christ will remain with us. Faith and hope pass away, but love does not, for Love is Christ Jesus.

---

[69] *trin.* 13.19.24; WSA I/5, 363–364.

As Augustine writes at *trin.* 4.18.24: "now we accord faith to the things done in time for our sakes, and are purified by it; in order that when we come to sight and truth succeeds to faith, eternity might likewise succeed to mortality."[70]

***

Again, let us take stock of the systematic implications of this way of viewing Christ's redemptive work. At base, we find here a description of Christ's place in the order of love. As a good deal of recent Augustinian theology has noted, Christ is the center of the order of love; it is in loving him that our hearts are conformed to the love of God.[71] More than that, we are to love all the things of the world in such a manner that our loves will be referred to him, so that we may love the creature who makes the God whom he is visible.[72]

Yet this picture allows us to see the work of redemption in its full scope. This *dispensatio similitudinum* – what I have called the regime of signs – is not extrinsic to the work of redemption. If it is Christ's human flesh that reveals the invisible God to us and draws our hearts to Her, it is this dispensation of creaturely likenesses that turns our hearts to Christ in his concrete particularity. In calling Christ the *Sapientia* of God, Augustine tells us not only that Jesus is the *patria* to which we hope to return and which we will contemplate eternally; Jesus is also the Wisdom of God that has providentially ordered all created signs to point back to Her. And so, if it is the redemption of the world that the Son wills in assuming flesh, She wills to work this redemption not solely through the preeminent sign of Her own human life, but through all the other signs that refer our loves to this center. From all eternity, the Word

---

[70] WSA I/5, 169–170.

[71] Especially significant here has been Eric Gregory, *Politics and the Order of Love: An Augustinian Ethic of Democratic Citizenship* (Chicago, IL: University of Chicago Press, 2008). See his discussion of the *uti/frui* distinction in Augustine (324–357), and especially his treatment of Christ's centrality within the order of love (327–330).

[72] Cf. *doctr. chr.* 1.33.37.

has willed that these creatures, in their relation to Christ, have a part to play in our redemption.

Though rendered in terms of the order of our loves, we should not let this recognition lapse into an abstraction – it concerns the beating heart of Christian piety. It tells us that each crucifix cut out of a tree is willed by God from before the foundation of the world to point to Christ; that every stone set into a country chapel, or each piece of drywall decorating the spare interior of a strip-mall church exist in part so that they may serve as signs of the Incarnate. Yet this is true not only of evident signs of devotion: It is no less true of the street sign at the end of your road, or of the stocked shelves at one's local supermarket. Not all of these in fact succeed at pointing us back to Christ, at present; I will have more to say in later chapters of why this is the case, and how we might come to see them in their place within the redemptive *dispensatio similitudinum*. Yet we should affirm that inasmuch as these things exist, they exist as signs of Christ's flesh – they exist as signs that may yet draw our hearts back to God. This is part of what it is for each thing to be the creature that it is; they are disposed by the Word for this very purpose from the foundation of their being. Theology must do more to reflect on the lived experience of those drawn to the love of Christ. If we actually speak to the faithful in the pews, I suspect we will find that our hearts are turned to the love of God at least as much by what seems a coincidence as they are by the oldest and grandest prayers of the Church. Sometimes, all we need is a well-timed child's voice: *Take and read, take and read.*

If this is the case, though – if all this is included in the Word's providential disposition of created history, if all these significatory relations are intended to point us back to Christ's flesh – all this must be included in the work of incarnation. Through the imitation of Christ, we become like Christ. But this is not all: In becoming like him, we become the very likenesses by which he redeems us – and in so doing, accomplishes and assumes the full shape of his *own* identity, becomes the Redeemer. The likenesses our lives become and the redemptive work he accomplishes through them tell us *who Christ is*, and *make him thus*. He is not only the Galilean rabbi walking along the coast of Tiberias, he is also the one who wills to save us through many and varied means of grace: the child's voice telling us to read; the grand chorale that moves our spirit heavenward; the tacky print of a doe-eyed Christ in a church basement that breaks down our defenses during a twelve-step meeting. All of these compose the identity of the Christ who is our Redeemer, because they (and many other signs) are how he redeems us. And if our redemption will only be perfected when all creatures signify to us the incarnate Wisdom who created them, then we must say that the existence of all creatures, and the agency and causality of the created order, are drawn into God's redemptive work. Precisely in being employed to effect our salvation, they are included within the work of incarnation – they are included within the Word's will to assume human flesh, to become the particular historical person Jesus Christ, who is the true sign of God to which all signs point. *This* is how Jesus wills to redeem us: by relating our lives to his; by assuming a human flesh to which our lives may point. This, too, is the work of incarnation.

This is not alien to or outside the Word's act of assuming our nature. As Graham Ward has written, "Redemption is the fulfillment of the economy of the incarnation ... Jesus is the Christ only in relation to other human beings; the act of redemption is a relational act; Christology needs to pay more attention not only to the identity of the God-man, but to the redemptive operation effected in and through this complex co-abiding."[73] Christ's own identity is at issue here, his identity as the Redeemer, the one who wills and accomplishes the salvation of all things. Though he wills this redemption from all eternity, he accomplishes it only through his human flesh, precisely as it is related to the signs of him that are the created order.

[73] Graham Ward, *Christ and Culture* (Oxford: Wiley-Blackwell, 2005), 106.

We should distinguish this claim, however, from a philosophical account that would make all these relations intrinsic to Christ himself. As John Heil writes,

> A view of this kind implies that objects have all of their properties essentially: if Socrates has a bruise on his left shin, he could not have failed to have a bruise on his left shin. Why? A change in a single property of a single object changes relations among every object. Objects in Socrates' world would no longer be related in endless ways to bruised Socrates. So, whatever is, is what is of necessity and could not have been otherwise.[74]

Better, Heil thinks, to distinguish between internal and external relations: It is an internal relation that the number 6 be greater than 5, but it is an external relation that Simmias is taller than Socrates. Had Simmias failed to exist (with the relation of Simmias' being taller than Socrates consequently failing to obtain), Socrates himself would be no different. We may – and should – distinguish between such internal and external relations in Christ; he does not necessarily possess all the qualities or relations that are his own. Yet we should observe how many of these external relations offer us the signs by which we are redeemed: He does not necessarily call Peter and Andrew, but he does, and this has been critical for the historical development of the churches in which so many worship each Sunday; he does not necessarily meet the Syrophoenician woman, but he does, and his sense of calling is changed by the encounter; he does not necessarily hang upon the Cross, but he does, and death is put to death as a result. It is quite possible to say – particularly in awareness that all things hold together in him, that he is the sign to which all signs refer – that *all* the "extrinsic" relations he bears throughout creation potentially signify him; and further, that the fullness of our redemption requires that they do in fact come to signify him

---

[74] John Heil, "Relations," in *The Routledge Companion to Metaphysics*, eds. Robin Le Poidevin, Peter Simons, Andrew McGonigal, and Ross P. Cameron (London: Routledge, 2009), 310–321, 313.

concretely for us. In this case, the relations he bears throughout the whole of the created order are necessary not properly to him *qua* human, but to the work of redemption he accomplishes – and thus, to his enacted identity as the Redeemer of the world.

There is, then, nothing strictly necessary about the shape of these relations; indeed, it is not beyond the power of God to save us in another manner entirely, without any need for our lives to play a role in drawing our hearts back to God. Yet this is the way the triune Lord *has* willed to redeem us. Not only Christ's humanity, but the lives and existence of both the human and nonhuman world are made the instruments through which God accomplishes the redemption of the world. Even more strongly, each creature that plays a part in giving Christ's life its redemptive shape assumes an *unsubstitutable* role in God's redemptive work.

Were these unsubstitutable signs different – had St. Bartholomew never met Christ, or had there been no swine grazing in the region of the Gerasenes – the shape of Christ's life would have been different, and would thus have redemptively pointed humanity back to God in a slightly different manner. The difference for Christ's own human life in these instances might have been small (though the former might have made the history of the Church in India very different, and even the latter would alter any number of Christian works of art, allegorical exegeses, or resonances of seeing pigs in the course of our daily lives), but we can appreciate something of the scope of this point if we try to imagine a Christ not born to Mary, or not born to the people of Abraham. While the power of God gives Christ's life its redemptive efficacy, we should not underestimate the extent to which these creatures give to Christ's life its redemptive shape. Here again, we may say that, while God might have brought about the redemption of the world through Christ's flesh under many different conditions, in fact God has willed to effect the reconciliation of sinful humanity only in *this* way – God has willed that redemption should be complete only with the creatures that give Christ's life its shape.

Yet to this point, we have been speaking of the redemptive shape of Christ's life as if he were any other human person: living in a particular place and time, bounded by birth and death. If Christ is risen, if Christ still abides with the Church, if Christ may validly be considered as the *totus Christus* uniting head and body, then we will need to revise this estimation. If Christ's human life continues still today, and if his human agency continues to work redemption through the Church which is his body, then his life is *still being given* its shape through the work of his body in the world. As the redeemer of the world, the full shape of Christ's life – the relations his human flesh enters into, the outworking of his human will in the world – must include all those acts by which human desires are drawn back to God through the sole mediator of Christ's humanity. The shape of Christ's human life will only be complete eschatologically, as all the redeemed enter into the intimacy of life in him.

Christ cannot himself be fully the redeemer unless and until the full scope of God's redemptive will is accomplished in humanity.[75] All the created signs that God uses to point to the flesh of Christ – the one sign that is both our true home (*patria*) and the way that leads there (*via*), both *scientia* and *sapientia* – are drawn into the work of incarnation by which Christ's life receives its redemptive shape. These signs play an unsubstitutable role in accomplishing the

---

[75] So Ward, *Christ and Culture*, 149: "Jesus Christ as God incarnate can of himself only reveal to the extent he is recognised; he can only reconcile and redeem all to the extent he is responded to. Christology begins with the operation of Christ 'between'"; and Niels Henrik Gregersen, "*Cur deus caro*: Jesus and the Cosmos Story," *Theology and Science* 11.4 (2013), 389: "the cosmic relations are co-constitutive of Christ. In this view, the incarnate Christ cannot at all be the incarnate Logos, *unless* he is internally related to the cosmos at large; one cannot make a division between Christ and the cosmos, once they have obtained their internal relations. Expressed in theological language, Jesus could not be savior without actually being there for those who are to be saved by him. Just as a message cannot be a gospel, unless it is actually good news for people, so the body of Christ cannot be genuinely incarnate apart from the entire nexus of the world of Energy, Matter, and Information."

work of reconciliation, and so of making it the case that Christ is in fact the redeemer of the world.

Put provocatively, in the spirit of the shocking and paradoxical statements that play so important a role in Augustine's nativity sermons: Jesus is a divine-human person in virtue of the act of incarnation, but he is only the Redeemer in virtue of the work of incarnation. He is human because the Word has assumed human nature, but he is the human that he is – the Christ of God – only with us and alongside us, as we are redeemed in him and granted a role in furthering his redemptive work. In its own life, the body of Christ fills up all that is lacking in the sufferings of Christ – not because Christ's work is insufficient, but because God has willed that Christ's redemption should be complete *with* us, making use of our lives and agency to accomplish the salvation of the world.[76]

Following after Augustine's insights, we may see in the theology of the *totus Christus* something far bolder than a mere metaphor or hermeneutical strategy. There is a real union that exists between Christ and the created world, as his human flesh is determined by its relations to the human and nonhuman world around it.[77] So too is there a real extension of Christ's human life in the life of the Church, as (in a manner still to be worked out) his human agency increasingly works through the lives of those joined to him by the Spirit. As Body is joined to Head, not only is the heavenly city reconciled to God, but the shape of Christ's human life is completed as others are drawn into relation to him, serving as signs of God by pointing others to his humanity. Because the flesh of Christ still lives and continues to make an active difference in the world, the final shape of Christ's life that the Word eternally wills to assume must still be worked out, as the infant in Bethlehem had still to

---

[76] Augustine deploys Colossians 1.24 as a Pauline affirmation of the *totus Christus* at, *inter alia*, *s. Dolbeau* 22.20, *en.Ps.* 61.4, and *en.Ps.* 86.5; see Chapter 11, below, for more extensive consideration of the christological significance of this verse.

[77] Cf. DeHart's description of "the fusion of Jesus and his followers into a single event of meaning or symbolic communication"; *Unspeakable Cults*, 111.

become the Galilean rabbi. Only with his body is Christ fully the one who accomplishes the salvation of the world, the one whose name is above all names, the one before whom every knee will bow. Before this end without end, there is an important sense in which the work of incarnation remains unfinished. Jesus and the Church together make one whole Christ, for he has willed that his life should not be complete without theirs.

7 | The Work of the Cross

The Cross is the center of the work of redemption, for Augustine no less than for the majority of the Western Christian tradition.[1] It is, as St. Paul writes, the act of righteousness that leads to justification and life for all, the death which communicates life to us as we are baptized into it; we are crucified with Christ, and so he lives in us. It is through the blood of the Cross that God has reconciled all things to Herself, and Christ's sufferings are completed in us as we fill up in our bodies what is lacking in them. We are meant to know nothing but Christ, and him crucified. At the last day, we will.

To speak of Augustine's "theology of the Cross," however, or even an "Augustinian theology of the Cross," is no simple matter.[2]

---

[1] I have preferred the language of "work of redemption" over the many other options that the Christian tradition provides – reconciliation, atonement, and so on – as I believe it best conveys the full scope of the implications of Augustine's christology. While the Atonement is clearly a central concern of this chapter in particular, attention to the "work of redemption" broadens the focus beyond the question of what is accomplished on the Cross to include the Holy Spirit's work in the life of the believer and in the Body of Christ (as we will see in the next several chapters). Reconciliation, while essential to Augustine's account of redemption, does not as effectively communicate the true victory and overthrow of sin accomplished through Christ's life. For my purposes, the essential feature of the language of "redemption" is not the economic metaphor, but the reality of liberation from a hostile oppressive force, and a fundamental alteration in the state of one's being. See, for instance, the way the language of redemption functions in the texts from Isaiah Richard Hays has collected at *Reading Backwards: Figural Christology and the Fourfold Gospel Witness* (Waco, TX: Baylor University Press, 2014), 73: Is. 41.14; Is. 43.14–5; Is. 44.24, 26b; Is. 49.7.

[2] John Cavadini has arguably come closest; see his "Jesus' Death Is Real: An Augustinian Spirituality of the Cross," in *The Cross in Christian Tradition: From Paul to Bonaventure*, ed. Elizabeth A. Dreyer (New York: Paulist Press, 2000), 169–191. Also

Even measured against the standard of his christological reflection, Augustine's discussions of Christ's crucifixion are especially unsystematic. This is, it must be said, more a feature than a bug. Augustine makes use of all the resources at his disposal to describe this mystery. John Cavadini has outlined the many different metaphors Augustine employs to describe the significance of Christ's passion – the Cross as mousetrap, lampstand, classroom, boat, a "tree of silly fruit."[3] Each of these metaphors conveys a slightly different theological emphasis, and would need to be considered fully if we were to pursue a synoptic view of Augustine's theology of the Cross. Attempting to bring systematic order to such a diverse range of theological expressions can only be a betrayal of the nuances and discontinuities of Augustine's reflections on the Crucifixion – a betrayal that this book has been perpetrating, to a greater or lesser extent, all along.

Such treachery may be required, however (or at least permitted), by fidelity to the object of contemplation on which Augustine focused ever more intently throughout his career as priest and bishop: the mystery of the Cross. Like all the *sacramenta* by which God draws human loves back to Himself, the Cross both reveals our redemption and effects that very redemption in its being revealed. It would be a mistake to carve this too neatly into categories of "subjective" or "objective" effects – precisely in transforming our subjectivity, Christ's sacrifice objectively draws us back to God. Even so, there is a distinction to be drawn in the vicinity. The Cross is, on the one hand, the *sacramentum par excellence*, the very heart of the significatory economy by which our loves are led

instructive are Matthew Drever, "Images of Suffering in Augustine and Luther," *Dialog: A Journal of Theology* 51.1 (2012): 71–82; and Matthew Drever, "Entertaining Violence: Augustine on the Cross of Christ and the Commercialization of Suffering," *The Journal of Religion* 92.3 (2012): 331–361.

[3] Cf. John C. Cavadini, "'The Tree of Silly Fruit': Images of the Cross in Augustine," in *The Cross in Christian Tradition: From Paul to Bonaventure*, ed. Elizabeth A. Dreyer (New York: Paulist Press, 2000), 147–168.

back to God. On the other hand, Christ's sacrifice truly does, as the precondition of the transformation of our desires, effect a new possibility of fellowship with God and our neighbor. In the Cross, space is opened within Christ's Body, enabling our new life in him.

***

If, then, the Cross is as a sign, what does it reveal to us? Augustine's theology of the Cross consistently maintains that Jesus' self-offering shows us the profound humility of the Word – the very same humility that we will require if we are to be restored to God. Even at the height of Augustine's sense of the continuity between Christian faith and Platonic philosophy,[4] he contrasts the pride of the sinful with the crucifixion and death of Christ.[5] More famously, at *conf.* 7.18.24, Augustine says of his youth that he was not yet "humble enough to grasp the humble Jesus as my God, nor did I know what his weakness had to teach." Through the "humble dwelling" which he builds "from our clay," Christ comes to sinful humanity and "heals their swollen pride and nourishes their love, that they may not wander even further away through self-confidence, but rather weaken as they see before their feet the Godhead grown weak."[6]

In a sermon roughly contemporary with the *Confessions*, Augustine tells his congregation that "On every side the humility of the good master is being most assiduously impressed upon us, seeing that our very salvation in Christ consists in the humility of Christ. There would have been no salvation for us, after all, if Christ had not been prepared to humble himself for our sakes."[7] Christ's

---

[4] Cf. *vera rel.* 4.6–7, in which Augustine states that had the Platonists been alive in his own day, they surely would have become Christians.

[5] *vera rel.* 16.31: *Contumelias superbissime horrebant; omne genus contumeliarum sustinuit . . . Dolores corporis exsecrabantur; flagellatus atque cruciatus est. Mori metuebant; morte multatus est.*

[6] *conf.* 7.18.24; WSA I/1, 178.

[7] *s.* 285.4; WSA III/8; 97–8. Cited at Deborah Wallace Ruddy, "The Humble God: Healer, Mediator, Sacrifice," *Logos: A Journal of Catholic Thought and Culture* 7.3 (2004): 87–108, 88.

humility is the surgery that he himself has endured: "If he in whom there was no disease submitted to the surgeon's knife, if he who is himself our healing did not refuse this searing remedy, should we be rebellious against the doctor who cauterizes and cuts, the doctor who trains us through all our troubles and heals us of our sin?"[8] The theme is still present among his latest works, as at *ench.* 28.108. Throughout Augustine's works, then, the life of Christ, and particularly his death on the Cross, stand as a sign of humility, manifesting to us the dependence upon God's act that is required if we are to be redeemed.[9]

So too does the Cross teach us of God's disposition toward sinful humanity: "First we had to be persuaded how much God loves us, in case out of sheer despair we lacked the courage to reach up to him."[10] This too is tied to humility; God saves us through the weakness of humility so that we will not become swelled up with pride and trust in our own strength.[11] To learn hope, without our hoping in ourselves: This is the first step on our path back to God.

Above all, the Cross reveals to us, in one and the same moment, our condition of estrangement from God and God's assumption of that condition. This is the particular significance of the Cry of Dereliction, one of the key sites where Augustine's theology of the *totus Christus* comes into focus:

> *O God, my God, look upon me, why have you forsaken me? . . .* What did the Lord mean? God had not abandoned him, since he himself was God . . . For what other reason was this said than that we were there, for what other reason than that Christ's body is the Church? Why did he say, *My God, my God, look upon me, why have you forsaken me?* Unless he was somehow trying to catch our attention, to make us understand, "This psalm is about me"? *The tale of my sins*

---

[8] *en.Ps.* 40.6; WSA III/16, 231.

[9] Babcock, "Christ of the Exchange," 164–171.

[10] *trin.* 4.1.2; WSA I/5, 153.

[11] *trin.* 4.1.2.

leaves me far from salvation. What sins could these be, when it was said of Christ, *He committed no sin, nor was any guile found on his lips* (1 Pt 2.22)? How, then, could he say, *the tale of my sins*, except because he himself intercedes for our sins, and has made our sins his own, in order to make his righteousness ours?[12]

Christ is trying to catch our attention, to teach us that these words are about us, and that we are the ones who are godforsaken; that much is clear. Michael Cameron speaks of the "voice exchange between savior and sinner that engineered an astounding trade of life for death" as the "very engine of human redemption," and marks the "several layers of impersonation" in Christ's words here.[13]

Yet this raises the natural question: Is this revelation merely for show? Is this simply an instructive sign that Christ provides us, or does it manifest something deeper about Christ's own experience of the Cross? In his *Enarratio in Psalmum* 30, likely preached between 394 and 395, in the last days of his priesthood,[14] Augustine is ambiguous on whether Christ's soul was actually moved by fear:

> Surely we cannot attribute fear to Christ as his passion loomed, when we know that was what he had come for? When he had reached that suffering for which he had come, was he afraid of imminent death? Surely even if he had been human only, not God, he could have been more joyful at the prospect of future resurrection than fearful because he was about to die, couldn't he? . . . Facing death, then, because of what he had from us, he was afraid, not in himself but in us.[15]

His implication seems to be that Christ experiences this fear *only* in his mystical Body the Church, but not in his own soul. Christ says

---

[12] *en.Ps.* 21.2.3; WSA III/15, 229.
[13] Michael Cameron, *Christ Meets Me Everywhere: Augustine's Early Figurative Exegesis* (Oxford: Oxford University Press, 2012), 198.
[14] Cameron, *Christ Meets Me Everywhere*, 166.
[15] *en.Ps.* 30(2).3; WSA III/15, 322–323.

that he is sorrowful to the point of death, but this expresses the reality of his spiritual union with the Church, rather than his own affective state. Certainly Augustine's Christ was not afraid of his own death at this point in his writings; but does being "afraid in us" signify *any* movement of Christ's soul at all, a disturbance of his affections on account of the judgment we must face? Perhaps; but Augustine remains unclear on this point.

By Book 14 of the *City of God*, written in the late teens or early twenties of the fifth century, Augustine is prepared to make much bolder claims about Christ's emotions.[16] It is in the context of his reevaluation of the place of emotion in the lives of the redeemed that Augustine turns to consider Christ's own life:

> Even the Lord himself, when he condescended to live a human life in the form of a servant (although wholly without sin), showed these emotions where he judged that they ought to be shown. For there was nothing fake about the human emotion of one who had a true human body and a true human mind ... Rather, for the sake of his fixed purpose, he took on these emotions in his human mind when he willed, just as he became man when he willed.[17]

Christ parallels – and is in fact the archetype and completion of – the claims that Augustine makes of Paul's redeemed affections: A righteous person experiences "emotions and feelings, which spring from love of the good and holy charity" (*hi motus, hi affectus de amore boni et de sancta caritate venientes*), and "these emotions are in accord with right reason when they occur where they ought properly to occur."[18] How much more, then, should the incarnate

---

[16] Carole Straw provides an excellent summary of the development of Augustine's thought on *timor mortis* at "Timor Mortis," in *Augustine through the Ages: An Encyclopedia*, ed. Allan D. Fitzgerald (Grand Rapids, MI: Wm. B. Eerdmans, 1999), 838–842.

[17] *civ.* 14.9; WSA I/7, 112. John C. Cavadini offers a careful reading of this passage with reference to Christ's emotions at "Feeling Right: Augustine on the Passions and Sexual Desire," *Augustinian Studies* 36.1 (2005): 195–217, 202.

[18] *civ.* 14.9; WSA I/7, 112.

Wisdom of God experience these movements of the soul as he is joined to the condition of sinful humanity? Augustine concludes, "as his Passion was approaching his soul was sorrowful; and certainly these affections are not ascribed to him falsely."[19] There is a difference, though, between our experience of these passions and Christ's: Our "tears come ... from the infirmity of our human condition; but this was not true of the Lord Jesus, Whose very weakness came from His power."[20]

Augustine explicitly draws the connection between Christ's vulnerability and his emotional state, writing at *en.Ps.* 87.3 that "The Lord Jesus took upon himself these feelings of human weakness, just as he also took on weak human flesh with its liability to death."[21] The logic of his position suggests that Christ's expression of godforsakenness on the Cross similarly expresses some emotional state – certainly not the Son of God's being cut off from the presence of God (just as his sorrow unto death does not require that he actually fear death in the way we do), but rather some participation in our experience of God's absence.[22] Christ suffers our godforsakenness both as the God from whom we have attempted to withdraw, and as the human who has taken our part for our redemption. As Rowan Williams has written, "in the state of spiritual darkness, we are tempted to think that God is absent, yet when we hear Christ speaking 'our' words of anguish, we know that this cannot be so. His humanity is inseparably united with God so that, if he gives voice to our suffering, we know that such suffering does not silence God."[23] The Cross shows us God's fellowship with sinners – shows us that

---

[19] *civ.* 14.9. My translation.

[20] *civ.* 14.9; translation from Augustine, *The City of God against the Pagans*, trans. Robert W. Dyson (Cambridge: Cambridge University Press, 1998), 599. See also *en. Ps.* 87.3.

[21] WSA III/18, 260.

[22] Augustine's denial that Christ was truly abandoned by God "does not signify that Augustine meant to deny the reality of the experience itself; but it does compel us to recognize the special and somewhat external sense in which he makes it Christ's experience"; Babcock, "Christ of the Exchange," 328. Cf. also 180–182.

[23] Rowan Williams, "Augustine and the Psalms," *Interpretation* 58.1 (2004): 17–27, 19.

the Word has put Herself under the knife, and humbled Herself by taking on our sinful condition.

In the terms of my own theological project, then: If we consider Jesus solely in his union of divinity and humanity, his cry of god-forsakenness is wholly inappropriate to him. He is not truly abandoned by the Father; what could it even mean for the Son to be so abandoned within the changelessness of the divine life? These are words proper only to sinful humanity; how, then, can he utter them without falsehood?

Christ can only speak these words because he has truly united himself to our sinful condition. He can only speak this way because, in the work of incarnation, he has truly taken our lives into his own. He is not who he is, he is not the one able to utter these words truly, without us. On the Cross, Christ reveals his life to be marked by the life of *every* sinner – not only those who were his family and friends and adversaries in the course of his Galilean ministry, but each person whose life is sheltered in Christ's own through the Crucifixion. When Christ cries out in godforsakenness, he shows his life to be determined by the lives of sinners – of all sinners, if it is right to say that he is the Lamb of God who takes away the sin of the world. His sorrow is the sorrow of my godforsakenness; his tears are shed over your sins. The shape of his life – his teaching, his prophetic acts, his self-surrender, even the words he speaks on the Cross – is impossible apart from his union with those who are his Body. So also, only by dwelling within this world can he open to us a new life within his own. What is ultimately revealed on the Cross is our union with Christ: A union born of love; enacted in humility; consummated in his flesh, his affections, and the whole shape of his life.

***

Yet the Crucifixion does not simply reveal this fellowship between God and humanity; it effects this union. In this sense, the Cross must be viewed as the consummation of the Incarnation – not because incarnation is a historical process that ebbs and flows throughout the course of Christ's life, but because it is on the Cross that Christ abandons himself most fully to our condition of godforsakenness. As Karl Barth writes, "If Jesus Christ has followed our way as sinners to the end to which it leads, in outer darkness, then we can say with [Isaiah 53, the Song of the Suffering Servant] that He has suffered this punishment of ours."[24] Barth echoes the sensibility apparent in Augustine's exegeses of the psalms subtitled "of David, to the end": The Cross truly does liberate us from the power of death; it truly does effect the forgiveness of sins, and restore the possibility of right relation to God.

To pull on one particularly important thread of Augustine's understanding of the Crucifixion's objective significance within the work of redemption, Augustine tells us that it is Christ's sacrifice which liberates us from the power of the devil. Adam and Eve were not alone – or even original – in their fall; Augustine tells us that "The devil was the mediator of this road, persuading to sin and hurling down into death; he too brought his own single death to bear in order to operate our double death."[25] Interwoven with the inner cleansing effected by the *sacramentum* of Christ's offering is an account of the breaking of the devil's power over humanity, "who had yielded to his seduction, and whom he had thus as it were acquired full property rights over, and being himself liable to no corruption of flesh and blood had held in his thrall in his weakness and poverty and the frailness of this mortal body, like one seemingly rich and powerful, and all the prouder for that, lording it over a wretched ragged slave."[26]

Clearly, this does not occur outside the purview of God's providence: As Augustine goes on to write in *De trinitate* 13, "As for the way in which man was handed over into the devil's power, this should not be thought of as though God actually did it or ordered it

---

[24] Karl Barth, *Church Dogmatics* IV/1, 253 (§59.2).

[25] *trin.* 4.13.16; WSA I/5, 163.

[26] *trin.* 4.13.17; WSA I/5, 165.

to be done, but merely that he permitted it, albeit justly. When he withdrew from the sinner, the author of sin marched in."[27] The crucial link forged here is the one between the devil's mediation of sin to us and his rights over us. In the relationship between Satan and humanity, we see a perversion of our relation to God and Christ. We are, at root, created to be receivers of God's gifts. In teaching humanity to sin, the devil offers us a sort of deceptive gift – not quite a new pattern of action so much as a pattern of inaction, a deficient cause (*causa deficiens*) as Augustine writes in *De civitate dei*.[28] Even so, the devil teaches us to behave as he does – proudly, maliciously, slothfully, and so on – and in so doing, mediates to us the nothingness that increasingly characterizes his and our lives. We become bound to him in a twisted image of the gratitude we ought show to God, and come to resemble him ever more fully. As the author of sin, the devil is the head of a degenerate and degenerating community; the *civitas terrena* is also *civitas diaboli*.[29] Inasmuch as the devil has rights over us, it is because he is the model of our sin, and he will pursue his advantage over us until this power is broken.

The account of our justification Augustine offers in *De trinitate* 13 hinges on a contrast between power and justice. God is, of course, all-powerful, and had God wished simply to break the power of the devil over us by claiming us as Her own, no creature could resist. Yet Augustine seems to think that effecting salvation in this way would serve as a final confirmation of what we might call the "satanic impulse": "The essential flaw of the devil's perversion made him a lover of power and a deserter and assailant of justice,

---

[27] *trin.* 13.12.16; WSA I/5, 355–356.
[28] *civ.* 12.7. On the *causa deficiens*, see Charles T. Mathewes, *Evil and the Augustinian Tradition* (Cambridge: Cambridge University Press, 2001), 78–80, 92–3; and Jesse Couenhoven, who emphasizes that the condition of possibility of our fall away from the good in the fact that we are created from nothing; cf. Jesse Couenhoven, "Augustine's Rejection of the Free-Will Defence: An Overview of the Late Augustine's Theodicy," *Religious Studies* 43.3 (2007): 286–290.
[29] *civ.* 17.16; *en.Ps.* 61.6.

which means that men imitate him all the more thoroughly the more they neglect or even detest justice and studiously devote themselves to power, rejoicing at the possession of it or inflamed with the desire for it."[30] This desire for domination will be familiar to readers of *De civitate dei* as the *libido dominandi*, the dominating lust;[31] but here Augustine ventures to imagine what it would be like if God were also characterized above all by the will to exercise power, irrespective of the justice of Her actions. Had God liberated humanity from Satan's tyranny through coercive force, She would begin to appear to us uncomfortably similar to the devil, only incomparably more powerful. And this revelation of the ultimacy of power would, in itself, seem to confirm us in our lust for domination, rather than loosening its grip on us. Instead of God's redemptive work serving as an attractor to desires rightly ordered by the love of God and neighbor, this conquest of hell would only reinforce that power is the final word, and that we are justified in pursuing it over all other things. The problem is not that redemption would be impossible – another act of power would undoubtedly be sufficient to convert our hearts forcibly – but rather that God's saving acts would be a stumbling block, deepening us in sin before freeing us from it.

As a result, Augustine tells us that "it pleased God to deliver man from the devil's authority by beating him at the justice game, not the power game, so that men too might imitate Christ by seeking to beat the devil at the justice game, not the power game."[32] This is what Christ's death accomplishes: a just judgment against the devil that strips him of his right to exercise power against us. One of the most

---

[30] *trin.* 13.13.17; WSA I/5, 356.

[31] *civ.* 1.1.

[32] *trin.* 13.13.17; WSA I/5, 356. Sean Larsen has developed this strand of Augustine's thought into a very convincing theology opposing patriarchy and heterosexism as modes of diabolic life; see Sean Larsen, "The Word Was Always Flesh," *Syndicate: Symposium on Mark D. Jordan's* Convulsing Bodies (Jun 5, 2016): https://syndicate .network/symposia/theology/convulsing-bodies/.

significant features of Christ's death in *De trinitate* 13 is that it was a travesty of justice, an offering that the devil had no right to accept. The miscarriage of justice that the devil allows removes, as it were, the legal standing by which he was granted power over sinful humanity. Stripping away the devil's rights over us is the heart of Augustine's description of justification in this text: "this blood of his, of one who had no sin at all, was shed for the remission of our sins, and the devil, who once held us deservedly under the sentence of death as we were guilty of sin, was deservedly obliged to give us up through him he had most undeservedly condemned to death, though guilty of no sin."[33] Once this power is broken, "it is therefore perfectly just that he should let the debtors he held go free, who believe in the one whom he killed without being in his debt. This is how we are said to be justified by the blood of Christ."[34]

As an act of God's power over the devil no less than as a redemptive sign to us, the Cross must be seen as a fundamentally communal enterprise. Our lives are ordered by communion with God, thus allowing us to love our neighbor; or they are ordered by the simulacrum of communion that the devil allows, a diabolic mediation of life in the world that inevitably collapses in on itself. The Cross reveals to us that our lives together are lived under the power of sin, inescapable by our own resources; and the Cross breaks that power, through mediating new life to us.

---

[33] *trin.* 13.15.19; WSA I/5, 358. Patout Burns notes this is true across Augustine's thought: "Augustine's primary explanation of the process of redemption is usually identified as a forensic analysis which addresses the rights of the devil. This theory was proposed early, middle, and late in his writing career, and with little significant change"; J. Patout Burns, "How Christ Saves: Augustine's Multiple Explanations," in *Tradition & the Rule of Faith in the Church: Essays in Honor of Joseph T. Lienhard,* eds. Ronnie J. Rombs and Alexander Young (Washington, DC: The Catholic University of America Press, 2010), 193–210; 193. Yet Burns identifies two further motifs of redemption: Christ's dissolution of death in his own body, and Christ's kindling a new love in our hearts through his witness. My account of the Cross in this chapter strives to hold together each of these three threads.

[34] *trin.* 13.14.18; WSA I/5, 357.

Extending the point, we may say that the Cross reveals God's judgment against creaturely powers of domination. Christ preaches of the coming of a new Kingdom whose borders are not secured by violence. He proclaims the rule of the God of Israel, a sovereignty that does not depend upon the exploitative authorities by which our systems of power are maintained. In the prophetic acts of his final days, Christ challenges the justice of Roman rule and the complicity of the Temple authorities in the violence inflicted against the powerless. He is arraigned as a blasphemer and executed by the Empire for insurrection. The humility of the Incarnation is also a sign that God Herself takes the side of those who are humiliated and brutalized by others. The Word shows us not only that She has taken the part of sinful humanity, but that She has decisively rejected the sin that the powerful inflict upon the vulnerable.

Here again, the whole shape of Christ's life leads us to this conclusion. The Word assumes the flesh of Israel, a politically oppressed ethnic minority within the Roman Empire.[35] He inaugurates his ministry by proclaiming good news to the poor and liberation to the imprisoned.[36] His ministry is conducted within a context of economic exploitation, and oriented to the disadvantaged and exploited.[37] As Rosemary Radford Ruether has observed, "the protest of the Gospels is directed at the concrete sociological realities in which maleness and femaleness are elements, along with class, ethnicity, religious office, and law, that define the network of social status."[38] The more that the redemptive sign of Christ's life is viewed in the context of the whole work of incarnation – which is to say in part, the more that Christ's life is viewed in his historical

---

[35] James H. Cone, *Black Theology and Black Power* (Maryknoll, NY: Orbis Books, 1997), 64.

[36] James H. Cone, *God of the Oppressed* (Maryknoll, NY: Orbis Books, 1997), 69.

[37] Gustavo Gutiérrez, *A Theology of Liberation*, 15th Anniversary ed. (Maryknoll, NY: Orbis Books, 1988), 102–105.

[38] Rosemary Radford Ruether, *Sexism and God-Talk: Toward a Feminist Theology* (Boston, MA: Beacon Press, 1993), 137.

connection to the lives of those around him – the more that the liberatory significance of Christ's work comes into focus.

The significatory function of the Cross and its concrete effect in liberating us from the power of sin thus cannot be separated. The power of the devil is, in part, broken by the Cross as sign. Signification, justification, and liberation should thus be held together in a contemporary Augustinian christology. More concretely, for a twenty-first-century white citizen of the United States, the redemptive efficacy of the Cross requires us to see Christ in the black bodies who are victims of lynching. To echo the argument of Black and womanist theologians, and to anticipate my development of an Augustinian theology affirming their insights, it is *only* by coming to see the face of Christ in the lynched bodies that a white supremacist social order has taught us to despise that we may be saved.[39] What it is to know Christ crucified, what it is to see his life as redemptive within the work of incarnation, is to see him as one who has drawn the lives of the victims into his own. As M. Shawn Copeland has written, "the only body capable of taking us all in as we are with all our different body marks – certainly, the queer mark – is the body of Christ."[40] It is to this end that the Augustinian theology of the *totus Christus* necessarily leads.

***

The whole Christ is born out of the Cross, precisely as the place where the reality of human sin is met and overcome. This suggests, as Christians since St. Paul have known, that we must look to the Cross if we are truly to understand the sin from which we are redeemed. That Christ's single death opens the space for a new form of communal life suggests to us, however, that we must understand death itself as an inherently social enterprise. A hypothesis, then: The Cross shows us

[39] M. Shawn Copeland, *Enfleshing Freedom: Body, Race, and Being* (Minneapolis, MN: Fortress Press, 2010), 117–124; and James H. Cone, *The Cross and the Lynching Tree* (Maryknoll, NY: Orbis Books, 2011).

[40] M. Shawn Copeland, *Knowing Christ Crucified: The Witness of African-American Religious Experience* (Maryknoll, NY: Orbis Books, 2018), 79.

that death, suffering it and meting it out, is a form of human community. More than that, death is the *only* mode of community available to sinful and unredeemed humanity. As Augustine writes at *civ.* 13.10, our whole life is a *cursus ad mortem* – a race to death, a feature of human life as true of our communities as it is of each of our biological existence.

Death is the end toward which all our sinful attempts at community are necessarily directed; the desire toward which we have set our hearts, whether we know it or not. Dealing death and receiving it – *donner la mort*, Derrida would say – is the paradigmatic act of the sort of community we sinners share, the only gift that can truly be given.[41] To give death, or to receive it – this is the way we fallen humans are able to share our lives together; and, I argue, the only way, if we are considered in ourselves and apart from our union to Christ's flesh. The *coup de grâce* is, in practice, rarely delivered: Our communal interactions rarely rise to the level of explicit murder. Yet as part of its significatory work, the Cross enables us to see the death-dealing that is inherent in all our unredeemed communal interactions, to a greater or lesser degree.

Consider, for instance, why the language of death seems irreplaceable in our descriptions of some of the most grievous wounds that humans have inflicted upon one another. Orlando Patterson, in describing slave-holding societies throughout human history as societies in which "relations of domination" are sustained through violence,[42] has made use of the language of "social death."[43] Slavery is, Patterson notes, a "substitute for death" – often throughout human history, slavery has been the substitute for "death in war. But almost as frequently, the death commuted was punishment for

---

[41] Jacques Derrida, *The Gift of Death and Literature in Secret*, 2nd ed., trans. David Wills (Chicago, IL: University of Chicago Press, 2008).

[42] Orlando Patterson, *Slavery and Social Death: A Comparative Study* (Cambridge, MA: Harvard University Press, 1982), 2.

[43] The phrase itself comes from Michel Izard by way of Claude Meillassoux; cf. *Slavery and Social Death*, 38.

some capital offense, or death from exposure or starvation."[44] Consequently, "the definition of the slave, however recruited" is that of "a socially dead person," "excommunicated" from all the social relations (legal rights to marry or over children, for instance) she properly bears to others as her birthright.[45] The new slave was even generally stripped of her name and given a new one to mark the death that had taken place.[46]

This death is social not only in extinguishing the social relations the slave should rightly have to her family and neighbors – it is social in that it is cultivated and maintained by the broader slave-owning political order of which she is a part. Social death is not dealt once and for all; it is inflicted daily, through vicious patterns of action in which those who think they are living constitute the dead as dead. In describing the "necropolitics" of such societies, Achille Mbembé has written that "the ultimate expression of sovereignty resides, to a large degree, in the power and the capacity to dictate who may live and who must die."[47] Both slave societies and "late-modern colonial regimes"[48] are contexts of "living death"[49] or "death-in-life,"[50] circumstances in which one's agency can only be exercised as the recipient of social death or, as in the suicide bomber, by receiving social death in such a manner that one also inflicts death upon one's oppressor.[51]

Yet this way of speaking is not found only in situations of slavery and colonialism. Both Mbembé and Susan Brison point to the Holocaust as a similar instance of death-in-life.[52] Susan J. Brison

---

[44] Patterson, *Slavery and Social Death*, 5.

[45] Patterson, *Slavery and Social Death*, 5.

[46] Patterson, *Slavery and Social Death*, 55.

[47] Achille Mbembé, "Necropolitics," trans. Libby Meintjes, *Public Culture* 15.1 (2003): 11–40, 11.

[48] Mbembé, "Necropolitics," 38.

[49] Mbembé, "Necropolitics," 40.

[50] Mbembé, "Necropolitics," 21.

[51] Mbembé, "Necropolitics," 36.

[52] Mbembé, "Necropolitics," 12, quoting Hannah Arendt's *The Origins of Totalitarianism*.

quotes Charlotte Delbo: "I died in Auschwitz, but no one knows it."[53] Brison discusses many of the same dynamics to which Patterson and Mbembé point, noting, for instance, how many survivors of the Shoah are so distant from their lives before the death camps that they take new names (Jean Améry, Paul Celan),[54] or whose experiences of social death eventually lead them to take their own lives (again Améry and Celan, Primo Levi).[55] No less harrowing is Brison's way of describing her own rape and attempted murder: "For months after my assault, I had to stop myself before saying (what seemed accurate at the time), 'I was murdered in France last summer.'"[56] She writes, "I felt as though I had outlived myself, as though I had stayed on a train one stop past my destination."[57] While we should not suppress the singular horrors of the experiences of enslavement, rape (itself a ubiquitous feature of slave-holding societies), or the Holocaust, we may observe with Brison that each of these experiences can produce "a similar disintegration of the self."[58]

It would be a grievous mistake, I think, to dismiss the voices of these survivors as mere metaphor or hyperbole. In the midst of unimaginable – and unimaginably different – contexts of violence, they tell us that, at the limits of the suffering humans are able to inflict upon one another, human persons experience something that can only be described as a death. The specific features of each

---

[53] Susan J. Brison, "Outliving Oneself: Trauma, Memory, and Personal Identity," in *Gender Struggles: Practical Approaches to Contemporary Feminism*, eds. Constance L. Mui and Julien S. Murphy (Lanham: Rowman & Littlefield, 2002): 137–165, 137. I am very grateful to Julia Feder for directing me to Brison's work.

[54] Brison, "Outliving Oneself," 144.

[55] Brison, "Outliving Oneself," 158.

[56] Susan J. Brison, *Aftermath: Violence and the Remaking of a Self* (Princeton, NJ: Princeton University Press, 2002), xi.

[57] Brison, "Outliving Oneself," 144. Brison also writes that "the victim's inability to be – and assert – herself in the context of a rape constitutes at least a temporary social death" (143).

[58] Brison, "Outliving Oneself," 159 n.3.

experience vary, but they are all-encompassing: a sense of utter alienation from the person one was before this experience; a sense of one being stripped of all agency; a sense of being reduced to a mere object or target of abuse; a sense of separation from all other people; a lack of control over one's own bodily functions or emotional reactions, and a related sense of the dissolution of one's identity; a sense of the vulnerability of one's body, and the experience of it as an enemy; a sense of being fastened to the present, without the possibility of a livable future; the compulsive repetition of traumatic memory; a breakdown of one's world.[59] As Brison summarizes, quoting Judith Herman, "'The traumatic event . . . destroys the belief that one can *be oneself* in relation to others' . . . Without this belief, I shall argue, one can no longer *be oneself* even to oneself, since the self exists fundamentally in relation to others."[60] That many victims of slavery, rape, and the Holocaust (as well as any number of other traumas) frequently manage to find subversive and life-giving ways to exercise agency does not undermine the central point: the power that they are up against, the power exercising dominion in their suffering, is death.

In situations such as these, we must speak of death as a phenomenon that is social both in the manner it is inflicted and in its effects; but can it make sense here to call death a mode of *community* – a mode of shared life between those who are dealing death and those who are suffering it? I have no wish to temper the obscenity of such a statement. By calling death a mode of community, I aim to identify the human good of which it is a privation: We are meant to live together, and are meant to find in one another the God who is the source of all life. That our relations to one another can become so marred beyond human semblance that they plunge us into solitude and death is surely one of the most horrifying consequences of the deformation of the grace by which God grants

---

[59] Brison, "Outliving Oneself," *passim*.

[60] Brison, "Outliving Oneself," 139. Citing Judith Herman, *Trauma and Recovery* (New York: Basic Books, 2002), 53; emphasis original.

us life. Death – this social death, this death by which we share our lives together, this death by which we dissolve one another's possibility of life – is the first and final consequence of sin.

Indeed, death is, as I have said, the *only* mode of community available to sinful and unredeemed humanity. We must be very careful at this point: Just as my claim is not that enslavement or rape or the Shoah are commensurable experiences, neither is my claim that sin inducts all people into the social death that characterizes these experiences. The hideousness of these atrocities are found in their particularities: the singular way that slaveholding in the American South tore children away from their parents for sale; the qualitatively different way that a rape victim is shorn of his or her agency and reduced to an object of violence; the icy industrialism by which so much of the Jewish population of Europe was stripped of its humanity. It would be abhorrent and absurd to say that these experiences are on the same moral plane as the white heteropatriarchal *ennui* of the global privileged. These sufferings are not the same, and are not comparable.

Yet if we are to take the suffering of the victims as a starting-point for understanding sin and death, neither can we say that the suffering of *these* victims has nothing to show us about the hell from which the Cross redeems humanity. We can perhaps speak of these instances of social death as "concretizations" of the dynamics of sin regnant throughout fallen and unredeemed humanity. In the language of the phenomenological tradition, our lived experience is not simply a stream of sense data: The manner in which phenomena give themselves to us teaches us not only about the intentional object of our experience, but about our own lives as those to whom such phenomenal manifestations can appear.[61] The concrete

---

[61] John E. Drabinski offers one of the most sophisticated analyses of phenomenological concretion at *Sensibility and Singularity: The Problem of Phenomenology in Levinas* (Albany, NY: State University of New York Press, 2001), 18–9, 55–8. See also Levinas' discussions of concretion in the lectures "Reflections on Phenomenological 'Technique'" and "The Ruin of Representation," in *Discovering Existence with Husserl,*

is the phenomenon in its immediacy and alterity, prior to any conceptualization of it; but in manifesting itself to us, the phenomenon brings to visibility features of our own constitution as those able to receive it. As Levinas writes, "The senses *make* sense."[62]

My claim, then, is that these occasions of social death and the dissolution of identity manifest to us the dynamics of *all* human life and experience under the condition of sin. Precisely because these experiences of death follow the path of sin to its end, to the extremity of human sociality marred by sin, they bring to visibility the death-dealing and -receiving that is inherent to all community between sinful persons. It is not simply a matter of degree, of these moments being *worse* than the casual harms we inflict on one another every day. In the force and inescapability with which this sense of outliving oneself imposes itself on those who suffer it, social death is qualitatively different than other experiences of death dealt and received. Precisely in its difference, social death reveals the necrotic dynamics of all sinful human community – a dynamic faced and overcome on the Cross.

***

All human community, then, is necrotic; "Whichever way you turn, everything is uncertain, except for one sole certainty: death."[63] Let me anchor this claim in two further moments of Augustine's thought. The first, in the realm of his political theology; the second, in his moral psychology. It is frequently noted that Augustine offers two definitions of a republic in the *City of God*. The first, from Book 2.21, is Cicero's: He defines "a people is not just any assembly of a multitude but rather an assembly joined together by a common sense for what is right and a community of interest."[64]

trans. Richard A. Cohen and Michael B. Smith (Evanston, IL: Northwestern University Press, 1998), 91–121.

[62] Levinas, *Discovering Existence with Husserl*, 98; emphasis mine.

[63] *en.Ps.* 38.19; WSA III/16, 190.

[64] *civ.* 2.21; WSA I/6, 58.

Even as he forecasts that if a republic is defined by the common good, Augustine admits that "according to more plausible definitions, [Rome] was a republic in a way."[65] It is a functional definition of this sort, presumed but never explicated, that allows him to describe Rome as a city ordered by its common love for glory, and to describe not only the *civitas Dei* but also the *civitas terrena* as communities, the heavenly city constituted by "love of God, even to the point of contempt for self," and the earthly city constituted by "love of self, even to the point of contempt for God."[66]

Yet famously, Augustine offers another definition of a republic in Book 19 of the *City of God* that undercuts the Ciceronian one: Here, Augustine tells us that when Cicero speaks of "a common sense for what is right," he presumes that "a republic cannot be maintained without justice. Thus, where there is no true justice there can be no right ... it follows beyond any doubt that where there is no justice there is no republic."[67] By this criterion, the only true human community is the heavenly city, the only republic ordered by true justice, because its life is wholly ordered by the love of God.

Augustine is teaching us to see fallen human community as inherently unstable, ever collapsing in on itself. This collapse is not merely incidental to the *civitas terrena*: Because this community has been ordered by the love of self extending to the contempt of God, this motion toward dissolution is intrinsic to it. The condition of the earthly city, as Augustine argues throughout the *City of God*, is one of fracture: Its life is governed by patterns of domination, and only offers the appearance of true community inasmuch as it helps protect one from the domination of others and dominate them more effectively in turn. In itself, the earthly city is founded upon and governed by murder: Cain, Romulus, the military state; take your pick. In eschatological view, the earthly city can only lead to the violent opposition of each member to each other; this is the

---

[65] *civ.* 2.21; WSA I/6, 59.
[66] *civ.* 14.48; WSA I/7, 136.
[67] *civ.* 19.21; WSA I/7, 378.

lesson that we should learn from demonic attempts to draw humans away from God.[68] The logic of the earthly city is death: death given first to our enemies, then to our neighbors, and finally to ourselves. To the extent that our loves are not turned to God by grace, desire for this death is the movement expressed in all our dealings with our neighbors; all our interactions tend toward this promised end.

So too does Augustine's moral psychology underwrite the conclusion that death is the mode of our lives together as sinners. Within Augustine's view of the soul, all our ability to know and act within the world emerges through the soul's threefold activity of memory, intellection, and love. In the beatitude proper to our created nature, our knowledge and love of the world are meant to be ordered by the soul's orientation to God. We are able to know the world as it truly is, to know each thing as the unique creation God has made it, for we are able to know it in the light shed on our intellects by the Word of God's presence within us. So also, we are able to know its created goodness as it participates in and serves as a likeness of God's own transcendent Good, and to love it as the good creature it is. When, however, our loves are improperly ordered to God, all these operations of the soul are undermined. Because our souls no longer cleave to God, the presence of the Word to our intellects is darkened; ignorance creeps into our knowledge of the world. Rather than perceiving the world truly as God created it, we perceive a distorted image of it.[69]

Our lives are lived in ignorance of the true value of things, leading us to value some created goods (say, wine or food) more highly than they deserve, and other goods (the virtues, for instance) less highly

---

[68] *civ.* 2.10.

[69] Cf. Robert Dodaro, *Christ and the Just Society in the Thought of Augustine* (Cambridge: Cambridge University Press, 2004), 29: "the moral object of knowledge is also in some respect an object of love, and, conversely, that which is not known cannot be loved." This is closely related, Dodaro argues, to our *timor mortis*: The fear of death both stems from our inability to understand ourselves as the creatures of God and produces in us an inability to see our own lives included in Christ's death (30).

than we should. As we continue to make these misguided judgments, we become habituated to them, developing an undue attachment to wine or an aversion to those who are too honest. Not only, then, are our evaluative judgments compromised, but in many cases even when we correctly identify the higher good our habits chain us to the objects of our inordinate loves, leaving us powerless to will the good that we perceive.[70] This weakness of will is, as we have seen, thoroughly tied to our ignorance, the corruption of our acts of intellection. We love it not as it is, but a fantasy image of it, projected by and bent to our disordered desires. This is what it is to love the world wrongly: To love it as what we would have it be, rather than as God has made it. This also is why Augustine characterizes our relations to the world as animated by the *libido dominandi*, the "lust for domination" that is, at the same time, the lust that masters us.[71]

The upshot of this compressed Augustinian account is that, when we sinful humans encounter our neighbor, we never see her as she really is. We do not know her as the creature God has made her, and we do not love her as such. Our loves are directed not toward God, but toward the nothing – the misguided self-love that believes we can take ourselves as our own ground, that we can exist without receiving our existence from God. Just as this phantasmal self-love is actually the orientation of our loves to the *nihil*, so also our attempt to love our neighbor is directed not toward her as the creature she is, but toward our own heart's illusory projection of her as we would have her be. It is not that we love nothing at all – in loving our neighbor wrongly, we are indeed loving *her* in a disordered fashion; but precisely *in* loving her wrongly, the weight of our loves draws us ever closer to the nothing that is the true object of all our disordered affections. The proximate objects of our loves may be quite varied, but as Augustine observes in the *City of*

---

[70] This is a central theme of Wetzel's *Augustine and the Limits of Virtue*; see especially pp. 135–139.

[71] *civ.* 1.1.

God, the architecture of our loves is binary, either drawing us deeper into participation in the triune life of God, or locking us in a degenerative spiral away from God.

We prefer the simulacrum of her fashioned by our disordered loves to the truth of her life as God has made her. To the extent that the truth of her life fails to match the image of her I have projected, my disordered love of her will be a *libido dominandi*. It is worth noting that I cannot make her an object of domination *without* loving her as other than she is, for God has made her the sort of creature that should not be subjected to domination. And so long as I love my neighbor in disordered fashion, she will *always* fail to measure up the project of my misshapen loves. In loving our neighbor wrongly, then, we implicitly but necessarily long for her extinction. I will continue loving my illusion and dominating my neighbor until I have destroyed her, and will finally, if surrendered to my loves, come to the point of my own destruction. Not only as a result of our mutability, but just as truly in light of our lives together, should we say with Augustine, "From the very moment when a person first comes into existence in this body that is doomed to die, there is never a time when death is not at work in him."[72]

To repeat my original point, then, death is the only mode of human community available to sinful humanity. It is the structuring principle of all our interactions with one another, to the extent that those interactions are not included within the history of God's redemptive work in Christ. It is the origin and completion of all our various communities, to the extent that those communities are not destined to be sanctified and incorporated into the one true community of the heavenly city. But in saying that all moments of unredeemed community are ultimately moments of death-dealing, I also intend to affirm the vitiated good that such moments still exemplify: In giving and receiving death, we really *are* seeking fellowship; we really *do* seek to share our lives with one another. But

---

[72] *civ.* 13.10; WSA I/7, 75.

we can do so only by attempting to bring our neighbor and ourselves to nothing.

***

From this vantage point, we may see the outlines of a new understanding of the Cross's redemptive significance. The Cross is not merely the expression of God's condemnation of sin, or the tragic result of humanity's rejection of God's grace. It is the act in which the Word consummates Her union with fallen humanity, entering fully into communion with us. In making himself vulnerable to suffering and death, Christ opens himself to the truest possible fellowship with us – which is to say, he receives us in the only way we can meet him: as death-dealers. He allows us to meet him as we truly are, to bring ourselves to this encounter without reserve, without deception. He offers himself over to us to be made into nothing, just as we would aim to make of the whole of God's creation. Christ's experience of fellowship with us follows our wicked attempts at communion to their natural conclusion – to the end, as Augustine would say.

On the Cross, the Word surrenders Himself wholly to union with us. The Word is wholly united to our *nature*, of course, solely in virtue of the act of incarnation, identical to the act of the divine life. Yet it is only on the Cross that the life of Christ becomes fully transparent to our sinful condition. Within the work of incarnation, our lives and agency give shape to Christ's own – and because our desires tend toward the annihilation of our neighbor and ourselves, it is in his death that our lives as sinners are included most fully in Christ's own. In this way, the single death that Christ suffers comes to match the double death we suffer – the death of the body when separated from the soul, and the death of the soul when separated from God – in what Augustine calls a *coaptatio* or ἁρμονία, a "harmony of salvation."[73] The sign of Christ's life reflects to us our death, so that his resurrection may give us hope in our own.

---

[73] *trin.* 4.2.4–3.5; WSA I/5, 155.

Within this redemptive economy, the Cry of Dereliction is an especially potent sign, showing us that there is no depth of god-forsakenness that the Word cannot match in Her human life. At this point, the conclusions of the preceding chapters become particularly important. There is nothing, humanly, that it "feels like" to be the divine person of the Son. Accordingly, the union of human nature to the Word places no limit on what Christ is able to experience, excepting only that Christ's desires are perfectly ordered to God, rendering him incapable of sin.[74] Yet if Christ's ignorance, alongside the corruptibility of his flesh, can serve a purpose within God's work of redemption, it seems that he can experience the very "undoing of the self" that victims of trauma have undergone.[75] His embodied experience is not excluded from this experience ("I thirst"), and the purpose of much of the Passion narratives of the Gospels seems to be to render his body an object of violence. He is paraded through the streets of Jerusalem; he is

[74] Natalie Carnes is characteristically insightful in describing how the eternal God can nevertheless be seen in Christ's suffering on the Cross: "God remains fully and unchangingly God all the way through brokenness. This is why the cross is such a profound source of hope: By remaining God even in brokenness, Christ on the cross images the breaking of brokenness ... In this way, vulnerability is not opposed to the impassibility of God. It is impassibility's anterior side. God's naked, suffering, vulnerable body on the cross is the impassibility of love made visible. Breakingness comes with brokenness as the negation of the Image is negated"; Natalie Carnes, *Image and Presence: A Christological Reflection on Iconoclasm and Iconophilia* (Stanford, CA: Stanford University Press, 2018), 88–89.

[75] Brison, "Outliving Oneself," 138. Shelly Rambo offers an even more capacious sense of the trauma of the Cross, writing: "traumatic suffering is not contained in a single event ... If we interpret the suffering of the cross traumatically, the trauma cannot be isolated to the cross. Instead, the site of suffering extends to the middle space, which means that theological discourse about trauma must press beyond interpretations of the cross – the death event. Instead, the death and resurrection events must be brought together around a new question, 'What persists between them?'"; *Spirit and Trauma: A Theology of Remaining* (Louisville, KY: Westminster John Knox, 2010), 156. I take this perspective to be profoundly consonant with my understanding of the works of incarnation and redemption as encompassing the whole of cosmic history, even if the Cross remains the center of this history. The Cross is not the end of Christ's suffering – it "haunts" history, filled up in the *totus Christus*.

repeatedly scourged; he is stripped naked, and stripped of the ability to protect himself from this public humiliation. He undergoes social death as he is subsumed within Rome's techniques of imperial control; his body is made someone else's speech, as his flesh and then corpse are made warnings to all those who would resist Rome's version of peace.[76] The theological duality of this moment goes some distance toward explaining Christ's words from the Cross: He both cries out in godforsakenness and prays for the forgiveness of the world. The Crucifixion is both Christ's abandonment and his self-emptying into communion with sinful humanity; indeed, it is the latter only inasmuch as it is principally the former. There is no reserve to the depths of loneliness and despair that Christ can humanly experience as he surrenders himself to our damnation.

The Cross then manifests to us Christ's union to our condition.[77] Yet his death does not only speak to us of our spiritual death – it is also God's means of overcoming our separation from Him. By entering into community with us truly, in the only manner available to us, Christ also opens the possibility of a new fellowship with God and one another. In the midst of the death-dealing that defines all sinful human community, Christ brings resurrection – the possibility of restored communion, of a life together that is not ordered to extinction. Christ's cross is itself our reconciliation: In refusing to let our defection from God persist, in drawing our lives into his own, in drinking to the last the cup of death that inevitably results from our turning from God toward the nothingness, Christ has accomplished the forgiveness of sins, opening for us a path back to God by his own flesh.

We should note an important feature of this account: The death of Christ is indeed, in itself, redemptive; but it is not redemptive

---

[76] Brison speaks of victim's bodies "being used as another's speech" at "Outliving Oneself," 150.

[77] Kimberly Baker emphasizes the unitive aspects of Augustine's theology of the Cross at "Augustine on Action," 84–88, 97–99, 117–125; proposing that for Augustine "the union of the Head and Body is culminated in this moment [on the Cross] because it is in this moment that Christ's solidarity with humanity is undeniable" (87).

because it is suffering.[78] Rather, it is redemptive because through entering into our communities of death-dealing, in receiving death at our hands, Christ has conquered the death that reigns in all unredeemed community. Christ bears the full weight of our attempts to reduce him and ourselves to nothing, and is nevertheless raised triumphant by the power of God. Through letting his life be shaped by ours within the work of incarnation, Christ's human flesh becomes the key site of mediation by which the power of his divinity is communicated to our humanity.

In fact, we may say that, in suffering death at our hands, Christ has joined himself to the condition of all creation. Christ's death joins him, as Niels Henrik Gregersen has observed, not only to all humans, but to all biological life: the evolutionary ancestors that produced his human form through a history of predation that spans hundreds of millions of years; the doves sacrificed to bring him into Israel's covenant; the fish he eats on the shores of the Sea of Galilee.[79] Indeed, if we take the entropy and decay we see throughout the created order to be an index of the consequences of creation's defection from its Creator, then Christ's reception of death at our hands unites him at least to the whole of the material world, and perhaps to all of creaturely temporality.[80]

[78] This emphasis is motivated, in my account, by a desire to offer what Kathryn Tanner has described as "a model of atonement based on the incarnation" that is responsive to the critiques of feminist and womanist scholarship decentering the Cross within christology; see Kathryn Tanner, *Christ the Key* (Cambridge: Cambridge University Press, 2010), 252; and Delores S. Williams, *Sisters in the Wilderness: The Challenge of Womanist God-Talk* (Maryknoll, NY: Orbis Books, 1993), 178–199 for a classic critique of the soteriological significance of the Cross. Without valorizing innocent death and suffering as such, I do take the death of Christ to be soteriologically necessary precisely because of the "nature" of sin (or, more precisely, because of the precise way that sin distorts God's good creation). It is fellowship with us *as sinners* that is required if the Incarnation is to be redemptive, and thus Christ must confront the communal march toward nonbeing if sinners are to be reconciled to God.

[79] See "The Cross of Christ in an Evolutionary World," *Dialog: A Journal of Theology* 40.3 (2001): 192–207, 203–204.

[80] In this, I agree with Paul Griffiths' description of all creation, including temporality itself, as metronomically damaged: "The rule, in the devastation, is the tick-tock that brings death. The other things, the acts of life and growth, do not belong to the

From this standpoint, we can see also why the Resurrection is the necessary seal of the Cross's redemptive effect.[81] The Resurrection reveals the heart of the Cross: the restoration of divine-human community, purged of the death-dealing intrinsic to all sinners' lives together. On the Cross, Christ walks the way of our violent fellowship to its end, uniting himself unreservedly to the horror of human community, in order that he might institute a new pattern of resurrected sociality as one so bound to us. It is not simply that he has returned to life, having conquered death; it is that he has returned to life *with us,* conquering the social death that patterns (to a greater or lesser extent) all human community on this side of the eschaton. Just as he has willed not to be incarnate without us, he has not willed to conquer death alone – we have been baptized into his death, so that we also might be united to his resurrection. By refusing to abandon us to the godforsakenness we have chosen, we are incorporated by God's grace into the whole Christ, made his living members as he extends his incarnate life in us. Indeed, Christ's resurrection bears significance for all creation, as death is overcome in all things, and as we are reconciled to it.[82]

This recognition that the whole Christ must be considered internal to the work of redemption opens new possibilities for understanding how the Cross justifies us. Internal to Augustine's own texts, *iustificare* clearly means "to be made righteous," rather than anything like the later forensic understandings of justification

metronome, and they are, now, in the devastated world, occasional contradictions of it, signs that it is not everything"; Paul J. Griffiths, *Decreation: The Last Things of All Creatures* (Waco, TX: Baylor University Press, 2014), 92.

[81] On Augustine's understanding of the Resurrection as bringing death to an end, see Babcock, "Christ of the Exchange," 144–150.

[82] Elizabeth Johnson has argued in this vein that "deep incarnation" must be matched by a "deep resurrection"; see Elizabeth A. Johnson, "Jesus and the Cosmos: Soundings in Deep Christology," in *Incarnation: On the Scope and Depth of Christology*, ed. Niels Henrik Gregersen (Minneapolis, MN: Fortress Press, 2015), 133–156 (especially 145–150); and *Creation and the Cross: The Mercy of God for a Planet in Peril* (Maryknoll, NY: Orbis Books, 2019), 187–194.

proposed by the Reformers.[83] Certainly there is little evidence in Augustine of anything like a justification that does not accomplish and accompany the transformation of those so justified. Yet, by recognizing the way that the whole Christ is intrinsic to the work of redemption (to be explored more fully below), my contemporary Augustinian account also departs from a more characteristically Roman Catholic understanding of Christ's work creating a storehouse of merits that is then communicated one-sidedly through the Sacraments and the Spirit's work. On my account, justification – being made righteous – is worked out historically with fear and trembling, through a noncompetitive relation of divine and human agency not only in Christ, but in us.[84] For this reason, we should say that justification is not fully accomplished until the end of all things, when the risen Christ has received the full measure of his glory through being united to and completed in his Body.

Christ transfigures our ability to relate to one another. By assuming our suffering and death into his own life, Christ opens to us the possibility for redeemed fellowship even in the midst of our isolation. His life mediates our presence to one another: a presence that, to the extent that we meet one another as members of the Body of Christ, does not participate in the death-dealing that marks all unredeemed human community. Our lives themselves become bodily signs of our Lord's presence to us: We are given to one another as gifts, our lives coming to serve as sacraments that effect the redemption to which they

---

[83] See here Isaac Chae, "Justification and Deification in Augustine: A Study of his Doctrine of Justification" (Unpublished Ph.D. Dissertation, Trinity Evangelical Divinity School, 1999), 82–89; though Chae notes the presence of some language of sinful humanity being declared righteous at 87–88.

[84] While I agree, then, with Kathryn Tanner's assessment that "What justification refers to in us is the fact of our unity with [Christ], our incorporation within his own life, which brings about our being born again to a new identity in him," I cannot agree that "Nothing about us, in and of ourselves, therefore has to change in order for us to be justified"; *Christ the Key*, 86. Our justification is our incorporation into Christ's life, but our agency is ingredient to this incorporation – though it is an exercise of agency that is founded upon grace, and thus ever secondary to the work of the Spirit.

testify. As we share this new life together, our loves joined together by the work of the Holy Spirit, we meet one another as fellow members of one Body, united under one Head; we become sites in the world where Christ encounters Christ. To understand how the Cross redeems us, it is not enough to describe the death of one human, even if that human is also God. Christ has willed that our redemption should be complete only *with* us, a "whole redemption" – whole with our lives together, empowered by the Spirit, and not otherwise.

Part III | The Body of Christ

8 | The Spirit of Christ

Jesus' cross and resurrection are inherently social realities. They function redemptively only as we are bound to them – bound to Christ. Nothing is lacking in or incomplete in the work Christ accomplishes on the Cross or in the eschatological life he breathes into creation on Easter morning, for all things are folded into them. Yet for these realities to be what they are, they must include us not only prospectively, but also actually. Even as the Incarnation is not a process (it is not something that needs to be completed historically, but is perfect from the moment Christ's flesh is brought into being in union with the Word in Mary's womb), it is a *work* – it touches, is intrinsically related to, and affects every moment of created history. In the same way, God's fellowship with sinful humanity and the new life opened in the Resurrection are fully and finally wrought on Golgotha and in the empty tomb, and yet these realities *already include* the histories by which we are bound to Christ more and more intimately throughout our lives.

This dynamic alerts us to the fact that we have to do, here again, with a divine reality – not simply the time-bound unfolding of creaturely existence, but a work unified across time by virtue of its origin in the eternity of the divine life. Even as the effects of this work are known in our lives as a halting growth in sanctity, because it is the work of *God*, the noncompetitive operation of this redemptive grace must be acknowledged as the selfsame triune act of God's life, eternity refracted into temporality in a manner that shows us the incomprehensible coact in being of the divine life. If Christ's life, death, and resurrection redeem us, they do so only because the same

Spirit who proceeds from Father and Son in eternity binds our hearts to the Father through the Son in history. Redemption is not a process, but it does proceed.

Just as attention to the place of Christ in Augustine's thought corrects a misreading of Augustinian anthropology as rooted in a "solipsistic egotism" or of Augustine as "forefather of the modern, Western idea of the individual, autonomous self,"[1] our Augustinian christology corrects a persistent inattention to pneumatology and a disconnection of Christ's work from the work of the Spirit. As is so often the case in Augustine's thought, the hinge is love: The God who is Love binds us to Herself through Christ by a love She sheds in our hearts. For as Augustine writes, "the love which is from God and is God is distinctively the Holy Spirit; through him the charity of God is poured out in our hearts, and through it the whole Trinity dwells in us (*per quam nos tota inhabitet trinitas*)."[2]

This chapter, and this third part more broadly, marks another turn in my argument. The frame of theological noncompetition in the relation of Christ's divine and human natures remains the same; but where previously we were focused upon how *Christ's* life receives its shape, here we begin to consider in more sustained fashion how Christ's life grants *ours* shape. Where the last part traced the Word's eternal act of assuming flesh and the consequences of His union with sinful humanity on the Cross, this part follows the Spirit's work as it redemptively reforms individual, human communities inclusive of but not limited to the Church, culminating in the Body of Christ in its eschatological fullness (inclusive of the nonhuman world). In this third and final part, we take as a central focus how we come to complete Christ: How our loves, our actions, our social bodies, our relations to the nonhuman world are made instruments of salvation,

---

[1] Charles Mathewes and Matthew Drever have both noted the critiques of Augustine along these lines; see Charles T. Mathewes, "Augustinian Anthropology: *Interior intimo meo*," *Journal of Religious Ethics* 27.2 (1999): 195–221, 213; and Drever, *Image, Identity, and the Forming of the Augustinian Soul*, 4.

[2] *trin.* 15.18.32; WSA I/5, 421 (modified).

the accomplishment of which grants Christ's life its full redemptive character and significance.

Yet here, too, we must hold in mind the lessons of my argument's earlier stages. Our agency is a proper focus of christology, particularly as we hold it to mediate Christ's human agency and thus accomplish his identity as Redeemer; but this agency is always in a responsive, noncompetitive relation to the priority of God's agency, even internally. We may turn to consider the Spirit's action in the world, but this work in our hearts remains the created effect of the simple act of the divine life in its Third Person, no less timeless than Christ's divinity in the Incarnation, and theologically inseparable from this Word in the unknowability of the divine life. The Spirit's acts are Her own, as a Person whose agency exists as a relation to the agency of Father and Son; yet the Spirit's acts are also Christ's, for there is only one will and one agency in the life of the God who is a simple multiplicity and a multiple simplicity. Even as we examine the outworking of Christ's identity in the Body in whom he lives, we cannot speak as if the relation between Head and Body is unidirectional, such that what is "objectively" accomplished in Christ is only later "subjectively appropriated" in those joined to him.[3] The work Christ accomplishes in us affects him in his humanity, extending and completing his life. It is not sufficient to consider only his agency in relation to ours; we must reckon also with *our* agency in relation to *his*, if we wish to approach him in the fullness of his eschatological divine-human identity.

This chapter begins this trajectory, attending to the Spirit's work in reforming the loves of those being joined to Christ. We will find that, rather than leading us to a solipsistic focus on interiority, our loves are the key points of connection to the world – both drawing us away from, and finally back to our Creator. It is the Holy Spirit *through* our loves who binds us to God and empowers us to cleave to Christ in our neighbor, and to our neighbor in Christ. It is thus in

---

[3] As, complicatedly, in Barth; cf. George Hunsinger, *How to Read Karl Barth: The Shape of His Theology* (Oxford: Oxford University Press, 1991), 35–42, and *passim*.

our loves – in coming to love with Christ's loves – that we are made members of him, the fullness of his Body.

***

Augustine offers two great schematizations of love – *De doctrina christiana* 1's *uti/frui* distinction, and *De civitate dei* 14's description of the "two loves" animating the beatific and diabolical modes of human sociality. As different as these two schematizations may be, they depend upon a common presupposition: that our love cannot finally rest in any finite good. For the Augustine of *De doctrina* 1, the triune Lord is the only object, the only "that toward which," that can be loved for its own sake. God alone is properly enjoyed; all other loves are intermediary, loved truly but not finally, since loving them rightly means loving them as creatures and signs of the infinitely lovable God. All other loves are "referred" to God, moving us by the weight of our love toward Him in the same movement by which we are drawn closer to the creatures He has made.[4] *De civitate dei* 14 draws out the contrary implication: If we take any object but God as the endpoint of our loves, our loves are referred away from God, to their only other possible terminus: the nothingness from which we have been drawn in creation, the natural endpoint of any love misdirected away from God.[5]

The startling claims that Augustine makes at times – that God alone is to be enjoyed, that there can be no true virtue apart from Christ – spring from his overriding interest in the consequences of our loves: namely, whether our lovings unite us to the triune Lord, or seduce us away from Her loving embrace. Augustine's controversial writings on the possibilities of pagan virtue, frequently treated by interpreters under the rubric of "splendid vices," make this feature of Augustine's thought apparent.[6] The very same action,

---

[4] *doct.* 1.22.21.

[5] *civ.* 14.28.

[6] See *civ.* 5.19. Jennifer Herdt has carefully assessed Augustine's teaching on pagan virtue and splendid vice at Jennifer A. Herdt, *Putting on Virtue: The Legacy of the Splendid Vices* (Chicago, IL: Chicago University Press, 2008), 45–71.

committed in the same moral context, may be virtuous or sinful depending on the quality of love from which the action springs.[7] Does this loving draw the lover closer to a stable beatitude, cleaving to God in Christ? Or does it, for all the admirability of any individual action performed on its basis, further deform the lover's affective constitution, damaging her very capacity to love the true Good in which all loves finally rest?

This attention to the teleology of love is foundational to Augustine's moral psychology. *Amor motus quidam sit*, he famously writes – love is a kind of movement.[8] At least equally well-known is his description of the *pondus amor* – the weight of our love.[9] At each point, Augustine is concerned to emphasize the directionality of love – love's purpose is to cross distance, uniting us to that which we love. Yet love is inertial: With two exceptions, an affective act does not simply bring us to its object and hold fast; it continues carrying us to the love for the sake of which we were – explicitly or implicitly – loving some intermediary good. This is no reflection on the desirability of that intermediary good itself, but rather uncovers for us the *nature* of that good. Of anything in creation, it is true that it has been drawn from nonbeing and is sustained in its existence by its participation in the triune Lord. Intrinsic to each creature is this twofold reference: to its origin, the nothing it is in itself; and to the Source of its life.

In loving some creature, we either love it as it actually *is* – namely, as a creature whose very existence speaks to us of the highest Good – or we love it as something it is not. And, in trying to love something other than what God has created, we find ourselves loving nothing at all – only a figment, a missed mark (ἁμαρτία) that ends up moving us away from God and back into the void. It is intrinsic

---

[7] *ep.Io.tr.* 5.7; WSA I/14, 82.

[8] *div. qu.* 35.1; WSA I/12, 49.

[9] *conf.* 13.9.10. This metaphor is deeply rooted in Augustine's thought from even his earliest writings; see Joseph Torchia, "'*Pondus meum amor meus*': The Weight-Metaphor in St. Augustine's Early Philosophy," *Augustinian Studies* 21 (1990): 163–176.

to the life of each creature that loving it should draw us closer to the Creator, for we are meant to love it as a sign of God. So Augustine: God alone "was able to say in the fullest possible sense, *I am who I am*; and, *You shall say, He who is has sent me to you* (Ex 3.14), which means that everything else that is, not only could not be unless it came from him, but also can only be good insofar as it has received its being so from him."[10] We are able to love creatures rightly – we might go further, and say we are only really able to love *them* at all – only if we love them as *sent*.

Far more than any Augustinian emphases on the unity of the soul,[11] this ontological feature of created existence accounts for the unity of knowing and loving in Augustine's thought. Loving rightly requires knowing the beloved truly (absent hypostatic union, at least), a problem that generates the many reflections of the *De Trinitate* – for how can one love what one does not know? To love some creature truly is to love it in its particularity, to love it in all the distinctness and complexity with which it has been brought into existence. It is a responsal movement of the soul toward the singularity in which God has created *that particular creature*. This response is elicited not only by the creature's intellectual availability to us, but at least as importantly, by its bodily availability: We taste the sweetness of the cherry, and are gladdened by it; we love the sea as we hear its churning waters and feel its buoyancy enveloping us; the softest caress from the hand of our lover can summon a flood of delight within us.

The incredible density of Augustine's moral psychology, and the central metaphors of an "order of love" or a "chain of love" or an "ascent" by means of love, are each given shape precisely by the particularity of each creature. One does not – or at least, should not – proceed helter-skelter through a series of creaturely lovings. Our lovings can appear to us as ordered precisely because they are

[10] *doct.* 1.32.25; WSA I/11, 121.
[11] On which, see Peter Burnell, *The Augustinian Person* (Washington, DC: The Catholic University of America Press, 2005), Chapter 2.

responsive to the providential order in which God has established creation. The true order of love simply loves things as they are, complete in the relationships within the created order in which God has set things. Because creation is complex, because we are set in many different relationships to one another and throughout the realm of finite being, many true "orderings" of love are possible; even apart from sin, we may be conveyed by our loves to God along many different pathways. Sin introduces a nearly limitless number of false orderings of love by which we can move to the only other end finally possible for us: extinction. But the work of redemption introduces a genuinely new possibility: a darkened peregrination through the world that, by grace, leads us finally home, at which point we are given a retrospective but no less truthful view of the good creation where we had wandered so long.

***

To sin, then, is to love wrongly – to fail to respond properly to the world, and more basically, to fail to respond properly to God's loving advent through it. In failing to love God as They should be loved, and in failing to love the world as God has made it, God is no longer the ultimate end to which all my affections are turned. I thus do not "move toward" God, becoming united to the Good that is identical to the divine life: I do not enter into a deeper intimacy with Them, I do not participate more fully in Their life, I am not made holier as my soul cleaves to Their perfect Good. Because our loves are turned to something other than God as their final end, each instance of sinful loving can only move us further away from God. This is just what it is for sin to be sin: It damages our relationship to the source of our life, introducing distance where once there was intimacy and creating a rift that calls for reconciliation.

This seems to me a commonsense account of the effects of sin: How could we imagine a sinful act drawing us closer into union with God of itself? *Qua* sin, mustn't a sinful act necessarily increase the spiritual distance between the sinner and God? Holding forth the possibility that some sinful act might draw us closer to God indicates that we have not sufficiently appreciated the gravity of sin. As Newman remarked,

> it were better for sun and moon to drop from heaven, for the earth to fail, and for all the many millions who are upon it to die of starvation in extremest agony, so far as temporal affliction goes, than that one soul, I will not say, should be lost, but should commit one single venial sin, should tell one wilful untruth, though it harmed no one, or steal one poor farthing without excuse.[12]

These words should not, I think, be discounted as hyperbole. They appear callous to us only if we forget or dispute that all these evils enter into God's good creation through sin. Each sin, even the most minor, carries in itself the seed of all the world's sufferings. Until we recognize this fact, we will not yet properly grieve our sin.

Sin, as it relates to our willing, is perhaps best understood as a sort of degenerative condition. The problem is not simply that we are unable to will the right thing; it is that our willing itself has been compromised, such that even when we will the right thing, we cannot will it rightly. However good the end of my desire, my willing of this end cannot, *post lapsum*, be perfectly ordered to God's goodness. To a greater or lesser extent, my willing will be marked by some trace of falsehood. For Augustine, this falsehood is paradigmatically that of inordinate self-love – of a refusal to know the world as God has created it and a preference for my own distorted projection of the world as I would have it be.[13] Yet, as I will argue below, this falsehood may also be an inordinate self-love

---

[12] John Henry Newman, *Certain Difficulties Felt by Anglicans in Catholic Teaching, Vol. 1: In Twelve Lectures Addressed in 1850 to the Party of the Religious Movement of 1833* (London: Longmans, Green, 1918 [1850]), 240.

[13] So Rowan Williams, *On Augustine*, 83, 88: "To see evil as privation is to see it as something that affects my own perception of what is good for me: If evil is the absence of good, it is precisely that misreading of the world which skews my desires"; Consequently, "if evil itself is never a subject or substance, the only way in which it can be desired or sought is by the exercise of the goods of mental and affective life swung

that undervalues the dignity and moral agency with which we have been created. We can believe the world's lies that we are less worthy, less capable, less qualified to respond to God's call to faithful action in the world. Though not the prideful self-assertion commonly associated with the Augustinian tradition, this is a natural extension of Augustine's account of disordered loves: whether we occupy the position of the dominator, or can only see ourselves and our world through the lies imposed on us through the domination of others, our willing is compromised; as a result of this disorder, we cannot see the world truly, or love it for what God has created it to be. Sin thus introduces a constitutive defect in our willing.

Because our fallen wills can only produce volitions that are more or less marked by sin, even our noblest acts – considered in themselves – can only move us farther away from God. To take a crude analogy: Imagine a complicated machine, with one loose part. Initially, the machine's operation will not be greatly affected; but as it continues to run, the loose part will introduce various irregularities in the ways that parts relate to one another. Gradually, other parts will become loose too, and the structural integrity of the whole mechanism will weaken. Eventually, as a result of that one loose part, the whole machine will decompose.

We are not, of course, machines, and our affective constitution does not function so mechanically. Our moral decohesion does not unfold as a consistent march toward wickedness: Even if left to our own devices, wholly lacking any assistance beyond the grace of our creation, we can imagine that the progressive derangement of our wills would proceed in fits and starts, sometimes plunging dramatically away from God, sometimes plateauing as we consolidate our moral losses and the ontological corruption of our natures. Yet the most determinative feature of these splendid vices is the instability of the constellation of desires that produce them. Though

around by error to a vast misapprehension, a mistaking of the unreal and groundless for the real."

the lust for glory may restrain for a time other vicious impulses, providing for an apparent growth or even heroism in virtue, the incoherence of these affective orderings only increases underneath the placid surface.

What is most important from the standpoint Augustine offers in *De civitate dei* is the orientation of one's desires, not the snapshot of one's affective order that could be made at any particular moment: Do your desires draw you into deeper intimacy with God, or do they release you into incoherence and the *nihil*? For Augustine, the answer for any sinful heart not turned to the love of God by grace must always and only be the latter, regardless of whatever apparent virtues might otherwise be manifested, and even if those virtues might be of such a quality that they can inspire others to greater devotion to God.[14] For Augustine, the "death of the soul leads to sin, since its life, that is, its God, abandons it, and it necessarily produces dead works until the grace of Christ brings it back to life."[15]

By their own power, then, our sinful wills cannot draw us closer to God.[16] In that our wills can only produce more or less sinful volitions *post lapsum*, our exercises of agency necessarily diminish our capacity to participate in the life of God. Rather than understanding the slide into nothingness as an unrelenting plunge downward, we might take instead the image of a satellite's degenerate orbit: At any one moment, the satellite might be moving at a velocity and course that are closer or farther away from those that would be appropriate to a stable orbit, but the inner trajectory of the system considered as a whole leads inexorably to orbital decay. So it is with the love of self to the contempt of God, qualitatively distinguishable from the proper ordering of one's desires to

---

[14] *civ.* 5.14.
[15] *nat. et gr.* 23.25; WSA I/23, 229. See also *gr. et lib. arb.* 4.7 and. 6.13; *corrept.* 2.3; and *praed. sanct.* 3.7.
[16] Han-Luen Kantzer Komline, *Augustine on the Will: A Theological Account* (Oxford: Oxford University Press, 2020), 148; cf. also 151–155, 248–249.

God as their final referent; and, though in our experience they are always mixed, two cities are founded on these loves.

Recognition of our condition should leave us profoundly skeptical of any self-directed projects of moral reformation. Again, under the proviso that we consider them merely as human enterprises and so absent any further grace beyond the (sinfully compromised) grace of creation, even our most admirable habits, actions, and dispositions – our generosity, our community-building, our care for and solidarity with the marginalized, our liturgical practices – can only hasten our destruction.[17] For these acts, or even other less obviously admirable acts, to succeed in drawing us back to God, there must be some redemptive efficacy added to them in excess of what they properly merit.[18] This is the logic of Augustine's much-maligned later anti-Pelagian works, and it is a logic I take to be the only one consistent with his understanding of sin as constitutive defect: No instance of sinful willing can draw our hearts closer to God, unless it is empowered by the Holy Spirit to produce a redemptive effect in excess of what the act itself possibly could.

The love of God that founds the *civitas Dei* is not, and indeed cannot be, a natural human orientation of the will after the Fall; any imperfect love of God compromised by sin could only lead to further derangement of our will. The love of God that animates the Church can only be the love that is God Herself shed abroad in our hearts, the Holy Spirit.[19] Only as this Love dwells within us, and communicates to us a grace that restores the damage done to our nature, can we be restored to God.[20]

***

---

[17] Augustine denies that the grace of creation is sufficient for the conversion of our wills at *praed. sanct.* 5.9–10.

[18] Komline, *Augustine on the Will*, 188.

[19] *ep.* 194.3.10. Cf. J. Patout Burns' *The Development of Augustine's Doctrine of Operative Grace* (Paris: Études Augustiniennes, 1980), 145ff, on the increasing importance of the Holy Spirit in Augustine's account of redemption.

[20] *ep.* 194.4.18.

Within Augustine's writings, this theme emerges in what has come to be called Augustine's "doctrine of operative grace," with particular attention to the question of the *initium fidei*, the beginning of faith.[21] His mature position, the position most consistent with his understanding of our willing as itself compromised by sin, may be summarized in a few lines of his late letter to the monks of Hadrumentum, *De gratia et libero arbitrio*:

> It is certain that we will when we will, but he causes us to will what is good, of whom were said the words I cited a little before, *The will is prepared by the Lord*. Of him it was said, *The Lord will direct the steps of human beings, and they will choose his path* (Ps 37:23); of him it was said, *It is God who produces in you the willing as well* (Phil 2:13). It is certain that we do an action when we do it, but he who says,

---

[21] The classic study of this topic is Burns, *Operative Grace*. Burns argues that after the year 418, a period in which Augustine composed the important texts *De gratia Christi*, *epistula* 194, and *Contra duas epistulas Pelagianorum*, he comes to believe that, as God grants those whom He chooses the "grace of conversion": "The divine operation reverses a contrary disposition towards evil in bringing a person to faith in Christ. Moreover, it actually produces the consent of faith. Those whom the Father teaches, who hear Christ's words of life, who receive the Spirit of faith invariably repent and receive the gift of charity" (157). Alongside Burns' study, a standard presentation of a significant shift in Augustine's understanding of God's elective purposes can be found in Peter Brown's description of Augustine's "lost future"; see *Augustine of Hippo: A Biography*, 2nd ed. (Berkeley, CA: University of California Press, 2000), 139–150. While such a shift does seem present to me in Augustine's thought, particularly on the question of whether our intellects are capable of driving our ascent to union with God or whether our desires take precedence as they are animated by grace, Carol Harrison offers important reminders on the continuity of Augustine's thought from early to late at *Rethinking Augustine's Early Theology: An Argument for Continuity* (Oxford: Oxford University Press, 2006). While Burns' study is undeniably helpful, it will become clear that my sympathies are with the reading of James Wetzel, whose critique of Burns may be found at James Wetzel, *Augustine and the Limits of Virtue* (Cambridge: Cambridge University Press, 1992), 190. Most recently, and most fully, Han-Luen Kantzer Komline has charted how Augustine's sense of the will's role in the *initium fidei* changes throughout Augustine's literary career, eventually reaching his mature stance that the fallen will can contribute nothing to the beginning of faith; see Komline, *Augustine on the Will*, chapters 2, 3, and 4, especially her presentation of Augustine's final position at 126.

I shall make you walk in my ordinances and observe and carry out my judgments (Ex 36:27), makes us do the action by offering fully efficacious strength to the will (*sed ille facit ut faciamus, praebendo vires efficacissimas voluntati*).[22]

Some of the defining features of the Hadrumentum correspondence are in plain view in this passage: Rather than extensive appeal to philosophical argument, the language of this text and the later texts *De correptione et gratia, De praedestinatione sanctorum*, and *De dono perseverantiae* is almost overwhelmingly Scriptural, even relative to Augustine's other writings. This decision is likely motivated both by awareness of his audience, and by a need to play defense against worries that the Augustinian doctrine of predestination was unfounded in Scripture.[23] He is concerned in these texts primarily to show that his doctrine of grace does not undermine the monastic life, and specifically practices of moral striving and correction. Without attention to Augustine's audience, it can appear that he has retreated into a sort of Scriptural fundamentalism – never mind that pressures in Augustine's conception of God, from his understandings of divine simplicity, timelessness, and omniscience through to his conception of sin's effects on our willing, that push him toward this conclusion.[24]

Here and elsewhere in his later works, Augustine is unambiguous: Our hearts are, because always sinful until fully restored to union with God, never able to produce anything but dead works,

---

[22] *gr. et lib. arb.* 16.32; WSA I/26, 92–3.

[23] See Augustine's response to his critics in *gr. et lib. arb.* 2.2; WSA I/26, 71: "he has revealed to us through his holy scriptures that there is free choice of the will in human beings. I remind you, however, how he revealed this, not by human words, but by the words of God."

[24] Though Augustine does not explicitly raise the nexus of concerns of simplicity, timelessness, and foreknowledge in the Hadrumentum correspondence, this is likely a concession to a readership that had already shown itself philosophically unsophisticated in the questions the community posed him; he discusses these concerns together at *civ.* 11.

and so must at each moment be drawn by the operation of grace beyond their own capacities. In order to succeed in our desire to draw closer to God, God Herself must assist us in adding "fully efficacious strength to the will." At each moment of our redemption, "both in its beginning and in its completeness,"[25] "both in its increments and in its beginnings faith is a gift from God."[26] This work of grace persists throughout our lives, strengthening our wills and illuminating our intellects with as much consistency as God desires, but always in excess of what our knowing and loving could produce on its own. To the extent that we come to desire God's renovating work, this too is a product of the Holy Spirit's activity within us.

Yet emphasizing the Spirit's priority in our redemption should not lead us to understand this divine work improperly – denying, for instance, that any external reality can play a role in our conversion, or that external signs can contribute to turning our hearts back to God.[27] On such an account, the advent of the Holy Spirit would be a wholly internal affair, one that would mark a clear before and after in the life of faith.[28] Before, we would be autonomous in our sin; after, moved irresistibly by an interior activity of God. Before, *sub lege*; after, *sub gratia*. Each moment after grace's advent would define a before and after, in fact, as each new gracious intervention creates a capacity to will a good that we could not before. Such an

---

[25] *praed. sanct.* 8.16; WSA I/26, 163.

[26] *praed. sanct.* 11.22; WSA I/26, 167.

[27] This is the heart of Wetzel's disagreement with Burns, particularly as the latter contrasts Augustine's earlier theology of congruent vocation with his later doctrine of operative grace. Phillip Cary has similarly argued that Augustine's doctrine of grace precludes his holding to the redemptive efficacy of outward signs at Phillip Cary, *Outward Signs: The Powerlessness of External Things in Augustine's Thought* (Oxford: Oxford University Press, 2008), 191.

[28] Augustine does, of course, frequently speak of this as an inward transformation, as at *praed. sanct.* 8.13. This section is also interesting for its emphasis on the Father's role as internal teacher, drawing together both the Son's revelatory work and the Spirit's conversion of the affections, stressing (as John 6.43–6 suggests) that the source of the divine salvific agency is to be appropriated to the Father.

account might be thought necessary to avoid any suggestion that we are responsible for the change in the orientation of our loves.

James Wetzel has noted, however, a surprising feature of Augustine's doctrine of grace: The more he stresses our powerlessness to turn our loves to God, the more hesitant he is to identify the beginnings of grace's work in our hearts. "Once he finds himself in the midst of redemption, the beginning of the process will elude the reach of his memory, much in the way that its completion extends beyond his expectation."[29] God's grace is experienced as "anachronistic": Rather than seeing a qualitatively new operation of grace at work in the moment of our conversion, we come to see grace as always preceding our activity, without being able to isolate any moment of our lives when this work began.

On Wetzel's telling, Augustine's account of grace is intended to rule out any suggestion that our own activity might come prior to God's act in our redemption. The anachronism of grace is not a contingent feature of our experience – a mere inability to isolate the moment when grace did, in fact, begin working within us – but rather a *structural* feature of the relation between divine and human activity. We must learn to see God's gracious activity as irreducibly prior to our own working, whether our wills remain in bondage to sin and thus tending to our dissolution or whether our wills are drawing us back to the love of God.

The upshot of Wetzel's presentation is that our whole lives, and all our willing, come to be seen as dependent upon the grace of God and included within God's redemptive work. No firm distinction can be drawn between God's use of external realities to draw us back to Him and God's work enlivening our desires through operative grace. The God who offers us creaturely signs pointing us back to Him is not separate from the one who is *interior intimo meo*, and so God's gracious work through these things is also the work in which God operates within. Though the moment in which our hearts are

---

[29] Wetzel, *Limits of Virtue*, 194.

converted to the love of God does indicate a qualitative shift in the ordering of our desires, the work by which God accomplishes this conversion need not be seen as more internal or more external than the preparatory work which began before our births.

This approach does nothing to undermine our reliance on grace: Our condition when desirous of the *nihil* is as dire as it seems, and our conversion really is as dependent upon grace as Augustine claims. Yet Wetzel's account allows us to view this work of the Holy Spirit in its proper relation to human freedom. Our dependence upon grace does not undermine our autonomy or diminish our freedom, but rather intensifies the only freedom worth having.[30] At the base of Augustine's understanding of human freedom is a simple claim: "If God's power always lies at the bottom of ours, then we must cease trying to mark self-determination at the point where unadulterated human power begins to assert itself."[31] It is not our ability to resolve an inward indeterminacy between willing good or willing evil that marks our creaturely freedom. On the contrary, we are most free when we will in the way God has created us to will – when we will what God wills that we should will. In sinful willing, we see the bondage of our incapacity to will according to our nature;[32] in our freedom, we are able to will the good perfectly, and are thus most fully ourselves.

This is, fundamentally, a logic of noncompetition between divine and creaturely agency, one that teaches us to see all our willing and indeed our very existence as a response to the ever-prior work of

---

[30] We may describe his position as a compatibilist one, as at Lynne Rudder Baker, "Why Christians Should Not be Libertarians: An Augustinian Challenge," *Faith and Philosophy* 20.4 (2003); Katherin A. Rogers, "Augustine's Compatibilism," *Religious Studies* 40.4 (2004): 415–435; and Couenhoven, "Augustine's Rejection of the Free-Will Defence." As Wetzel writes at *Limits of Virtue*, 216, however, "the issue of contention is not whether grace and freedom are compatible, but whether freedom is even intelligible apart from grace."

[31] Wetzel, *Limits of Virtue*, 126.

[32] So Wetzel, *Limits of Virtue*, 206: "Freedom to resist grace is not . . . genuine freedom but bondage to sin."

God.[33] We must make the leap of viewing freedom as being defined by the freedom to do what God wills. As Augustine notes in a letter at the end of his life,

> entrust yourself without delay not to yourself . . . but to that powerful one who is able to do all things. Do not wait until he wills it, as if you were going to offend him if you willed it first. For, whenever you have willed it, you will be willing it with his help and by his working. His mercy, of course, anticipates you so that you may will it, but when you will it, you yourself will it. For, if we do not will when we will, then he does not give us anything when he makes us will.[34]

It is God who creates us, and God who creates a new will in us as we are redeemed. Only grace can draw our desires back to God, enabling us to will the good, know the world and our histories truly, and receive our lives and world as gift. Grace enables us to love the world more truly than we know, and empowers the fragile offering of our still-sinful volitions to bring us – otherwise impossibly – closer to God.

Yet this does not trample on our will or autonomy. To think it does would, as Wetzel cautions against, be to understand our wills as the one part of our existence that is most truly our own only when God is absent from it. It would be to understand the sinful will as paradigmatic of our freedom. Instead, for Augustine, our wills are most fully our own when they perfectly reflect God's own, when we will as the redeemed creatures we are. Our freedom is not exclusive of God's willing, but is founded upon it. There is no constraint that God's will imposes on our own; it is sin that holds our will in

---

[33] Couenhoven has carefully marked how this shift from a libertarian to a compatibilist understanding of freedom led him to abandon the free will defense against the problem of evil, and to focus instead on the deficient cause of a sinful will and the condition of possibility of the fall in our changeability; see "Augustine's Rejection of the Free-Will Defense," 286–290.

[34] *ep.* 2*.7; WSA II/4, 236. Cited at Wetzel, *Limits of Virtue*, 195. See also *gr. et lib. arb.* 21.42.

bondage, making us powerless to return to God. Her enlivening of our will is a work of liberation.

We misunderstand the nature of our dependence upon God if we wait passively for this work to take place in us before striving for holiness. Our wills – really *our* wills – are made vehicles of our sanctification by the power of the Spirit, and even the desire for greater faith and love of the good are signs of the Spirit's work within us. Yet because both our existence and our power to will our redemption are utterly dependent upon God's own redemptive will, there can be no question of our willing this good with an autonomy contrasted with God's agency. From the beginning of salvation to its completion, our redemption is the work of God, and it is *because* of that fact that it is also truly ours.

It is this truth that extends soteriologically a dynamic that has been well identified in Augustine's theological anthropology. To speak of a "self" in Augustine's thought is not to speak of a reality closed off from the world, a place to which we might retreat in solitude, but is rather to speak of a life constitutively open to and actively dependent upon God.[35] For the Augustinian, there is no "self" at all that is not created for active and ecstatic contemplation of God. To the extent we do not turn to God in knowledge and love, we do not exist – we really are nothing. This is the conclusion to which Augustine leads his readers in the *De trinitate*: We are only

[35] Charles Taylor and Phillip Cary offer classic presentations of Augustine as the progenitor of the modern "self" at Charles Taylor, *Sources of the Self: The Making of the Modern Identity* (Cambridge, MA: Harvard University Press, 1989); and Phillip Cary, *Augustine's Invention of the Inner Self: The Legacy of a Christian Platonist* (Oxford: Oxford University Press, 2000). Contrasting proposals emphasizing the instability of any notion of the self in Augustine may be found at Michael Hanby, *Augustine and Modernity* (London: Routledge, 2003); John C. Cavadini, "The Darkest Enigma: Reconsidering the Self in Augustine's Thought," *Augustinian Studies* 38.1 (2007): 119–132; James Wetzel, "The Force of Memory: Reflections on the Interrupted Self," *Augustinian Studies* 38.1 (2007): 147–159; Matthew Drever, "The Self Before God? Rethinking Augustine's Trinitarian Thought," *Harvard Theological Review* 100.2 (2007): 233–242 and *Image, Identity, and the Formation of the Augustinian Soul*; Rowan Williams, *On Augustine*, 163–5; and Jean-Luc Marion, *In the Self's Place*, 96.

truly the image of God when we are engaged in active contemplation of the triune Lord.[36] Before that end without end, our "self" is
not a settled matter, but always in progress. As John Cavadini has
written, "Someone who is self-aware is aware not of 'a self' but of
a struggle, a brokenness, a gift, a process of healing, a resistance to
healing, an emptiness, a reference that impels one not to concen-
trate on oneself, in the end, but on that to which one's self-
awareness propels one, to God."[37] This is the fundamental character
of the Christian life on an Augustinian account: a continual turning
back to God; a recognition of the failure properly to love God and
the world; a deepening awareness both of one's sin and of the
goodness of one's created nature; a halting journey through which
we are opened to the presence of God, and the others whom God
has given us.

This tension at the heart of our notions of selfhood or identity has
been commented upon by Wetzel as one of the animating insights
of Augustine's theological project. Speaking specifically of the
Confessions, Wetzel writes, "The basic imperative of confession
holds constant throughout Augustine's thirteen tries at self-
recollection and knowledge of God, and that is for him to face the
great question of himself. Part of what it means for him to face this
question is to suffer the death of his straying self; the other part is to
surrender to the life that works through this death."[38] On this
account, our lives are lived confessionally, caught in a cyclical
movement of dispossession, reception of God's gift, and responsive
self-offering.[39]

As with Wetzel's caution about Augustine's theology of grace,
however, we must not think that we can identify a beginning of this
process. It is not that we are first dispossessed of the false identity we

---

[36] *trin.* 14.8.11; 14.12.15; Williams, *On Augustine*, 175.
[37] Cavadini, "The Darkest Enigma," 123.
[38] Wetzel characterizes Augustine's writings as taking place in a "confessional mode" at
Parting Knowledge, 61; the quotation is found at *Parting Knowledge*, 60.
[39] Wetzel brings these three terms together at *Parting Knowledge*, 262.

have constructed for ourselves, only to receive a true sense of ourselves in relation to God subsequently. Rather, it is through the death of the old human that we receive the new human, and in the very reception of new life in Christ that the old human is shown to be phantasmal. This recognition does nothing but repeat in our own lives what is true of Christ's death and resurrection: This death is only redemptive inasmuch as it is the means by which we are united to Life itself, and in so doing, Life puts death to death. The grace that works to turn our hearts back to God is the same grace, working inseparably, that leads the Son of God to the Cross.

***

Indeed, more than this: the grace by which we are born into new life is the work of the same Spirit that gives Christ's own human life its redemptive shape. Augustine says as much at *De praedestinatione sanctorum* 15.31:

> let this fountain of grace be seen from which grace is poured out through all his members according to the measure of each. Each human being becomes a Christian from the beginning of his faith by the same grace by which that man became Christ from his beginning. Each person is reborn by the Spirit by whom he was born. The same Spirit produced in us the forgiveness of sins who brought it about that he had no sin.[40]

Augustine subtly invokes the inseparability of the trinitarian operations here; he does not go so far as to say that the Spirit Himself accomplishes the Incarnation, or that the Spirit is all that prevents Christ from sinning. Yet the Son is never who He is apart from the work of the Spirit, and so the Spirit (and, by extension, the Father) must be affirmed to work the Incarnation and to sustain Christ's sinless life as well. It is not that they act "alongside" the Son; what it *is* for the Son to act is for Him to act in union with the Spirit and the Father. The Word's human birth is unthinkable apart from the

---

[40] WSA I/26, 174.

divine action of the Spirit – the same Spirit that dwells in the hearts of believers, regenerating their loves and drawing their hearts back to God.

But this entailment of work and presence of course runs both ways.[41] Even as we speak of the Spirit's operative grace empowering us to love God, we must also identify this action as the work of the divine Son. Indeed, the grace by which Christ creates faith within us is the same grace by which he willed to assume human flesh. It is significant in this connection that one of Augustine's preferred titles for Christ in his later writings is the "predestined man": "There is ... no more illustrious example of predestination than the mediator himself"; apart from any merit or good willing, this human was called into being as the recipient of the grace of union with God.[42] Our predestination is inextricable from his own: God "predestined both him and us, because he foreknew not our merits, but his future works both in him in order that he might be our head and in us in order that we might be his body."[43] It is not merely union with humanity that the Word predestines, but the whole redemptive shape of Christ's life – God predestines our lives united with His, all the redemptive works he will accomplish through our lives.

---

[41] On Christ as the source of operative grace, see *corrept.* 11.32.

[42] *persev.* 67; WSA I/26, 236. See also *corrept.* 11.30 and *persev.* 15.31. Keech, *Anti-Pelagian Christology*, 222–228. In his description of Christ as "predestined man," I would add Augustine's account of Christ the predestined human to the convergence between Barth and Thomas identified at Matthew Levering, "Christ, the Trinity, and Predestination: McCormack and Aquinas," in *Trinity and Election in Contemporary Theology*, ed. Michael T. Dempsey (Grand Rapids, MI: Wm. B. Eerdmans, 2011), 244–273; and Bruce L. McCormack, "Processions and Missions: A Point of Convergence between Thomas Aquinas and Karl Barth," in *Thomas Aquinas and Karl Barth: An Unofficial Catholic-Protestant Dialogue*, eds. Bruce L. McCormack and Thomas Joseph White (Grand Rapids, MI: Eerdmans, 2013), 99–126. In this vein, see Komline's identification of the Augustinian roots of Barth's doctrine of election at Han-Luen Kantzer Komline, "Barth and Augustine," in *Wiley Blackwell Companion to Karl Barth*, Vol. 2, eds. George Hunsinger and Keith L. Johnson (Hoboken, NJ: John Wiley, 2000), 421–434; 425–428.

[43] *persev.* 67.; WSA I/26, 236.

To be redeemed, to have our hearts turned back to God by the work of the Spirit and to participate more deeply in the triune life of God, is thus to find our own place within the shape of Christ's life. As the Word's eternal will to assume flesh is also the origin of the grace that regenerates our hearts, our progression in faith must be a progression into the concrete reality of Christ's human life. As Augustine writes in the sixtieth of his *Enarrationes in Psalmos*: "Christ has made himself a pattern for the life you live now by his labors, his temptations, his sufferings, and his death; and in his resurrection he is the pattern for the life you will live later."[44] This very movement into Christ, driven by the weight of our loves, is the confessional movement by which we receive our lives anachronically, in a beginningless giving to which we are always late. It is the same movement by which we are dispossessed of the false conceptions of the world born of our misshapen desires – a dispossession experienced sometimes with the gentleness of a pleasant dream dissipating as we wake into a quiet morning, and sometimes with the world-shattering force of the crucifixion of our intellects. Both this reception of our lives at Christ's hand and the collapse of the lie that sin has made our perception of the world are necessary if we are to respond to the gift God has given, meeting the divine love of God with the burning of our own perfected desires. Finding ourselves in Christ, uncovering the deceptions into which our sin had led us, offering ourselves over to the triune Lord – this is Christ alive in us.

***

In the midst of Augustine's *epistula* 194 to Sixtus, he includes a reminder in the course of interpreting Christ's discourse in John 6:

> *And he said, For this reason I told you that no one can come to me unless it has been given to him by my Father* (Jn 6.66). This is why some of those who heard him speaking of his flesh and blood went away scandalized, but some remained because they believed, because

---

[44] *en.Ps.* 60.4; WSA III/17, 195.

no one can come to him unless it has been given to him by the Father and, hence, by the Son and by the Holy Spirit. For the gifts and works of the inseparable Trinity are not separate.[45]

In describing the operation of grace in the heart of the elect as the work of the Holy Spirit, we must always remember that the Spirit's activity is inseparable from that of the Father and the Son. Yet this is far more than a formal reminder of the eternal triunity of God's life, even in the heart of the believer. In recognizing the trinitarian shape of the Spirit's action, we affirm that God's love poured out in our hearts is none other than Christ's loves.

In the life of Christ and the gift of the Holy Spirit, we find two temporal manifestations of the eternal life of God. The life of Christ offers us the true image of God, a human life exhaustively determined by the love of God – in fact, a human life which finds its subsistence solely as the human life of the Word. In the Holy Spirit, we find that this very same power of God comes to dwell within us, creating in us the love of God and conforming both our desires and the actions that proceed from them to the will of God.[46] Throughout the writings of the anti-Pelagian period, Augustine increasingly comes to describe Christ as the only just human.[47] Christ is unique in his perfect love of God, a love that properly orders all his other desires as referring finally to the *summum bonum*.

In the integrity of his person, the divine will is perfectly united to a human will. Christ's human will is God's will, no less than the will of the Word is one with the will of the Father and the Holy Spirit; and to the extent that it is possible within the created order, the human will and desires of Christ reflect and perfectly express all that is contained in Christ's divine will. Christ's human will and

---

[45] *ep.* 194.3.12; WSA II/3, 294.
[46] Komline considers the Holy Spirit as the divine will that conforms our wills to itself at *Augustine on the Will*, 352–363.
[47] Dodaro underlines the importance of Augustine's descriptions of Christ as uniquely just at *Christ and the Just Society*, 78.

desires are thus intrinsically related to the will of the Holy Spirit, just as is true of Christ's divinity. We see moments of this interrelation in the Scriptural witness, as when Christ is driven into the wilderness by the Spirit, or preaches in the synagogue at Nazareth the year of the Lord's favor.[48] Throughout his ministry, the Holy Spirit empowers Christ's human nature as a reflection of the Spirit's differentiated identity with the Son who is incarnate in Christ.[49] The Son and Spirit (along with the Father's act of sending, expressed temporally as the Father's commanding of Christ) therefore operate inseparably not only in eternity, but also in enabling the responsive and perfect human love of God in Christ.[50] Christ's human desires exist not only as those of the human life assumed into unity with and dependent for its personal subsistence upon the Word, but as human desires answering to the indwelling of the Holy Spirit.

In a very real sense, then, the desires created in *us* by the power of the Holy Spirit are Christ's own desires – inseparably united to his human affections. As Augustine writes at *en.Ps.* 32.ii.2, "In his human will he embodied ours in advance, since he is our Head and we all belong to him as his members . . . in displaying the will proper to a human being he displayed your nature, and straightened you out."[51] In this sermon, Christ's redemptive effect is principally figured as exemplary and educative, even as he recognizes the Spirit to be with Christ and the Father "one in godhead, so there can be no disparity of will."[52] By the time of *De trinitate* 4, he will speak more expansively of the *totus Christus* being bound together "by virtue of

---

[48] See Eugene F. Rogers Jr., *After the Spirit: A Constructive Pneumatology from Resources outside the Modern West* (Grand Rapids, MI: Wm. B. Eerdmans, 2005), 61.

[49] Bruce L. McCormack has highlighted the importance of the Spirit's ministrations to Christ's human nature at "Karl Barth's Christology as a Resource for a Reformed Version of Kenoticism." *International Journal of Systematic Theology* 8.3 (2006): 243–251.

[50] Cf. Komline, *Augustine on the Will*, 335–336.

[51] WSA III/15, 393.

[52] WSA III/15, 393.

one and the same wholly harmonious will reaching out in concert to the same ultimate happiness, and fused somehow into one Spirit in the furnace of charity," connecting this unity of will explicitly to God's consubstantiality.[53] The later discussion in the same book of the *filioque* makes clear that the Spirit shed in our hearts who conforms our will to Christ's will is indeed the Spirit of the Son as well as the Father.[54] In *trin.* 15, it is the Spirit of Christ, "God the Holy Spirit *proceeding from God* who fires man to the love of God and neighbor when he has been given to him, and *he himself is love.* Man has no capacity to love God except from God."[55]

Inasmuch as we will what the Spirit wills – an always-imperfect identity on this side of the eschaton – we will the content of Christ's divine-human will. Inasmuch as our loves are ordered properly by and to the love of God, our loves correspond to Christ's own human loves, enlivened by the presence of God in him.[56] It is perhaps not too misleading to imagine that, as our wills come to be shaped ever more fully by the gracious activity of the Spirit, our wills come to reflect (again, always imperfectly) what Christ himself would have done had the circumstances of his life been exchanged with our own. Just as Christ's will is the Word's perfect human repetition in time of what She wills eternally, so also our wills come to resemble more and more a responsive human willing of the Spirit that dwells within us – a Spirit which is the Spirit of Christ, willing none other than Christ wills.[57]

The relevant difference is that what we will by grace, Christ wills by nature; or, more precisely, we will by grace what Christ wills

---

[53] *trin.* 4.9.12; WSA I/5, 161, modified.

[54] *trin.* 4.20.29.

[55] *trin.* 15.17.31; WSA I/5, 421 (emphasis added).

[56] Cf. Komline, *Augustine on the Will*, 308.

[57] Cf. Paul J. DeHart, *Unspeakable Cults: An Essay in Christology* (Waco, TX: Baylor University Press, 2021), 185: "because both the Word (in Jesus) and the Spirit (in the communities of faith) are self-relations of the selfsame God, a single respiration organically unites with Jesus' new body the communal body that continues to represent Jesus as a sign in the old world."

necessarily in his humanity by virtue of that humanity's hypostatization by the Word. The Spirit enables us to will what Christ wills. Indeed, because Christ reigns in heaven even now united to his human flesh, we must say that in drawing our loves to God and teaching us to will what God wills, the Spirit conforms us to what Christ actively *does* will for any particular situation. In this way, the lives of the saints are lived not only in imitation of Christ, but as an extension of Christ's own life – his will becoming ours through the Spirit's activity.

It is in this sense that we must speak of the love of God as the means of our union with Christ. The Spirit creates in us the love of God; but we cannot come to love God without loving also the human who is God. "Because now you are unable to see," Augustine tells us,

> let your task consist in desiring. The entire life of a good Christian is a holy desire. What you desire, however, you don't yet see. But by desiring you are made large enough, so that, when there comes what you should see, you may be filled ... This is how God stretches our desire through delay, stretches our soul through desire, and makes it large enough by stretching it. Let us desire, then, brothers, because we have to be filled.[58]

We have seen already that Christ is the center of this *dispensatio similitudinum*, this regime of signs. We have seen too that he is the point in created history to which all created signs refer, and in so doing, show us visibly how all created signs refer to the invisible God. It is love that carries us to God, stretching our soul and fitting us for the blessed vision of God in His heavenly city.

Though all this is critically important, it is incomplete if not supplemented by the conclusions of this chapter: The love by which our souls are stretched, the desire that forms the "entire life" (*tota vita*) of the Christian, is the work of the Holy Spirit within

---

[58] *ep.Io.tr.* 4.6; WSA I/14, 69.

us. Not in abstraction from Christ, for this renovating grace is accomplished by the divine person who is consubstantial with and proceeds from both Father and Son – it is truly the Son's work as well, in that the Spirit never works except inseparably from Son. Yet also not in competition with our own agency; for as we noted in Chapter 2, God's agency is utterly prior to our own even as eternity has priority (without having temporal precedence) to any moment of time.

By the Spirit's work, it may truly be said that it is no longer we (sinners) who live, but Christ who lives in us. His loves are made our loves as our souls are animated by his Spirit. His actions are accomplished historically as our actions, as they spring from his holy loves which have taken root in our heart. His glorified knowledge of the world becomes our own, as we learn to see truly for the first time the world God has created. Leaving aside the self-deceptions that characterize our experiences as sinners, we learn to see the purposes of God threading through our lives, God's gracious activity always preceding our own. In this new understanding of our lives in God, we find that our own judgments about our lives come to reflect ever more deeply God's own – we see our sin as sin, and our flailing desires as inchoate longings for God.

Christ's life is repeated in our own, novel in circumstance, and in that we are freed to live our lives fully the more he lives in us. Though Christ remains unique in that his human flesh exists only as the human life of the Word, we find in our own lives a movement toward the same perfect responsiveness of our human wills to the will of God working within us. The "blurred form" of our sinful lives passes into the "clear form" of our life in Christ (*transimus de forma obscura in formam lucidam*).[59] Our lives become an extension of the Incarnation.

∗∗∗

---

[59] *trin.* 15.8.14.

And yet, the mystery extends still further; for the human whose life provides redemptive form to our own is a human like we are, a man whose life exists not in splendid isolation but in generative commerce with the world.[60] If Christ still lives, even more if he lives in us, our willings and lovings have the potential to mark his own willings and lovings in the world today.

It is worth being precise on this point. From all eternity, the will and desire of Christ are the will and desire of the Word, the eternal Son of God. In Jesus Christ, this eternal will and love is manifested in a human life. Yet precisely because it is a *human* life, the manifestation and historical accomplishment of the Word's eternal love occurs only in responsiveness to the world. In his divine nature, the Word's love is utterly complete before all ages; but in his human nature, Christ's desires are responsive to and shaped by the existence and agency of the world. This is no threat to Christ's ability to manifest the divine will that is his own from all eternity; indeed, the historicity and responsiveness of Christ's human will are *precisely how* his divine love is made known in creation.

This puts us in an interesting position when considering his relation to the individual Christian, whose desire is enlivened by the work of the Holy Spirit and empowered for the love of God and neighbor. As true as it is that both Christ's divine love and his human loves are present and made known in the hearts of individual Christians (and indeed, in the hearts of all those whom the Spirit is drawing closer to the Father – perhaps not identical groupings), it is *also* true that Christ's human loves are *responsive* to the agency of those in whom he lives. The influence is not unidirectional, from Christ to the Church; it is also the case that, because he is human,

---

[60] Cf. DeHart's hypothesization of a theological outlook in which "the Word's presence and the Spirit's act are not juxtaposed against the human dynamics of history but utilize just those dynamics, in their autonomy and fragility. God 'speaks' the Word into history and is heard there, and the divine 'meaning' is truly made humanly meaningful; but the humanly meaningful means the historically meaningful, and historical meaning occurs as culture" (*Unspeakable Cults*, 104).

the lives of those who are his Body give shape to his own life, affect his own risen and glorified loves and desires across the history of the Church.

It is not simply that Christ loves my neighbor in me. It is also the case that, empowered by the love of God shed in my heart through the Holy Spirit, I come to love my neighbor in a manner that is unique to me, my creaturely particularity delighting in her creaturely particularity. Inasmuch as my loving is also Christ's loving in me, he comes to delight in *my* delight in my neighbor – his human love of my neighbor is perfected, made a true manifestation of the divine love he has had for my neighbor from all eternity, as it is informed by my human love for my neighbor. This is not to say there was any deficit in his love of my neighbor that is corrected by his loving my neighbor through me; or indeed, that there is any sense in which I love my neighbor "better" than Christ does. But it is to say that the way Christ comes to love my neighbor in the particularity of his human life is marked, *in saecula saeculorum*, by the way he has loved my neighbor through the particularity of my human life.

Call it the particular intensity and intimacy of a love shared in difficult circumstances; call it the indelible bond that is formed when one acts sacrificially for the good of another. We know these experiences to be among the most lasting traces one life can leave on another. As we participate redemptively in Christ, Christ participates in the love that members of his Body share amongst themselves in their most joyful and desperate moments. His human life is marked by these moments, as surely as it was marked by the care of the Blessed Virgin.

To the extent that my life and actions spring from the love of God that the Holy Spirit has cultivated in my heart, Christ has made himself known to my neighbor through me; and who he will be for my neighbor in the City of God – indeed, who he will be for the whole of his Body, the particularity of his human life itself – is shaped by loving my neighbor through me. By the work of the Holy Spirit, Christ loves the world through us, and is changed by the experience.

9 | A Crucified People

There can be no solitary Christian. To be redeemed just is to be forgiven and restored to loving fellowship with one's neighbor and God, by the neighbor who is God.

It would be a mistake, then, to see the Holy Spirit's work in the heart of each believer as a two-stage process, first healing the heart of each believer and then fashioning a new community out of those who are being redeemed. *Caritas* is the gift that the Spirit sheds in our hearts – an inherently directed gift, moving us and uniting us to God by way of Christ's humanity. It is not Christ in the abstract to whom we are united – it is to Christ the Head, complete with his Body. Within the work of redemption, there is no union with God or Christ that can take place without uniting us by the same movement to the many diverse neighbors who compose Christ's body. Fellowship and solidarity with our neighbor is not the outflow or consequence of our redeemed life; it is the substance of that life. Life together is what it is for us to have been redeemed.

If we have treated the internal work of the Spirit first in the preceding chapter, it cannot be because that work precedes Her work within human communities. Indeed, in the order of being, the priority runs the other direction: It is Christ who is the primary reality in the work of redemption; we are saved only as he unites us to him in one *totus Christus*. Only in the order of knowing, as we learn to see our sin and the ways our disordered lovings have separated us from one another, might it appear that the Spirit's work in the individual Christian comes first. It appears this way to us because sin has convinced us that we can be creatures of God by ourselves.

The confessional movement of dispossession, reception of God's gift, and responsive self-offering that marks our conversion and wandering return to God must accordingly be seen not only as a feature of the individual's life, but of our life together. As M. Shawn Copeland has written, "self-dispossession is the price solidarity exacts."[1] We sinners cannot simply make an inward retreat from the world and ascend upward to God. We must be taught whom to love through the signs God has given us: the sign of Christ's human life, the cosmos that testifies to his divinity, the neighbor in whom we encounter his humanity. We have no way of loving the God whom we cannot see that is not also and intrinsically love of the world that shows us God. And this love will cost us: cost us our sense of ourselves, cost us the patterns of communal life we have built, cost us the false world our sin has fashioned for us, so that we may live truly in the world God has made.

***

As Augustine sees, our inward disintegration both stands at the root of our social fracture, and is hastened by it. The inner and outer effects of sin are mutually reinforcing; nevertheless, it makes sense to begin here by moving from a consideration of how our inward disorder creates a disordered communal life. Robert Dodaro has noted the consequences of sin visible in our ignorance (the "incapacity to know oneself, others, and God with utter moral clarity"), weakness in willing the good,[2] and fear of death (*timor mortis*).[3] The three are, in fact, related: As Dodaro writes, "the moral object of knowledge is also in some respect an object of love, and, conversely, that which is not known cannot be loved,"[4] while the fear of death is both partially motivated by our inability to understand ourselves as

---

[1] M. Shawn Copeland, *Knowing Christ Crucified: The Witness of African-American Religious Experience* (Maryknoll, NY: Orbis Books, 2018), 145.

[2] Robert Dodaro, *Christ and the Just Society in the Thought of Augustine* (Cambridge: Cambridge University Press, 2004), 28.

[3] Dodaro, *Christ and the Just Society*, 30.

[4] Dodaro, *Christ and the Just Society*, 29.

the creatures of God and produces in us an inability to see our own lives included in Christ's death.

Perhaps most perniciously, the anxiety that the ever-present fear of death produces in us makes us dread the loss of that which we possess. We are aware of the impermanence of our possessions, and thus attempt to secure them from a world that threatens on every side. Our lives become a sustained effort in crisis management, seeking to safeguard that which we always imperfectly know and value as good. This is the logic of empire, as Augustine traces throughout the *De civitate dei* under the rubric of the *libido dominandi*.[5] Yet the *libido dominandi* also functions significantly in our attempts to understand one another, enter into social relations with one another, and attempt to know ourselves in light of these interactions. In being (mis)directed to, for instance, glory, wealth, or safety as the ultimate end of our love, we come to desire other subsidiary goods inasmuch as we take them to bring us greater glory, wealth, or safety.

These evaluative judgments grant a provisional intelligibility to our lives. Sin creates a world for us – a world we are able to inhabit, if only for a time.[6] We are able to narrate the goals we are pursuing in acting the way we do; we can give an account of what the world is like, and what we value within it; we can give an account of what might make our own lives meaningful. Yet this intelligibility is inherently unstable; no finite good can ultimately stand in God's place. We will find that glory in the eyes of our peers is fleeting and easily lost, that the accumulation of wealth is insufficient to satisfy the deeper needs of our souls, or that we cannot predict and plan against all the dangers that threaten our safety. These losses and

---

[5] Dodaro, *Christ and the Just Society*, 32–43.

[6] So Jesse Couenhoven: "Patriarchy, for example, is not simply a choice individuals make but a way of seeing and being in the world; for those raised in it, sexism becomes second nature. Thus, the dynamics of patriarchy parallel those of original sin – both can be transmitted through social means and enslave persons involuntarily"; *Stricken by Sin, Cured by Christ*, 202.

unsatisfied longings are the cracks in the self-understanding sin has forged; they are the moments when the world pushes back on our misshapen desires, when God's creation forces through the lies we tell to reveal the falsity of the desires, the perceptions, and the histories we have made for ourselves. Instead of receiving my neighbor and my world as the good creation of God, my need to protect my unstable self-understanding or to secure the goods I believe will bring me happiness forces me to receive them as enemy, as obstacle, as tool, as resource. And I begin to seek out others who can be conscripted into the project of ordering my life such that my desires will not be challenged, my understandings of myself and the world will not be threatened, and I may maintain the intelligibility of my life and history in the light of the finite goods I pursue.

It is thus the fear of death – the fear of losing the goods I have come to value and the self-understanding I have constructed in light of valuing them – that most directly comes to undermine and dissolve the social relations we are meant to bear to one another as created by God. The destructive social orderings of racism, patriarchy, heterosexism, and unrestrained environmental depredation exist precisely as the product of a sinful attempt to overcome the effects of sin, my effort to expand and secure the goods I possess and the borders of my identity against that which might challenge me. Similarly, these hegemonies are aligned (and the struggles against them are necessarily intersectional) not only because they together function to the benefit of a racist ableist colonialist heteropatriarchy, but because that form of life is produced and maintained by the same lust for and logic of domination. This is not to say that countering these hegemonies does not require tools of analysis and strategies of resistance particular to each struggle; resisting colonialism and patriarchy are intimately related, but very different tasks. But neither can the redemptive work of overcoming evil and healing our sinful natures be reduced to attaining justice in any of these realms in isolation from the broadest reach of God's redemptive purpose. Without the reconciliation to God of the whole person, body and soul, even real advances in justice or equal provision for the material conditions of one's life are bound to be fleeting and unstable, eventually devolving into a substantially different but no less dominative social order.

The *libido dominandi* is thus, first and foremost, an attempt at self-possession. Yet because it is ingredient to our created natures to be open to God, as well as to the neighbors and contingent events that grant our lives their shapes, this attempt at self-possession is directly called into question by the relations we bear to God and the world around us. To maintain the illusion we have crafted for ourselves, we must attempt to keep these challenges in check through careful circumscription of the ways we relate to one another. Our interactions pass through the filters of race, gender, sexuality, and culture, with our social institutions, personal habits, conceptualities, and deployments of coercive power functioning to insulate us from any challenge our neighbor might pose to our self-understanding. These social realities are not merely tools we have carefully wrought through the mechanisms of law, custom, and constant formal and informal policing of our behavior according to communal norms, but take on a life of their own, continuing to shape our desires and entrench in us estimations of what is good and praiseworthy or aberrant and threatening. The logic of the *libido dominandi* is one of stasis: Our hope is that we may preside over our lives as the custodians of our own providential ordering, keeping the machine we have fabricated moving frictionlessly in perpetuity. Our aim, most basically, is not to be surprised.

We do not begin, then, by viewing others as mere objects of our desire, or as instruments or obstacles that can enable or hinder our pursuit of what we love. Nevertheless, those who become habituated to the misapprehensions that enable us to see those who bear the image of God only as threats or tools will, in some cases, cease to view others as challenges to their agency at all. My suggestion that domination is most basically about insulating oneself from surprise at encountering another may give the impression that even the most oppressive relationships bear within them a recognition of common humanity, an implicit recognition that the life of another may really call my own life into question. This likely gives us too much credit. While I think something like this account is necessary to describe how we come to see one another as threats or instruments in the first place, it also seems true to say that as we become increasingly fixed in our wicked desires and ignorant of the created order in its relation to God, our relations to (some) others come to exemplify less and less the mutuality that is proper to our created natures. Though the goods inherent in our relations to one another cannot be fully eradicated without our being subsumed entirely in the nothingness toward which sin pushes us, the *libido dominandi* not only distorts our sociality, but tends ever to its dissolution. Hell is not only privation, but privacy.

While this dominative tendency is the product of the sinful orientation that is common to all people, it is at the same time important to note that the power to dominate others is not evenly distributed. What's more, domination itself becomes a habit: As I find that I may bend others to my will, any resistance to my will seems more and more to merit violent reprisal. The history of the world that Augustine offers in *De civitate dei* is one of war, conquest, enslavement, and empire: These histories mark off particular configurations of the power to dominate, configurations that nurture the violent impulses of some and condemn others constantly to bear the consequences of injustice. It is important to keep in mind that there is no "perfect dominator" or "perfect dominated" here; history offers abundant examples of those who are profoundly oppressed by one set of social realities nevertheless occupying a standpoint where they are oppressors in relation to others. Contemporary intersectional politics and theologies aiming at the liberation of oppressed peoples have quite skillfully shown how, for instance, the voices of women of color have been marginalized within the struggles for both racial and gender equality.[7] Even so, it is undeniable that as the *libido dominandi* functions at an expansive scale to enable the dominance of some members of a community, so also it works to place others consistently in the role of the dominated. And just as this social location supports the self-possession of some, it leaves those oppressed in a state of enforced dispossession.

***

It seemed natural to Augustine – as, I admit, it seems natural to me – to follow this confessional imperative to what is by now a familiar end: the way of humility, an affective and intellectual participation in the crucifixion of Christ that sacrifices our attempts at self-possession so as to understand more completely our dependence upon grace. Our desires must be chastened, and our view of the world broken apart, so that we may find our true identity in open responsiveness to God's advent. This way of humility serves as the common source of some of the most compelling insights of the modern Augustinian tradition: Pascal's rigorous attention to self-deception in others and himself;[8] Rowan Williams' abiding sense of the incompleteness and perpetual instability of theological language;[9] Jean-Luc Marion's reformulation of the subject as one constituted by a love that always precedes it;[10] James Wetzel's restless attempt to find the difficult truths unstated but structuring the texts he interprets;[11] Susannah

---

[7] Cf. Jacquelyn Grant, *White Women's Christ and Black Women's Jesus: Feminist Christology and Womanist Response* (The American Academy of Religion, 1989), 37, 195.

[8] Blaise Pascal, *Penseés*, trans. A. J. Krailsheimer (London: Penguin Books, 1995), 63: "Such is our true state. That is what makes us incapable of certain knowledge or absolute ignorance. We are floating in a medium of vast extent, always drifting uncertainly, blown to and fro; whenever we think we have a fixed point to which we can cling and make it fast, it shifts and leaves us behind; if we follow it, it eludes our grasp, slips away, and flees eternally before us. Nothing stands still for us."

[9] See Rowan Williams, *On Christian Theology* (Oxford: Blackwell, 2000), Chapter 9.

[10] Jean-Luc Marion, *The Erotic Phenomenon*, 20–24.

[11] See the various interpretations of Augustine, Anselm, Dante, Kant, and Wittgenstein (*inter alia*) throughout Wetzel, *Parting Knowledge*.

Ticciati's use of the apophasis to repair our theologies of predestination, opening us to the love of Christ and our neighbor;[12] Natalie Carnes' dialogical reinvention and renewal of the *Confessions* through the lens of motherhood.[13]

Each of these thinkers displays the Augustinian "confessional movement" that Wetzel has described. The self, confident in itself and its understanding of the world, suffers a moment of dispossession as it yields to the gracious self-offering of God and the rough ground of a world that exceeds our constructions of it.[14] In the reception of God's grace and of our lives in the world, we come to understand ourselves anew, not as self-grounding subjects but as those whose lives are intrinsically open to and constituted in relation to God and the world. Finally, in receiving this grace and the gift of the world's presence, we are empowered for a responsive self-offering, as we seek to live in the world anew and offer an account of our place within it.[15] What makes this movement so powerful is the recognition that, since it is founded in the unanticipatable self-giving of God and the world, this movement can never be final. There is no safe place to stand and rest here, only the for-now

[12] Susannah Ticciati, *A New Apophaticism; and On Signs, Christ, Truth, and the Interpretation of Scripture* (London: T&T Clark, 2022).

[13] Natalie Carnes, *Motherhood: A Confession* (Stanford, CA: Stanford University Press, 2020).

[14] Natalie Carnes offers one of the most acute contemporary presentations of confession: "In confession, the self is broken, so that it, too, might resist closing in on the visible. It is broken as a false image and as a false beholder of images. For if what an idol names is a wrong relation to the beheld, then the self relating to what is beheld must also be addressed"; *Image and Presence: A Christological Reflection on Iconoclasm and Iconophilia* (Stanford, CA: Stanford University Press, 2018), 80–81. Carnes names here the proper relation between what I have called the confessional movement and the regime of signs, discussed above in Chapter 6.

[15] Though she makes no claim to operate self-consciously within the Augustinian tradition, my understanding of this confessional movement is also quite indebted to Judith Butler, *Giving an Account of Oneself* (New York: Fordham University Press, 2005). Butler writes: "The 'I' is the moment of failure in every narrative effort to give an account of oneself" (79); and notes, "I begin my story of myself only in the face of a 'you' who asks me to give an account" (11).

ceaseless movement by which we stretch out to the world in pursuit of God and neighbor, and finding them, are always surprised. Within the life of Christian faith, this way of humility thus cultivates in us an abiding awareness of our dependence upon God's grace.

Accordingly, we should be quite wary of thinking that we will be successful in any of our own attempts to reorder our loves to God. Ought does not imply can: The darkening of our intellects by sin remains a persistent obstacle for us, so long as our love and knowledge of God – and in this primal love, of the world and our neighbors within it – remains imperfect. We should not expect that we will be able to see truly where our loves are disordered; we should not expect that even our attempts to turn our hearts to God will not end up doing more harm than good to our affective constellation. How much violence, how much abuse, debasement, suffering, and enslavement has been inflicted in the name of love and sanctification?

This is the shadow side of Augustine's comforting dictum "Love, and do what you will" (*dilige, et quod vis fac*).[16] On the one hand (and in Augustine's original intent), it is a hopeful statement that if our loves are properly guided by the love of God, our hearts will naturally be drawn to act justly toward our neighbor. On the other hand, so long as we have not been fully purged of sinful desire, it carries a note of tragedy. We will, at best, do what it seems good to us to do. Often, the good will be hidden from us, and we will not be able to act upon it. Sometimes, we will manage to see the good clearly, but our desire to act in accordance with it will not be sufficiently strong to bring about a good action, a result of the concupiscent habits that chain us to our sin. Our intellects are darkened, and our wills are weak; one way or another, we will do what we love, even if it is against our better judgment.[17]

---

[16] *ep.Io.tr.* 7.8.

[17] I am indebted to conversations to Jim Wetzel for this insight.

This aspect of Augustine's thought suggests that an Augustinian ethic should be accented somewhat differently than a great deal of contemporary moral theology. The foundational (though far from the only) task of the Christian moral life must be prayer, as slender a reed as this may often seem. This dynamic is clearly visible in Augustine's late correspondence with the monks of Hadrumentum. By the end of his life Augustine was clear that neither the summons to holiness nor the struggle to act righteously is sufficient in itself to restore us to the love of God. At *De correptione et gratia* 2.3, Augustine writes,

> The apostle does not say: We warn, teach, exhort, or reprove; rather, he says, *We pray to God that you may do no evil, but that you may do what is good.* And he was, nonetheless, speaking to them and doing all those things which I mentioned: He warned, taught, exhorted, and reproved. But he knew that all these things which he was doing in an obvious way by planting and watering did no good unless he who gives the increase in a hidden way heard him praying for them.[18]

Why, then, undertake to exhort or reprove at all? Certainly, the reproof of others can serve as an occasion in which God distributes grace; for as we saw in the last chapter, God's work and the work of external signs are not exclusive of one another, but rather are noncompetitively related.[19] Yet even here, whether or not one is moved to holiness depends not on the mere fact of the rebuke, but on God's work in it.[20]

---

[18] WSA I/26, 110.

[19] Cf. also *corrept.* 9.25; WSA I/26, 126: "Let no one, then, say that we should not rebuke someone who wanders from the right road, but that we should only ask of the Lord for his return and perseverance . . . For, if this person has been called according to his plan, God undoubtedly makes his being rebuked also to work for his good."

[20] I am substantially in agreement with Paul Kolbet when he writes of *corrept*, "It is a fundamental theological misunderstanding of God's relationship to the world to see divine agency as competing in history with human agency and art. No matter how robust one's notion of divine grace is, its transcendent quality prevents it from being a simple substitute for human effort"; Paul R. Kolbet, *Augustine and the Cure of Souls:*

Augustine's moral psychology faces us with the recognition that even our most laudable works, even our most righteous beliefs and actions, may nevertheless spring from a diseased will. The very actions that the world – even we ourselves – take as signs of growth in the good and as motivated by the love of justice may in fact be actions that move our hearts away from God and deeper into the darkness. Indeed, even accounting for the goodness of our natures and the grace of creation, all our actions *will* – as the actions of those not yet perfect in the love of God – move us toward the abyss unless assisted by a special work of the Spirit. By a charity that comes to us as gift, we are drawn to God in a manner that cannot be accounted for as the effect of any love proceeding from a sinful heart.

Prayer, as a political act, beseeches God that our fatally compromised desires may nevertheless be redemptive, may nevertheless further the goal of a true and lasting justice, may nevertheless bring human society to resemble more closely the City of God. We pray that our self-deceptions may be revealed, that our inattention to the suffering of our neighbor may be rectified, that we will be enabled to see and resist the violence that characterizes our life together.

Revising a Classical Ideal (Notre Dame, IN: University of Notre Dame Press, 2010), 137. Two qualifications, however. First, as Kolbet has framed the issue through grace's "transcendent quality," he is entirely right to say that grace cannot replace effort; indeed, the whole purpose of grace is to *activate* effort, the desire for good and the just action that follows from it. Yet this must not be taken to compromise the priority of grace's operation, or the feedback-loop in which sin holds us: Our effort is powerless if we understand it to anticipate grace, or even to be cooperative in any way that imagines grace and our will to each contribute a part of what is needed in order to produce some result in our willing. Second: I am convinced by Conrad Leyser that, by the end of his life, and without modifying the noncompetitive framework of grace's operation to which Kolbet directs our attention, Augustine had a fairly dim view of his own ability to discern what words might move his congregants and monastic brethren toward the love of God; cf. Conrad Leyser, *Authority and Asceticism from Augustine to Gregory the Great* (Oxford: Oxford University Press, 2000), 23–27. This need not imply any crisis of confidence in his ability to preach words of correction, rebuke, or exhortation, precisely because Augustine understood preaching to be so deeply shaped by the language of Scripture. When one doubts that one can effectively choose the right words to lead another to faith, it is best to rely on the words God has given us.

We pray in the knowledge that the whole life of the Church is a history of sinful actions that lead by grace to a forgiven and sinless common life, and we pray in the hope that the broken lives we offer to God may nevertheless be used to bind up the wounds of others.[21] In contrast to the Early Modern "hyper-Augustinianism" Jennifer Herdt so effectively critiques, however, the aim of this ethical outlook cannot be the achievement of a pure faithfulness free of the self-deception of the sinful heart that might subsequently be contradistinguished from the duplicity of pagan virtue.[22] The Christian's moral self-opacity is not an error that might be purged on this side of the eschaton, but rather a persistent feature of any heart that has not yet been made perfect by the Spirit's work. We know that sin compromises our ability to see our loves clearly, and so we know that we cannot know where we are self-deceived and acting from misshapen loves. Neither does this counsel to prayer lead us to a quietism that would ignore the ways that even our inaction is implicated in the injustice and harm of a fallen world, thus benefiting from it and extending it.[23]

The purpose of grounding Christian ethical practice in prayer is rather to cultivate a very particular sort of disposition in the moral agent: an awareness that the success or failure of any ethical endeavor, the progression or eclipse of justice in one's heart and in one's society, cannot depend upon our own righteousness, but solely upon the grace of God. The outstanding exemplar of virtue may nevertheless, precisely motivated by the desire for justice, bring about untold harm; the notorious sinner may be granted an unexpectedly pivotal role in the furtherance of an egalitarian and

---

[21] I share Jonathan Teubner's dim view of the possibilities for our moral advance, and have enjoyed talking with him about it rather more than is seemly; see his *Prayer after Augustine* for an expansive account of Augustine's theology of prayer.

[22] Jennifer A. Herdt, *Putting on Virtue: The Legacy of the Splendid Vices* (Chicago: Chicago University Press, 2008), 350.

[23] Paul J. Griffiths comes, in my estimation, too close to this outlook at "The Quietus of Political Interest," *Common Knowledge* 15.1 (2009): 7–22.

mutualistic common life. Prayer cultivates in us a properly Christian humility, a recognition that if there is to be any growth in justice in our world, it will be a consequence of our actions only secondarily to God's providential bestowal of charity and knowledge of the good. This humility recognizes that, as real as the virtues are and as integral as they will be to the life of the heavenly city, habit in itself is powerless to cultivate virtue in us if it is abstracted from the active intervention of the Spirit. Simply put, placing prayer at the heart of the Christian moral life acknowledges the irreducible priority of God's action in our sanctification, and the fragility of our own assessments of what will make us holy or our society just.

Even as emphasizing prayer as the foundational act of the Christian moral life continually returns attention to our dependence on the work of the Holy Spirit, we must recognize that our prayer is not exclusive of concrete action that seeks to cultivate virtue in us or bring about a more just social order.[24] As Augustine observes at *en.Ps.* 37.14, "there is another kind of prayer that never ceases, an interior prayer that is desire. Whatever else you may be engaged upon, if you are all the while desiring that Sabbath, you never cease to pray ... Your continuous desire is your continuous voice."[25] The very desire from which we act for the good of our neighbor should thus be seen as prayer. Similarly, the actions born of this desire continue the very prayer born out of our recognition of our dependence upon the Spirit.

Prayer and confession of our dependence upon the Spirit's work do not supplant the struggle to live a holy life or to bring about a just society, but generate these struggles *as* prayer. To the extent that our actions derive from the charity that the Spirit graciously sheds in our hearts, these actions are themselves our prayer – they themselves cry

---

[24] Cf. Aaron Stalnaker, "Spiritual Exercises and the Grace of God: Paradoxes of Personal Formation in Augustine," *Journal of the Society of Christian Ethics* 24.2 (2004): 137–170, 143–144.

[25] WSA III/16, 157.

out for God to bring about a just world and to cleanse us of our sin. Such actions include our participation in habits of worship and moral formation by which grace is communicated to us: participation in the sacraments; practices of communal prayer and worship; participation in local community groups advocating for the right of prisoners, or for just treatment of workers, or against unjust policing. Whether or not these habits actually cultivate righteousness in us depends utterly upon the free action of the Spirit; yet as expressions of our desire for our lives and our societies to be made holy, they at least constitute a prayer offered up for the Spirit's transformation, an attempt to ready our-selves for the work of individual and collective sanctification.

This prayer, this desire, this holy struggle lifts our hearts to God in recognition of the grace that the Spirit has already communicated to us, and in hope that this grace may be renewed. We are bold to work out our salvation through such practices only because this work is conducted always in fear and trembling, always aware that even our best efforts may result in catastrophe if not supported at each moment by the Spirit's work. In all our striving for justice, we follow the way of the Cross, knowing ourselves to be powerless if not animated by a charity that comes to us from beyond us. And we pray, both in word and deed, in the humble awareness that our sanctification is far from complete.

***

So far, all this operates well within the bounds of Augustinian orthodoxy. The emphases on our self-deception and the bondage of our wills, the awareness of our dependence upon the Spirit's work within, the commendation of prayer and the way of humility as the remedy for the malady of self-love – all of this seems to me the natural endpoint of Augustine's meditations on our being drawn into participation in Christ's cross.

Yet precisely by directing our attention to the places where we know and love the world falsely, this Augustinian outlook also focuses me upon what does *not* seem natural to me, demanding my consideration of what I suspect I would never have come to know about the world without having learned it from others. At this point (and perhaps at many other points in this study that I have not been able to recognize), even the invitation of a dialogic "we" cannot be sustained.[26] We have to do here with you and me, we two who are (I hope and pray) being drawn together into Christ's Body; but we may inhabit very different places in the world sinful humanity has fabricated.

Neither is it sufficient to remain long in a discursive register in which you or I are united to my neighbor, to the stranger, to the Other, with no further specification. As Emilie Townes has reminded us, "In postmodern America, discourse on 'the Other' often becomes an excuse to remain ignorant and arrogant about our illiteracy of other peoples – their thoughts, their religions, their politics, their values, their social structures, their moral landscapes – their isness/ontology – both mundane and radical."[27] If "the Other" remains only an abstract posit of our theological accounts, our theologies simply repeat the errors of our sin. We do not come to see this Other truly, as she has been created by God, or love her in our particularity. Rather than coming to see her distinctly and in her proper dignity as the particular creature she is, she remains ill-defined – an abstract neighbor, to be loved sooner or later, in circumstances that we feel no pressure to examine with any care. We may, of course, say that loving this Other our neighbor is necessary for us to be conformed to Christ, but the neighbor herself fails to appear here. She is, instead, a theological promissory note: that eventually, some particularity or other will open us to the love of God. She would be reduced for us to her redemptive function as a sign of Christ. Yet, by the lights of my approach, redemption through such an ill-defined sign is an impossibility, for our neighbor's life is only a redemptive sign *in its particularity*, and as this

---

[26] See above, Introduction, n.1.

[27] Emilie Townes, *Womanist Ethics and the Cultural Production of Evil* (New York: Palgrave Macmillan, 2006), 31.

particularity is used by the Spirit to heal us of the effects of sin and turn us to God.[28]

It is not sufficient, then, simply to observe that our disordered loves have distorted our relations to our neighbors; we must attend to specifics of *how* we have failed to love our neighbors, for this will also give concrete shape to our discussions of our redemption – of what it will mean for us to be restored to the love of God. We require attention to the specific others we characteristically tend to fail – and the others whom I am predisposed to fail are potentially quite different from the others whom you are likely to fail.

Recognition of your and my differences should not, however, lead us to fall into the trap of imagining our sins to be wholly novel. The particular constellation of my desires, the ends toward which I am turned, the vigor with which I pursue them – all of these are given a distinct cast by the particularity of my creatureliness, the singular way in which my participation in the divine life is distorted through the lens of sin's privation. Yet in significant respects, I learn these desires through imitating others: I learn that my greatest glory is to kill and die for the Eternal City; I learn that children may be valid sources of profit if employed within unsafe working conditions; I learn what it is to be a slaveowner or trader; I learn what it is to have a hated ethnic other and how to murder them most efficiently.

It is not enough to say that our desires are disordered and need to be reordered; we must also say that, depending upon one's social location, they are disordered along fairly consistent lines.[29]

---

[28] Cf. Ticciati, *A New Apophaticism*, 223.

[29] Sarah Coakley has noted Christian philosophy of religion's inattention to this sort of epistemic malformation along gendered lines; see Coakley, "Analytic Philosophy of Religion in Feminist Perspective: Some Questions," in *Powers and Submissions: Spirituality, Philosophy, and Gender* (Oxford: Blackwell, 2002), 98–105, drawing particularly on the resources afforded by Anglo-American feminist standpoint epistemology. More recently, Erin Kidd has demonstrated the generative theological possibilities of Miranda Fricker's concept of "epistemic injustice"; see Miranda Fricker, *Epistemic Injustice: Power and the Ethics of Knowing* (Oxford: Oxford University Press, 2007); Erin Kidd, "Theology in the Wake of Survivor

And since, as we discussed in the last chapter, the endpoint of sinful human community is death, we must affirm that the lives of some within any social body of sinful human persons are far more resolutely exposed to the forces of death than others. If sin in social relationships appears inevitably as a *libido dominandi*, then what it is to be redeemed as a dominator will be a far different matter than being redeemed as one dominated. The matter is only made more complex by the recognition that the number of standpoints according to which one can occupy the position of either dominator or dominated is as numerous as the many conflicting desires in your own heart and that of your neighbor.

Within the social order that I, and presumably you, inhabit, the distortions of knowledge and desire of the world communicated from person to person consistently make some rather than others the objects of domination: people of color, with unique histories and modulations of violence directed against groups including indigenous peoples, members of the African diaspora, Asian-Americans, and Latinx peoples; women; the poor; lesbian, gay, transgender, bisexual, and genderqueer persons; the disabled; children; non-Christians, and particularly Jews and Muslims; and the nonhuman creatures with whom we share our lives. None of these patterns of domination are accidental or innocent. They are the product of a centuries-long (sometimes millennia-spanning) process of habituation according

Testimony: Epistemic Injustice and Clergy Sex Abuse," *Journal of Religion and Society* suppl. 21 (2020): 161–177; and especially Erin Kidd, "A Feminist Theology of Testimony," *Theological Studies* 83.3 (2022): 424–442. Sameer Yadav has also importantly highlighted epistemic and affective failures to address the critiques of theologies of liberation in contemporary analytic theology, similarly working from sources in Anglo-American philosophy and Christian theologies of liberation; see Sameer Yadav, "Toward an Analytic Theology of Liberation," in *Voices from the Edge: Centring Marginalized Perspectives in Analytic Theology*, eds. Michelle Panchuk and Michael Rea (Oxford: Oxford University Press, 2020), 47–74. These sources offer in my judgment an ideal entry point to some of the most important and exciting work being done in my own small corner of the theological landscape: contemporary theology in dialogue with the Anglo-American philosophical tradition.

to which the loves of some – especially those who, like me, take themselves to be white, male, heterosexual, normatively abled, and Christian – are so misshapen that their neighbors can no longer appear or be encountered in their full humanity.

Let me state plainly: This failure of love, and its attendant failure to know the world as it is, is the source of every evil that one person has inflicted on another, and on our environment. Every blow to which a parent has subjected their child; every massacre that has been inflicted against indigenous peoples within a program of ethnic cleansing; every woman's body claimed as a prize for victory in battle; every hushed violation forced upon a child by priest or trusted elder; every slur directed at a person of color, or a gay, lesbian, or trans-gender person; every lash delivered by a slaveholder and every family torn apart for profit; killing fields, death chambers, suppressed uprisings; each of these have as their necessary precondition this failure to know and love. These acts, all the horrors of our history and all the trivial knives we slip into the hearts of those we love on a daily basis – all of them are a denial of the good creation of God. All of them require a turning from the knowledge and love of the world as God has made it; all of them are a refusal – known or unknown, but culpable in either case – to live the lives God has given us.

The disordering of our loves is never a private affair. We should expect that the fears and hatreds and dominating lusts of one person will be communicated from one person to another, for we are habituated into our vices no less than our virtues. We should expect, too, that as they come to function as gathering centers of our communal action, as they are marshaled into conquest and settlement and apartheid, they will form the very bases of our social institutions. Such institutions, if described truly, *must* be described as collective expressions of white supremacy, or patriarchy, or heterosexism, or colonialism, or ableism, for the love of sameness and consequent domination of these particular stripes of otherness according to each of these vectors of oppression is among the loves animating these communities. Indeed, it does not go too far to say that the early twentieth-century social order of the

United States is *called together* by the distorted loves that valorize white heterosexist colonialist patriarchy, and dominate those who do not satisfy this violently established norm. Two cities called together by two loves; these loves *are* – not exhaustively, but quite significantly – the loves that have called together the *civitas terrena* in our own day. The only surprise to be found in this account is that contemporary Augustinians have been so intransigent in their refusal to engage modes of theological analysis that call these distorted loves and patterns of domination to the fore. With few exceptions, Augustinians have failed seriously to engage the work of scholars writing in a broadly liberationist mode who have uncovered the distortions and dehumanizations performed within the Western Christian tradition.[30] Engagement with black, queer, and womanist theology in particular has been almost wholly absent within the modern Augustinian tradition.[31]

[30] Resources such as the essays collected in *Feminist Interpretations of Augustine*, ed. Judith Chelius Stark (University Park, PA: The Pennsylvania University Press, 2007) model serious engagement with feminist theology, but are underutilized within Augustinian scholarship. Eric Gregory provides a notable counterexample to this tendency in his engagement with feminist ethics of care Gustavo Gutiérrez, Martin Luther King, Jr. at *Politics and the Order of Love*, 157–175 and 188–196. Luke Bretherton similarly (to the extent he would describe his project as Augustinian) instructively engages Black Theology at *Christ and the Common Life*, 82–118. David E. Wilhite has brought Augustine productively into conversation with postcolonial thought at "Augustine the African: Post-colonial, Postcolonial, Post-Postcolonial Readings," *Journal of Postcolonial Theory and Theology* 5.1 (2014): 1–34; and Justo L. González has drawn attention to Augustine's ethnic hybridity at *The Mestizo Augustine: A Theologian between Two Cultures* (Downers Grove, IL: InterVarsity Press, 2016). Susannah Ticciati begins her most recent book expressing deep worry about postmodern identity politics, which makes it all the more surprising to find her lauding James Cone as providing an exemplary analysis of the self-reflexive substitution for the sake of another's justice that issues from her reading of the *totus Christus*; see Ticciati, *On Signs, Christ, Truth, and the Interpretation of Scripture* (London: T&T Clark, 2022), 179–184. Most bracingly, but offering to my mind the most challenging and promising way forward, see Matt Elia, *The Problem of the Christian Master: Augustine in the Afterlife of Slavery* (New Haven, CT: Yale University Press, forthcoming).

[31] For a particularly egregious example of this tendency of contemporary Augustinianism, see *The T&T Clark Companion to Augustine and Modern Theology*, eds. C. C. Pecknold and Tarmo Toom (London: Bloomsbury T&T Clark, 2013), which

Yet it is the work of these liberationist scholars that, to my mind, best evidences the confessional imperative of Augustinian thought. In calling attention to the pervasive violence in which Christian theology is and has been complicit, works of critical theology have uncovered the persistent effects of sin within God-talk, opening the opportunity for confession and repentance among those in positions of domination. In working for the dignity and liberation of oppressed peoples, these theologians have truly confessed the goodness of God's creation for what it is, rather than uttering the dehumanizing falsehoods that have been passed down within the theological tradition as the natural order of things. My aim is not to assimilate these liberatory theological projects to that of the Augustinian tradition – they have their own aims, procedures, and integrity, as diverse and conflicting as any other broadly considered theological approach. Rather, it is to note that the Augustinian tradition – if it is to be true to itself – must confessionally undertake a self-scrutiny every bit as rigorous as the critiques leveled against Augustine, and the dominant Western theological tradition more generally, by many varied and diverse theologies of liberation. To the extent that Augustinians have failed to uncover the racism, sexism, homophobia, ableism, and colonialism of the Christian theological tradition, they have failed to follow the way of the Cross, and failed to join themselves to Christ's humility.

Meditation upon the damage done to our knowledge of the world by sin's distortive effects tells me that the points of my moral life most significant to me in the work of redemption may be those aspects of the world that I still see only dimly today. It tells me that the lives in whom it is most necessary for me to see Christ in my neighbor, and to see my own sin reflected in their eyes, are the lives of those whose experiences, affective formation, and window onto the world is very different than my own. More precisely, my salvation requires that

(excepting Susannah Cornwall's fine essay) includes virtually no engagement with feminist, womanist, black, queer, postcolonial, ecological, or Latin American theologies of liberation.

I come to see Christ and the Spirit's redemptive work in the lives of exactly those people whom my moral formation has led me to love deficiently, those whom I have failed to see clearly as lives through which Christ is offering himself to the world.

The Augustinian tradition's culpable inattention to the full scope of the work of redemption has been observed even in its most basic conceptions of human sin. Whether or not Augustine himself held that prideful self-love was the root of every sin,[32] much of the Augustinian tradition has taken pride as the source from which all other sinful desires spring. As feminist critics of this tradition have observed, however, centering our attention on pride makes a patriarchal masculine conception of sin normative: Sin is a matter of aggressive self-assertion over-against God, striving to occupy the judgment seat of the Lord; it is an attempt to exist without dependence on God, without dependence on anyone, but rather to found our own identity. Yet as Valerie Saiving has noted against some representatives of the Augustinian tradition (Reinhold Niebuhr, specifically), sin characteristically assumes very different forms in the experience of women living within patriarchal societies: Their temptations more commonly

> are better suggested by such items as triviality, distractibility, and diffuseness; lack of an organizing center or focus; dependence on others for one's own self-definition; tolerance at the expense of standards of excellence; inability to respect the boundaries of privacy; sentimentality, gossipy sociability, and mistrust of reason – in short, underdevelopment or negation of the self.[33]

Saiving's presentation bears of course the marks of her own racial and gendered intellectual and affective formation: It shows little awareness

---

[32] Jesse Couenhoven has convincingly argued that he did not: See "'Not Every Wrong Is Done with Pride': Augustine's Proto-Feminist Anti-Pelagianism," *Scottish Journal of Theology* 61.1 (2008): 32–50.

[33] Valerie Saiving, "The Human Situation: A Feminine View," *The Journal of Religion* 40.2 (1960): 100–112; 109.

of the very different experiences characteristic of women in poverty, women of color living under white supremacy, women living under colonialism, or of the very different temptations to which these experiences might expose them. Yet this acknowledgment only confirms her central point: It is a mistake to view all sin through the prism of prideful assertion of one's own desires against the will of God. Based on the particularities of our society's affective malformation, some – women especially – more commonly experience sin not as a rebellion against God's will for one's life, but as an acquiescence to another's attempt to determine one's life or pursue one's desires. Our society teaches women what Susan Nelson Dunfee has called "the sin of hiding," an aversion to exercise their own agency and assert their own value in the face of those who would question it.[34]

In analogous fashion, the hegemonic white supremacy of our society pervasively calls into question the dignity and value of black life. At the heart of black theology's critique of white Christian complicity in slavery and racism is its suppression of voices that would declare and defend the sanctity of black life, beginning from the experience of African-Americans. Can it be any wonder that a theological tradition defined by the liberatory struggle to reclaim agency and self-determination would find little to affirm in a piety that stresses humility and uprooting pride above all else?

We may put it simply: The Augustinian tradition has been too preoccupied, for far too long, with the experiences of sin and redemption that resonate most strongly with the intellectual and affective formations of white men. Even the characteristic

---

[34] Susan Nelson Dunfee, "The Sin of Hiding: A Feminist Critique of Reinhold Niebuhr's Account of the Sin of Pride," *Soundings* 65.3 (1982): 316–327. Saiving's insights have also been developed by, *inter alia*, Daphne Hampson, "Reinhold Niebuhr on Sin: A Critique," in *Reinhold Niebuhr and the Issues of our Time*, ed. Richard Harries (Oxford: Mowbray, 1986), 46–60; Judith Plaskow, *Sex, Sin, and Grace: Women's Experience and the Theologies of Reinhold Niebuhr and Paul Tillich* (Washington, DC: University Press of America, 1980); and more recently (and critically) Jodie L. Lyon, "Pride and the Symptoms of Sin," *Journal of Feminist Studies in Religion* 28.1 (2012): 96–102.

Augustinian description of sin as self-love can be dangerously misleading if it prevents us from seeing the much wider array of disordered desires that are possible and describable by means of an Augustinian theological anthropology.

The problem of our love is not that we love ourselves too much; it is that we have believed a story about ourselves other than the story God tells us. Sometimes this is a story we tell ourselves – a story of our innocence, a story of our uprightness, a story in which we are ill-used by others and therefore justified in the injustice we return to them. At other times, however, it is a story told to us by others: that we are unworthy, that we are lesser, that we do not belong and thus do not deserve the dignity and agency that is given to others.[35] To the extent that the former is true of us, we require the way of purgation and humility that Augustine so frequently counsels. But to the extent that our lives are determined by the violent and degrading stories told by others – to the extent that the wickedness and domination endemic within our social order already places us on the cross alongside Christ Jesus, making both my neighbor and I members of a crucified people – participation in the sufferings of the incarnate Word will take on a very different cast. In this case, the proper ordering of our loves will mean throwing off the lies that the world has told to us, and breaking thereby the chains with which we are bound.[36] It will involve the people who are disproportionately marginalized throwing off the lies of patriarchy, and white supremacy, and heterosexism, and colonialism, and subverting a social politics that teaches them to be quiet and submissive.[37]

---

[35] Cf. Joy Ann McDougall, "Rising with Mary: Re-visioning a Feminist Theology of the Cross and Resurrection," in *The Strength of Her Witness: Jesus Christ in the Global Voices of Women*, ed. Elizabeth A. Johnson (Maryknoll, NY: Orbis Press, 2016), 32–43, 37.

[36] Elizabeth A. Johnson, *She Who Is: The Mystery of God in Feminist Theological Discourse*, 10th Anniversary ed. (New York: The Crossroad, 2002), 64.

[37] As Erin Kidd writes: "feminist conversion experiences are always and already movements closer to God"; Kidd, "A Feminist Theology of Testimony," 433 (drawing upon the work of Nancy Dallavalle, Elizabeth Johnson, and Karl Rahner).

Analysis of particular instances of oppressive social orders show that they function precisely to control the humanity of those dominated, undermining their capacity for social relations so they cannot challenge the agency, self-understanding, or social world of the dominator. M. Shawn Copeland has mapped these processes with devastating clarity in her recounting of the way American slavery directly attacked the embodied social existence of black women. Slavery challenged black women's "freedom for God" in making white Christianity a pillar of white racial domination in preaching that God had willed the institution of slavery; it attacked their "freedom for being human" in subverting their agency and responsibility for their lives; it compromised their "freedom for loving without restraint" in destroying the relationships of loving mutuality within the marital bond; it "devalued motherhood and mother-love" by tearing apart the families of the enslaved for economic gain; it undermined "freedom for community and solidarity" in strictly policing the social interactions and assemblies of slaves; it attacked not only the soul's agency, but with particular force the black body through pervasive violence, sexual and otherwise; and in its aspiration of structuring the entire life of the enslaved, American slavery challenged the possibility of "psychic healing and growth," the self-love ordered to God that is intended for us as creatures.[38]

When, therefore, Copeland writes that "Slavery sought to desecrate and deform black bodies,"[39] we must see in this assertion the inverse of the *libido dominandi*'s attempt at self-possession. In order for that lie to be preserved, those who bear the weight of domination must be stripped as thoroughly as possible of the spiritual and bodily dignities that make them human; they must be rendered unthreatening by removing, as much as possible, true reciprocity in their interactions, the interdependence and vulnerability that I have argued is at the heart of human life in the world. In contrast to the

---

[38] M. Shawn Copeland, *Enfleshing Freedom: Body, Race, and Being* (Minneapolis, MN: Fortress Press, 2010), 47–50.

[39] Copeland, *Enfleshing Freedom*, 51.

oppressor's attempt at dominative self-possession, the one who is oppressed finds her life hemmed into a forced incoherence to the extent that her agency and humanity have been torn away. Her place within this social order is defined as the site where her humanity cannot appear, where her agency cannot be manifested – for the social order itself is predicated on the ability of others to control the way her humanity might challenge that of her oppressors. One may think here of the forced incoherence of "double-consciousness" as described by W.E.B. DuBois, or of his sense that his existence itself constitutes a problem for society.[40]

If the dominant society teaches you that you are nothing, the way of humility will be a way of self-assertion. This is not pride: It is a humility that believes God's story about one's value and worth more than the stories of the world, even if that worldly narrative of domination has been internalized. Humility, rightly ordered self-love, means to accept what God has created one to be and to live accordingly, even if that means vigorously contesting the injustices to which one is subject rather than accepting them quietly.[41] The way of the Cross, the way of humility, is as much a challenge to imperial authority as it is a *kenosis* of the Son. When Christ looked to the Kingdom of God, it was he, not Caesar, who sat on the throne. The proclamation that Christ's authority is set against the dehumanizing operations of empire is not an alternative to the way of humility, it is a recognition of what has been true of the Son of God's path to the cross all along: He has scattered the proud in the

---

[40] Brian Bantum insightfully notes the way that interracial bodies are themselves made problematic within societies ordered by white supremacy at *Redeeming Mulatto: A Theology of Race and Christian Hybridity* (Waco, TX: Baylor University Press, 2010), Chapter 2.

[41] I have in mind here the dynamic of receptivity to God mobilizing resistance to unjust created structures like patriarchy and white supremacy on display in Sarah Coakley, *Powers and Submissions*, Chapter 1; and Andrew Prevot, *Thinking Prayer: Theology and Spirituality among the Crises of Modernity* (Notre Dame, IN: University of Notre Dame Press, 2015).

imagination of their hearts, put down the mighty from their seat, and has exalted the humble and meek.

This Spirit-empowered reclamation of agency and dignity cannot be restrained to an inward, spiritualized resistance to modes of domination. It strikes at the very heart of the social orders that misshape the loves of those who inhabit, working to transform the material conditions that result from and further the domination of some by others.[42] As with any ethical action, we cannot know in advance what the effects of such striving may be: At times it may indeed bring about a relatively more just society, but at other times the struggle for liberation itself may eventuate in deeper injustice and oppression, committed even by the leaders of such struggles.[43] Such is the nature of human moral action under the condition of the ignorance and weakness brought about by the Fall.

This awareness cannot absolve us of action, however: We will, necessarily, love and act in accordance with our love. This is simply what human persons do. Whether we act or do not act, we are inheritors of and participants in social orders that lead to the exploitation of some and the vicious cocktail of violence and professed innocence by others. Precisely in our inability to know the consequences of our actions and whether we are contributing to the cause of justice or plunging deeper toward the *nihil*, we are called to love and work for the good of our neighbor – and this involves

---

[42] Hence Elizabeth Johnson's decision to begin her trinitarian theology by considering "Spirit-Sophia," who is "the source of transforming energy among all creatures. She initiates novelty, instigates change, transforms what is dead into new stretches of life ... It is she who is ultimately playful, fascinating, pure and wise, luring human beings into the depths of love ... Wherever the gift of healing and liberation in however partial a manner reaches the winterized or damaged earth, or peoples crushed by war and injustice, or individual persons weary, harmed, sick, or lost on life's journey, there the new creation in the Spirit is happening." Johnson, *She Who Is*, 135.

[43] Jean-Bertrand Aristide, onetime Roman Catholic priest and liberation theologian who exploited the people of Haiti after coming to power as the nation's president, offers an instructive example here.

contesting and dismantling the social patterns that deny her full humanity. We must struggle prayerfully, in the trust and hope that the Holy Spirit works within our striving, drawing us toward a justice that we cannot yet see. Here again, Augustine's injunction to "Love, and do what you will" is meant to teach us that any good our actions may bring about, any personal growth or social transformation, is dependent upon the active work of God not only in our hearts, but in our world.

All members of the Body of Christ are called to this struggle, for one cannot love God without also loving one's neighbor. Yet we should not underestimate the complexity of our affective constellations. We are never simply the oppressor or the oppressed. This is not meant to get anyone off the hook, for surely it is the case that those like myself inhabiting the socially dominative location within a white heterosexist patriarchal colonial order will require constant disavowal of these social patterns and their benefits through speech and action. Yet it is to admit a grim awareness that those who have been subjected to violence often put others to violence in turn: The abused becomes the abuser; the victim of racial oppression repeats patterns of patriarchy and heterosexism; the feminist struggling for agency overlooks her disempowerment of women of color. Some of the best thinkers of the Spirit's liberating work have recognized and confessed these failings in themselves, and incorporated this recognition into their understanding of the struggle for liberation.[44] Just as an Augustinian account of the work of redemption benefits from the insights of liberationist thinkers, engagement with Augustinianism may help liberationist thinkers thematize this reflexive move already present in their own theological tradition.

---

[44] Perhaps most famously, James Cone's acknowledgment of his own early writings' "complete blindness to the problem of sexism, especially in the black church community. When I read [*Black Theology and Black Power*] today, I am embarrassed by its sexist language and patriarchal perspective"; "Preface to the 1989 Edition" at James H. Cone, *Black Theology and Black Power* (Maryknoll, NY: Orbis Books, 1997), x.

For Augustinians, we must recognize that the way of humility has two faces: not only the crucifixion of our pride, but also the ennobling recognition that those who have been crucified by the world alongside him are welcomed by his stripes and resurrection into a new condition of eschatological blessedness. This understanding of the way of humility should not be surprising, for one of the central categories through which Augustine articulates his theology of redemption, *confessio*, is similarly bivalent. Confession is for Augustine not only the acknowledgment of our sins and failings, but also – perhaps even more deeply, as the final three books of the *Confessions* demonstrate – a work of praise: praise for the God who has made all things and remade us through the death and resurrection of Christ, and delight in the goodness of what God has made.[45] Confession marks the act by which the prideful man is moved by the Spirit to lower himself in humility, but no less than this, it marks the act by which the downtrodden stand and claim the fact that the life God has given them is far more than the subaltern life the world permits them. Indeed, if the God who sets the pattern for the way of humility is the same God who liberates Israel and avenges the widows, orphans, and strangers against those who exploit them, then the exaltation of the humble and meek is likely the more determinative revelation of the character of God's redemption than is God's sending the rich empty away.

Awareness of confession's fuller sense guards us against thinking that the confessional movement of dispossession, reception, and responsive self-offering is a unidirectional cycle through which we proceed in orderly fashion.[46] Yes, it may happen that in the experience of some, it is necessary that their sinfully distorted pictures of

---

[45] Cf. *en.Ps.* 29(2).19; WSA III/15, 313.

[46] I am grateful to Christina McRorie for pushing me on this point, and especially for suggesting the example of Serene Jones' reordering of the traditional Protestant *ordo salutis*, beginning with sanctification and moving to justification; see Serene Jones, *Feminist Theory and Christian Theology: Cartographies of Grace* (Minneapolis, MN: Fortress Press, 2000), Chapter 3.

themselves and the world must be shattered by the coming of God's grace before the gift of oneself can be received anew. Yet it may just as easily be the case that the advent of God's grace is experienced first through the reception of one's identity from God, a new life that enters into one's experience of social death. In this case, the moment of dispossession is secondary, as one is loosed from the prison of worldly expectations or the conditions – internal or material – of subjugation. Indeed, one might even begin this movement with a responsive self-offering to the presence of the Holy Spirit, drawing one almost unknowingly and spontaneously into a new spiritual condition marked by dispossession of the old human and the reception of new life. The point, above all, is that this confessional movement does not mark out three stages of the Christian life, as if one traces them out as one matures spiritually. Rather, this confessional movement is a generative whole, returning us again and again to each of its moments as we are drawn to union with God through the sanctification of our loves.

***

As the Spirit heals our souls by binding us to Christ, so also the Spirit's work restores our communities by giving us new life as members together of the one Body of Christ. Indeed, just as the Holy Spirit comes to each heart and animates it with charity, He comes also to serve as the *anima* of Christ's Body. It is the presence of Christ's Spirit which makes the whole Christ, Christ. Augustine is explicit with his congregation:

> Consider our own bodies and their parts. The body consists of many parts, and one spirit quickens all the parts. Look here, by the human spirit, by which I am myself this human being, I bind together all parts of my body; I command the limbs to move, I direct the eyes to see, the ears to hear, the tongue to talk, the hands to work, the feet to walk. The functions of the different parts vary, but the unity of the spirit coordinates them all. Many things are commanded, many things are done; but it's just one who commands, and one who is

served. What our spirit, that is our soul, is to the parts or members of our body, that the Holy Spirit is to the members of Christ, to the body of Christ.[47]

To the extent we have been redeemed, the members of the Body of Christ live from the same charity, Christ's very loves dwelling within our hearts. We come to act from the same desire for God that binds together the *civitas dei*. We move in the same directions, work toward the same end, thirst for the same righteousness and justice in our midst – and all because we live in common from one and the same Spirit who forges us into one whole.

This charity which the Spirit grants us (and is) serves as the foundation of the politics of the heavenly city. In loving other members of the body of Christ, we love our neighbors in whom Christ has come to dwell. Here, the divine love that God puts in our hearts for our neighbor is met with the divine love that God puts in our neighbor's heart for us. We are made one: I love my neighbor as Christ, and am loved as the same Christ. Commenting on the statement of the first Johannine epistle that *This is how we know that we love the sons of God* (5.2), Augustine asks,

> Which sons of God? The members of the Son of God. And he himself also becomes a member by loving, and through love he comes to be in the structure of Christ's body, and there shall be one Christ loving himself. For, when the members love each other, the body loves itself ... But, if you love your brother, perhaps you love your brother and don't love Christ? How can that be, when you love Christ's members? When you love Christ's members, then, you love Christ; when you love Christ, you love the Son of God; when you love the Son of God, you also love his Father. Love, then, cannot be separated.[48]

---

[47] *s.* 268.2; WSA III/7, 279. For a full study of this theme, see Stanislaus J. Grabowski, "The Holy Ghost in the Mystical Body of Christ According to St. Augustine," *Theological Studies* 5.4 (1944): 453–483.

[48] *ep.Io.tr.* 10.3; WSA I/14, 148.

The unique relation between Christ and the Church, and the unique relation that members of Christ's body bear to one another, is thus derived from the fact that the same love exists in each of them.[49] To the extent that the same Spirit illuminates their minds and sanctifies their desires, members of the Church perceive the same hurts in the world, and desire the same justice in it. The members of Christ's Body desire as one that their individual lives and their lives together should be made into signs of God's love for the world, and that God will use their words and actions to draw those outside the community of the Church into the new life shared by those who have entered into Christ.

The structure of the life of the redeemed is thus one of mutuality in difference, of Christ recognizing Christ in the other.[50] Difference, because each member has a particularity proper to her, a part in this blessed community that only she is fit to play by the grace of her creation and of God's providential disposition of created history. Mutuality, because in the unsubstitutability of her life and place in God's redemptive work, the same Christ lives and is made known by the indwelling of the same Spirit. She is restored to dignity and agency by the empowering presence of the Spirit; she is freed from the chains of domination, freed from the story a sinful world has told her of her own life; freed to proclaim in the distinct manner the good news that the power of sin and empire have been broken and that a new Kingdom has been born.

This proclamation will require that she and her neighbor are both dispossessed, willingly or unwillingly, of the world that sin has created, and will require that those who take themselves to be high and lofty should be cast down. As James Cone has written, in words especially important for those of my background (and those backgrounds overrepresented in the Augustinian tradition) to

---

[49] Cf. Philippians 2.2.

[50] Cf. Studer: "Christ Celebrates Christ in the Liturgy"; Basil Studer, *The Grace of Christ and the Grace of God in Augustine of Hippo: Christocentrism or Theocentrism?"*, trans. Matthew J. O'Connell (Collegeville, MN: The Liturgical Press, 1997), 57.

hear: "The coming of Christ means a denial of what we thought we were. It means destroying the white devil in us. Reconciliation to God means that white people are prepared to deny themselves (whiteness), take up the cross (blackness), and follow Christ (black ghetto)" – and to take up indigeneity, *mestizaje*, queerness, disability, a broader ecological consciousness, feminism – all the particularities through which Christ speaks in the world – and denying whatever there might be in us that opposes these works of the Spirit.[51] Only thus will we truly follow Christ's command to go out into all the world, finding him already present and gazing back at us in the face of our neighbor.

---

[51] Cone, *Black Theology and Black Power*, 150.

10 | A Resurrected Body

The Resurrection is the victory of the incarnate Word over death, and begins the glorification of his human flesh. In it, God teaches us that death cannot extinguish the life that is granted to us in Christ, for She lives even in the midst of death. In so doing, She accomplishes the forgiveness of sins, undoing our separation from Her. Having joined Herself as fully as possible to our godforsakenness, having arrested our fall into the *nihil*, She now begins the long process of drawing us into union with Her own divine life. There is no farther God can tread along the way of our sin; She has reached its endpoint, and overcome it. Just as Christ's ministry moves inexorably to the Cry of Dereliction, in which he is so joined to us in separation from God that even he cannot humanly see the triune beatitude he nevertheless enjoys, his Resurrection begins a movement in which the glory of God becomes so apparent in his flesh that, at its eschatological culmination, every knee shall bow before him.

Just as he joins himself to our condition on the way to the Cross, in his Resurrection, he joins *us* to *his* condition. This is why it is so important that his very same flesh, animated by the very same soul, is freed from the tomb on Easter morning.[1] What had been a corpse is alive again, and so it is a living body into which we are incorporated by the power of the Spirit. What had been a soul separated from its body by the "first death" animates that body again, just as Christ's human desires save us from the "second death" by the

---

[1] This is a persistent emphasis in Augustine's preaching on the Resurrection: See Gerald O'Collins, *Saint Augustine on the Resurrection of Christ: Teaching, Rhetoric, and Reception* (Oxford: Oxford University Press, 2017), 8; O'Collins quotes here *s.* 362.10.

Spirit's mediation.[2] It is not simply that we are made alive by God as a result of Christ's work; he lives, and lives in us.

***

Within Augustine's work, the Resurrection is the event of Christ's life that encompasses the whole of his human life, and manifests the union of all his fleshly particularities to the Son of God. As he writes in one of his richest Paschal homilies, preached on the Tuesday after Easter sometime after 412:[3]

> The resurrection of the Lord Jesus Christ is the distinctive mark (*forma*) of the Christian faith. After all, that he was born as a human being of a human being at a particular time, while being God from God, God apart from any time; so, that he was born in mortal flesh, *in the likeness of the flesh of sin* (Rom 8.3); that he endured infancy, passed through boyhood, reached young manhood and lived through this until his death – all this was at the service of the resurrection. I mean to say, he wouldn't rise again unless he had died, unless he had been born; and thus the fact that he was born and died led up to the resurrection. Many people, both alien to us and godless, have believed that the Lord Christ was born a human being, of a human being. Although they didn't know that he was born of a virgin, still both friends and enemies have believed that Christ was born a man; both friends and enemies have believed that Christ was crucified and died; that he rose again, only his friends have known.[4]

The Resurrection provides the *forma* of Christ's life – its shape or pattern, the moment toward which his whole life is leading, the end that gives the whole its intelligibility – and in so doing, serves also as the *forma* of the life that is being created in the hearts of those joined to him. From the standpoint of God's timeless eternity, all Christ's

---

[2] *civ.* 13.2; WSA I/7, 69: "The death of the soul occurs, then, when it is abandoned by God, just as the death of the body occurs when it is abandoned by the soul."

[3] WSA III/6, 295.

[4] *s.* 229H.1; WSA III/6, 295.

childhood interactions, all his travels throughout Galilee and Judea, all the moments when he spoke an Aramaic word or ate a simple meal or drank at a well, are leading to the moment in which new life is made from death.

Belief in Christ's resurrection sets apart Christians from non-Christians descriptively, and understandably: "there are two things we had always been familiar with: being born and dying . . . To rise again, though, and to live for ever, who was ever familiar with that?"[5] Belief in this shocking new fact *is itself* faith in Christ, the evidence of the Spirit's work. It not only marks off people who accept a certain description of historical events, but indicates God's creation of a new relationship: Only his *friends* have known. To trust that Christ has been raised from the dead is already to be united to his life, to trust that God is bringing new life in our death as well.

Augustine sees in the Resurrection the guarantee of our particularity. We are accustomed to thinking of death as the ultimate mark of finitude, the limit by which we recognize all the other limits and finite determinations of our lives. Yet the situation is precisely the opposite for Augustine:

> Nothing, after all, is so certain for anyone and everyone as death. Start at the beginning. People are conceived; perhaps they come to birth, perhaps they don't. They are born; perhaps they grow up, perhaps they don't. Perhaps they go to school, perhaps they don't; perhaps they marry, perhaps they don't; perhaps they'll have children, perhaps they won't; perhaps they'll have good ones, perhaps they'll have bad ones; perhaps they'll have good wives or husbands, perhaps bad ones; perhaps they'll be rich, perhaps they'll be poor; perhaps they will be of no account, perhaps they will be highly honored. Among all the other things, can this be said about them: "Perhaps they'll die, perhaps they won't"?[6]

---

[5] *s.* 229H.1; WSA III/6, 295.
[6] *s.* 229H.3; WSA III/6, 298.

In its universality, death threatens to bring all our particularities to naught, making us indistinguishable from all else that has passed from life. In the true death to which sin is leading us, this universality is realized exhaustively, as we pass into an identical nothingness. But against this, resurrection tells us that God will restore us to life. Christ exists in all the determinateness of his life, the very same flesh that had been laid in the tomb; and if Christ, then possibly us in Christ. In manifesting to us the invisible God who he is and who raises him from the dead, Christ shows us also the new life in him that we cannot yet see. These are not two revelations, but one, for the God that Christ signifies is the God who draws us into Her own incarnate life.

In another Easter sermon, Augustine dramatizes this action by which we are included in Christ's body: "I'm inviting you to my life, where nobody dies, where life is truly happy, where food doesn't go bad ... that's where I am inviting you, to the region of the angels, to the friendship of the Father and the Holy Spirit, to the everlasting supper, to be my brothers and sisters, to be, in a word, myself. I'm inviting you to my life."[7] The Resurrection shows us for the first time that God triumphs over the blank universalizing force of death, and truly defeats death by infusing the power of incorruptibility in a human life for the first time. This victory becomes ours too, as the work of the Holy Spirit creates in us the love of Christ, incorporating us into this Body that has overcome death.

***

It is no great surprise that the Resurrection figures so prominently in Augustine's thought; perhaps more striking, particularly when compared to the contemporary theological landscape, is the central place the Ascension occupies in his thought. Though it is relatively rare for the Ascension to take center stage in current discussions of Christ's redemptive work, it is a preoccupation of Augustine's writings, and is for him one of the key facts determining the

---

[7] *s.* 231.5; WSA III/7, 22.

shape of the Christian life.[8] As William Marrevee observes, the Ascension serves for Augustine as the theological complement of the Incarnation: In assuming human nature, Christ assumes the *forma servi*, foregoing the manifestation of the divine glory that is properly his due; in the Ascension, Christ displays in his flesh the *forma dei*, his example of humility completed in the glorification of his body.[9] The Ascension is thus understood to complete the glorification that began with the Resurrection; in rising from the Mount of Olives in full view of his disciples, Jesus is revealed fully and finally as the incarnate Lord, "mak[ing] the hidden divinity of Christ manifest for us."[10] With his glorification complete, Christ dwells in heaven and intercedes for us, serves as Great High Priest in the true *sanctum sanctorum*, and mediates between us and God.

Yet the Ascension's manifestation of divine glory is at the same time – and necessarily – an occlusion, the disappearance of Christ's flesh from our vision. On Augustine's account, Christ's departure removes from us what might have been a stumbling block: "it was necessary for the form of a servant to be removed from their sight, since as long as they could observe it they would think that Christ was this only which they had before their eyes."[11] Augustine understands both Christ's injunction to Mary "*Noli me tangere*" in the garden on Easter morning and Thomas' need to see himself the

---

[8] Two very different exceptions to this trend are Linn Marie Tonstad, *God and Difference: The Trinity, Sexuality, and the Transformation of Finitude* (New York: Routledge, 2016), Chapter 7, and Douglas Farrow, *Ascension Theology* (London: T&T Clark International, 2011). Perhaps the most fascinating recent treatment, however, may be found in Anthony J. Kelly, *Upward: Faith, Church, and the Ascension of Christ* (Collegeville, MN: Liturgical Press, 2014). In Chapter 4 particularly, as Kelly discusses the "The Body of the Ascended Christ and the Expanded Incarnation," Kelly anticipates some of the arguments of this book to the effect that the Church exists as an "extra-metaphorical" extension of the Incarnation; see pp. 74–75.

[9] William H. Marrevee, *The Ascension of Christ in the Works of St. Augustine* (Ottawa: University of Ottawa Press, 1967), 67.

[10] William H. Marrevee, *The Ascension of Christ in the Works of St. Augustine* (Ottawa: University of Ottawa Press, 1967), 68.

[11] *trin.* 1.9.18; WSA I/5, 78. Cited at Marrevee, *Ascension of Christ*, 98.

wounds of the cross as symptoms of our inability to love properly even the resurrected flesh of Christ: We are liable to hold to these physical signs too tightly, content to remain in sight without passing over to belief in the God who remains invisibly present in Christ's body. Even in the resurrection appearances, God remains hidden in Christ: "what had arisen was flesh, because it was flesh that had died; the godhead which could not die still lay concealed in the flesh of the Risen One. His human shape could be seen, his limbs grasped, his scars felt, but could anyone see the Word through whom all things were made? Could anyone hold onto that?"[12]

Here too, the work of the Holy Spirit is essential in creating faith in us. Not the empty tomb, not even seeing the resurrected flesh of Christ with our own eyes offers us a sign sufficient to break sin's hold over us and begin the therapeutic reordering of our desires back to God. Our knowledge of these signs must be enlivened by the presence of the Spirit. Yet even as this process of reordering begins, our loves remain bound by habit to the changeable things we have learned to desire inordinately. We are accustomed to seeing the world around us as the objects through which we seek the satisfaction of our desires, rather than as signs of God. On this score, Christ's flesh is no different; for his disciples, their habit was to view him as a teacher, a friend even, but certainly not as their creator. Augustine recasts Christ's statement in John 14.28 as his explanation of the need for the Ascension: "This is why I must go to the Father, because while you see me like this you assume from what you see that I am inferior to the Father, and thus with all your attention on the creature and on the adopted condition, you fail to understand the equality I enjoy with the Father."[13] In ascending from Mount Olivet, God assists our movement from unbelief to faith, preventing Christ's flesh from serving as a distraction.

---

[12] *en.Ps.* 49.5; WSA III/16, 384. Cited at Marrevee, *Ascension of Christ*, 94.
[13] *trin.* 1.9.18; WSA I/5, 78.

Framing the Ascension in these terms may make it seem that Christ's flesh serves a merely instrumental purpose in our redemption, and if Augustine left things there,[14] these suspicions would be well founded. Alongside the suggestion that seeing Christ with our own eyes might serve as an obstacle to faith, however, is the claim that the Ascension is necessary *precisely because* his resurrected flesh is the fullest possible creaturely sign of God. At *trin.* 1.9.18, Augustine writes, "His ascension to the Father signified his being seen in his equality with the Father, that being the ultimate vision which suffices us";[15] and similarly, at *en.Ps.* 49.5, he says that the disciples "went on gazing after him whom they had known; but it was in his lowly condition that they had known him and they did not know him yet in his radiant glory."[16] These passages suggest that the Ascension is not the end of God's revelation through the flesh of Christ, but rather the intensification of it. In being raised to heaven, the flesh of Christ receives to the greatest extent possible the glory that the Word has possessed from all eternity.

This does not entail any deeper or more intimate unity with the Word than Christ possessed throughout his life, but it is the conversion of the *forma servi* to the *forma dei*. Christ's flesh is no longer presented to us as milk in actions and wonders that we can interpret, but is the solid food for which we are not yet ready. In the *forma servi*, Christ's flesh was for us a visible sign of the God whom sin has made invisible;[17] in the Ascension, it becomes a sign without any accommodation for the weakness of our eyes, and so Christ's flesh too becomes invisible to our sinful eyes. We are dazzled by the glory of God in him, and he vanishes in our moral blindness; we are left staring where we had seen him just a moment ago. If we stand looking at the same place, hoping to see him again, we show that we

---

[14] As Marrevee comes close to doing, at points.

[15] WSA I/5, 78.

[16] WSA III/16, 385.

[17] To be distinguished from God's essential incomprehensibility, which persists eschatologically.

do not understand properly. Only perfect faith will allow us to see the overwhelming glory of God, hypostatically united to his flesh and dwelling within it maximally.

In disappearing from view, then, Christ teaches us to long for the deity manifested in flesh no longer visible to us. We do not lack for signs of Christ, from the obvious icons, statues, and paintings, to – as we have seen – potentially any creature. Yet after the Ascension, these signs point us to an invisible referent. Even the eucharistic host – fully and truly Christ's flesh – is marked off as a bodily presence of Christ that is visible only as bread; here, above all, we learn that only faith will allow us to see Christ in the world under the guise of bread and wine, and that this same faith is required if we are to see the glory of God fully manifest in his eschatological flesh. To attain this vision, we must set our loves on Christ, believing in what he taught and did in the *forma servi* and letting our desires carry us to heaven where the bodily sign of God's presence now dwells. Augustine captures this dynamic well at *en.Ps.* 58.i.10, asking, "What does he mean that he ascended to the Father? He ascends when he makes himself known to us as the Father's equal. We ascend by making progress until we have the capacity to see this, to understand it, in some degree to take it in."[18] Augustine characteristically speaks here of Christ ascending "to the Father," understanding this as his now being manifest with the same glory that the Father has possessed from all eternity, but which was hidden for the Word in the form of the servant.

Matching Christ's final manifestation in the *forma dei* is our own reception of God: As we make progress in faith and in setting our loves on Christ, we "take in" this mystery to the extent that we are able. Even at the Last Judgment, only those purified by charity will behold Christ in the form of glory.[19] We are warranted, I think, in seeing here not only an epistemic claim (that we take in the mystery

---

[18] WSA III/17, 157.

[19] Cf. *Io.ev.tr.* 21.14; WSA III/12, 386: "The form of a slave will be shown to slaves; the form of God will be reserved for sons."

of the Incarnation as we ascend to Christ, our minds being conformed to the truth of God's work in Christ), but that we actually take his mystery into ourselves. As Christ is manifested as God, so also we are made Christ: The Ascension begins to pattern our lives too as we rise to union with God. We are being drawn to a vision not only of Christ's flesh, but of our own – restored, transfigured, made everlastingly into the dwelling place of God.

In his theology of the Ascension, then, Augustine desires from us a fundamental reorientation of our view of the world and our understanding of our own lives. Drawing on one of the most prevalent christological metaphors of the *Enarrationes in Psalmos*, that of Christ as the cornerstone,[20] Augustine tells us that "God's Church, though established here below, strains toward heaven, and so our foundation is laid there, where our Lord Jesus Christ sits at the Father's right hand."[21] The Church is a temple founded upside down, its chief cornerstone laid in heaven rather than on Earth. We are meant to understand our lives on that basis, seeing our lives and our life together in the Church as beginning from Christ. We are called to act not on the basis of what we are, but on the basis of that into which we are being made.

The City of God in its earthly pilgrimage is thus caught between two realities: Christians are meant to understand the world and act within it on the basis of Christ, knowing the world and loving it as Christ does; yet Christ himself has disappeared from view, showing us that we lack at present the restored relation to God that would allow us to do so.[22] Our efforts at seeing Christ in the world are compromised from the start, and so the Church is meant to be

---

[20] Augustine's deployment of this metaphor is often tied to the Ascension, and is based primarily on two passages of Scripture: Psalm 117.22 ("the stone rejected by the builders has become the headstone of the corner") and Ephesians 2.20 ("with Christ Jesus himself as the true cornerstone").

[21] *en.Ps.* 29.ii.10; WSA III/15, 310.

[22] Sarah Stewart-Kroeker has called attention to the christological density of Augustine's language of *peregrinatio* throughout her *Pilgrimage as Moral and Aesthetic Formation*.

a community in movement, carrying lightly all its understandings of the world and the temporal goods it now possesses, but holding fast to the savior it cannot see but who nevertheless dwells within it. The Church's life at any moment of history is inherently provisional, a community committed both to its own revisability, and to the belief that any progress in its life is attributable to the Holy Spirit who animates it. All the Church's work is ordered to the end of reconciliation with God – which is to say, it is meant to fit us for the vision of God in Christ's ascended flesh. This dynamic informs Augustine's approach to the images offered to the Church by Scripture, an account of creaturely *similitudines* that I have argued extends to the significatory potential of every created particular:

> Whatever likenesses have been proposed to you, if you find them in Scripture, believe them (*Et si quae tibi similitudines datae fuerint; si inveneris in Scripturis, crede*). If what you find there is no more than a reflection of popular belief, do not put too much faith in that; it may accord with reality, or it may not. What matters is that you progress, and a likeness (*similitudo*) is meant to help you along to salvation. You do not find this particular image helpful? Very well, take another; the point is that you must act on it.[23]

Scripture serves as the bedrock of the language of divine signification, yet all created likenesses may assist us in our journey back to God. Our charge is to discern God's presence in the world, and to act on what we understand God's will to be; in all this, we are guided by our love for Christ. Yet we love him as crucified, and thus in the awareness that our understandings are flawed, our actions will be sinful, and our love is imperfect; we live in the constant awareness of our failure.

The Augustinian hope is that through both our successes and failures in the Christian life, through our twofold confession of sin and our delight in the world God has made, we may learn to depend

---

[23] *en.Ps.* 66.10; WSA III/17, 322–323. I have lightly revised Boulding's translation here.

ever more fully on the power of the Holy Spirit uniting us to Christ. This pilgrimage will be halting at best. To make a step toward God in this life is always and at the same time to discover a new way of missing the mark; yet if our loves are set on Christ, we may trust that God will eventually draw us to union with Herself. As we seek to discern Christ in worldly *similitudines*, we move from misunderstanding to misunderstanding, in the hope that we may eventually be brought to the Truth. Through this knowing enabled by love, "we are being changed from form to form, and are being passed from a blurred form to a clear one."[24] We are remade into the Christ who has ascended beyond the limits of our vision; we are fashioned into the form of the Resurrection, hoping that one day, we may clearly manifest our risen Lord in the world.

***

It is, above all, in the life of the Church that we come to reflect the form of Christ's resurrection in this *saeculum*. For Augustine, the Church is a community of mutual self-recognition: Ideally at least, each Christian knows herself to be made part of the Body of Christ, and recognizes the Church's other members as this same Christ. It is no longer I who live, but Christ who lives in me, and this enables me to recognize that the life of my neighbor within the Christian community is inseparable from my own. As Augustine writes at *s.* 236.3, "Learn to take in strangers as guests, where Christ can be recognized ... when a Christian takes in a Christian, members are serving members; and the head rejoices, and reckons as given to himself whatever has been lavished on a member of his."[25] Above all, and as we have seen in the last chapter, it is the work of the Holy Spirit that creates this reality, binding us to Christ in charity. By Her work, our lives are made Christ's loves, and my and my neighbor's loves are inseparable as the loves of the whole Christ.

---

[24] *trin.* 15.8.14; WSA I/5, 406.
[25] WSA III/7, 45.

This does not mean, incidentally, that all my neighbor's loves will be directly identical to my own: To use a Pauline metaphor, I may be a foot, while my neighbor is an eye in Christ's Body. We may, on the surface, love very different things, and act in very different ways. The action by which the Spirit sheds Christ's loves in our hearts is not an action that makes us one homogeneous lump, with all our loves guiding us to live and act identically. The image of a constellation of loves is useful here: just as our own affective movements of the soul are best conceived as a constellation of loves, more or less harmoniously balanced with one another, so also Christ's Body is capable of many loves harmonized with one another. It is the same love of God joined with a love of neighbor that is the primary love shared by all who are being redeemed, and ordering the individual expression of their other loves. Yet the other loves attendant to and ordered by the love of God will be as diverse as the particular circumstances of Christians' lives. To the extent our other loves are ordered by the love of God, our loves will repeat Christ's own human desires in the situation in which we find ourselves – to the extent our sanctification has been accomplished, we will desire precisely what he desires in that situation, as surely as if he alone were present and active in that situation, rather than him being present and active in us. Consequently, my loves will be intelligible to other members of the Body of Christ as the actions *of* Christ, the same Christ who dwells within me and animates my life. To the extent we are redeemed, we will see the face of Christ perfectly in one another.

Quite obviously, this is not yet the condition of the Church as it exists now. We catch glimpses of Christ – powerful, transformative ones – in the lives of our fellow Christians, but this charity must still be fostered in us. Augustine frequently writes of the sacraments as the gifts of God that both create the love of God in us by the Spirit's work, and as gifts that enable us to see that we are together members of the same Christ. It was clear to Augustine (clearer than it is to me, at any rate) that baptism uniquely conveys the regenerating work of the

Holy Spirit, and is necessary for salvation.[26] Whether or not we agree with Augustine on this point, his description of baptism's effects is no less powerful: "when you were baptized, then you were born members of Christ."[27] As James K. Lee has written, baptism "incorporates one into the body of Christ and has the effect of 'uniting the church in this time' (*quo in hoc tempore consociatur ecclesia*). The sacrament of baptism builds up the one body of Christ and binds together the members in faith, hope, and charity."[28]

The eucharist is no less determinative of the Christian life, for in this sacrament, we behold veiled in bread and wine the same mystical body of which we are a part.[29] Augustine frequently plays upon our likeness to the bread and wine: We are visible signs of Christ's ascended flesh no less surely than are the eucharistic elements.[30] In his justly famous *sermo* 272, Augustine weaves together the threads of the bread and wine, the risen and ascended flesh of Christ, and our own existence as Christ's Body. Augustine begins by directing attention to the bread and wine on the altar: "what you can see, then, is bread and a cup; that's what even your eyes tell you; but as for what your faith asks to be instructed about: The bread is the body of Christ, the cup the blood of Christ."[31] Yet, Augustine quite reasonably asks, how can this be? How can this bread and wine possibly be the body and blood of Christ? This question is bound up, for Augustine, with the awareness of the particularity of Christ's flesh:

> Some such thought as this, after all, may cross somebody's mind: "We know where our Lord Jesus Christ took flesh from; from the

---

[26] *an. et or.* 1.9.10. Augustine makes exception for martyrdom, a baptism of blood; see Stanislaus J. Grabowski, "St. Augustine and the Doctrine of the Mystical Body of Christ," *Theological Studies* 7.1 (1946): 72–125, 84–85.

[27] *s.* 72A.8; WSA III/3, 289.

[28] James K. Lee, *Augustine and the Mystery of the Church* (Minneapolis, MN: Fortress Press, 2017), 18.

[29] Cf. Kimberly F. Baker, "Augustine on Action, Contemplation, and their Meeting Point in Christ," (Unpublished Ph.D. Dissertation, University of Notre Dame, 2007), 137–141.

[30] See, for instance, *s.* 229.1 and *bapt.* 7.50.98.

[31] *s.* 272; WSA III/7, 300.

Virgin Mary. He was suckled as a baby, was reared, grew up, came to man's estate, suffered persecution from the Jews, was hung on the tree, was slain on the tree, was taken down from the tree, was buried; rose again on the third day, on the day he wished ascended into heaven. That's where he lifted his body up to; that's where he's going to come from to judge the living and the dead; that's where he is now, seated on the Father's right. How can bread be his body? And the cup, or what the cup contains, how can it be his blood?"[32]

It is not simply a question, then, of how bread and wine can be something other than what they seem – it is a question of how anything can truly be the Body and Blood of Christ without being the very flesh drawn from Mary. The key is the statement of St. Paul in 1 Cor. 12.27: *You are the body of Christ and its members*: "So if it's you that are the body of Christ and its members, it's the mystery meaning you that has been placed on the table of the Lord."[33] The eucharist points to the mystery of the Church's incorporation into Christ, and in receiving it, this mystery is accomplished: "what you receive is the mystery that means you."[34]

Here again, it is the work of the Holy Spirit that makes both the bread and those receiving it the Body of Christ:

> So why in bread? Let's not bring anything of our own to bear here, let's go on listening to the apostle himself, who said, when speaking of this sacrament, *One bread, one body, we being many are* (1 Cor. 10.17). Understand and rejoice. Unity, truth, piety, love. *One bread*; what is this one bread? The one body which we, being many, are. Remember that bread is not made from one grain, but from many.

---

[32] *s.* 272; WSA III/7, 300.

[33] *s.* 272; WSA III/7, 300. See Lee's very helpful discussion of Augustine's evolving use of the language of *mysterium* and *sacramentum* at *Augustine and the Mystery of the Church*, 10–24.

[34] *s.* 272; WSA III/7, 300.

When you were being exorcised, it's as though you were being ground. When you were baptized it's as though you were mixed into dough. When you received the fire of the Holy Spirit, it's as though you were baked. Be what you can see, and receive what you are.[35]

In receiving the sacraments, we thus receive the Holy Spirit, creating in us the love that makes us the Body of Christ. Indeed, what makes the sacraments distinct within the Christian life is that, first, they manifest to us the mystery of our redemption, offering Christ's body and blood to us in visible sign; and second, we can trust that the Spirit will use them graciously to communicate charity to us.

Both points together are significant. Augustine is well aware that the Spirit works outside the boundaries of the Church; he has no interest in placing limits on where the unanticipatable grace of God might make its presence known in history.[36] What makes the sacraments distinct is not that they are the sole manner by which God creates charity in us, but that they are uniquely reliable sites for encountering the power of God. Christ has promised to be present in the breaking of the bread; he, with the Holy Spirit, has elected these rites as the medicine by which grace is communicated to us. They are not, Augustine hastens to add, universally efficacious; we cannot count on them as a resource under our control, mechanically dispensing grace to all who come, without regard to whether they approach the Body and Blood of Christ with faith and love.[37] Yet they are places where we expect to meet our Lord, and where we can make ourselves available for the Spirit's transforming grace. However evident the Church's failures may be, we believe these sacraments convey grace, as we have been told by Christ himself.

---

[35] s. 272; WSA III/7, 301.

[36] Lee, *Augustine and the Mystery of the Church*, xix.

[37] *ep.Io.tr.* 6.10; WSA I/14, 98: "if you want to know that you have received the Spirit, question your heart, lest perhaps you have the sacrament and don't have the sacrament's power."

The first point is also quite important, for it constitutes the Christian community as one ordered by the task of loving witness. The members of the Church at any one moment of history are not uniquely recipients of God's redemptive grace; even on the most stringent Augustinian account of who will be redeemed, we must admit that many who are not yet part of the visible Church will one day be brought within this community.[38] What makes the Church distinct is that it *knows* of the love that it receives – it knows that this love is received from and properly directed toward Christ, whom we are becoming. What distinguishes the Church is that we are capable of true confession, confession of our own sins and of God's redemptive work in Christ. This is one reason why the eucharist is such a powerful representation of the Christian life: Just as it makes the Body of Christ visible to those who receive it, the Church is to make the Body of Christ which it is visible to the world. It does so erratically, characterized by all the imperfections and failures that remain endemic to its sinful life. But in its best moments, this flawed human institution is transfigured, the life of Christ radiates from within it, and all the spots and stains so readily apparent on most days are overpowered by the light of God.

This knowledge grants the Church a particular vocation in the world: As it is founded on the eucharistic self-offering of Christ's body, so also this community becomes a sacrifice offered to God.[39] As Christ is both priest and victim, the whole Christ offers itself up to God and to the world. The eucharist thus serves not only as the revelation of the Church's foundational mystery, but as the mystery of its eschatological consummation. As Augustine writes at *De civitate dei* 10.6, "The true sacrifice, then, is every act done in order that we might cling to God in holy fellowship, that is, every act which is referred to the final good in which we can be truly

---

[38] *civ.* 1.35.

[39] Augustine first speaks of the eucharist as the sacrament of Christ's passion at *Contra Faustum* 20; see Lee, *Augustine and the Mystery of the Church*, 105–106.

blessed."[40] By living according to the love shed in our hearts by the Holy Spirit, every aspect of our lives is offered to God, lifted to union with Him and cleaving to Him eternally even as this cleaving also commissions us to serve the world. The *totus Christus* becomes a *totum sacrificium.*[41]

In this sacrificial self-offering, the whole community of the Church is carried into Augustine's confessional movement. This dynamic of sanctification characterizes the lives of Christians in their mutual relations, not simply the heart of each individual enlivened by the Spirit's work. The life of the Church is meant to be characterized by dispossession, as this community works to renounce its surrounding society's chauvinisms, its nationalisms, its standing in high society, its fear of the stranger in the land, and the worldly aspirations incompatible with the way of the Cross. It throws off, too, the cultural scripts it has inherited and often propagated that deny the full humanity of all God's people. The Church's preaching, prayer, and sacramental piety each call the Church to throw off the old humanity put to death on the Cross, anything that would prevent them from cleaving wholly to God, and to their neighbor in God. As such, there are times when Christian preaching and prayer will be profoundly destabilizing for the members of the Body, calling them into an eschatological future caught in irregular eruptions into this *saeculum*, and in the reliable inbreaking of the Kingdom of God around the eucharistic table.

So also, the life of the Church is meant to be characterized by the reception of new life, as social relationships are refigured by the new humanity to which the Spirit gives birth. In this new humanity, the old world has passed away: There is no longer male or female, slave or free, Greek or Jew – not because these fleshly particularities are obliterated, but because the distinctiveness of our bodies and the

---

[40] WSA I/6, 310.

[41] As Lee translates *civ.* 10.6: "we ourselves are the whole sacrifice (*quod totum sacrificium nos ipsi sumus*)"; *Augustine and the Mystery of the Church*, 119.

histories that have marked us is given a radically new significance through incorporation into the *totus Christus*. The social relationships marked by these differences have been wholly reconfigured, allowing for new patterns of life together, new possibilities for reconciled and peaceful sociality. This new life is given as the crucified peoples of the world are raised to voice and agency within their wider community, as the harms and historical oppressions they have suffered are remembered and seen for the way they shape our societies today, and as those who had been despised within our world are finally granted by God's action equal standing as members of Christ's Body. This same life is given in the patterns of prayer and worship that cultivate disciples, by the Christian practices that cultivate in us faith, hope, and love, and by preaching and teaching that edifies the community and helps them understand more fully the incomprehensibly mystery of God's life.

This is not, except in fits and starts, what the social reality of the Church looks like in any given set of its members today – just as we glimpse the death-dealing at the heart of our life together only in occasional and terrible moments. Two cities, gathered together by two loves; any human community, just as any individual unperfected heart, will be a chaotic interlacing of some loves tending in the one direction, some loves tending in the other. If true growth in holiness is possible in this life it is only by the gracious action of God, and while we may hope and trust in the Spirit's work, we cannot expect a smooth or uniform progression toward virtue in Christ's Body. Some people receive the sacraments with great regularity, and viciously exploit their neighbors; in some ages, Christian communities are the originators of tremendous evil in the world.[42]

Yet as the Body of Christ, the Church – the visible Church, with all its institutional flaws – is ordered to and by the love of God. This is not to say that the Church is the only network of human sociality

---

[42] Lauren F. Winner, *The Dangers of Christian Practice: On Wayward Gifts, Characteristic Damages, and Sin* (New Haven, CT: Yale University Press, 2018), 20–21.

bound for glory, or even that it is the community of greatest sanctity in the world today; it is only to say that its existence does not depend upon itself, but rather, that it exists only as Christ's Body called together by the work of the Spirit. To the extent that any community is founded solely upon human love and agency, to the extent it is not animated by the same Spirit that joins the Church together by creating in us the love of God, that community can only be a constituent of the *civitas terrena*. The Church, as one social body animated by the loves of her Head, is called together *as* a community of responsive self-offering: "in the offering she makes, she herself is offered."[43]

Yet as Augustine makes abundantly clear in *civ.* 10, offering this true sacrifice to God entails also the Church's self-offering to the world, in *opera misericordiae* – works of mercy, or compassion, or fellow-suffering, even of solidarity.[44] "Mercy is the true sacrifice," not because works of mercy can be finally opposed to the worship of the Church, but because the eucharistic offering is only really complete if it leads us to follow where the Word has led in assuming flesh: into fellowship with the oppressed, into a true *misericordia* that compels us to place our bodies on the line alongside them.[45] Our responsive self-offering to the Spirit's work cannot be completed by the individual as such; we are only the Body of Christ – Christ himself is only made whole – inasmuch as the lives of the redeemed are bound to one another.

***

If we ask where the risen and ascended Christ is present in the world today, it is easy to answer that he dwells within his Body, the Church. Indeed, as Tarsicius van Bavel has identified, one of the

---

[43] *civ.* 10.6; WSA I/6, 312.

[44] *civ.* 10.1; see Lee's discussion at *Augustine and the Mystery of the Church*, 117–118.

[45] *civ.* 10.5; WSA I/6, 310. M. Shawn Copeland and Samuel Wells have each written of the eucharist as a reality that calls the Body of Christ into solidarity with the poor; see Copeland, *Enfleshing Freedom*, 109, and Samuel Wells, *God's Companions: Reimagining Christian Ethics* (Oxford: Blackwell, 2006), 209–210.

two texts most important for Augustine's understanding of the *totus Christus* is an affirmation from Christ's own lips of his identity with the Church: *Saul, Saul, why do you persecute me?*[46] Time and again, Augustine will use this passage to signal that the life of the Church is not external to Christ's own life, but that the Church is joined to Christ in such a way that its suffering is properly his own.[47] As he writes at *en. Ps.* 85.5, "The body of Christ cries out all day long, as its members give place to each other and succeed each other. One single person spans the ages to the end of time, and it is still the members of Christ who go on crying out."[48]

Yet the other text that figures so prominently in Augustine's imagination is no less revealing: "*I was hungry, and you fed me; I was thirsty, and you gave me a drink; I was a stranger, and you made me welcome; I was naked and you clothed me, sick, and you visited me. And the just will reply, 'When did we see you suffering all this, and minister to you?' He will say, 'When you did that for even the least of these who are mine, you did it for me.'*[49] Throughout his works, the poor, the stranger, the prisoner, and the desperate serve as one of the clearest signs of Christ's presence in the world. Here again, the general principle is that what happens to the members of Christ happens to Christ. Augustine frequently uses the metaphor of our own bodies: When our foot is trodden upon, it is the tongue that cries out.[50] Though it is Christ's Body that is subjected to suffering, either from persecution or from poverty and deprivation,

---

[46] Tarsicius J. van Bavel, O.S.A., "The Concept of the 'Whole Christ'," in *Saint Augustine*, ed. Tarsicius van Bavel and Bernard Bruning (Brussels: Mercatorfonds/ Augustinian Historical Institute, 2007), 268.

[47] Augustine is clear, however, that Christ suffers "he is afflicted on earth not in himself, but in his members"; *s.* 162A.5; WSA III/5, 156. With the Resurrection and Ascension, the glorification of his flesh ensures that his sufferings truly were finished on Golgotha.

[48] WSA III/18, 225.

[49] *en. Ps.* 86.5; WSA III/18, 251, citing Matthew 25.35–40. See van Bavel, "Concept of the 'Whole Christ,'" 268.

[50] *en. Ps.* 86.5; *s.* 137.2; *s.* 345.4.

nevertheless, these experiences are truly Christ's, because of the charity that binds this Body to its ascended Head.[51] Because of this charity – the love of Christ in joining himself to our sinful condition, and this same charity poured out in us by the Holy Spirit drawing us to where he is enthroned in glory – we must affirm "Christ is in want here, Christ is a stranger here, Christ is ill here, Christ is confined to prison here."[52]

The very substance of the Christian life is to meet Christ in these persons despised and rejected by the world: "Such are the needs of the journey; that's how we have to live in this wandering exile, in which Christ is in want. He's in want in his people, he's replete in himself. But being in want in his people, replete in himself, he brings those who are in want to himself."[53] Christ himself is the beggar who lays in his sores at the gates of those who follow him.[54] And indeed, these works of mercy that Christ demands of his Body will only be complete when the City of God has finished its earthly pilgrimage: "That rich man is in dire need until the end of the world."[55]

It is true that, as Augustine talks about these works of mercy, he frequently enjoins members of the Church to give especially to other Christians. In his use of Matthew 25, he stresses that we are to give to the least of these *who are mine*. There is a special grace conferred, it seems, when a Christian serves a Christian (cf. *s.* 236.3, above), for in these instances both the giver and the receiver are strengthened together in one and the same charity. They do not simply both love Christ, they love Christ in loving one another. Almsgiving within the Christian community is thus a near-sacramental reality that creates the love proper to the Body of Christ even as it manifests this love.[56]

---

[51] *s.* 162A.5; WSA III/5, 156: "our only connection with this head is charity."

[52] *en. Ps.* 86.5; WSA III/18, 251.

[53] *s.* 236.3; WSA III/7, 46.

[54] *en. Ps.* 48.i.16.

[55] *s.* 239.7; WSA III/7, 63.

[56] Kimberly Baker appropriately cautions that, for Augustine, "not every person is incorporated into Christ's body"; "Augustine on Action," 88. While this is undoubtedly the case for Augustine both at any moment in the City of God's earthly

Yet at times, Augustine seems to speak of the good of almsgiving in an unrestricted fashion. Even as he speaks of the benefits received by "the least of [Christ's] followers" as Christians give to the poor, he tells his listeners, "take notice, and don't ignore, so to say, disease-ridden Lazarus lying at your gate. Give to the poor, because the one who receives what you give is the one who wished to go in need on earth, and to enrich from heaven."[57] Even more straightforwardly: "No one should be afraid of spending money on the poor. Nobody should imagine that the one who receives it is the one whose outstretched hand he sees. The one who receives it is the one who ordered you to give it."[58] While giving to the Christian poor thus seems to have a special christological significance in Augustine's thought, giving to the poor as such may perhaps be regarded giving to Christ. The poor have a special intimacy with the Lord who has willed to become servant of all.

For the most part, Augustine seems content to rest this identification of Christ with the poor on Matthew 25. When Augustine does reflect on the spiritual benefits of involuntary poverty, he tends to emphasize that the poor are less likely to be sinfully attached to wealth, and thus rise more easily to God in love.[59] Yet, as Kate Ward has argued, "Augustine's mistrust of wealth, vigorous calls to almsgiving, and support for the poor's self-advocacy and agency make him a vital resource for modern proponents of distributive justice."[60] Joined to a liberationist understanding of the social effects and structures

---

pilgrimage and in its eschatological completeness, it is balanced by his sense of the impossibility of identifying who is – and even moreso, who will finally be – citizens of the heavenly city. At any rate, we need not follow him on this point, and Susannah Ticciati gives us good reason to think we should not; see *A New Apophaticism*, 67–71, where Ticciati gives the initial formulation of her argument that "A symmetrical treatment of grace and judgment . . . reintroduces the competitive logic Augustine has otherwise argued against" (69).

[57] *s.* 113B.4; WSA III/4, 186.

[58] *s.* 86.3; WSA III/3, 397.

[59] Kate Ward, "Porters to Heaven: Wealth, the Poor, and Moral Agency in Augustine," *Journal of Religious Ethics* 42.2 (2014): 216–242, 228–230.

[60] Ward, "Porters to Heaven," 237.

generated by sinful desire, we may see the poor as having a particularly important role within Christ's work of redemption precisely because they are regarded by the dominant society as of little value – they are the ones from whom the hegemonic imagination teaches those in power to withhold love, encountering them not as reflections of the image of God, but as insignificant or exploitable.

Within a contemporary Augustinian theology, we may say: It is precisely because our dominant society's affective formation has led the wealthy to despise the poor that the work of redemption requires that the wealthy see Christ in their faces. The purgation of wickedly ordered loves is not, or is not always, a slow process of attuning our desires; at times, it requires a chastening of our loves under the sign of contrariety, coming to behold the *summum bonum* incarnate in the faces of those we have been taught are of little value. This reasoning holds not only of the poor, but all those who are despised and oppressed by the hegemonic imagination: the stranger, the neighbor with disabilities, the one who (for one reason or another) does not live according to the modern logic of economic productivity, the religious or racial minority or oppressed majority, the person whose sexual identity or orientation does not fit society's normatively cis-hetero expectation. As Brian Bantum has argued, "Christ's body and life inhabit the neither/nor that marks all human lives, but that is particularly resonant in mulatto/a bodies. Yet Jesus inhabits this space in a different way. His presence as mulatto recreates the space around him. He is neither/nor – *but*."[61]

Analogously to the function of the mulatto/a body within American racialized society – indeed, in and as his own mulattic human life – Christ challenges all our presumptions of defining our own identities through practices of inclusion and exclusion. "Christ's life is a demand upon the disorientation of our lives that we have so long presumed to be oriented."[62] In this "redemptive

---

[61] Brian Bantum, *Redeeming Mulatto: A Theology of Race and Christian Hybridity* (Waco: Baylor University Press, 2010), 99.

[62] Bantum, *Redeeming Mulatto*, 112.

disruption," and in the particular life he lives, Christ opens to us a new possibility of life lived in the Spirit, inviting us "to enter into an identity of desire and dependence" upon one another.[63] The face of Christ must be seen, his agency and presence must be acknowledged and responded to, in the very fleshly particularities that mark off some bodies as objects of exclusion and violence.[64] Only in this manner may our loves be truly turned to Christ. The logic of Augustine's eucharistic theology carries through his theology of Christ's presence in the poor: Look to the poor and see the face of Christ; become what you see by receiving them.

This is not to instrumentalize the oppressed for the sake of their dominators' redemption. For one thing, this necessity of recognition of Christ's presence in the despised other is not limited to those in a dominant social position: ingredient to authentic liberation is not merely the alteration of the material conditions of one's oppression (though that is, of course, necessary), but the transformation of one's own subjectivity, shaking off the social scripts that legitimate one's own oppression. This is why the Black Christ, the Christa, the infant Christ and old Christ as the *orishas* Elegguá and Obbatalá have been such powerful liberatory symbols: They recognize the sanctity of one's own flesh, the special presence of Christ with the oppressed.[65] Second, the endpoint of this christocentric reordering of loves is not the wealthy climbing to heaven on the backs of the

[63] Bantum, *Redeeming Mulatto*, 131.
[64] Cf. again Carnes' account of prosoponic likeness: "God has chosen to share the divine face with the least of these, whether or not they are members of the body of Christ. And the Spirit, as the one who draws humans into the divine life, rests on the most vulnerable of society, giving them the face of God, making them God's own *prosopon*"; *Image and Presence*, 139.
[65] Kelly Brown Douglas, *The Black Christ* (Maryknoll, NY: Orbis Books, 1994); Nicola Slee, "Visualizing, Conceptualizing, Imagining and Praying the Christa: In Search of Her Risen Forms," *Feminist Theology* 21.1 (2012): 71–90; Clara Luz Ajo Lázaro, "Jesus and Mary Dance with the *Orishas*: Theological Elements in Interreligious Dialogue," in *Feminist Intercultural Theology: Latina Explorations for a Just World*, ed. María Pilar Aquino and Maria José Rosado-Nunes (Maryknoll, NY: Orbis Books, 2007), 109–124; 114–117.

poor, it is (as Ward notes is already the case in Augustine's own work) the creation of a mutualistic community, a leveling of the social relationships between those who had been privileged and those who had been oppressed. If the recognition of Christ in the poor or the oppressed other is truly redemptive, it can only lead to one place: The mutual acknowledgment of Christ in one another, the affirmation of one's identity and agency as the beloved of God.[66]

The central christological point is that the shape of our disordered desires informs the shape that our redemption takes: The medicine we require is, in many cases, the encounter with Christ in whom and what we had failed to love properly before. Christ does not simply meet us in the world or in flesh of the other – in giving himself to us through them, he restores us one to another. As Augustine writes at *en.Ps.* 44.20, "we ascend to the Head, and descend to his members. Christ is there, and Christ is here."[67] He teaches us of the incalculable value of our neighbor; he teaches us that every sparrow, every rock, every grove of trees, and every movement of the sea is the gift of God, to be loved for God's sake.

There is, then, a necessary ecclesiological correlate to the christological emphasis on the work of incarnation: To be what it is, the Church requires its relationship to extra-ecclesial human communities. Said differently, the indefinable boundaries between the earthly and heavenly cities during the world is a necessary feature of ecclesial existence.[68] Just as Christ only is who he is in responsive relation to the sinful humanity joined to him, the pilgrim life of the Church can only unfold in receptivity to the world unwashed by the waters of baptism. Mike Higton has diagnosed this point and its christological underpinnings most acutely, noting that Christ's receptivity to the world founds an ecclesial existence in which Christian sanctification

---

[66] Ward, "Porters to Heaven," 234.

[67] WSA III/16, 299.

[68] I have drawn the evocative phrase "during the world" from Charles T. Mathewes, *A Theology of Public Life* (Cambridge: Cambridge University Press, 2007), 15 (and *passim*).

is mediated also through the Church's enmeshment in human communities beyond it. "The church becomes what it is," Higton observes, "in interaction with all that surrounds it. Its identity as healed, as glorified, as transparent to the light, life, and love of God – to the extent that such an identify becomes visible at all – is not achieved by its protection from the world, nor by the influence of the Spirit rather than the influence of other creatures upon it."[69] Against a tendency Jennifer Harvey and Al Barrett diagnose within white (and perhaps especially Anglican) theology to center the agency of those in dominant social positions and identify it with Christ's agency, Higton pushes Christian theology to see its work within the world as, significantly, one of receptivity.[70]

Higton's proposed repair of Anglican social theology complements the proposals of prodemocratic Augustinian moral theology, which presents Christian life in the world as a fundamentally ascetical enterprise.[71] Such *askesis* is premised on the notion that the Church's sanctification requires, in part, difficult encounters with the non-Christian world in which the Church's own pursuit of the highest Good is refined through contest and collaboration with those presently beyond its bounds. The Church's faithfulness to Christ requires openness to the voices and experiences of non-Christians, and even participation in struggles led by them – for only as receptive to these lives can the Church enact the determination of Christ's own life by the world.[72] To the extent that

---

[69] Mike Higton, "Kathryn Tanner and the Receptivity of Christ and the Church," *Anglican Theological Review* 104.2 (2021): 134–147, 144.

[70] Jennifer Harvey, "What Would Zacchaeus Do? The Case for *Dis*identifying with Jesus," in *Christology and Whiteness: What Would Jesus Do?*, ed. George Yancey (New York: Routledge, 2012), 84–100; Al Barrett, *Interrupting the Church's Flow: A Radically Receptive Political Theology in the Urban Margins* (London: SCM, 2020). Here again, Elia, *The Problem of the Christian Master* serves as a model of this theological receptivity.

[71] See especially Mathewes, *Theology of Public Life*, and *The Republic of Grace: Augustinian Thoughts for Dark Times* (Grand Rapids, MI: Wm. B. Eerdmans, 2010).

[72] I am grateful to Eric Gregory for pushing me on this point.

democratic politics in the contemporary social order furthers the end of such ecclesial receptivity, the christological proposal I have outlined should fund further work in prodemocratic Augustinian political theology.[73]

While this "ecclesial correlate" of the work of incarnation fosters a general sense of the Church's need to learn from those outside it (to the extent that an "outside" can be provisionally identified in this *corpus permixtum*), Augustine's interpretation of Matthew 25 goes even further in authorizing a full-throated affirmation of struggle alongside the poor. If the downtrodden of the world are conformed to Christ by undergoing the suffering wrongly inflicted upon them, then their desire for liberation participates in and repeats Christ's own desire for the coming of the Kingdom of God. To the extent that the poor, marginalized, and oppressed desire that the proud should be scattered in their conceit, the mighty should be cast down from their thrones, the humble should be exalted, and the hungry should be filled with good things, they repeat in themselves Christ's own desire. This understanding, present in germinal form in Augustine, is outworked to a much fuller extent in a surprisingly wide range of contemporary theologies of

---

[73] Eric Gregory, Luke Bretherton, and Matt Elia have been particularly astute in recognizing the significance of christology for prodemocratic moral theology; see Gregory, *Politics and the Order of Love: An Augustinian Ethic of Democratic Citizenship* (Chicago, IL: University of Chicago Press, 2008), 287 and 324–350; and Bretherton, *Christ and the Common Life: Political Theology and the Case for Democracy* (Grand Rapids, MI: Wm. B. Eerdmans, 2019), 68: "Through contemplating the broken body of the suffering servant, the faithful become open to the realization that they have a common life, in and through Christ, with the poor. 'We' cannot be healed without 'them,' nor they without us." At 310 n.46, Bretherton – reflecting on the anthropological picture of the human as distinguishable between "the person, the person-in-relation-to-other-persons-and-non-human-life situated in a specific time and place, and the person-in-relation-to-the-whole-of-humanity-and-the-whole-of-creation" (310) – remarks: "A fully developed, systematic christological basis for the account of humanity set out here is needed but beyond the scope of this chapter." One hermeneutical lens through which one might productively approach the present work is as an attempt to answer this need.

liberation – often making explicit reference to the understanding of the oppressed as an extension or prolongation of the Incarnation.[74]

The oppressed enact in their flesh Christ's own longing for justice and perfect love between all people, and so in the Spirit's power present a sign to the world capable of directing the world's hearts and minds to the love and contemplation of God. By their lives, they actively participate in the world's redemption.[75] The crucified peoples cry out at injustice, insisting that our action is sin. We often render ourselves insensible to their voices – as is necessary to maintain a global economy that depends on working conditions close to if not indistinguishable from slavery. But in those moments when we hear their cry, the voice that comes to us is Christ's own, because it issues from those who are conformed to his life. It comes to us as a demand, teaching us little by little how we must love one another if we are to inherit together the Kingdom of God. And their struggle is a redemptive one, for it liberates them into the human dignity which has been endowed by God, and liberates their wealthy oppressors from the inhumanity by which they create and sustain social orders that crucify the powerless.

To the extent that we are not united and actively uniting ourselves to the crucified peoples, we fail to display Christ to the world. This entails that the Church's own life is intrinsically united to the life of

---

[74] So, for instance, James Cone has written, "If the Church is a continuation of the Incarnation, and if the Church and Christ are where the oppressed are, then Christ and his Church must identify totally with the oppressed to the extent that they too suffer for the same reasons persons are enslaved"; James H. Cone, *Black Theology and Black Power*, 69; M. Shawn Copeland writes, "We are the body raised up by Christ for himself within humanity; through us, the flesh of the crucified and resurrected Jesus is extended through time and space"; Copeland, *Knowing Christ Crucified*, 78; and the Jesuit martyr Ignacio Ellacuría observes, "The Son of Man is he who suffers with the little ones; and it is this Son of Man, precisely as incarnate in the crucified people, who will become judge"; Ignacio Ellacuría, "The Crucified People," in *Mysterium Liberationis*, eds. Ignacio Ellacuría and Jon Sobrino, trans. by Phillip Berryman and Robert R. Barr (Maryknoll, NY: Orbis Books, 1993), 580–603, 603.

[75] Cf. Ellacuría, "The Crucified People," 580, which speaks of "humankind's active participation in . . . salvation."

the oppressed; the degree of its separation from them is the measure of its failure to be what it is.[76] The poor, the widows, the orphans, all the crucified peoples of the world are the Body of Christ, the extension of the Incarnation; the degree of the Church's separation from them is the measure of its failure to be what it is, and to fulfill the coredemptive work to which Christ has called it.

Augustine himself suggests that actively working for justice is inseparable from our understanding of Christ's presence among us, telling us, "Our justice is Christ, as the apostle Paul says. And so whoever is hungry for this bread is hungry for justice – but for the justice which comes down from heaven, the justice which God gives, not the sort which human beings fashion for themselves."[77] In distinguishing the justice that God gives from that which we achieve, Augustine does not mean to suggest that this justice exists apart from the material conditions of our lives, but rather indicates the source of this justice. The human justice he rejects is "That for which they presumed on their own strength, claiming that they, with their own virtue, perfectly fulfilled the law." The justice of God, by contrast, is "that justice which [God] gives to someone so that he might be just with his help."[78] We must affirm, then, that our justice is always a gift of God; but we must also affirm that we live together as the Body of Christ only to the extent that our lives together are ordered by this justice.

As we long for the forgiveness of our sins and the vision of God and strive to live holy lives, so also we must thirst for justice and act on the basis of whatever we can perceive of justice's demands, trusting that our action will be empowered by the Spirit. To imagine a Church separated from the crucified peoples of the world is to imagine Christ at disunity with himself; it is a scandal akin to the sundering of the Church's visible unity. Christ wills to be complete only with us; Christ accomplishes salvation in and through us. Only as the Church seeks to love those who are banished from or

---

[76] Cf. Bretherton, *Christ and the Common Life*, 76–78.
[77] *Io.ev.tr.* 26.1; WSA III/12, 449.
[78] *Io.ev.tr.* 26.1; WSA III/12, 449–450.

degraded within the various orderings of our lives – the foreigner, the peasant, the culturally or racially hybridized – is it the Body of Christ, a community through which love courses without loss, returning always to God. Only as it becomes a sign of Christ in joining the crucifixion of these peoples does it become what it is: Christ himself, accomplishing the redemption of the world.

***

This is our resurrection, our homeland and the way that leads us there. We will see Christ finally in the *forma dei*, the knowledge we possess by faith (*scientia*) converted finally to that attained by sight (*sapientia*). God guides us through our journey, granting us at each moment the grace that accords with Her providential ordering of created history. Christ is active in this history not only as the Word which sustains all things in being and sets them in their relations to one another, but also in the assumed flesh: "our head is at the Father's right hand to intercede for us; some of his members he welcomes, others he chastises, others he is cleansing, others he consoles, others he is creating, others calling, others recalling, others correcting, others reinstating."[79]

Through Christ, we will, God willing, come to see Her face to face, no longer through a glass darkly. In this life in a new Jerusalem, we will be perfected in our ability to love one another, finally able to meet our neighbor face to face as well, without the deceit and self-deception that characterize our experience now, without the mis-recognitions and wounds that we pass one to another. We will be fully written into Christ's life, our lives conformed to his, and to his glory. Our every thought will be Christ's, our every desire his own, our very bodies made perfect signs of his flesh, and God in it. We will be the Body of Christ: Christ will finally be complete, the Head united to his Body, wholly our Redeemer as all are wholly redeemed, Christ made *totus Christus*. The Word will have accomplished in the Body his mediatory end; what relation will we then bear to the flesh of Christ?

[79] *en.Ps.* 85.5; WSA III/18, 225.

There is reason in Augustine's writings to worry that our eschatological relation to Christ will be functionally discarnate.[80] At times, he seems to suggest that when grace has made us fit for the unmediated vision of the invisible God, we will leave Christ's flesh behind as a pedagogue no longer needed. In his first homily on the Gospel of John, for instance, he tells his listeners, "Feed on milk, so as to be able to take solid food. Do not withdraw from Christ born in the flesh, until you reach Christ born of the one Father (*A Christo per carnem nato non recedat, donec perveniat ad Christum ab uno Patre natum*), the Word God with God, through which all things were made; because that is the life which, in him, is the light of all."[81] In what sense could we speak of our eschatological destiny as a withdrawal from Christ's flesh?

More worrisome still, in the *De trinitate* Augustine speaks in a manner that might suggest an eschatological caesura between the human nature of Christ and the divine life. Interpreting the puzzling words of 1 Corinthians 15.24, Augustine writes,

> We shall contemplate God the Father and Son and Holy Spirit when *the mediator of God and men the man Christ Jesus* (1 Tm 2.5) has *handed over the kingdom to God and the Father* (1 Cor 15.24), and hence no longer *intercedes for us* as our mediator and priest, son of God and son of man, but is himself subject as priest, in the *form of a servant* he has assumed for us (Phil 2.7) ... So inasmuch as he is God he will jointly with the Father have us as subjects; inasmuch as he is priest he will jointly with us be subject to him.[82]

As written, this passage suggests that the flesh of Christ is essentially, and exists everlastingly as, *forma servi*. We are not, in the City of God, to worship the glorified flesh of Christ, precisely because it is flesh; instead, we are to worship the triune God that stands over-against it. What are we to make of this?

[80] Cf. Babcock, "Christ of the Exchange," 348–352.
[81] *Io.ev.tr.* 1.17; WSA III/12, 53.
[82] *trin.* 1.10.21; WSA I/5, 80.

Augustine seems to me in these moments to stray from his best insights concerning the Incarnation. He seems concerned to emphasize the difference in our relation to God that begins as we are enabled by grace to see the incomprehensible essence of God, but in so doing portrays the flesh of Christ as irrelevant to our beatitude. Augustine's logic at this point lapses into placing the divine and creaturely planes in competition with one another: We can only pass to an unmediated encounter with the Lord to the extent that Christ's flesh recedes from view. We need not follow him here.

Even so, we should not dismiss too easily the consideration that leads Augustine to such a position. If we are in resurrected life rendered capable of perceiving the ever-incomprehensible nature of God, then Christ's humanity ceases to serve as the necessary mediator that our present sinful condition requires. As Augustine writes in *De trinitate* 1, "It is *when he cancels all sovereignty and all authority and power* that the Son will reveal the Father, that is, when there is no more need for the regime of symbols (*dispensatio similitudinum*)";[83] "We will not seek anything else when we reach that contemplation of him, which is not yet ours as long as we are rejoicing only in hope."[84] If we took Christ's flesh to be an eschatologically necessary mediator of the vision of God, we would find ourselves still requiring faith to see the invisible God in the Christ's human visible nature. Our desire to see God face to face would go unfulfilled, persisting throughout our everlasting life. We should thus affirm, with Augustine, that Christ's human nature ceases to serve as a necessary mediator of the beatific vision. In this sense, we do indeed pass from the milk of Christ's flesh to the solid food of contemplating the divine nature, and it is true to say that the incarnate Son carries us to sight of the Father. Though the Word remains everlastingly united Her flesh, it no longer plays for us the role it once did in our relation to God.

[83] *trin.* 1.8.16; WSA I/5, 76.
[84] *trin.* 1.8.17; WSA I/5, 77.

The question thus becomes, what significance *does* the flesh of Christ bear for us when our redemption is accomplished, and the answer here is easy: It is, in the end without end, the flesh of our Lord, and is worshiped and adored as He is. Rather than the object of our longing, the flesh of Christ becomes for us in glory an object of delight, the material presence of the God whom we adore also in the immaterial life which is properly and eternally His own. The Word's resurrected humanity is no longer necessary to bring us to some end, for we have arrived at our end, and it is him. His incarnate life with us is sheer gratuity, a creaturely regiving of what is already given to us in the beatific vision, God enabling our communion with Him not only as He draws our souls into union with Him, but also as he enfolds our bodies in his own.

This is analogous to Augustine's treatment of how we will see God in redeemed materiality more generally. Christ's flesh will no longer uniquely manifest the divine life within the material world; in the heavenly Jerusalem, *all* creaturely reality will be made transparent to the vision of God.[85] As Augustine tentatively advances in the *De civitate dei*,

> It is possible, and in fact highly probable, that in the world to come we will see the corporeal bodies of the new heaven and the new earth in such a way that, wherever we look, we shall see God with brilliant clarity, everywhere present and governing all things, including bodily things ... in the life to come, wherever we look with the spiritual eyes of our bodies, we shall, even by means of our bodies, behold the incorporeal God ruling all things.[86]

He tell us that our bodily eyes, made spiritual as the soul is united to God, will even see God when they are closed – that is, even the backs of our eyelids will reveal the divine nature to us in high definition.[87] In all things, we will behold God's Truth; and consequently, we will

---

[85] Though it remains the case that the Word's flesh is uniquely *Him*.

[86] *civ.* 22.29; WSA I/7, 550.

[87] *civ.* 22.29.

see creation without misrecognition, in all the particularity and unsubstitutability with which God has created it.[88] Even language will be unnecessary for us, as our very bodies will communicate our intentions perfectly and without need of interpretation.[89]

Yet we should affirm that, even eschatologically, the material world will reveal God precisely in being ordered by and to the flesh of Christ. What had been true in the economy of redemption – that a creature becomes a redemptive sign of God to the extent that it is recognized in its relation to the flesh of Christ – will be constitutively true of all material reality in the City of God. Just as each thing is made what it is by its participation in the Word, so also the materiality of the heavenly Jerusalem will reveal the triune God by being ordered to the flesh that Word has assumed. His body will be the Lamb on the throne at the center of the City of God; we will stand together around it, offering praises to him as God; we will receive his body in an unending eucharist. In this new creation, such bodies' "motion and their rest, like their form itself, will be fitting, for nothing unfitting will be there at all."[90] To say that these movements are ordered by the Word requires that we say also that they are ordered in relation to the flesh in whom that Word lives. Even eschatologically, he remains the one in whom all things hold together, and we are glorious only in likeness to him: As Augustine quotes the First Epistle of St. John, *"we are God's sons, and it has not yet been manifested what we shall be; we know that when he is manifested we shall be like him, for we shall see him as he is* (1 Jn 3.2)."[91] We will not only see God *in* Christ; we will see God *as* Christ, clearly as the Son of the Father and in union with the Holy Spirit.[92]

[88] *civ.* 22.30.

[89] *civ.* 22.29.

[90] *civ.* 22.30; WSA I/7, 551.

[91] *trin.* 1.8.17; WSA I/5, 77.

[92] See Babcock's discussion of the beatific vision of Christ's flesh at "Christ of the Exchange," 218–227.

Even in the heavenly Jerusalem, Jesus continues as our Great High Priest, no longer interceding for us (for we have been brought to the Father), but existing as who he always was: the one who assumes flesh in sheer gratuity, and then lives a human life as a perfectly responsive self-offering in his human will to his divine will. This is, perhaps, the limited sense in which we can say with Augustine that Christ is "subject" in his human flesh to his triune life: Even in Christ, the divine agency is always irreducibly prior to the response of the created order. Christ's human flesh serves as the paradigm of the responsal existence that all creation will possess eschatologically.

While in the *forma servi*, this meant that it was appropriate for Jesus to pray to his Father, to suffer, die, and be raised. We can only imagine what his fleshly life will be like *in forma dei*. In his glorified flesh, we will know him as the same one who accomplishes our glorification in his own human life. As the divine action comes always before us, so also we will know his human responsiveness to God to be irreducibly prior to our own; we will find that our own unmediated response to the gift of our existence God gives us is also and at once a response to his human life. In this sense, he will remain the celebrant at our everlasting eucharist, the one who both leads our prayer and is prayed to as God, but without standing between us and an immediate encounter with God. Whereas now we meet God first in the flesh of Christ, then our life with God shall inseparably issue in communion with the human Jesus Christ.

As we relate to one another – as we behold the beatific vision of God in one another, and in our own flesh – we will find that each movement and act of praise presents us with Christ. We may even hope to speak in the tongue of angels – language born not of the necessity of relating to one another in an opaque world, but springing from the glory of God radiating through a renewed and spiritualized materiality. The words of such a language would themselves be utterly gratuitous, existing solely as objects of delight, offered in and as response to God's transfiguring presence, ever the same, ever new. And our lives together will bear, all together and each in its own unique manner, the seal of Christ's life: "Nothing will give more joy to that city than this song to the glory of the grace of Christ, by whose blood we are delivered. Then the words of the Psalm will be fulfilled: *Be still, and see that I am God.*"[93] All creation will have been written into the flesh of Christ; all that will remain to us will be to live, to love, to set the air trembling with words of praise offered to the Lord.

[93] *civ.* 22.30; WSA I/7, 553.

11 | Extending the Incarnation

One deeply traditional christological image teaches us to regard Christ's humanity as an instrument, wielded by the power of God for the salvation of the world.[1] Imagine the Word as a surgeon, skillfully employing the scalpel of his human flesh to overcome in us the power of sin, to pour out the Holy Spirit upon us, and to bring us to the everlasting love of God. The analogy offers several christological advantages: It makes clear that the Word is the source and agent of all Christ's works; it preserves the distinction between Christ's divinity and humanity; it chastens any lingering proclivities to view Jesus' humanity as independently existent or causative.[2] This human *is*, and certainly is capable of bringing redemption,

---

[1] See, for instance, Khaled Anatolios, "'The Body as Instrument': A Reevaluation of Athanasius' Logos-Sarx Christology," *Coptic Church Review* 18.3 (1997): 78–84; Dominic Legge, *The Trinitarian Christology of St. Thomas Aquinas* (Oxford: Oxford University Press, 2017), 213–218, which emphasizes Thomas' reclamation of the language of the instrumentality of Christ's humanity from John of Damascus; and J. David Moser, "The Flesh of the Logos, *Instrumentum divinitatis*: Retrieving an Ancient Christological Doctrine," *International Journal of Systematic Theology* 23.3 (2021): 313–332.

[2] There are also potential worries that the language of instrumentality might raise. Paul Verghese specifically critiques Augustine's christology for wrongly instrumentalizing Christ's humanity; see T. Paul Verghese, *The Freedom of Man: An Inquiry into Some Roots of the Tension between Freedom and Authority in Our Society* (Philadelphia, PA: The Westminster Press, 1972), 51–59. Kimberly F. Baker has responded decisively to this critique precisely through appeal to Augustine's theology of the *totus Christus*; see Kimberly F. Baker, "Augustine on Action, Contemplation, and their Meeting Point in Christ" (Unpublished Ph.D. Dissertation, University of Notre Dame, 2007), 227–231.

only as he exists in the hand of the Word, moved by the Word's power. Apart from the surgeon, the scalpel sits dumbly on the table.

Yet a slight shift in perspective foregrounds the distinctive features of the christological proposal I have developed in these pages. For who forged the scalpel? Who was responsible for mining the raw materials, smelting and transporting them, alloying them, stamping out and sharpening them, shipping them across the world to the hospital where that scalpel was unwrapped from its sterile packaging by a nurse and placed into the surgeon's hand? What histories of medical development were necessary for the scalpel to take that particular form? Who built the hospital – laid the cornerstone, established the endowment, raised funds for the modernization of its surgical theaters? What of the custodial staff who cleans the operating room, mitigating the risk of infection and furthering the possibility of true healing there?

What of the surgeon herself? What childhood experiences, what frivolous TV dramas, what family friend or older peer led her to study medicine? Who were the partners and friends and pets who sustained her emotional health through the pressures of medical school? Who were the teachers who taught her anatomy – who taught her to cut into human flesh without bringing death? What institutions brought her to that surgery, licensing boards and hiring committees and hospital schedulers? Beginning from the particularity of the scalpel and the particularity of the surgeon swiftly carries us into a borderless network of particularities, all of which contribute to a greater or lesser extent to the precise shape of that surgical encounter – some of which are necessary for it to occur at all.

I do not mean to suggest that these two surgical images are exclusive of one another: The former effectively emphasizes the instrumentality of Christ's flesh. But the latter analogy emphasizes the *quality* of that instrument. When the tool under consideration is a human life, even the human life of the Word, it is not sufficient simply to accept the presence of the scalpel without further question. How it got there, why this instrument looks the way it does and is employed according to strict medical guidelines, is of tremendous significance. Rather than accepting the scalpel as a material given for the sake of emphasizing the Word's agency, this second analogy suggests that the surgeon wielding the scalpel is *herself* the argumentative correlate to Christ's humanity. Healing is only possible within the operating room because of the particularities of both surgeon and scalpel, informed and determined by the full sweep of the histories that have brought her to the moment where she is poised over the patient prepared to make the first incision.

This second analogy does not suggest that we need to grant independent existence or separable "personhood" to Christ's humanity (it comes into being and persists only in union with the person of the Word and as the Word's humanity), any more than it forces us to posit any change or development in the eternal life of the Son of God (the Word is who She is from all eternity, and all Christ's human experiences and acts and relationships are Hers). It does, however, broaden our understanding of what it might mean for a *human life* to be the instrument of God – if it is truly human, the shape of this life will be defined in significant part by and inseparable from the human and nonhuman world within which it is lived. Absent the systems of production that brought them to the hospital, neither scalpel nor surgeon could bring healing: Without its sterile packaging, the scalpel would bring infection; without the medical-grade alloy of steel, it would rust before making it to the operating theater; without her parents and friends and teachers, the surgeon would bungle her way into malpractice or fail to go to medical school at all. If the Word has elected to redeem us through the life of Christ, She has elected also the lives and the context that make Christ who he is.

What we require is an account of Christ's person and work that accounts for his receptivity to the world – to the way in which the existence and agency of the human and nonhuman world grant his life shape, moving beyond the attribution to him of a bare human essence and seeing him as a full-blooded, socially implicated human who is the Word. We require an account of how the world – and more precisely Christ's eschatological Body, with all its human and nonhuman constituents – *completes* Christ, making him the particular human who the Word has willed to be.

In his theology of the *totus Christus*, Augustine has long been regarded as one of the chief inspirations for the claim that the life of the Church should be described as an "extension of the Incarnation."[3] This teaching is far from having won unanimous approval throughout the contemporary theological landscape; indeed, some of the most distinguished and influential theologians of the last century have turned their ire upon it.[4] Even a theologian as measured in judgment

---

[3] Emile Mersch, *The Whole Christ: The Historical Development of the Doctrine of the Mystical Body in Scripture and Tradition*, trans. John R. Kelly, (Milwaukee, WI: The Bruce, 1938), 409, of Cyril of Alexandria and Augustine: "Thus, guided by the same Spirit in quest of the same truth, yet each intent upon the development of his own doctrine, the Doctor of the Incarnation and the Doctor of Grace unite in a common teaching, which represents Christianity as the Incarnation, extended by means of grace to the whole 'body' of Christ." See also Emile Mersch, "Deux traits de la doctrine spirituelle de saint Augustin," *Nouvelle Revue Theologique* 57.5 (1930): 391–410; and Jean Rivière, "Notre Vie dans le Christ selon Saint Augustin," *La Vie Spirituelle* 24 (1930): 112–134.

[4] So Karl Barth, *Church Dogmatics* IV/3.ii, ed. G. W. Bromiley and T. F. Torrance, trans. G. W. Bromiley (Edinburgh: T&T Clark, 1962), 729: "to speak of a continuation or extension of the incarnation in the Church is not only out of place but even blasphemous. Its distinction from the world is not the same as His; it is not that of the Creator from His creature. Its superiority to the world is not the same as His; it is not that of the Lord seated at the right hand of the Father. Hence it must guard as if from the plague against any posturing or acting as if in relation to world-occurrence it were an *alter Christus*, or a *vicarius Christi*, or a *corredemptrix*, or a *mediatrix omnium gratiarum*, not only out of fear of God, but also because in any such behaviour, far from really exalting itself or discharging such functions, it can only betray, surrender, hazard and lose its true invisible being, and therefore its true distinction from the world and superiority to world-occurrence." See also Karl Barth, *Church Dogmatics* IV/2, ed. G. W. Bromiley and T. F. Torrance, trans. G. W. Bromiley (Edinburgh: T&T Clark, 1958), 55. Jürgen Moltmann similarly writes that theologies of the *Christus prolongatus* "[blur] Christ's freedom with regard to his church ... in these ideas pneumatology and christology slide into one another and merge to such an extent that their difference and solidarity within the Trinity is no longer visible. The particular work of the Spirit is subordinated to Christ." Jürgen Moltmann, *The Church in the Power of the Spirit:*

as the late John Webster warns that one of Augustine's most acute inheritors comes close to "those 'extension of the incarnation' or *totus Christus* ecclesiologies with which Anglicans often flirt and by which they are sometimes seduced."[5] (The Augustinian – and Anglican – may reply: Lord, grant me chastity, but not yet.) Webster's comment reflects a wariness that these theologies wrongly confuse christology and ecclesiology, refusing to respect the singularity of the Word's human life.

This worry is not without merit: Even theologians sympathetic to this strong identification of the life of Christ with the life of the Church must ask, in what sense can Christ's Body *extend* the Incarnation? Surely the whole point of the doctrine of the Incarnation is to establish a relationship between the Second Person of the Trinity and the humanity of Christ that is utterly unique within the created order? Critics may observe with some justice that those who speak of an extension of the Incarnation frequently do so in a way that does not seem to justify so shocking a locution: The claim frequently appears as a mere theological intensifier, loudly declaring a mystical union between Christ and the Church that is capable of little further analysis. Rarely is any sophisticated account given of the christological under-pinnings of such a controversial claim.

The confession of Christ's eschatological Body as an extension of the Incarnation is not, as its detractors fear, an assertion that anything beyond the humanity of Christ is hypostatically united to the Word.[6] It is, rather, a recognition of the way that this

---

A *Contribution to Messianic Ecclesiology*, trans. Margaret Kohl (Minneapolis, MN: Fortress Press, 1993), 72–73.

[5] John Webster, "Rowan Williams on Scripture," in *Scripture's Doctrine and Theology's Bible: How the New Testament Shapes Christian Dogmatics*, ed. Markus Bockmuehl and Alan J. Torrance (Grand Rapids, MI: Baker Academic, 2008), 108–123, 110.

[6] At least, that is not *my* claim; but see Jordan Daniel Wood, *The Wholy Mystery of Christ: Creation as Incarnation in Maximus Confessor* (South Bend, IN: University of Notre Dame Press, 2022). Wood's book is dazzling, and shares some affinities with my own project. While there are conceptual worries I would wish to raise in response to it (that the logic of person and nature become so disconnected in his presentation of

humanity in its historical actuality is always already constitutively related to the human and nonhuman world. For Christ to be human, only the Word's action is necessary; but for Christ to be who he is, his life requires others. And if, in the simplicity of the divine life, the Son's act of assuming human nature in inseparable operation with Father and Holy Spirit is one and the same divine act with the Trinity's providential ordering of human history, then we should say that the lives of the redeemed are included within the full intension of the Word's assumption of human flesh. Christ's identity, the human identity that the Word wills to have from all eternity, can only be actual within the temporal and developing order of creation, and as Christ's Body is joined to him. It is not, then, exclusively the case that Christ's human life comes to determine the lives of the redeemed; our lives are made constitutive parts of the redemptive efficacy of *his* life, and of his human particularity. He has willed to be complete only with us, and his life assumes its full redemptive shape only as we are united to him in final eschatological glory. Unfolding the levels at which our lives contribute to Christ's is the task of this chapter.

***

Maximus – which seems entirely compelling, to this nonspecialist – that it is not clear how nature meaningfully informs personal existence, for instance, or that the metaphysical distinction between nature and person is univocally applied to both divinity and creation in a way that seems to undermine God's unknowability), I suspect my deepest disagreement with his project is a theologically basic one: While he has successfully articulated Maximian "Christo-logic" as a live christological option, his conclusion that all creation is hypostatically identical to the Trinity simply does not sufficiently preserve God's transcendence, "the distinction" (cf. David Burrell) that I take to be basic to the God/world relation. Wood, as is clear in his rejection of analogy, would disagree; and accordingly, would undoubtedly regard my project as implicitly Nestorian. But I would be in good company, for so he must similarly regard all christological proposals that do not arrive at the sheer identity of Jesus with the Second Person of the Trinity (cf. Wood, "Against Asymmetrical Christology: A Critical Review of Rowan Williams, *Christ the Heart of Creation*," in *Eclectic Orthodoxy*, August 2019: https://afkimel.wordpress.com/2019/08/04/against-asymmetrical-christology-a-critical-review-of-rowan-williamss-christ-the-heart-of-creation/).

It is easy enough to imagine how the human Word of God could be marked by the lives of those around him – by his family and friends, his Jewish religious culture and Roman political order, his natural environment. We are used to thinking of human life in this way: I am, and you are, affected by many of those in physical and temporal proximity to us, whether our acquaintance is emotionally profound and extended across years or if it is a chance event that brings us together, an accident or stroke of good luck. Even here, though, consider all those who in the course of a month will spend the vast majority of that time within the same square mile within which I live, but whom I will never meet, whose faces I will never see, who leave no lasting impression on my life. We can imagine situations in which our lives affect or are affected by those at much greater distance: the factory worker who makes the phone that distracts me as I write, the fisherman who catches the creature that will be filleted, frozen, shipped across the world, and winds up on your dinner table. At this degree of human distance, however, the number of people whose lives will come into contact with your own is vanishingly small compared to the number whose will not.

If we expand the circle still more widely in space and time, we can see that it is quite difficult to understand how Christ's life might be marked by your life and mine, lived thousands of years after his birth. Yet this is precisely the sort of relation that I wish to pursue in proposing how our lives might complete Christ's. We receive some encouragement in this effort from the fact that most Christian thinkers have affirmed some version of this universal relation between the life of Christ and all other humans: The Word has assumed our common nature in a manner that has affected all humanity; on the Cross, Christ has borne the sins of the world. In each case, the scope of these relations is such that they include all humans; and in the theology and piety of the Christian life, it has been of great significance that they touch each person individually. Christ has taken on *my* nature, vivifying it in some degree simply by the Word's presence to it. Christ has taken on *my* sins, bearing concretely the actions that have led to my estrangement from

God and the guilt for these actions. For most theology historically, it is not simply that Christ is nailed to the Cross because he refuses to back down in the face of imperial violence (though this is indeed integral to the Crucifixion), but that the sins of the whole *massa damnata* lead him to this end. In the account I have offered above, Christ's death does not simply occur as a result of the death-dealing endemic within Roman Palestine, but as a way of entering into true fellowship with the death-dealing of sinful humanity as such.

The logic of Christian soteriology thus depends on a universal and supra-temporal register in which Christ is affected by us: by taking on our nature, and by our sin. This universal scope is already presupposed by virtually all theological reflection on Christ, even if they do not thematize it as I propose to do here; and so my account only alters the contours of Christ's universal receptivity, rather than arguing for a sort of universal relatedness that theology might otherwise forego.

***

A second register of our affecting Christ: His human flesh is marked by the natural and artificial signs that refer our loves to him.

We have seen already how Christ is the center of the "regime of signs," the redemptive order of signification that directs our hearts and minds to the invisible God through Her visible human nature. In this, Christ's humanity makes visible the fact at the center of our own existence: We *are* only by participation in the Word. As this Word becomes manifest in history, this relation of dependence becomes visible too as a significatory ordering to Christ's flesh. This is, I suggest, the theological reality underlying a fully christocentric Scriptural hermeneutic like Augustine's: The eye's lens; melting wax; drums; pelicans, owls, and sparrows; all these are fit to be employed as Scriptural images of Christ, because all these created realities in their very being are ordered to his human flesh.[7] In their very being, and in being fellow-participants in physical and biological

---

[7] See, respectively, *en.Ps.* 16.8; 21.15; 33.i.9; and 101.i.7–8.

processes with Christ, oceans, whales, mountains, estuary grasses, pulsars, all point us back to him; or, if you catch them in a certain mood, respond back to us "We are not God, but She made us."[8]

At a basic level, these facts alone mark Christ's human life. The created signs that point to Christ are not external or incidental to the work of redemption: They, and their ordering to Christ, are among the means by which he redeems us. Though there is no necessity behind any particular sign – Christ would still be powerful to save even if no pelicans existed, or ever had – nevertheless these worldly signs *actually are* used by Christ to draw us to himself; and he wills that they should be. They are channels through which Christ, inseparable from the Spirit, dispenses grace, and so are used by him to accomplish our redemption. Without them, he might still have reconciled us to God; but in point of fact, he has used *them* to become the Redeemer, the one who through them actually accomplishes and will accomplish our salvation and union with God. These signs are integral to his human career as our Redeemer, integral to the way we are lovingly united to him as members of his body. If the whole Christ includes both Head and Body, and if we only become Body through the signs that Christ uses to draw us to his human flesh and to the altar where we receive what we are, then this providential ordering of signs – stretching from the beginning of creation through to its eschatological transformation – marks the human life of Christ and informs its shape.

At a deeper level, we should recognize that the lives of those who have been joined to Christ not only take a place within the regime of signs, but help fashion it. We should be mindful here of the priority of God's noncompetitive agency in relation to our own; yet this does nothing to curtail our freedom, or to constrain deterministically the contingency of natural events or our decisions at the level of secondary causality. Except that we are bound by sin, we are free to act in the world, free to respond by the power of the Spirit to

---

[8] *conf.* 10.6.9. Cf. Gregersen, *"Cur deus caro,"* 381–383.

God's loving advance, free to work as individuals and communities to witness to Christ's presence among those subjected to domination and injustice.

We are free, as well, to use our agency to *make* created signs that point our hearts to Christ – indeed, the conversion of the material world into signs of Christ is one of the most important aspects of the Church's mission in the world. The paradigmatic instance of this is of course the eucharist, in which the agency of the priest in concert with that of the assembled Body of Christ offers up bread and wine and receives back the flesh and blood of Christ. The redemptive efficacy of this sign is evident: In offering up these creatures of bread and wine, we also offer ourselves, our souls and bodies; in the conversion of the eucharistic elements to the body and blood of Christ, we become what we receive, being digested into Christ's body.[9] As Sarah Coakley has noted, the priest stands at the threshold between God and the people: In her own mediatorial and sacrificial vocation, she points to the true sacrifice, and the one true Mediator.[10] Yet in standing at this threshold, we may add that the priest directs attention not only to the God beyond all knowing, but to Christ present in the people. By virtue of her calling to the sacramental priesthood, she calls the people to a recognition of their own priestly ministry, a vocation to awaken all the world to a new capacity to speak of Christ.

This vocation is accomplished in the labor of the woodworker, fashioning a tree into a crucifix that will be used in liturgical procession. It is lived out in the stonecutters and glaziers who fashion sacred images so far distant from the people below that their details can be seen only by saints and angels as the people of God gather in worship. It is performed as chalk blessed at Epiphany and candles blessed at Candlemas sanctify the spaces within which we live. It is enacted as travelers tramp out pilgrimage paths through

---

[9] *s.* 57.7.
[10] Sarah Coakley, "The Woman at the Altar: Cosmological Disturbance or Gender Subversion?", *Anglican Theological Review* 86.1 (2004): 75–93, 89–91.

a wild countryside, sanctifying a route along which prayers will be offered for hundreds of years to come. It is realized in the paintings and frescoes that help us imagine and inhabit the narratives of Scripture and the lives of the saints. And, in fact, in much less exalted or pious signs of Christ: stone crosses serving as distance markers; children's toys of Noah's ark; glow-in-the-dark Madonnas and other tchotchkes; Halloween costumes of Pope Francis and, as Natalie Carnes has argued, Rihanna's regalia at the Met; even the tree pulp turned into the pages of a theology book.[11]

As many of these examples make clear, the production of such signs often contains a sacrificial element: Something is transformed, something offered over or destroyed as human agency fashions a creature into a new sign of Christ.[12] Yet this is not always the case: When Hopkins writes of the windhover, it is not just the printed words on the page which come to serve newly as a sign of Christ. In hearing the poem, in remembering or even memorizing its lines, the lives of all kestrels everywhere are opened to a new possibility of christological signification. This involves no change in the kestrel itself; what Hopkins or our teacher or friend who introduced us to the poem have changed for us is our relation to the bird. Our lives – my life and that of the windhover – have been newly coordinated around Christ our common center. Yet what I wish to emphasize here is the *contingency* of this connection within my relation to the bird. Hopkins need not have written this poem; he need not have taught me to see the kestrel anew. Though the bird by the very goodness of its

---

[11] Paul J. Griffiths, "A Defense of Christian Kitsch," *Divinity: Duke University* (Fall 2011): 36; Natalie Carnes, "The Charge of Blasphemy and Pope Rihanna," *Church Life Journal: A Journal of the McGrath Institute for Church Life*, June 15, 2018: https://churchlifejournal.nd.edu/articles/the-charge-of-blasphemy-and-pope-rihanna/.

[12] Joshua S. Nunziato argues convincingly that this "parting" should not be understood as a loss to the one performing the sacrifice, for "the work of parting teaches us to make sacrifices as offerings, which acknowledge that what we offer is not – and never was – ours to give up." *Augustine and the Economy of Sacrifice: Ancient and Modern Perspectives* (Cambridge: Cambridge University Press, 2020), 6.

existence may serve as a sign of Christ, Hopkins has introduced something new and decidedly unnecessary in the kestrel's significatory reality. And such sign-making can even make a material difference on the lives of those creatures made into signs: How many albatrosses have been saved from a violent end by *The Rime of the Ancient Mariner?*

This new form of signification is not totally separated from the bird's material reality. Indeed, the determinate features of the bird's life are what make it so vivid as a sign of Christ. Its ability to ride the wind's currents, hanging in place; its dramatic and lightning-fast plunge to catch prey below; the color of its beak that recalls the cold encrustation over a glowing ember; these are not mere windowdressing on the kestrel's ability to signify Christ, but the very details that make it such a unique sign pointing our hearts back to God. It does not go too far to say that Hopkins has recognized and made use of the very features of the kestrel's existence that intrinsically point back to Christ: Through his free poetic agency, he has seen the kestrel's true connection to Christ, and rendered it in a culturally and linguistically determinate form.[13]

This use of agency is not exclusive of further, even wildly different poetic acts in which the same features of the bird's life might be made into signs that convey otherwise, but it does generate a new redemptive sign: The windhover's life – all windhovers' lives – are bound to the words of Hopkins' sonnet. For those whose hearts are turned to God by this poem, the place of the windhover itself in the work of redemption has been transformed: I see one dipping overhead, and my heart is drawn to the heart of Christ. By making them for me a sign of Christ, Hopkins has given them a role in my own sanctification that they otherwise would not have held, and meaningfully altered who Christ is for me – how he redeems me, how he appears for me in the world.

---

[13] Cf. Natalie Carnes, *Motherhood: A Confession* (Stanford, CA: Stanford University Press, 2020), 176: "Lambs in texts signify Christ because all lambs do."

This may all seem rather extrinsic to Christ's humanity: After all, the kestrel itself seems perfectly content to go about its business, utterly unaffected by whether or not I take it to be a sign of Christ. Yet within the work of incarnation, it is otherwise. In assuming flesh, the Word has willed to enter into the order of creaturely signification. This is, in part, how Christ wills to redeem us, by drawing our hearts back to God through loving the creation that refers all loves to his human flesh. This is what it means for the Word to take a place within the order of creation, for the Word in the eternal will of God to take on a life with a determinate shape, rather than merely the bare reality of human nature. From this perspective, we may say that in willing to assume flesh, the Word enters into a creation in which the windhover's existence intrinsically points to Christ, and enters into the order of history knowing that Hopkins will even further intensify the windhover's ability to point us to Christ. All this is included in the shape of Christ's life, known and willed in Word's eternity to be Her own particular historical life. All this is included within the work of incarnation.

But surely, some created signs are too far removed from God's redemptive work to signify Christ truly? Here, we may adapt a familiar Augustinian dictum: Insofar as a thing exists, it bears the potential to signify God. Further specified, insofar as a thing exists, it bears the potential to signify the *human* Word, to whom all signs which exist by participation in the divine life refer. This opens the door to what Marcella Althaus-Reid has called the "obscene Christ," portrayals of Christ that break apart our expectations of sacrality and profanity so as to depict Christ's presence with ever-shocking novelty.[14] While the structure of participation entails the significatory potential of even the most surprising images, this point is not all that must be said: Such images are furthermore required

---

[14] Marcella Althaus-Reid, *Indecent Theology: Theological Perversions in Sex, Gender, and Politics* (London: Routledge, 2001), 111. Even in their intentionally transgressive nature, these obscene Christs should be regarded as what Natalie Carnes calls "iconoclasms of fidelity"; see *Image and Presence*, 12 and *passim*.

precisely in light of the lives and human particularities that have been joined to Christ, required by the marginalization and violence they have suffered precisely at the hands of others not yet fully incorporated into his Body, required by the fact that these lives have brought their own loves and desires and kinks into his identity and into his human love of the world. As we think and speak and meet God enfleshed, we need "God, the Faggot; God, the Drag Queen; God, the Lesbian; God, the heterosexual woman who does not accept the constructions of ideal heterosexuality; God, the ambivalent, not easily classified sexuality."[15] The recognition that even intentionally scandalous signs may mediate Christ's redemptive presence and lead one to cleave to God calls attention to a corresponding warning: Even the most traditional and pedigreed signs and depictions of Christ from the Christian tradition can draw our hearts away from God and toward the *nihil* if loved wrongly – as, for instance, if meaningfully separated from love of one's neighbor.

The relation between the work of incarnation and the work of redemption thus begins to come into focus: The work of redemption, the concrete circumstances through which the Word wills to redeem humanity, are included *within* the work of incarnation. These are not two separable divine acts: They are one act, considered on the one hand as the Word's entry into history, and on the other considered as the grace that draws us back to God through Christ's human flesh. This is not to say that we are redeemed by the Incarnation simply as such, any more than it is to say that the redemption accomplished in the Cross and Resurrection are wholly separable from the Incarnation. But it is to say that in the determinate life of Christ – connecting him in the order of signs to all creatures from the beginning of creation to its eschatological completion – the full shape of Christ's life becomes redemptively significant. In the resurrected body, all flesh will tell

---

[15] Althaus-Reid, *Indecent Theology*, 95.

us of God, and God in Christ; everywhere we look, we will see his presence clearly, radiating out from a source more inward than the interiority of each creature.[16] We will not be fully and finally joined to God until, by the Spirit's work, we are able to see the whole of created history pointing to the Creator who has entered into it – until we are able to see all creation as caught up in the redemptive shape of Christ's life, knowing as we are known.

***

The order of signification is essential in understanding Christ's redemptive work, but the theology of the *totus Christus* cannot be reduced to it. Christ is really present within the life of the Church, within the lives of all those who are being drawn to him by the Spirit's work. At a third register of Christ's receptivity, we must think of Christ's active presence within the lives of the faithful, as we encounter him through the lives and agency of others.

Who is Christ for me, apart from my neighbor? I can read any number of theology books, can look at any number of artistic representations of Christ's ministry or the Crucifixion, can read any number of sonnets teaching us to find his face in any number of animals, and still be unmoved by encounter with him. We move rather closer to the point in reading the Scriptural narratives of Christ's life: Here, we encounter him in all the vividness of human particularity. We trust that in reading these texts, we are not only reading *about* Christ, but that he himself is present to us by the work of the Holy Spirit. Yet Christ's presence to us in Scripture lacks the corporality of his eucharistic presence. And this eucharistic presence, while undoubtedly the fullest reception of Christ possible to us in this life, is inherently communal – the sacrament does not compete with my neighbor as a source of Christ's presence, but requires her for its validity. It is the

---

[16] *civ.* 22.24; WSA I/7, 542: "How great, how lovely, how certain will be its knowledge of all things, without error and without effort, when it drinks in God's wisdom at its very source, with supreme happiness and with no difficulty at all!"

eucharist that proves the centrality of my neighbor in the mediation of Christ's presence.

This will, I suspect, come as no surprise to the vast majority of Christians. For most, the face of Christ is given most powerfully in the face of the neighbor: the Sunday school teacher, the youth minister, the retiree who single-handedly sustains the parish soup kitchen, the recovering addict who vulnerably confesses his struggles at coffee hour. These are the ones who teach us who Christ is, and how he lives today. The Christian life is nurtured and sustained through encounter with Christ in these lives; indeed, without these living faces of Christ, the Christian life threatens to feel hollow. Even when spiritual hollowness creeps in (as it inevitably does), it is often the faith and faithful living of others that sustains us through these times. Where there is living faith, there is encounter with Christ in the neighbor: the priest on Sunday morning; the young family at wits' end who nevertheless prioritize teaching their children to worship; the elderly gentleman who has suffered profound loss and is willing to share this pain and wisdom with others. These are Christ, severally and together.

Such lives bring us into the presence of Christ's love; indeed, because they only possess these loves through the mediation of Christ's Spirit, we may say that their loves *are* Christ's loves, the human desires of the Word's humanity created in our hearts by the Spirit's gracious work. Their lives extend Christ's because they love as he loves, they act as he acts – imperfectly, perhaps, but evidently and transformatively. As Charles Gore has written of Christ, "He is a person who while human, has yet, in virtue of His Godhead, access into the innermost parts of our being, into the very roots of our personality; and He has become, even in His manhood, 'quickening spirit.'"[17] Our hearts are transformed not simply by Christ's divinity, but by his humanity as well; it is this fact that makes each person

---

[17] Charles Gore, *The Incarnation of the Son of God: Being the Bampton Lectures for the Year 1891* (London: John Murray, Albemarle Street, 1912), 223.

enlivened by Christ's indwelling such a powerful sign of his presence in the world. The Church continues the Incarnation because it extends into our lives the divine-human personality of the Word – our words, acts, and desires are truly Christ's own, and proceed from him. There is no confusion here: Only the humanity of Christ is hypostatically united to the Word, and Christ's life in us does not compete with our own agency, for it is Christ's Spirit that empowers our agency. Yet there is real unity, as the human loves and desires of Christ become truly our own.

This allows us to state clearly a truth that I suspect will resonate with the experience of virtually every Christian: We are not saved without our neighbor. Indeed, in most cases, our redemption, our coming to love and cleave to the heart of God, is accomplished mostly through encounter with our neighbors. True enough, we may think here of the heroic witness of the saints, of the Blessed Virgin Mary, of Martin of Tours, of Becket and Richard of Chichester, even of St. Augustine himself, all of whom enjoy the blessed vision of God and intercede for us even now; but following the incarnational movement that allows us in flesh to meet God enfleshed, we must think also of those who have mediated Christ to us through their bodily presence. I mean the servants of God who sit on vestries and church councils, the people who volunteer for church cleanup days, the church sextons who arrive before dawn on a Sunday morning to spread salt on the sidewalks in winter.

We should not over-romanticize these imperfect Christians: It is to be expected, by the Augustinian above all, that some of these same servants of God may be found any given Sunday spreading gossip about their neighbors, speaking shortly with a child who runs unrestrained through the parish hall, slipping in their pocket a bit of cash as they count the morning's offering. This is to be deeply lamented, as all sin is; at times, grievous abuses of trust may require an individual to remove themselves from the community. Churches can unquestionably be places of harm, and the harm is made even more profound by the fact that the wounded have come there to meet the loving source of their existence in word, sacrament, and neighbor. Augustine does not permit the easy disidentification of these sins from Christ; he admits that "in Christ's body there are, in a manner of speaking, evil humors, inasmuch as his body is still in the process of being healed and won't be in perfect health until the resurrection of the dead."[18] The Body of Christ remains wounded, is even now diseased, precisely because our lives are so fully identified with Christ's own. But the miracle is how often our humble self-offering to God *is* employed by the Spirit to enflame the hearts of our neighbors, how often we ourselves encounter Christ in the imperfect lives of those with whom we share in Christian fellowship.

We are saved, in significant part, by the work of Christ in one another: by the church rallying around a member whose home has burned down, or helping recent immigrants secure housing and work; by sermons and Bible studies in which we come to understand God's history with Israel and the life of Christ more deeply; by communities that take the sign of the cross figuratively and often literally into the streets, struggling against racism and fascism even as these actions place their lives in danger. These actions, these prayers, are caught up in the work of the Spirit, used by Christ to create his love in us, drawing us, *Deo volente*, into union with God. These actions cannot be taken for granted, and they are not interchangeable: It means something different to see one's Sunday school teacher protesting against the removal of a city's homeless shelter than it does to march alongside a stranger; it means something different to kneel in prayer alongside a family member or adult guardian than it does to sit through prayer over a loudspeaker at a Christian school. The point is not that the stranger at a march or the intercom prayer have no potential to move one's heart to God – the point is that the particularities of our relationships to one another *matter* as God uses our lives to draw our hearts to Her. The concrete realities of our lives and our relationships, the timing

---

[18] *ep.Io.tr.* 3.4; WSA I/14, 54.

and circumstances of the actions we perform, all these are inseparable from the redemptive efficacy by which the Spirit uses these
actions to reshape the constellation of our desires. Sometimes
knowingly, sometimes unknowingly, our very lives, the very agency
with which we choose how to live our lives, are used to effect our
redemption.

If it is in his humanity that Christ is truly our mediator, if he is
our healer and savior not solely in his divinity but preeminently in
his humanity, then he cannot in his humanity be untouched,
unaffected by this work of redemption. He is the one who lives in
us; he is the one who redeems us through one another, by extending
the human loves of his human nature. As he binds us to himself, he
is bound to us as well, animating our agency and life in the world
that he has made. The redemption he effects in us through his life in
our neighbor is truly the work of *his* human agency, as truly as is his
willing to go to the Cross. The Word has willed in the simplicity of
the divine life that our lives and agency should be included within
the work of redemption; in so doing, the Word has willed too that
our lives should help give His own human life its shape, that the
reconciliation with God accomplished in the humanity of Christ
should include within it our action in the world. Our lives, our
agency, have been drawn into the work of incarnation. Christ has
chosen not to be the Redeemer without us.

We can even speak here of our agency as co-redemptive with
Christ. This is certainly not the way that Augustine would have
spoken, not least at the height of the Pelagian controversy; the
situation was simply too fraught, even if he had wished to. In
a less guarded moment, something of this dynamic could be
observed in Ambrose's reflections on the Blessed Virgin Mary:

> While the apostles were in flight, she stood before the Cross, ani-
> mated by sentiments worthy of the Mother of Christ. She contem-
> plated with love the wounds of her Son, for she was less preoccupied
> with the death of her child than with the salvation of the world.

Perhaps indeed, knowing that by the death of her Son the redemption of the world was worked, she hoped to be able by her own death-to-herself to contribute some little to what was accomplished for the profit of all.[19]

Such an estimation of Mary's place is not wholly absent even in Augustine's work: In *De sancta virginitate*, he writes, "she was born spiritually from him, as everyone who believes in him, including her, is rightly called a child of the bridegroom. On the other hand, clearly she is the mother of his members, which is ourselves, since she has cooperated with charity (*quia cooperata est caritate*) for the birth of the faithful in the Church."[20] If the Blessed Virgin is indeed the model of the Christian life, a model of human nature wholly suffused with the grace of God, we may find an echo of our own inclusion in the work of redemption by considering her. She occupies a unique place within Christ's Body, yet part of this distinctiveness is to show paradigmatically what is true to a greater or lesser degree of all those joined to the whole Christ his members – as seems to be the case in the way Augustine writes of his mother Monica.[21]

In spite of how alien a phrase like "co-redemptive" might initially seem to Augustine's thought, it is ironically his doctrine of grace that allows us to use it without fear of undermining the gratuity of

---

[19] Ambrose, *Expositio evangelii secundum Lucam* 10.132; cited and translated at Aidan Nichols, *There Is No Rose: The Mariology of the Catholic Church* (Minneapolis, MN: Augsburg Fortress Press, 2015), 72.

[20] *virg.* 6.6; WSA I/9, 70. This passage was highlighted by John Paul II in a General Audience on April 9, 1997; *L'Osservatore Romano*, English ed., April 16, 1997, p. 7, cited by Mark Miravelle, *With Jesus: The Story of Mary Co-redemptrix* (Goleta, CA: Queenship, 2003), p. 75 n.25.

[21] Anne-Marie Bowery has identified parallels both to Mary and Christ in Augustine's presentation of Monica: "If we view Monica as a symbolic representative of Mary, then she cooperates in Augustine's conversion with Christ" (74); "In her role as spiritual mother, Monica function as more than a symbol for Mary. She becomes a Christ-like mediator between Augustine and God" (81); finally arguing that "Monica functions as the feminine face of Christ" (87); see Anne-Marie Bowery, "Monica: The Feminine Face of Christ," in *Feminist Interpretations of Augustine*, ed. Judith Chelius Stark (University Park, PA: The Pennsylvania University Press, 2007), 69–95.

our redemption.[22] The utter priority of God's grace, and the utter responsiveness of our agency, means that there can be no confusion here: As our lives and agency are drawn into God's redemptive work and used as the tools by which we draw one another to the heart of God, there is never any doubt that we accomplish this on the same plane of activity as the Holy Spirit. Even in the eschatological life of the saints, when our loves will be perfectly conformed to Christ's own, our agency will always and only follow upon the grace of God. There can be no question here of the ultimate merit of our actions accruing to us, for God's work always precedes us. And as there can be no "cooperation" (strictly construed) between creatures and a God whose agency lies along a transcendently other plane of existence, we cannot say our work is co-redemptive with the agency of Christ in his divinity.[23] Yet because Christ's will and action are also human, and because redemption is accomplished in his humanity as well as his divinity, we may say that our agency is co-redemptive with *his* human agency. Out of sheer grace, the Word has willed that we should play a part in one another's redemption alongside Christ. It is the very scandal of the Incarnation that allows us to speak of Creator of all things nursing at his mother's breast, of the one who is outside all time living as a child, of the Redeemer of the world empowering us to give new life to one another.

This casts a particular tenor on the Church's life: If the life of this Body is completed through our lives and agency, it can never be considered a settled reality. The life of Christ is responsive to our agency, and always has been. Consequently, the life of the Church is not simply an established repetition of what has come before. Even

---

[22] Cf. for instance, *s.* 121.4: "The first birth is from man and woman; the second birth, from God and the Church."

[23] In rejecting "cooperation (strictly construed)," I intend no more and no less than what Kathryn Tanner writes at *God and Creation in Christian Theology: Tyranny or Empowerment?* (Minneapolis, MN: Fortress Press, 1998), 93: "Divine *concursus*, God's working with creatures who work, should first of all not be talked about as a concord, a convergence of divine and created agencies productive of a single created effect."

as the Church faithfully receives and hands down the teaching and fellowship of the apostles, it is committed also to development, even novelty, in response to the Spirit's work. From the decision to baptize Gentiles, through new developments of lay piety in the Middle Ages, through to the unfortunately belated decision to welcome women and LGBT persons in all its orders of ministry, the Church Catholic realizes its co-redemptive vocation as it recognizes who Christ is and is becoming.[24] This implies no change in the Word or the Incarnation: Only the recognition that the human flesh through which the eternal God is revealed exists in the midst of historical development, and in intimate interconnection with the historical life of Her Body.

Yet, far from authorizing an overly triumphalist reading of the Church's agency or a one-sided valorization of her practices, an emphasis on the co-redemptive character of Christ's Body makes clear the judgment under which Christians stand. It is not enough to observe that Christians have been participant in horrors; their faith has authorized and motivated their horrors. They have not simply contributed imperfectly to Christ's redemptive work; they have actively vitiated it, flailing satanically to repeat the Fall with this new grace they have been given.[25] To the extent that Christians remain unredeemed, their sins strike more blasphemously at the heart of Jesus. This is true of every act of violence or exclusion

---

[24] That the inclusion of persons regardless of gender or sexual orientation in the threefold order of ministry is not yet the majority report of all the bishops within the apostolic succession is surely to be judged a grave sin in the long view of the Church's history. I offer this judgment not out of liberal Anglo-Catholic triumphalism or party spirit, but out of my recognition of the Spirit's work in the lives of women and queer persons called to and serving in ordained ministry. I write of their full inclusion in ministry as a *fait accompli* in awareness that, in many Christian communions (and even in my own), this remains an ongoing struggle – but in the hope and trust that the Holy Spirit cannot fail to accomplish all churches' recognition of the blessing of their lives and vocations. I am grateful to Matthew Whelan for pushing me on this point.

[25] Winner's *Dangers of Christian Practice* offers such a striking and important theological meditation precisely in concentrating on the sins to which the reception of the grace of the sacraments open us.

which Christians have taken their faith to authorize; it is true, also, of the Church's division itself, which presents a counter-testimony to the Cross.[26] If we risk describing our agency as co-redemptive with Christ's, we must say in the next breath that our work perpetually betrays him.

***

A final register of our effect upon Christ's humanity comes through meditation on Augustine's theology of the Ascension. Stated simply: Christ's human life has not ended. When Christ appears to Saul on the road to Damascus and asks, "Saul, Saul, why are you persecuting me?," when Christ tells us that when we have clothed the least of these we have clothed him (and so, presumably, when Christ appears Stephen in the breath between confession and martyrdom, or to St. Martin of Tours holding half a cloak, or to St. Julian in her sickness), these appearances constitute true encounters between a human Christ and the members of his Body – encounters in which both Head and Body may develop and change.[27]

---

[26] This is not to say all difference – even institutional difference – in the Church is exhaustively sinful. It may be that the varied institutional forms of Christian communities present opportunities for the flowering of the gifts of the Spirit that might otherwise fail to occur. While pursuing this intuition would require a more focused ecclesiology, we might say as a starting point: Salutary differences in Christian communions build up the love of God and one's ecclesial neighbor, while harmful divisions undermine them. The distinction between a truly Catholic Church and a sinfully divided one may thus depend less on the particularities of institutional forms than upon how we hold our differences, with schism being occasioned and sustained by a refusal by one or both sides of ecclesial difference to meet the other in love.

[27] In this respect, my Augustinian account dissents from the otherwise quite salutary christological proposal of Ian McFarland, who denies that "the resurrection inaugurates a further stage of Jesus' life, replete with new experiences, such that God's self-revelation in Jesus would not be defined by the completed time span extending from Christmas to Good Friday"; see *The Word Made Flesh: A Theology of the Incarnation* (Louisville, KY: Westminster John Knox Press, 2019), 169. This emphasis on the continued development of Christ's human identity is anchored in Augustine's lively sense of the union between Christ and the Church. As Kimberly Baker writes of "the relational dimension of the *totus Christus*," "The union of Christ and the Church

Though he has ascended to the right hand of the Father, and though his resurrected body has transfigured the materiality of his human flesh beyond mere spatiotemporal location, he has not become discarnate or decamped from historical narratability.[28] Indeed, quite suggestively, the representation of Christ's human flesh that we receive in the stories of the *Parousia* differs in important respects from the familiar images of Jesus we receive in the Gospels, both before and after the Resurrection. Before, he is a wandering rabbi, preaching or eating fish with his disciples on the shores of Galilee. After, he is enthroned in glory, seated in the clouds of the eastern sky; in the vision of St. John the Divine, he is the Lamb, praised by angels and martyrs, opening the seals of the heavenly scrolls, wearing many diadems and with eyes like flame at the head of the army of God, with a robe dipped in blood and the names Lord of lords, King of kings inscribed on his thigh.

It is, of course, quite difficult to know what to do with all this, and it would be a clear misreading of Revelation's genre and style to take this as a physical description of Jesus in the Second Coming. Yet it suggests to us that, at the end of all things, his aspect will have been changed: However we encounter him, he will appear to us quite differently even than he appeared to the disciples on the Mount of Olives. Indeed, it is likely that this changed aspect in Christ's presentation is already at work on Easter Sunday, as he is not immediately recognizable to Mary or to the disciples on the road to Emmaus. He has been touched and transformed by the power of God, but he has also been permanently marked in his flesh by the spear and nails on Golgotha. Rather than simply suggesting to us that Christ's flesh bears everlastingly the consequences of what happened before his death, we may take this as an indication that his flesh persists in its changeability. If Christ can be robed in the torn half-cloak St. Martin offers the beggar, how much more will

---

is a relationship, not a static concept. It grows and develops over time through Christ's life and the life of the Church"; "Augustine on Action," 89.

[28] *Pace* McFarland, *The Word Made Flesh*, 165.

Christ be clothed and marked through millennia of Christian worship and prayer? How much more will Christ's flesh be transformed
by the new thing God will accomplish at the eschatological consummation of the world, the "great deed" of St. Julian in which God
will bring about a new creation and wipe the tear from every eye?
Our experience of both his divinity and humanity will be reshaped
and renewed as we gather around the throne of God.

How will Christ's humanity be changed by our lives being united
to it? How will he be changed by living in us? Consider how readily
we acquire the verbal tics and physical bearing of family and friends
around whom we spend any significant amount of time. Over the
course of several months, I hear a friend beginning many sentences
with the word "So . . . ," and before long, I find myself unconsciously
repeating the same pattern of speech. I hear my brother inflecting
a word with a particular tone that I find amusing, and years later
reflect back on the words I've just spoken and realize, "That's
exactly the way John would say that." Perhaps you have adopted
the upright carriage of a parent who has served in the military, or
the precise slouch over a keyboard of a mentor in computer pro-
gramming. All these are common enough aspects of our experience,
and can lead to delightful or even surreal moments when meeting
for the first time the people who have influenced the people we love:
type and archetype, both standing before us.

Why should the same not be true of Christ's humanity? Can we
not expect, or at least hope, that when we meet Christ face to face,
we will find in him some trace of the bearing or habits of speech of
those in whom he has lived, and lives still? Just as Christ undoubtedly picked up the accent of a Galilean or the gestures his parents
taught him as he learned to pray as a child, we may hope that the
new physicality, the new patterns of his speech in his glorious return
may reflect something of the embodied habits of the Church in our
own day. We may hope to catch a glimpse of those who have been
Christ for us when he returns in final victory. In some cases, the
aspect of mercy seen in a neighbor's face or a quiet, unassuming

gesture will have been the very creaturely signs that mediated Christ's redemptive work to us. Perhaps we may hope that these especially will leave a mark on the human face of Christ.

If we find new birth in Christ's flesh, if we are made members of a Body that is born through the wound in his side, perhaps we may imagine the change wrought in his flesh by this delivery as a christological kind of fetal microchimerism.[29] Fetal cells can be found "in maternal blood and tissues during and for years after pregnancy. It has been proposed as 'a state of balance between host versus graft and graft versus host reactions, leading to the acceptance of the allogenic fetus.'"[30] For the fetus to thrive within the mother's body, it is necessary that some number of fetal cells become the mother's own in a manner that persists long after birth. Analogously, we may say that the living cells of our lives – our experiences, our moments of joy or heartbreak, our moments of moral heroism or weakness – are incorporated into the atomic structure of Christ's humanity, made lasting pieces in the composition of his eschatological identity. Christ is changed in our reception of him, and "the believers in Jesus as God must have the courage to keep 'reacquiring' Jesus interpretively" – above all, in the interpretation offered by the sign of their lives.[31]

Yet, as McFarland notes, this lively sense of Christ's continuing history raises an uncomfortable possibility: "if Jesus' earthly life were incomplete" in the way I am proposing, "then his coming in judgment would necessarily be a matter of dread, for how could one know whether the triumphant return of one whose story is

---

[29] I am indebted to Rhody Walker-Lenow for this image.

[30] Keelin O'Donoghue, "Fetal Microchimerism and Maternal Health during and after Pregnancy," *Obstetric Medicine* 1.2 (2008): 56–64; https://doi.org/10.1258/om .2008.080008. Citing Liegeois, Alain Liégeois, Marie-Claire Gaillard, E. Ouvre, D. Lewin, "Microchimerism in Pregnant Mice," *Transplantation Proceedings* 13.1.2 (1981): 1250–1252.

[31] Paul J. DeHart, *Unspeakable Cults: An Essay in Christology* (Waco, TX: Baylor University Press, 2021), 19.

incomplete were truly good news?"[32] This is an appropriate worry, only superficially addressed by the bare assertion that, however he might change, Christ is the same yesterday, today, and forever. Yet there is a better answer available to us. It is not the case that Christ remains utterly hidden from us, such that we have reason to fear that he will be unrecognizable to us in his return. Christ shows us his face *constantly* – in the poor, in the marginalized, in the faithful choir director who leads the congregation in song each week, in the widow who bakes the wafers to be offered in the sacrifice of the Mass. As we meet him in these many lives in whom he lives, we meet him *as* the same yesterday, today, and forever: We meet him with the same mercy, the same forgiveness, the same good news on his lips for the scorned and the oppressed. We hope for his return not because his history is concluded, frozen in amber, but because as we meet him anew in the world we find him bringing the same judgment and healing and restoration that the faithful have found in him for generations. We long for his mercy and cleansing fire precisely because he has accompanied the sinner in her repentance, and the marginalized of every generation in their struggle for liberation.

More than this: It is not the case that the continuing course of Christ's human development unfolds apart from God, either in his session at the right hand of the Father, or in his appearance among his pilgrim Body. The new determinations of his humanity are animated by and superintended by the very Holy Spirit that he breathes into his apostles. Christ's present incompleteness does not produce dread, because his is a Body enlivened by the Third Person of the same divine life that Christ incomprehensibly is. It is the Holy Spirit, working through his Body, who fully completes Christ's human identity.

The Christ signified by the life of the Church, the Christ who lives in his Body, is thus not final, not settled. In the vitality of the

---

[32] McFarland, *The Word Made Flesh*, 180.

members of his Body and in the particular contributions they continue to make to his identity as Lord, Christ's responsive human flesh manifests his continued development along with those he has joined to him. Even as the Church and those little ones in whom Christ is present signify him to the world, the Church does so in the knowledge that – by the particularity and agency of those being joined to Christ, and by his often-unpredictable responses to them in the promptings of the Holy Spirit – Christ may always show them a new face, something in his humanity unforeseen by those who are his members. He remains the one who tells us parables that we do not understand, the one whom – like the disciples on the way to Emmaus – we often recognize only belatedly. Christians live in the trust that Christ is present where two are three are gathered together, and will manifest himself both reliably (in, for instance, the eucharist) and unpredictably. We trust that, as the very one he was, he will come nonetheless to resemble those whom he has joined and is joining to himself.

There is a question by which members of Christ's Body should rightly be worried, however: As he unites himself to us, what are we doing to him? If we can robe him in glory by our faithfulness, can we also mar and disfigure his face by our apostasy – our disregard of the poor, our participation in the suffering of the oppressed, our continued acquiescence to the injustices of the earthly city? How, precisely, does the Church in our day further the work by which Christ is made truly our Redeemer, and where does it stretch his bones out of joint into a macabre simulacrum of the one who is rightly our Lord and King? Answering this question will require textured analysis of both the Church's faithful witness in the world, and its furtherance of the evils still endemic within our fallen world. If this account is right, however, such work is critical in answering the question of who Jesus Christ is today, in a very realist sense.

***

On the Cross, Christ has joined himself to our condition of estrangement from the Father, entering into the fellowship of our death-dealing and thereby opening a new possibility of community with God and neighbor. By the gracious indwelling of the Spirit, Christ has created within us loves conformed to his own, drawing us in one and the same movement to raise our hearts to God and to follow Christ into a new solidarity with the despised of the world. Through this new intimacy, Christ has created a new spiritual reality in which he may truly be said to speak in his Body, in which the sufferings of his Body are truly his own, in which there is an indissoluble reality of one person, one *totus Christus*. This Body is built up and sustained through Christ's own continual self-offering, the sacrament in which his flesh and blood are consumed so that we might be digested by him and made his members. All this adds up to quite a strong doctrine of Christ's Mystical Body – but can it justify calling the life of the Church an extension of the *Incarnation*?

No. For this to be anything more than a rhetorical overreach that risks confusing the life of the Church with the human flesh hypostatically united to the Word, something more is required: the recognition that the existence and agency of creation, and especially of the Church, are included within the Word's very will to assume flesh. The whole Christ, Head and Body, are included within the work of incarnation. The concrete particularity of Christ's life, and the redemption he accomplishes, require his union with existence and agency of his Body.

Within the canon of Scripture, this christological outlook comes to clearest expression in the Epistle to the Colossians. Paul – or the writer influenced by him who has taken up his name, if we take this epistle to be pseudonymous – famously incorporates within the letter's first chapter one of the most rousing and expansive portrayals of Christ's work. Christ is the εἰκὼν (image) of the invisible God, the one ἐν αὐτῷ and δι᾽ αὐτοῦ and εἰς αὐτὸν – in whom and through whom and for whom – all things have been created, the one before all thing and in whom all things hold together (συνέστηκεν). He is the Head of his Body the Church, and πᾶν τὸ πλήρωμα – all the fullness – was pleased to dwell in him. The lack of an obvious referent is suggestive here: All the fullness of the invisible God, whose image he is? The fullness of all things created in and through and for him? The fullness of his Body the Church? Yes, πᾶν τὸ πλήρωμα. And for this Pauline writer, the blood of the Cross is the guarantor of reconciliation and community, drawing all things to union with God in the outpouring of Christ's life. It should be clear how deeply this passage has patterned the christological proposal I have offered here.

The all-encompassing and completed sense of God's redemptive work that we encounter in the "Christ hymn" makes all the more surprising the turn Colossians 1 takes at the chapter's end: "I am now rejoicing in my sufferings for your sake, and in my flesh I am completing what is lacking in Christ's afflictions for the sake of his body, that is, the church" (Νῦν χαίρω ἐν τοῖς παθήμασιν ὑπὲρ ὑμῶν, καὶ ἀνταναπληρῶ τὰ ὑστερήματα τῶν θλίψεων τοῦ Χριστοῦ ἐν τῇ σαρκί μου ὑπὲρ τοῦ σώματος αὐτοῦ, ὅ ἐστιν ἡ ἐκκλησία).[33] But this makes no sense: How could anything be lacking in the sufferings of the one in whom all creation hangs together? How could Paul complete the work in which God has already reconciled to Himself all things through the blood of the cross?

The Greek of Colossians 1.24 is remarkable in several respects: This is the only point where the word ὑστέρημα is employed to indicate any lack or deficiency associated with Christ; it is similarly the only use of the word θλῖψις to describe Christ's sufferings;[34] this verse is the only place in either the New Testament or the

---

[33] NRSV; *The Greek New Testament*, 3rd ed., ed. Kurt Aland, Matthew Black, Carlo M. Martini, Bruce M. Metzger, and Allen Wikgren (Münster: United Bible Societies, 1975).

[34] On these two points, see Andrew T. Lincoln, "The Letter to the Colossians," in *The New Interpreter's Bible*, Vol. XI, ed. Leander E. Keck (Nashville, TN: Abingdon Press, 2000), 551–670, 613.

Septuagint where the crucial verb ἀντανaπληρόω – to fill up or complete – is used.[35] Liddell and Scott provide two parallel usages of this verb.[36] An early use of the term may be found at Demosthenes' περὶ τῶν Συμμοριῶν 17 (*On the Navy-Boards*, 354 B.C.), where, in the context of dividing naval conscripts into battle sections, he says that the number of wealthy men in the unit should be filled up (ἀντανaπληροῦντας) with a similar number of poor men, so as to preserve the balance of each unit.[37] The second is found at Apollonius Dyscolus' Περι Συνταχεως (*On Syntax*) 1.19 (2nd c. A. D.), where he uses the term to describe the way that pronouns complete and render determinate the sense of verbs, as in the difference between "I write" and "you write."[38] The English language is importantly different than Greek here: where in English, the word "write" remains identical in both usages, thus leaving the pronoun to do all the work of specification, the Greek ἐγὼ γράφω, σὺ γράφεις incorporates the difference of subject in both pronoun and verb. When Dyscolus speaks of the pronoun "completing" or "filling up" the verb, we should understand the pronoun performing a kind of repetition or confirmation that makes the subject of the word newly concrete in the grammar of the sentence. Each of these parallel Greek usages of ἀντανaπληρόω may be instructive for our reading of Colossians 1.24, emphasizing the sense in which the verb may be used to suggest, on the one hand, the completion of some insufficient quantity, and on the other, completion as informing something in its particularity.

[35] Lincoln, "Colossians," 613.
[36] Henry George Liddell and Robert Scott, *A Greek-English Lexicon/with a supplement* 1968 (Oxford: Clarendon Press, 1985), 149
[37] Demosthenes 14.17: *Demosthenis Orationes*, ed. S. H. Butcher (Oxford: Clarendon Press, 1903).
[38] Apollonius Dyscolus, *De Constructione Libri Quattuor (Peri Suntaxeos)*, Vol. II.2, in *Grammatici Graeci*, ed. Gustav Uhlig (Leipzig: B. G. Teubner, 1910), 21.

Modern Biblical scholarship is, predictably, of many minds on the proper interpretation of this verse.[39] It does, however, help us identify a set of theological *desiderata* in interpretations of Colossians 1.24. Among these are (1) clarity in the extension of the referent of the phrase ἁι θλίψεις τοῦ Χριστοῦ; (2) some understanding of how ὑστέρημα may be predicated of ἁι θλίψεις τοῦ Χριστοῦ without implying deficiency or insufficiency in Christ's own performance of the work of redemption; (3) attention to the performance of these sufferings ὑπὲρ τοῦ σώματος, offering some description of how Paul's suffering contributes something to the body; following Richard Bauckham's association of Paul's sufferings with the "messianic woes" that precede the final advent of God's Kingdom,[40] (4) some account of the role such suffering plays in the internal constitution of the Body of Christ, of these tribulations as the inevitable result of a life lived in conformity to Christ in the midst of a sinful world, and as following necessarily from the proclamation of the Gospel; and (5) an account of the relation between Paul's sufferings and Christ's such that the use of the term ἀνταναπληρόω is justified.

It is my hope that the Augustinian christology I have proposed in this book answers these challenges in a compelling fashion. On my account, (1) the θλίψεις τοῦ Χριστοῦ refer not only to the Passion of Christ, but also to the sufferings undergone by Christ in his body, the

---

[39] See Yates' still important mapping of the interpretive options for this text at Roy Yates, "A Note on Colossians 1:24," *The Evangelical Quarterly* 42 (1970): 88–92; and a more recent employment of Yates' map at Jerry L. Sumney, "'I Fill up What Is Lacking in the Afflictions of Christ': Paul's Vicarious Suffering in Colossians," *The Catholic Biblical Quarterly* 68.4 (2006): 664–680. Other important recent entries on the literature on Colossians 1.24 include Paul L. Trudinger, "A Further Brief Note on Colossians 1:24," *The Evangelical Quarterly* 45 (1973): 36–8; Andrew Perriman, "The Pattern of Christ's Sufferings: Colossians 1:24 and Philippians 3:10–11," *Tyndale Bulletin* 42.1 (1991): 62–79; and Richard J. Bauckham, "Colossians 1:24 Again: The Apocalyptic Motif," *The Evangelical Quarterly* 47.3 (1975): 168–170, alongside Lincoln's evaluation of this literature at "Colossians," 613–614.

[40] Bauckham, "Colossians 1:24 Again," 169.

Church – and here it is important that the term θλῖψις is nowhere else in the New Testament used to refer to the sufferings which are proper to Christ alone as head. In a far more realist sense than is commonly seen in contemporary christology, this Augustinian outlook tells us that we are Christ: Our lives are conformed to his only as he dwells within us and is created within us by his Spirit; our lives, our bodies, souls, and agency, are drawn into his own life and will to save the world, and his redemptive work is accomplished through us as we become vital signs of him. His life is given its complete shape, he becomes our Redeemer, as he makes us into the very signs by which he redeems us. By his gracious will, he has chosen not to accomplish this work apart from us; though complete as *vere Deus* and *vere homo* by virtue of the Word's timeless act of assuming flesh, he wills to be the person that he *is* only with us, inclusive of our agency and the course of finite causality. Because of this intimacy between Christ's life and our own, we may even go so far as to say that he suffers in us, affirming the reality signified in the words *Saul, Saul, why persecutest thou me?* As he wills to take on human flesh interdependent with and vulnerable to our own flesh, he unites himself to all our suffering. As he undergoes suffering in his own body as head, he transfigures all suffering, teaching us that it will be overcome not only in his flesh but in ours as well.

When we thus speak of our own lives as filling up what is lacking in Christ's own sufferings, (2) no deficiency or incompletion is suggested, for Christ receives our wounds as his own. Because Christ has two natures, our lives and agency are doubly related to his: We are noncompetitively related to Christ in his divine nature, and interdependent with him in his human nature. The fact that we can be both at once is due to Christ's humanity, for he too is noncompetitively related to the eternal act of God's life as the Word's own human life and will. By the work of the Holy Spirit, we are made into the extension of Christ's life: Our lives become responsive to the dwelling of God's power within us in a manner closely related to the dwelling of the Word's power in Christ.

Where we differ is that the human life of Christ is the very life of God – Christ's personhood is the personhood of the Word, who has united human nature to itself and hypostatizes that nature in the human life of Christ. Though we live always in dependence upon God's gift, we are granted the possibility of existing as individual human persons. However much our lives come to be noncompetitively enlivened by the presence of Christ's Spirit in us and determined by Christ's life as we come to desire with his desires and act with his will, there will always be a qualitative difference between his divine-human personhood and our human personhood in union with God. Yet the human nature the Word assumes exists interdependently with us, and the work of redemption that the Word wills in assuming flesh is only completed as our human lives enter into relation with Christ's human life. He has willed to include our own lives and action in his redemptive work, and so Christ's own work is not full and final until we are joined to it. His flesh draws our hearts back to the invisible God, and as our affections are pulled heavenward, we ourselves come to serve as signs of Christ's flesh that draw others back to God, and they us. Our sufferings (3), both those inflicted unjustly by the sin of others and those entered upon gladly ὑπὲρ τοῦ σώματος in our testimony to the possibility of a just city, serve as redemptive signs for others as we repeat the pattern of Christ's life in our own. Until this city comes (4), the Church is called to reflect in its own life and through faithfulness in the midst of tribulation the possibility of a life ordered by love of God and neighbor. Though it enacts this possibility only imperfectly, defined as much by its own failures in love as by the successes in loving it receives as the gift of the Spirit, the Church's collective life at its most faithful (and thus, inseparable from those who are dehumanized by the forces of human wickedness) teaches us that on the other side of violence, death, and sin is a life lived wholly in response to God's gift, a life of mutual recognition, a restored relation between a healed soul and incorruptible body, an everlasting communal life of embodied loving contemplation in the City of God.

On this basis, (5) we can employ the term ἀνταναπληρόω in both of the senses explored above in Demosthenes and Apollonius Dyscolus. As we undergo suffering in the body of Christ, we render the full extent of Christ's sufferings newly determinate, completing them just as a pronoun completes a verb. We need not say that Christ suffered imperfectly in the events of the Passion, just as the verb γράφω is perfectly well-formed in itself; but the verb's subject attains a new concreteness in the sentence structure when it is accompanied by the pronoun ἐγώ. Analogously, we may say that though Christ underwent his sufferings perfectly on Good Friday, we see the full extent of his afflictions as he suffers in our lives as well. It is in this sense that we can even speak with Demosthenes about our sufferings "filling up" Christ's sufferings in a quantitative sense – there is, even now, more for Christ to suffer, as the downtrodden of the world and those groaning under the weight of sin suffer on the cross of the world. There will continue to be a lack in Christ's sufferings until the necessarily painful work of reconciliation is accomplished, as the surgeon's hand cuts away our malignity and restores us to health.

***

Colossians 1.24 is certainly not among the verses Augustine cites most frequently in his christological reflections; reference to it is dwarfed by the number of times Augustine returns to Christ's cry of dereliction or his words to Saul on the way to Damascus. In his extensive *corpus*, he cites it only eight times: at *Io.tr.eu.* 98.5 and 108.5; *en.Ps.* 61.4, 86.5, 87.15, and 142.3; *s. Dolbeau* 22.20; and at *trin.* 4.3.6. Frequency is not the only measure of importance, of course, and we have already encountered a number of these texts as being among the most important sites of Augustine's christology. One of the passages I have not yet discussed offers perhaps Augustine's most striking discussion of the verse from Colossians. At *en.Ps.* 61.4, Augustine writes,

If you are numbered among the members of Christ, whoever you are, mortal sufferer who hear these words (and whoever you are who do not hear them, for that matter; though in fact you do hear them if you are a member of Christ), then whatever you may suffer at the hands of those who are not Christ's members was lacking to the sufferings of Christ. This statement that it 'was lacking' means that you are filling up the appointed measure: not that you are causing it to spill over, but that you are suffering just so much as was necessarily to be contributed from your passion to the universal passion of Christ. He suffered as our head, and he suffers in his members, which means in us. We each pay what we owe into this commonwealth of ours, according to our limited means; we contribute our quota of suffering from the resources allotted to us. There will be no final balancing of accounts in the matter of suffering until this world ends.[41]

In condensed form, we see in this passage the central dynamic of Augustine's theology of the *totus Christus*. As we are written into the life of Christ, we find our sufferings made his, and his made our own. Yet these sufferings are not *added* to Christ's: They are part of the "appointed measure," they were *already* contained in his sufferings. In like manner, I have argued, a contemporary Augustinian christology should understand us completing Christ's life or extending the Incarnation not in such a manner that it would "spill over" into that which it is not, but in the sense of our lives *already* being included proleptically in the determinateness of Christ's human particularity.

We may put it this way: The life of the Church can only be an extension of the Incarnation, because the existence and agency of Christ's Body is already included within the *intension* of the Incarnation.[42] When we speak of the Incarnation, we do not simply

---

[41] WSA III/17, 204.

[42] I am self-consciously appealing to the contrasted terms of intension and extension as employed within Anglo-American philosophy (though my use comes closer to contemporary accounts of "hyperintensional" logic); see Daniel Nolan,

speak of the bare act of assuming human nature; we speak of the triune Lord's will that the Second Person should live a determinate human life, at home in the natural world, surrounded by family, friends, disciples, revilers, worshippers. The Word's will to assume flesh is the very same will by which the Word desires to redeem sinful humanity – but this redemptive purpose is only accomplished alongside, even with the active participation of Christ's Body. In the eternal God, all the contributions of the creaturely order that will play a part in accomplishing Christ's redemptive purpose are drawn into the will to assume flesh. The Word wills to live as a particular human, in a particular time and a particular place. This sets some in very direct relations to him, opening his human life to being affected by others around him just as ours is; it sets the whole of creation into distinct spatiotemporal and significatory relations to him that may themselves be used to draw our hearts to God; and if the Church truly is Christ's Body, it suggests that his human life may still be affected by the agency of those in whom he lives in the world today. The life of the Church is included within the intension of the Incarnation: Our lives and agency, which themselves exist only by the good pleasure of God, are presupposed by the Word's will to assume flesh, and help give Christ's human life its distinctive redemptive shape.

There is good reason within the Augustinian tradition to be skeptical of this way of expressing things. Does this not elevate us to the level of Christ, stealing away the gratitude for our redemption that is properly due to him alone? This concern is obviated by the recognition of the noncompetitive relation of divine and human agency: The priority, and thus the unquestioned source of our redemption, is the act of God. Because Christ is this same God, gratitude and worship are due to him alone. Indeed, quite to the contrary, my purpose in emphasizing the work of incarnation is

"Hyperintensional Metaphysics," *Philosophical Studies* 171.1 (2014): 149–160. My use of the term also comes close to Hopkins' notion of "inscape," the inward distinctiveness of a thing.

precisely to *intensify* our thanksgiving. Not only do we meet our incarnate Lord face to face, our lives have marked the human life of God. Not only are we redeemed by the work of Christ, we have been granted a(n irreducibly secondary and dependent) place in Christ accomplishing the salvation of our neighbor. Not only do we live, but Christ lives in us. All this, *all this*, is to be received and returned in offering to God.

It is only this reality that authorizes us to speak of the life of the Church as an extension of the Incarnation, for in drawing us to himself as members of his Body, Christ's own human identity is completed. Only in eschatological view, and thus only as our lives are united to his in the whole Christ, does Jesus become who he is, and who he has eternally willed to be: fully the Redeemer of the world, the one who has healed us of the effects of sin and united us to the Father. Only with us is this work completed, and so only with us does the Word's will to assume flesh and live this determinate redemptive life reach its consummation.[43] The Church is the extension of the Incarnation because without it Christ's redemptive work is unfinished, and he is not the one before whom every knee bows. This is the order of redemption that the triune Lord has willed in the eternal simplicity of the divine life; this is what it means for the Word to live a human life. We extend the Incarnation because by our own decisions, and friendships, and prayers, we are granted a place in making Jesus who he is, both in the time of his Galilean ministry and in the present day, as he lives in us. Christ is not Christ without his Body, without the effects of others upon him; he never was.

***

---

[43] While I am sympathetic to DeHart's claim that "if ... one of the missions [namely, that of the Spirit] is still historically in process, then so is the history of the incarnation itself," and his attendant emphasis on the "endlessly extended" reception of him (*Unspeakable Cults*, 157), my distinction between the act of incarnation and the work of incarnation allows me to further specify the sense in which the Incarnation *qua* act of the Word's timeless life is eternally complete, while the work of incarnation as history founded in God's providential order still requires completion.

A question remains: What are the limits of this Body that is an extension of the Incarnation? Throughout this chapter, I have used the phrase "the Church is an extension of the Incarnation" as a sort of shorthand, for while the visible community of the Church is indeed bound into the work of incarnation and those baptized into it are made true members of Christ, it is most properly the eschatological City of God which is the Body of Christ in its fullest extent. This City includes not only the visible community gathered below, but saints and angels gathered around the heavenly throne of God; and, in full eschatological view, includes many who are today separated from or even hostile to the community of the visible Church.

What's more, the account that I have offered above suggests that the lives of many who seem actively opposed to Christ contribute, by their lives and agency, to giving his life its shape. Consider, for instance, the Roman centurions who executed him: One of them, Mark tells us, was moved to declare that he was the Son of God, but the preponderance of them did not. They express no faith in him, there is no transformation of their lives that Scripture records – and yet Christ's confrontation with death does not occur without their agency. They, as much as anyone, have played a part in making Christ's life the redemptive sign that it is, and they have left marks on his flesh that persist eschatologically in glorified form. Are they, too, an extension of the Incarnation?

Any answer must reckon with the fact that even the signification of *their* lives is not final. At present, before the redemption of the world is perfected, their act of violent execution may only be able to signify for us under the aspect of judgment: In Christ's *Parousia*, these acts will be judged as wicked and condemned, consigned to nothingness as the sinfulness of all sinful acts must be. Yet if it is permissible to hope that these Roman soldiers may also be found among the redeemed at the end of all things, these acts may come to signify otherwise, as signs of God's refusal to permit the death we bring to one another to remain final – as sins that have been *forgiven*. Without these acts, Christ would not be the lamb who was slain. If the slaying is the last word, then all is lost; but if this lamb still lives by the power of God, the damnation of this sin *qua* sin becomes permanent absolution in the one whose sin it is. The forgiveness of these centurions consists in part in the fact that they are joined to Christ precisely as the ones who have committed these sins – and yet, by coming to dwell in him as he dwells in them, their sins take on a significatory and thus redemptive possibility that they did not previously contain.

Even the white supremacist? (To take an example that may be uncomfortably contemporary.) The first thing to be said, of course, in awareness of the physical and spiritual violence that such persons have inflicted on racially marginalized persons, is that their lives confront us now with an icon of what is damned on the Cross. Presently, they function most frequently as contorted signs that lead those who love them to delight in hatred and death, and draw those who follow the chain of loves in which they are links toward nothingness. Yet – we should say as a theological limit case – inasmuch as the white supremacist is an existent thing by the good pleasure of God and as he receives life from Him, even the white supremacist potentially signifies Christ. Certainly, we hasten to add, he does *not* signify Christ in his white supremacy; this signifies only perdition. He signifies Christ, at least, as a human, a bearer of the very nature assumed by the Word; and to the extent that we are unable to see Christ in him, it is because of the insensibility consequent to our sin, or attending the violence born of sin he inflicts upon those he encounters. To the extent he serves as an image of Christ at all, it is surely an image marred almost to the point of unrecognizability. And yet, he may in this damaged image signify Christ precisely as the one who comes in judgment of the harm he sinfully inflicts. He may point to Christ – scornfully but really – as the centurions did, hanging his lynched body upon the tree and speaking truthfully in his mockery: Truly this is the Son of God.[44] Stepping back from the particular example of the white supremacist, we should also note that it is not always the kind and generous souls whom God uses to work transformation in us; sometimes the Spirit can lead us to the most vivid and sanctifying encounters in those who show us a face of Christ almost wholly disfigured.

Speculatively, then, we may say: The eschatological perfection of the *totus Christus* seems to include the whole community of creation. This is, indeed, a "deep incarnation." By assuming flesh that is implicated in an expansive domain of physical processes and relations – cosmological, subatomic, ecological, evolutionary, to name a few – and that is socially extended as both the recipient and agent of human influence, a full account of the Word's humanity absolutely requires attention to the broad sweep of the nonhuman creation. These relations are not epiphenomenal to the true redemptive center of Christ's work: They are the growing edges of our awareness of this work, the place where it becomes progressively manifest that the redemption he has accomplished on behalf of sinful humanity is also the means by which he brings life and transformation to all creation. It is not simply the case that we will eventually be able to see how his death and resurrection matter for, say, the Amazonian pink river dolphin; it is that the fullness of our resurrected knowledge and love of God in Christ will not be complete until we know this creature – every creature – as a sign of him, and love him in loving its particularity.

As all creation is written into Christ's Body as a redemptive sign of his flesh, he is manifest in both divinity and humanity throughout all creation. This is as true of animal life and the inanimate natural world as it is of the human persons who willingly participate in Christ's redemptive work in service to

[44] For the fullest development the striking identification of lynched black bodies with Christ crucified, see James H. Cone, *The Cross and the Lynching Tree* (Maryknoll, NY: Orbis Books, 2011).

the world.[45] According to the potentialities of their natures, all things are capable of participating in Christ's redemptive work – and indeed, that redemptive work will not be complete until all these redemptive potentialities have been actualized, until creation is drawn to the heart of God by all things testifying to Christ in their very created particularity. Each creature reflects its creator's face unsubstitutably; each creature, within the work of incarnation, is granted a vocation within Christ's redemption that only it can realize. The whole creation comes to be the embodied sign of the God who, in the very Second Person of Her eternal life, assumes flesh; and this body of the cosmos is made Hers through the flesh that is Her own.[46] This is the whole Christ: all of creation gathered into the one in whom, and through whom, and for whom all things are made.

---

[45] With far greater attention to the racialized and colonial histories that mediate various enculturated encounters with Christ in the natural world than deep incarnation often affords, see Lee Miena Skye, "Australian Aboriginal Women's Christologies," in *The Strength of Her Witness: Jesus Christ in the Global Voices of Women*, ed. Elizabeth A. Johnson (Maryknoll, NY: Orbis Books, 2016), 162–171. See also Rebecca Copeland's *Created Being*, exemplary for her christological attention to the inanimate world.

[46] Natalie Carnes makes the point elegantly (drawing on Maximus) at *Motherhood*, 171: "I could narrate You this way: In creation, as in and because of the incarnation, the Logos seeks to realize the mystery of Her embodiment. She who bodies forth in the incarnation bodies forth in creation."

Conclusion

What has this book accomplished? Final judgment, of course, resides with the reader; but I hope two things.

First, I hope that this study has made a case that the writings of St. Augustine of Hippo offer a compelling and underutilized resource for contemporary christology. My method – evident in the final shape of my argument, if not in its discursive presentation – has been to work backward from what I take to be the heart of Augustine's christology: If Jesus Christ is the Word of God who can cry out in godforsakenness on the Cross as a result of his union with sinful humanity; if he is the one who can ask Saul truly why Saul is persecuting *him*, and to teach his disciples that whatsoever they have done to the least of them, they have done to *him* – then what must be true of his person and work? Pursuing this line of questioning has pushed us to examine what may otherwise have seemed like many diverse emphases of Augustine's expansive theological reflection, showing in so doing how Christ stands as their center and meeting point. In Christ, we come to encounter personally the triune Lord who always exceeds our comprehension and resists final description. In Christ, we meet in flesh the Wisdom that, from all eternity, patterns creation, is present in and to it, and sets all times and things in their proper relations to one another. In his human flesh, Christ is the sign to which all signs refer; the object of love to which and by which all loves are ordered. He redeems us by opening a new possibility of human fellowship in his body on the Cross, and draws us into this fellowship as his Spirit creates his very loves within us. In his election, he prefigures and is the precondition for our own predestination, as the unmerited nature of the Word's assumption of human nature is repeated in the Holy Spirit's gracious inauguration of our faith and charity. As his love is shed in our hearts by the Spirit's indwelling, the Church is called into being as a holy city, animated by Christ's love so it may finally attain to the one who loved it first. All this is accomplished through the mediatory humanity of Christ – through the way his humanity, and the bonds to the Church it makes possible, serve as the focal point of God's redemptive work in created history.

Augustine's achievement is not merely in coordinating all these theological *loci* through his reflection on Christ (though that alone would be sufficiently impressive to make study of his christology quite rewarding to contemporary christology), but in the *way* he coordinates them. In his resolute emphasis on the distinction between divinity and humanity in Christ, Augustine preserves the mystery and incomprehensibility of God even as he leaves no doubt we meet the Lord Herself face-to-face in Jesus. In his textured sense of the Holy Spirit's mediation of Christ's presence to us, Augustine joins together the inner and the outer, letting our affective, embodied, communal lives carry faith's knowledge in its train. On Augustine's account, the redemption Christ brings cannot be disconnected from the community of the Church and the lives of the poor, for the Word has made His human life inseparable from them, a Head bound by grace to its temporally extended Body. For all these reasons, Augustine's christology should be considered a fruitful resource for further engagement by those theological approaches that attend to the destabilizing nature of our God-talk, that want to carve out room for a lively sense of Christ's historical and ecological implication within the bounds of christological orthodoxy, that wish to expand our understandings of faith and salvation to include the affective and the embodied, and that wish to foreground Christ's liberating presence in and responsiveness to the lives of the poor and oppressed.

Yet second, I hope that this generative dialogue with Augustine has brought into focus my own christological proposal, one that begins from the recognition that Christ's humanity is bound up with the lives of the people and the world around him, and ends with an acknowledgment that his very human identity and redemptive work are inseparable from the creation he has joined to himself. This outlook complicates or overcomes many of the classical distinctions employed within christological reflection. A distinction between Christ's person and work is revealed to be so abstract as to be unserviceable for many of the purposes to which it has sometimes been turned in the past – for beyond the bare fact of his metaphysical constitution in two natures, what we take to be definitive of Christ's person as historically enacted is shown to be worked out in responsive relation to the created order. As such, Christ's personal identity unfolds in history in response to very concrete and contingent (though providentially ordered) actions and encounters, and he is *shaped* by them in a way that might have failed to obtain in their absence. This is not to say that Christ is not fully and truly, by the act of incarnation, the person of the Word – but it *is* to say that in redemptively *manifesting* Christ as the person of the Word, She has chosen to make use of the things of this world in fashioning Her humanity *thusly*. Christ's humanity is the Word's own human life, and She has willed to be in Her humanity who She is only in mutualistic relation with Her Body.

Or again, a distinction between the objectivity of Christ's salvation and the subjective appropriation of that salvation is undone by my proposal – for the objectivity of Christ's salvation is only accomplished in and through our sanctification. The Cross has broken the power of sin over us, and it is Christ's self-giving on the Cross that is completed as joins himself to us fully in the indwelling of his Spirit; yet it is through our lives and actions that he gives this Spirit to us, and to others. We are included within the objectivity of salvation as the tools of its accomplishment, for it is through our graced subjective appropriation of salvation that we are healed of sin's consequences and joined to God.

In all this, I hope to present an understanding of Christ as one who is truly united to us, from the first moment of his birth, to the climax of his saving work on the Cross, to his eschatological dwelling within us; a Christ who is no less divine for learning as we learn, struggling as we struggle, and loving as we love. I wish to present a Christ who is inextricable from the lives of those whom he has made his own, and to know that – as truly human – even God's humanity must be bound up with other lives in order to meet Him in it. I wish not only to see Christ in my neighbor, but to behold the face of the one whom I will praise in the heavenly city, and see my neighbor in Him.

Body and Head: one person. One person who is both our way and homeland: the God who utterly transcends us, the neighbor we serve, the giver of my own ecstatic identity who is *interior intimo meo*. He is our Sabbath; he is our rest. He is the one in whom the fullness of God dwells; he is the one in whom all things hold together, the one who has reconciled in his Body all things through the blood of the Cross. He enfolds all our particularity without eroding it, giving us our own lives and particularity through our creaturely differences, as we receive together the life of Christ. He is Lord, Messiah, child, friend, neighbor, stranger, the one who suffers as a result of my own and our social sin, the one who raises us together from the grave. He is the one in whom our life is hid, and the one with whom we will appear in glory; the one whose life we complete and extend. At the last, as we receive his flesh and blood and recognize his presence in one another, he is the one before whom we will bow, as our tongues confess: Christ is in all, and is all.

Bibliography

Adams, Marilyn McCord. *Christ and Horrors*. Cambridge: Cambridge University Press, 2006.

Aleixandre, Dolores. "Jesus and the Syrophoenician Woman: A Tale from the Margins," in *Concilium: Frontier Violations*, ed. Felix Wilfred and Oscar Beozzo. London: SCM Press. (1999/2): 73–79.

Allison, Dale C. Jr. *Constructing Jesus: Memory, Imagination, and History*. Grand Rapids, MI: Baker Academic, 2010.

Alonso, Pablo. "La Mujer Sirofenica en la Interpretación Patrística." *Estudios Ecclesiásticos* 80.314 (1995): 455–483.

"The Woman Who Changed Jesus: Text and Context," in *Jesus of Galilee: Contextual Christology for the 21st Century*, ed. Robert Lassalle-Klein. Maryknoll, NY: Orbis Books, 2011: 121–134.

Althaus-Reid, Marcella. *Indecent Theology: Theological Perversions in Sex, Gender, and Politics*. London: Routledge, 2001.

Anatolios, Khaled. "'The Body as Instrument': A Reevaluation of Athanasius' Logos-Sarx Christology." *Coptic Church Review* 18.3 (1997): 78–84.

Anderson, James F. *St. Augustine and Being: A Metaphysical Essay*. The Hague: Martinus Nijhoff, 1965.

Apollonius, Dyscolus. *De Constructione Libri Quattuor (Peri Suntaxeos)*, in *Grammatici Graeci*, ed. Gustav Uhlig. Leipzig: B.G. Teubner, 1910.

Aristotle. John Lloyd. *Categories and De Interpretatione*, trans. J. L. Ackrill. Oxford: Oxford University Press, 1963.

Augustine. *Vingt-six sermons au peuple d'Afrique*, ed. François Dolbeau. Paris: Institut d'études augustiniennes, 1996.

Augustine. *The City of God against the Pagans*, trans. Robert W. Dyson. Cambridge: Cambridge University Press, 1998.

Ayres, Lewis. "Remember That You are Catholic (serm. 52.2): Augustine on the Unity of the Triune God." *Journal of Early Christian Studies* 8.1 (2000): 39–82.

Nicaea and its Legacy: An Approach to Fourth-Century Trinitarian Theology. Oxford: Oxford University Press, 2004.

Augustine and the Trinity. Oxford: Oxford University Press, 2011.

Babcock, William. "The Christ of the Exchange: A Study in the Christology of Augustine's Enarrationes in Psalmos." Unpublished PhD dissertation, Yale University, 1972.

Baergen, Rene Alexander. "Re-Placing the Galilean Jesus: Local Geography, Mark, Miracle, and the Quest for Jesus of Capernaum." Unpublished PhD dissertation, Toronto School of Theology, 2013.

Bailey, Kenneth E. *Jesus Through Middle Eastern Eyes: Cultural Studies in the Gospels.* Downers Grove, IL: IVP Academic, 2008.

Baker, Kimberly F. "Augustine on Action, Contemplation, and their Meeting Point in Christ." Unpublished PhD dissertation, University of Notre Dame, 2007.

Baker, Lynne Rudder. "Why Christians Should Not Be Libertarians: An Augustinian Challenge." *Faith and Philosophy* 20.4 (2003): 460–478.

Bantum, Brian. *Redeeming Mulatto: A Theology of Race and Christian Hybridity.* Waco, TX: Baylor University Press, 2010.

Barnes, Michel René. "The Arians of Book V, and the Genre of De Trinitate." *The Journal of Theological Studies* 44.1 (1993): 185–195.

"Augustine in Contemporary Trinitarian Theology." *Theological Studies* 56 (1995): 237–250.

"De Régnon Reconsidered." *Augustinian Studies* 26.2 (1995): 51–79.

"The Visible Christ and the Invisible Trinity: Mt. 5:8 in Augustine's Trinitarian Theology of 400." *Modern Theology* 19.3 (2003): 329–355.

Barrett, Al. *Interrupting the Church's Flow: A Radically Receptive Political Theology in the Urban Margins.* London: SCM, 2020.

Barth, Karl. *Church Dogmatics*, 14 vols., ed. G. W. Bromiley and T. F. Torrance, trans. G. W. Bromiley. Edinburgh: T&T Clark, various.

Bauckham, Richard J. "Colossians 1:24 Again: The Apocalyptic Motif." *The Evangelical Quarterly* 47.3 (1975): 168–170.

Bavel, Tarsicius Jan van. *Recherches sur la christologie de saint Augustin, l'humain et le divin dans le Christ d'après Saint Augustin.* Fribourg en Suisse: Editions universitaires, 1954.

"The Concept of the 'Whole Christ'," in *Saint Augustine*, ed. Tarsicius van Bavel and Bernard Bruning. Brussels: Mercatorfonds/ Augustinian Historical Institute, 2007: 263–271.

Beeley, Christopher A. *The Unity of Christ: Continuity and Conflict in Patristic Tradition.* New Haven, CT: Yale University Press, 2012.

"Christological Non-Competition and the Return to Chalcedon: A Response to Rowan Williams and Ian McFarland." *Modern Theology* 38.3 (2022): 592–617.

Bevan, George A. "Augustine and the Western Dimension of the Nestorian Controversy." *Studia Patristica XLIX* (2010): 347–352.

Blount, Douglas. "On the Incarnation of a Timeless God," in *God and Time: Essays on the Divine Nature*, ed. Gregory E. Ganssle and David M. Woodruff. Oxford: Oxford University Press, 2002: 236–248.

Blowers, Paul M. *Maximus the Confessor: Jesus Christ and the Transfiguration of the World.* Oxford: Oxford University Press, 2016.

Bluck, Richard S. "Forms as Standards." *Phronesis* 2.2 (1957): 115–127.

Boersma, Gerald P. *Augustine's Early Theology of Image.* Oxford: Oxford University Press, 2016.

Bowery, Anne-Marie. "Monica: The Feminine Face of Christ," in *Feminist Interpretations of Augustine*, ed. Judith Chelius Stark. University Park, PA: The Pennsylvania University Press, 2007: 69–95.

Boyarin, Daniel. *The Jewish Gospels: The Story of the Jewish Christ.* New York: The New Press, 2012.

Bradshaw, David. "Augustine the Metaphysician," in *Orthodox Readings of Augustine*, ed. George E. Demacopoulos and Aristotle Papanikolaou. Crestwood, NY: St. Vladimir's Seminary Press, 2008: 227–252.

Bretherton, Luke. *Christ and the Common Life: Political Theology and the Case for Democracy.* Grand Rapids, MI: Wm. B. Eerdmans, 2019.

Brison, Susan J. *Aftermath: Violence and the Remaking of a Self.* Princeton, NJ: Princeton University Press, 2002.

"Outliving Oneself: Trauma, Memory, and Personal Identity," in *Gender Struggles: Practical Approaches to Contemporary Feminism*, ed.

Constance L. Mui and Julien S. Murphy. Lanham: Rowman & Littlefield, 2002: 137–165.

Brown, Peter. *Augustine of Hippo: A Biography*, 2nd ed. Berkeley: University of California Press, 2000.

Bultmann, Rudolf. *Theology of the New Testament II*, trans. Kendrick Grobel. New York: Charles Scribner's Sons, 1955.

Burkett, Delbert Royce. *The Son of Man Debate: A History and Evaluation*. Cambridge, MA: Cambridge University Press, 1999.

Burnell, Peter. *The Augustinian Person*. Washington, DC: The Catholic University of America Press, 2005.

Burns, J. Patout *The Development of Augustine's Doctrine of Operative Grace*. Paris: Études Augustiniennes, 1980.

"How Christ Saves: Augustine's Multiple Explanations," in *Tradition & the Rule of Faith in the Church: Essays in Honor of Joseph T. Lienhard, S.J.*, ed. Ronnie J. Rombs and Alexander Young. Washington, DC: The Catholic University of America Press, 2010: 193–210.

Burrell, David. *Knowing the Unknowable God: Ibn-Sina, Maimonides, Aquinas*. Notre Dame, IN: University of Notre Dame Press, 1986.

Aquinas: God and Action. Scranton, PA: University of Scranton Press, 2008.

Faith and Freedom: An Interfaith Perspective. Oxford: Blackwell, 2004.

Butler, Judith. *Giving an Account of Oneself*. New York: Fordham University Press, 2005.

Byassee, Jason. *Praise Seeking Understanding: Reading the Psalms with Augustine*. Grand Rapids, MI: Wm. B. Eerdmans, 2007.

Cameron, Michael. *Christ Meets Me Everywhere: Augustine's Early Figurative Exegesis*. Oxford: Oxford University Press, 2012.

Carabine, Deirdre. "Negative Theology in the Thought of Saint Augustine." *Recherches de théologie ancienne et médiévale* 59 (1992): 5–22.

Carnes, Natalie. *Image and Presence: A Christological Reflection on Iconoclasm and Iconophilia*. Stanford, CA: Stanford University Press, 2018.

"The Charge of Blasphemy and Pope Rihanna." *Church Life Journal: A Journal of the McGrath Institute for Church Life*. June 15, 2018: https://churchlifejournal.nd.edu/articles/the-charge-of-blasphemy-and-pope-rihanna/.

Motherhood: A Confession. Stanford, CA: Stanford University Press, 2020.

Carter, J. Kameron. *Race: A Theological Account*. Oxford: Oxford University Press, 2008.

Carter, Jason W. "St. Augustine on Time, Time Numbers, and Enduring Objects." *Vivarium* 49.4 (2011): 301–323.

Cary, Phillip. *Augustine's Invention of the Inner Self: The Legacy of a Christian Platonist*. Oxford: Oxford University Press, 2000.

Outward Signs: The Powerlessness of External Things in Augustine's Thought. Oxford: Oxford University Press, 2008.

Caulley, Thomas Scott. "Notable Galilean Persons," in *Galilee in the Late Second Temple and Mishnaic Periods*, Vol. 1, ed. David A. Fiensy and James Riley Strange. Minneapolis, MN: Fortress Press, 2014: 151–166.

Cavadini, John C. "Jesus, Symbol of God." *Commonweal* 126.17 (1999): 22–24.

"'The Tree of Silly Fruit': Images of the Cross in Augustine," in *The Cross in Christian Tradition: From Paul to Bonaventure*, ed. Elizabeth A. Dreyer. New York: Paulist Press, 2000: 147–168.

"Jesus' Death Is Real: An Augustinian Spirituality of the Cross," in *The Cross in Christian Tradition: From Paul to Bonaventure*, ed. Elizabeth A. Dreyer. New York: Paulist Press, 2000: 169–191.

"Simplifying Augustine," in *Educating People of Faith: Exploring the History of Jewish and Christian Communities*. Grand Rapids, MI: Wm. B. Eerdmans, 2004: 63–84.

"Feeling Right: Augustine on the Passions and Sexual Desire." *Augustinian Studies* 36.1 (2005): 195–217.

"The Darkest Enigma: Reconsidering the Self in Augustine's Thought." *Augustinian Studies* 38.1 (2007): 119–132.

Chae, Isaac. "Justification and Deification in Augustine: A Study of his Doctrine of Justification." Unpublished PhD dissertation, Trinity Evangelical Divinity School, 1999.

Chancey, Mark A. *The Myth of a Gentile Galilee: The Population of Galilee and New Testament Studies*. Cambridge: Cambridge University Press, 2002.

Greco-Roman Culture and the Galilee of Jesus. Cambridge: Cambridge University Press, 2005.

"The Ethnicities of Galileans," in *Galilee in the Late Second Temple and Mishnaic Periods*, Vol. 1, ed. David A. Fiensy and James Riley Strange. Minneapolis, MN: Fortress Press, 2014: 112–128.

Chester, Andrew. "High Christology: Whence, When, and Why?" *Early Christianity* 2.1 (2011): 22–50.

Choi, Agnes. "Urban-Rural Interaction," in *Galilee in the Late Second Temple and Mishnaic Periods*, Vol. 1, ed. David A. Fiensy and James Riley Strange. Minneapolis, MN: Fortress Press, 2014: 297–311.

Chrétien, Jean-Louis. *The Call and the Response*, trans. Anne A. Davenport. New York: Fordham University Press, 2004.

Coakley, Sarah. *Powers and Submissions: Spirituality, Philosophy, and Gender.* Oxford: Blackwell, 2002.

"What Does Chalcedon Solve and What Does It Not?," in *The Incarnation*, ed. Stephen T. Davis, Daniel Kendall, and Gerald O'Collins. Oxford: Oxford University Presss, 2002: 143–163.

"Re-Thinking Gregory of Nyssa: Introduction – Gender, Trinitarian Analogies, and the Pedagogy of the Song." *Modern Theology* 18.4 (2002): 431–443.

"The Woman at the Altar: Cosmological Disturbance or Gender Subversion?" *Anglican Theological Review* 86.1 (2004): 75–93.

Cobb, John B. Jr. *Christ in a Pluralistic Age.* Eugene, OR: Wipf and Stock, 1998.

Cobb, John B. Jr. and David Ray Griffin. *Process Theology: An Introductory Exposition.* Louisville, KY: Westminster John Knox Press, 1976.

Cone, James H. *Black Theology and Black Power.* Maryknoll, NY: Orbis Books, 1997.

God of the Oppressed. Maryknoll, NY: Orbis Books, 1997.

The Cross and the Lynching Tree. Maryknoll, NY: Orbis Books, 2011.

Copeland, M. Shawn. *Enfleshing Freedom: Body, Race, and Being.* Minneapolis, MN: Fortress Press, 2010.

"Meeting and Seeing Jesus: The Witness of African American Religious Experience," in *Jesus of Galilee: Contextual Christology for the 21st Century*, ed. Robert Lasalle-Klein. Maryknoll, NY: Orbis Books, 2011: 67–84.

Knowing Christ Crucified: The Witness of African-American Religious Experience. Maryknoll, NY: Orbis Books, 2018.

Copeland, Rebecca L. *Created Being: Expanding Creedal Christology.* Waco, TX: Baylor University Press, 2020.

Couenhoven, Jesse. "Augustine's Rejection of the Free-Will Defence: An Overview of the Late Augustine's Theodicy." *Religious Studies* 43.3 (2007): 279–298.

"'Not Every Wrong Is Done with Pride': Augustine's Proto-Feminist Anti-Pelagianism." *Scottish Journal of Theology* 61.1 (2008): 32–50.

Stricken by Sin, Cured by Christ: Agency, Necessity, and Culpability in Augustinian Theology. Oxford: Oxford University Press, 2013.

Crossley, James. *Why Christianity Happened: A Sociohistorical Account of Christian Origins (26–50 CE).* Louisville, KY: Westminster John Knox Press, 2006.

Jesus and the Chaos of History: Redirecting the Life of the Historical Jesus. Oxford: Oxford University Press, 2015.

Cross, Richard. *The Metaphysics of the Incarnation.* Oxford: Oxford University Press, 2002.

Cruess, Gregory Michael. "Augustine's Biblical Christology: A Study of the *In Ioannis Evangelium Tractatus CXXIV.*" Unpublished PhD dissertation, University of Notre Dame, 2019.

Daley, Brian E. "A Humble Mediator: The Distinctive Elements in Saint Augustine's Christology." *Word and Spirit* 9 (1987): 100–117.

"A Richer Union: Leontius of Byzantium and the Relationship of Human and Divine in Christ." *Studia Patristica* 24 (1993): 239–265.

"The Giant's Twin Substances: Ambrose and the Christology of Augustine's Contra Sermonem Arianorum," in *Augustine: Presbyter Factus Sum,* ed. Joseph T. Lienhard, Earl C. Müller, and Roland J. Teske. New York: Peter Lang, 1993: 477–495.

"Making a Human Will Divine: Augustine and Maximus on Christ and Salvation," in *Orthodox Readings of Augustine,* ed. George E. Demacopoulos and Aristotle Papanikolaou. Crestwood, NY: St. Vladimir's Seminary Press, 2008: 101–126.

Leontius of Byzantium: Complete Works. Oxford: Oxford University Press, 2017.

God Visible: Patristic Christology Reconsidered. Oxford: Oxford University Press, 2018.

Daly, Daniel J. "Structures of Virtue and Vice." *New Blackfriars* 92.1039 (2011): 341–357.

DeHart, Paul J. *Unspeakable Cults: An Essay in Christology.* Waco, TX: Baylor University Press, 2021.

Deines, Roland. "Religious Practices and Religious Movements in Galilee: 100 BCE–200 BCE," in *Galilee in the Late Second Temple and Mishnaic*

Periods, Vol. 1, ed. David A. Fiensy and James Riley Strange. Minneapolis, MN: Fortress Press, 2014: 78–111.

Demosthenes. *Demosthenis Orationes*, ed. S. H. Butcher. Oxford: Clarendon Press, 1903.

Denzinger, Heinrich. *Compendium of Creeds, Definitions, and Declarations on Matters of Faith and Morals*, 43rd ed., eds. Peter Hünermann, Heinrich Denzinger, Robert L. Fastiggi, and Anne Englund Nash. San Francisco, CA: Ignatius, 2012.

Derrida, Jacques. *The Gift of Death and Literature in Secret*, 2nd ed., trans. David Wills. Chicago, IL: University of Chicago Press, 2008.

Dewan, Lawrence. "Saint Thomas, Alvin Plantinga, and the Divine Simplicity." *The Modern Schoolman* 66.2 (1989): 141–151.

Diepen, Herman. "La psychologie humaine du Christ selon saint Thomas d'Aquin." *Revue Thomiste* 50 (1950): 82–118.

"L' 'Assumptus Homo' patristique." *Revue Thomiste* 71 (1963): 225–245.

Dodaro, Robert. "Christus iustus and Fear of Death in Augustine's Dispute with Pelagius," in *Signum pietatis. Festgabe für Cornelius P. Mayer OSA zum 60 Geburtstag*, ed. Adolar Zumkeller. Würzburg. Würzburg: Augustinus-Verlag, 1989: 341–361.

Christ and the Just Society in the Thought of Augustine. Cambridge: Cambridge University Press, 2004.

"Light in the Thought of St. Augustine," in *Light from Light: Scientists and Theologians in Dialogue*, ed. Gerald O'Collins and Mary Ann Meyers. Grand Rapids, MI: Wm B. Eerdmans, 2012: 195–207.

Dorner, August Johannes. *Augustinus. Sein theologisches System und seine religionsphilosophie Anschauung*. Berlin: Wilhelm Hertz, 1873.

Douglas, Kelly Brown. *The Black Christ*. Maryknoll, NY: Orbis Books, 1994.

Drabinski, John E. *Sensibility and Singularity: The Problem of Phenomenology in Levinas*. Albany, NY: State University of New York Press, 2001.

Drever, Matthew. "The Self before God? Rethinking Augustine's Trinitarian Thought." *Harvard Theological Review* 100.2 (2007): 233–242.

"Images of Suffering in Augustine and Luther." *Dialog: A Journal of Theology* 51.1 (2012): 71–82.

"Entertaining Violence: Augustine on the Cross of Christ and the Commercialization of Suffering." *The Journal of Religion* 92.3 (2012): 331–361.

Image, Identity, and the Forming of the Augustinian Soul. Oxford: Oxford University Press, 2013.

Drobner, Hubertus. *Person-exegese und Christologie bei Augustinus: zur Herkunft der Formel "Una Persona."* Leiden: Brill, 1986.

Dubarle, André-Marie. "La conaissance humaine du Christ d'aprés Saint Augustin." *Ephemerides Theologicae Lovanienses* 18 (1941): 5–25.

Dube, Musa W. *Postcolonial Feminist Interpretation of the Bible.* St. Louis, MO: Chalice Press, 2000.

Dunfee, Susan Nelson. "The Sin of Hiding: A Feminist Critique of Reinhold Niebuhr's Account of the Sin of Pride." *Soundings* 65.3 (1982): 316–327.

Edwards, Denis. *Deep Incarnation: God's Redemptive Suffering with Creatures.* Maryknoll, NY: Orbis Books, 2019.

Ellacuría, Ignacio. "The Crucified People," in *Mysterium Liberationis*, ed. Ignacio Ellacuría and Jon Sobrino, trans. by Phillip Berryman and Robert R. Barr. Maryknoll, NY: Orbis Books, 1993: 580–603.

Elia, Matt. *The Problem of the Christian Master: Augustine in the Afterlife of Slavery.* New Haven, CT: Yale University Press, forthcoming.

Emerton, John Adney. "The Origin of the Son of Man Imagery." *Journal of Theological Studies* 9 (1958): 231–232.

Evans, Craig A. "Patristic Interpretations of Mark 2:26 'When Abiathar Was High Priest.'" *Vigiliae Christianae* 40.2 (1986): 183–186.

Farrow, Douglas. *Ascension Theology.* London: T&T Clark International, 2011.

Faus, José Ignacio González. "Sin," in *Mysterium Liberationis: Fundamental Concepts of Liberation Theology*, ed. Ignacio Ellacuría and Jon Sobrino. Maryknoll, NY: Orbis, 1993: 532–542.

Fiedrowicz, Michael. *Psalmus Vox Totius Christi Studien Zu Augustins Enarrationes in Psalmos.* Freiburg: Herder, 1997.

Finn, Daniel K. "What Is a Sinful Social Structure?" *Theological Studies* 77.1 (2016): 136–164.

Fredriksen, Paula. *Augustine and the Jews: A Christian Defense of Jews and Judaism.* New Haven, CT: Yale University Press, 2010.

Frei, Hans W. *The Identity of Jesus Christ: The Hermeneutical Bases of Dogmatic Theology.* Eugene, OR: Wipf and Stock, 1997.

Freyne, Seán. *Jesus, a Jewish Galilean: A New Reading of the Jesus Story.* London: T&T Clark International, 2004.

"Jesus in Context: Galilee and Gospel," in *Jesus of Galilee: Contextual Christology for the 21st Century*, ed. Robert Lasalle-Klein. Maryknoll, NY: Orbis Books, 2011: 17–38.

Fricker, Miranda. *Epistemic Injustice: Power and the Ethics of Knowing*. Oxford: Oxford University Press, 2007.

Furstenberg, Yair. "Defilement Penetrating the Body: A New Understanding of Contamination in Mark 7.15." *New Testament Studies* 54 (2008): 176–200.

Gaine, Simon Francis. *Did the Saviour See the Father? Christ, Salvation and the Vision of God*. London: T&T Clark, 2015.

Geest, Paul van. *The Incomprehensibility of God: Augustine as a Negative Theologian*. Leuven: Peeters, 2011.

Gioia, Luigi. *The Theological Epistemology of Augustine's De Trinitate*. Oxford: Oxford University Press, 2008.

Gonzélez, Justo L. *The Mestizo Augustine: A Theologian between Two Cultures*. Downers Grove, IL: InterVarsity Press, 2016.

Goodman, Martin. "Galilean Judaism and Judaean Judaism," in *The Cambridge History of Judaism, Vol. 3: The Early Roman Period*, ed. William Horbury, William David Davies, and John Sturdy. Cambridge: Cambridge University Press, 1999: 596–617.

Gore, Charles. *Dissertations on Subjects Connected with the Incarnation*. London: John Murray, 1895.

The Incarnation of the Son of God: Being the Bampton Lectures for the Year 1891. London: John Murray, Albemarle Street, 1912.

Grabowski, Stanislaus J. "The Holy Ghost in the Mystical Body of Christ According to St. Augustine." *Theological Studies* 5.4 (1944): 453–483.

"St. Augustine and the Doctrine of the Mystical Body of Christ." *Theological Studies* 7.1 (1946): 72–125.

Grant, Jacquelyn. *White Women's Christ and Black Women's Jesus: Feminist Christology and Womanist Response*. The American Academy of Religion, 1989.

Gregersen, Niels Henrik. "The Cross of Christ in an Evolutionary World." *Dialog: A Journal of Theology* 40.3 (2001): 192–207.

"*Cur deus caro*: Jesus and the Cosmos Story," *Theology and Science* 11.4 (2013): 370–393.

Gregersen, Niels Henrik (ed.). *Incarnation: On the Scope and Depth of Christology.* Minneapolis, MN: Fortress Press, 2015.

Gregory, Eric. *Politics and the Order of Love: An Augustinian Ethic of Democratic Citizenship.* Chicago, IL: University of Chicago Press, 2008.

Griffiths, Paul J. *Intellectual Appetite: A Theological Grammar.* Washington, DC: The Catholic University of America Press, 2009.

"The Quietus of Political Interest." *Common Knowledge* 15.1 (2009): 7–22.

"A Defense of Christian Kitsch." *Divinity: Duke University* (Fall 2011): 36.

Decreation: The Last Things of All Creatures. Waco, TX: Baylor University Press, 2014.

Christian Flesh. Stanford, CA: Stanford University Press, 2018.

Grillmeier, Aloys. *Christ in Christian Tradition,* Vol. 1, trans. J. S. Bowden. New York: Sheed and Ward, 1964.

Gunton, Colin E. *The Promise of Trinitarian Theology.* Edinburgh: T&T Clark, 1991.

Gutiérrez, Gustavo. *A Theology of Liberation,* 15th Anniversary ed. Maryknoll, NY: Orbis Books, 1988.

Haight, Roger. *Jesus, Symbol of God.* Maryknoll, NY: Orbis Books, 1999.

Haley, James P. *The Humanity of Christ: The Significance of the Anhypostasis and Enhypostasis in Karl Barth's Christology.* Eugene, OR: Pickwick, 2017.

Hampson, Daphne. "Reinhold Niebuhr on Sin: A Critique," in *Reinhold Niebuhr and the Issues of our Time,* ed. Richard Harries. Oxford: Mowbray, 1986: 46–60.

Hanby, Michael. *Augustine and Modernity.* London: Routledge, 2003.

Harnack, Adolf. *History of Dogma,* Vol. 5, trans. Neil Buchanan. Boston, MA: Little, Brown, 1905.

Harris, Harriet A. "Should We Say That Personhood Is Relational?" *Scottish Journal of Theology* 51.2 (1998): 214–234.

Harrison, Carol. *Rethinking Augustine's Early Theology: An Argument for Continuity.* Oxford: Oxford University Press, 2006.

Hart, David Bentley. "The Hidden and the Manifest: Metaphysics after Nicaea," in *Orthodox Readings of Augustine,* ed. George E. Demacopoulos and Aristotle Papanikolaou. Crestwood, NY: St. Vladimir's Seminary Press, 2008: 191–226.

Hart, Kevin. "The Unbloody Sacrifice." *Archivio di Filosofia* 76.1/2 (2008): 189–197.

Harvey, Jennifer. "What Would Zacchaeus Do? The Case for Disidentifying with Jesus," in *Christology and Whiteness: What Would Jesus Do?*, ed. George Yancey. New York: Routledge, 2012: 84–100.

Hasker, William. *Metaphysics and the Tri-Personal God*. Oxford: Oxford University Press, 2017.

Hauerwas, Stanley. *God, Medicine, and Suffering*. Grand Rapids, MI: Wm. B. Eerdmans, 1990.

Hays, Richard B. *Reading Backwards: Figural Christology and the Fourfold Gospel Witness*. Waco, TX: Baylor University Press, 2014.

Heil, John. "Relations," in *The Routledge Companion to Metaphysics*, ed. Robin Le Poidevin, Peter Simons, Andrew McGonigal, and Ross P. Cameron. London: Routledge, 2009: 310–321.

Helm, Paul. *Eternal God: A Study of God without Time*, 2nd ed. Oxford: Oxford University Press, 2010.

Herdt, Jennifer A. *Putting on Virtue: The Legacy of the Splendid Vices*. Chicago, IL: Chicago University Press, 2008.

Herman, Judith. *Trauma and Recovery*. New York: Basic Books, 2002.

Heyer, Kristin E. "Social Sin and Immigration: Good Fences Make Bad Neighbors." *Theological Studies* 71.2 (2010): 410–436.

Hick, John. *The Metaphor of God Incarnate: Christology in a Pluralistic Age*. Louisville, KY: Westminster John Knox Press, 2005.

Hick, John (ed.). *The Myth of God Incarnate*. London: SCM Press, 1977.

Higton, Mike. "Kathryn Tanner and the Receptivity of Christ and the Church." *Anglican Theological Review* 104.2 (2021): 134–147.

Hill, Jonathan. "Incarnation, Timelessness, and Exaltation." *Faith and Philosophy* 29.1 (2012): 3–29.

Himes, Kenneth R. "Social Sin and the Role of the Individual." *The Annual of the Society of Christian Ethics* 6 (1986): 183–218.

"Human Failing: The Meanings and Metaphors of Sin," in *Moral Theology: New Directions and Fundamental Issues: A Festschrift for James P. Hanigan*, ed. James Keating. New York: Paulist Press, 2004: 145–161.

Hooker, Morna D. *The Gospel According to Saint Mark*. London: A&C Black, 1991.

Horsley, Richard A. *Galilee: History, Politics, People*. Norcross, GA: Trinity Press International, 1995.

"Social Movements in Galilee," in *Galilee in the Late Second Temple and Mishnaic Periods*, Vol. *1*, ed. David A. Fiensy and James Riley Strange. Minneapolis, MN: Fortress Press, 2014: 167–174.

Hume, David. *An Enquiry Concerning Human Understanding: A Critical Edition*, ed. Tom L. Beauchamp. Oxford: Oxford University Press, 2000.

Hunsinger, George. *How to Read Karl Barth: The Shape of His Theology*. Oxford: Oxford University Press, 1991.

Hurtado, Larry W. *One God, One Lord: Early Christian Devotion and Ancient Jewish Monotheism*, 3rd ed. Edinburgh: T&T Clark, 1998.

Jeffrey, Anne, Asha Lancaster-Thomas, and Matyáš Moravec. "Fluctuating Maximal God." *International Journal for Philosophy of Religion* 88.3 (2020): 231–246.

Jennings, Willie James. *The Christian Imagination: Theology and the Origins of Race*. New Haven, CT: Yale University Press, 2011.

Jenson, Robert W. *Systematic Theology, Vol. 1: The Triune God*. Oxford: Oxford University Press, 1997.

Systematic Theology, Vol. 2: The Works of God. Oxford: Oxford University Press, 1999.

Johnson, Elizabeth A. *She Who Is: The Mystery of God in Feminist Theological Discourse*, 10th Anniversary ed. New York: The Crossroad, 2002.

"Jesus and the Cosmos: Soundings in Deep Christology," in *Incarnation: On the Scope and Depth of Christology*, ed. Niels Henrik Gregersen. Minneapolis, MN: Fortress Press, 2015.

Creation and the Cross: The Mercy of God for a Planet in Peril. Maryknoll, NY: Orbis Books, 2018.

Johnson, Junius. *Christ and Analogy: The Christocentric Metaphysics of Hans Urs von Balthasar*. Minneapolis, MN: Fortress Press, 2013.

Jones, Paul Dafydd. *The Humanity of Christ: Christology in Karl Barth's Church Dogmatics*. London: T&T Clark, 2008.

Jones, Serene. *Feminist Theory and Christian Theology: Cartographies of Grace*. Minneapolis, MN: Fortress Press, 2000.

Keech, Dominic. *The Anti-Pelagian Christology of Augustine of Hippo, 396–430*. Oxford: Oxford University Press, 2012.

Keith, Chris and Anthony Le Donne (eds.). *Jesus, Criteria, and the Demise of Authenticity*. London: T&T Clark, 2012.

Keller, Catherine. *On the Mystery: Discerning Divinity in Progress*. Minneapolis, MN: Fortress Press, 2008.

Cloud of the Impossible: Negative Theology and Planetary Entanglement. New York: Columbia University Press, 2015.

Kelly, Anthony J. *Upward: Faith, Church, and the Ascension of Christ*. Collegeville, MN: Liturgical Press, 2014.

Kidd, Erin. "Theology in the Wake of Survivor Testimony: Epistemic Injustice and Clergy Sex Abuse." *Journal of Religion and Society* suppl. 21 (2020): 161–177.

"A Feminist Theology of Testimony." *Theological Studies* 83.3 (2022): 424–442.

Kilby, Karen. "Perichorsis and Projection: Problems with Social Doctrines of the Trinity." *New Blackfriars* 81.956 (2000): 432–445.

"Is an Apophatic Trinitarianism Possible?" *International Journal of Systematic Theology* 12.1 (2010): 65–77.

God, Evil and the Limits of Theology. London: T&T Clark, 2021.

King, Peter. "The Semantics of Augustine's Trinitarian Analysis in De Trinitate 5–7," in *Le De Trinitate de Saint Augustin: Exégèse, logique et noétique*, ed. Emmanuel Bermon and Gerard O'Daly. Paris: Institut d'Études Augustiniennes, 2012: 123–135.

Kinukawa, Hisako. *Women and Jesus in Mark: A Japanese Feminist Perspective*. Maryknoll, NY: Orbis Books, 1994.

Klausner, Joseph. *Jesus of Nazareth: His Life, Times, and Teaching*. New York: Macmillan, 1929.

Kloos, Kari. *Christ, Creation, and the Vision of God: Augustine's Transformation of Early Christian Theophany Interpretation*. Brill: Leiden, 2011.

Kolbet, Paul R. *Augustine and the Cure of Souls: Revising a Classical Ideal*. Notre Dame, IN: University of Notre Dame Press, 2010.

Komline, Han-Luen Kantzer. "The Second Adam in Gethsemane: Augustine on the Human Will of Christ." *Revue d'études augustiniennes et patristiques* 58 (2012): 41–56.

Augustine on the Will: A Theological Account. Oxford: Oxford University Press, 2020.

"Barth and Augustine," in *Wiley Blackwell Companion to Karl Barth*, Vol. 2, ed. George Hunsinger and Keith L. Johnson. Hoboken, NJ: John Wiley, 2020.

Kripke, Saul A. *Naming and Necessity*. Cambridge, MA: Harvard University Press, 1980.

Kwok Pui-Lan. *Discovering the Bible in the Non-Biblical World*. Eugene, OR: Wipf and Stock, 2003.

LaCugna, Catherine Mowry. *God for Us: The Trinity and Christian Life*. San Francisco, CA: HarperCollins, 1991.

Lang, Uwe M. "Anhypostatos-Enhypostatos: Church Fathers, Protestant Orthodoxy and Karl Barth." *Journal of Theological Studies* 49 (1998): 630–657.

Larsen, Sean. "The Word Was Always Flesh." *Syndicate: Symposium on Mark D. Jordan's* Convulsing Bodies (Jun 5, 2016): https://syndicate .network/symposia/theology/convulsing-bodies/.

Lázaro, Clara Luz Ajo. "Jesus and Mary Dance with the *Orishas*: Theological Elements in Interreligious Dialogue," in *Feminist Intercultural Theology: Latina Explorations for a Just World*, ed. María Pilar Aquino and Maria José Rosado-Nunes. Maryknoll, NY: Orbis Books, 2007.

Lee, James K. *Augustine and the Mystery of the Church*. Minneapolis, MN: Fortress Press, 2017.

Leftow, Brian. "Is God an Abstract Object?" *Noûs* 24.4 (1990): 581–598.

"A Timeless God Incarnate," in *The Incarnation*, ed. Stephen T. Davis, Daniel Kendall, and Gerald O'Collins. Oxford: Oxford University Press, 2004: 273–299.

"Presentism, Atemporality, and Time's Way." *Faith and Philosophy* 35.2 (2018): 173–194.

Legge, Dominic. *The Trinitarian Christology of St. Thomas Aquinas*. Oxford: Oxford University Press, 2017.

Lenow, Joseph E. "Christ, the Praying Animal: A Critical Engagement with Niels Henrik Gregersen and the Christology of Deep Incarnation." *International Journal of Systematic Theology* 20.4 (2018): 554–578.

"Following the Deeply Incarnate Christ: Discipleship in the Midst of Environmental Crisis," in *God in the Natural World: Theological Explorations in Appreciation of Denis Edwards*, ed. Marie Turner and Ted Peters. Adelaide: ATF Theology, 2020: 313–328.

"Shoring up Divine Simplicity against Modal Collapse: A Powers Account." *Religious Studies* 57.1 (2021): 10–29.

Levering, Matthew. "Christ, the Trinity, and Predestination: McCormack and Aquinas," in *Trinity and Election in Contemporary Theology*, ed. Michael T. Dempsey. Grand Rapids, MI: Wm. B. Eerdmans, 2011.

Lévinas, Emmanuel. *Otherwise than Being: or, Beyond Essence*, trans. Alphonso Lingis. Dordrecht: Springer Science and Business Media, 1991.

Discovering Existence with Husserl, trans. Richard A. Cohen and Michael B. Smith. Evanston, IL: Northwestern University Press, 1998.

Leyser, Conrad. *Authority and Asceticism from Augustine to Gregory the Great*. Oxford: Oxford University Press, 2000.

Liddell, Henry George and Robert Scott (eds.). *A Greek-English Lexicon/ with a Supplement 1968*. Oxford: Clarendon Press, 1985.

Liegeois, Alain, Marie-Claire Gaillard, E. Ouvre, and D. Lewin. "Microchimerism in Pregnant Mice." *Transplantation Proceedings* 13.1.2 (1981): 1250–1252.

Lincoln, Andrew T. "The Letter to the Colossians," in *The New Interpreter's Bible, Volume XI*. Nashville, TN: Abingdon Press, 2000: 551–670.

Lindbeck, George A. *The Nature of Doctrine: Religion and Theology in a Postliberal Age*. Louisville, KY: Westminster John Knox Press, 1984.

Lonergan, Bernard. *The Collected Works of Bernard Lonergan, v. 7: The Ontological and Psychological Constitution of Christ*, trans. Michael G. Shields. Toronto, OH: University of Toronto Press, 2002.

Lyon, Jodie L. "Pride and the Symptoms of Sin." *Journal of Feminist Studies in Religion* 28.1 (2012): 96–102.

MacKendrick, Karmen. *Divine Enticements: Theological Seductions*. New York: Fordham University Press, 2013.

Madec, Goulven. *Le Christ de Saint Augustin: La Patrie et la Voie, nouvelle édition*. Paris: Desclée, 2001.

Malbon, Elizabeth Struthers. *Hearing Mark: A Listener's Guide*. Harrisburg, PA: Trinity Press International, 2002.

Marcus, Joel. *Mark 1–8*, Vol. 27 of *The Anchor Bible*. New York: Doubleday, 1999.

Marion, Jean-Luc. *The Erotic Phenomenon*, trans. Stephen E. Lewis. Chicago, IL: University of Chicago Press, 2007.

Being Given: Toward a Phenomenology of Givenness, trans. Jeffrey L. Kosky. Stanford, CA: Stanford University Press, 2002.

In the Self's Place: The Approach of St. Augustine, trans. Jeffrey Kosky. Stanford, CA: Stanford University Press, 2012.

Markus, R. A. *Signs and Meanings: World and Text in Ancient Christianity*. Liverpool: Liverpool University Press, 1996.

Marrevee, William H. *The Ascension of Christ in the Works of St. Augustine*. Ottawa: University of Ottawa Press, 1967.

Mathewes, Charles T. "Augustinian Anthropology: *Interior intimo meo*." *Journal of Religious Ethics* 27.2 (1999): 195–221.

Evil and the Augustinian Tradition. Cambridge: Cambridge University Press, 2001.

A Theology of Public Life. Cambridge: Cambridge University Press, 2007.

The Republic of Grace: Augustinian Thoughts for Dark Times. Grand Rapids, MI: Wm. B. Eerdmans, 2010.

Mbembé, Achille. "Necropolitics," trans. Libby Meintjes. *Public Culture* 15.1 (2003): 11–40.

McCabe, Herbert. "The Myth of God Incarnate." *New Blackfriars* 58.687 (1977): 350–357.

McCormack, Bruce L. *Karl Barth's Critically Realistic Dialectical Theology: Its Genesis and Development 1909–1936*. Oxford: Clarendon Press, 1995.

"Karl Barth's Christology as a Resource for a Reformed Version of Kenoticism." *International Journal of Systematic Theology* 8.3 (2006): 243–251.

"Processions and Missions: A Point of Convergence between Thomas Aquinas and Karl Barth," in *Thomas Aquinas and Karl Barth: An Unofficial Catholic-Protestant Dialogue*, ed. Bruce L. McCormack and Thomas Joseph White. Grand Rapids, MI: Wm. B. Eerdmans, 2013.

The Humility of the Eternal Son: Reformed Kenoticism and the Repair of Chalcedon. Cambridge: Cambridge University Press, 2021.

McDougall, Joy Ann. "Rising with Mary: Re-visioning a Feminist Theology of the Cross and Resurrection," in *The Strength of Her Witness: Jesus Christ in the Global Voices of Women*, ed. Elizabeth A. Johnson. Maryknoll, NY: Orbis Press, 2016: 32–43.

McDowell, John. *Mind and World*. Cambridge, MA: Harvard University Press, 1996.

McFarland, Ian A. "'Willing Is Not Choosing': Some Anthropological Implications of Dyothelite Christology." *International Journal of Systematic Theology* 9.1 (2007): 2–23.

The Word Made Flesh: A Theology of the Incarnation. Louisville, KY: Westminster John Knox Press, 2019.

McGuckin, John. "Did Augustine's Christology Depend on Theodore of Mopsuestia?" *The Heythrop Journal* 31.1 (1990): 39–52.

McIntosh, Mark A. *Christology from within: Spirituality and the Incarnation in Hans Urs von Balthasar*. South Bend, IN: University of Notre Dame Press, 1996.

McWilliam, Joanne. "The Influence of Theodore of Mopsuestia on Augustine's Letter 187." *Augustinian Studies* 10 (1979): 113–132.

"Augustine's Developing Use of the Cross: 387–400." *Augustinian Studies* 15 (1984): 15–33.

Mersch, Emile. "Deux traits de la doctrine spirituelle de saint Augustin." *Nouvelle Revue Theologique* 57.5 (1930): 391–410.

The Whole Christ: The Historical Development of the Doctrine of the Mystical Body in Scripture and Tradition, trans. John R. Kelly. Milwaukee, WI: The Bruce, 1938.

Meyers, Eric M. "The Cultural Setting of Galilee: The Case of Regionalism and Early Judaism." *Aufstieg und Niedergang der römischen Welt* 19.1 (1979): 686–702.

Michelson, Jared. "Thomistic Divine Simplicity and Its Analytic Detractors: Can One Affirm Divine Aseity and Goodness without Simplicity?" *Heythrop Journal* 63.6 (2022): 1140–1162.

Milbank, John. "The Name of Jesus," in *The Word Made Strange: Theology, Language, and Culture*. ed. John Milbank. Oxford: Blackwell, 1997: 145–168.

Miravelle, Mark. *With Jesus: The Story of Mary Co-redemptrix*. Goleta, CA: Queenship, 2003.

Moloney, Francis J. *The Gospel of Mark: A Commentary*. Peabody, MA: Hendrickson, 2002.

Moloney, Raymond. *The Knowledge of Christ*. London: Continuum, 1999.

Moltmann, Jürgen. *The Trinity and the Kingdom: The Doctrine of God*, trans. Margaret Kohl. Minneapolis, MN: Fortress Press, 1993.

The Church in the Power of the Spirit: A Contribution to Messianic Ecclesiology, trans. Margaret Kohl. Minneapolis, MN: Fortress Press, 1993.

Moser, J. David. "*Totus Christus*: A Proposal for Protestant Theology and Ecclesiology." *Pro Ecclesia* 29.1 (2020): 3–30.

"The Flesh of the Logos, *Instrumentum divinitatis*: Retrieving an Ancient Christological Doctrine." *International Journal of Systematic Theology* 23.3 (2021): 313–332.

Mulhall, Stephen. *Inheritance and Originality: Wittgenstein, Heidegger, Kierkegaard*. Oxford: Oxford University Press, 2001.

Mynatty, Hormis. "The Concept of Social Sin." *Louvain Studies* 16 (1991): 3–26.

Nagasawa, Yujin. *Maximal God: A New Defense of Perfect Being Theism*. Oxford: Oxford University Press, 2017.

Nagel, Thomas. "What Is It Like to Be a Bat?" *The Philosophical Review* 83.4 (1974): 435–450.

Nelavala, Surekha. "Smart Syrophoenician Woman: A Dalit Reading of Mark 7:24–31." *The Expository Times* 118.2 (2006): 64–69.

Newman, John Henry. *Certain Difficulties Felt by Anglicans in Catholic Teaching, Vol. 1: In Twelve Lectures Addressed in 1850 to the Party of the Religious Movement of 1833*. London: Longmans, Green, 1918.

Newton, John Thomas Jr. "The Importance of Augustine's Use of the Neoplatonic Doctrine of Hypostatic Union for the Development of Christology." *Augustinian Studies* 2 (1971): 1–16.

Nichols, Aidan. *There Is No Rose: The Mariology of the Catholic Church*. Minneapolis, MN: Augsburg Fortress Press, 2015.

Nolan, Daniel. "Hyperintensional Metaphysics." *Philosophical Studies* 171.1 (2014): 149–160.

Novenson, Matthew V. *Christ among the Messiahs: Christ Language in Paul and Messiah Language in Ancient Judaism*. New York: Oxford University Press, 2012.

The Grammar of Messianism: An Ancient Jewish Political Idiom and Its Users. New York: Oxford University Press, 2017.

Nunziato, Joshua S. *Augustine and the Economy of Sacrifice: Ancient and Modern Perspectives*. Cambridge: Cambridge University Press, 2020.

Nutt, Roger W. "Thomas Aquinas on Christ's Unity: Revisiting the *De Unione* Debate." *Harvard Theological Review* 114.4 (2021): 491–507.

Oakman, Douglas E. "Late Second Temple Galilee: Socio-Archaeology and Dimensions of Exploitation in First-Century Palestine," in *Galilee in the Late Second Temple and Mishnaic Periods*, Vol. *1*, ed. David A. Fiensy and James Riley Strange. Minneapolis, MN: Fortress Press, 2014: 346–356.

O'Collins, Gerald. *Saint Augustine on the Resurrection of Christ: Teaching, Rhetoric, and Reception.* Oxford: Oxford University Press, 2017.

O'Connell, Robert J. *Images of Conversion in St. Augustine's Confessions.* New York: Fordham University Press, 1996.

O'Daly, Gerard. *Augustine's Philosophy of Mind.* London: Gerald Duckworth, 1987.

O'Donoghue, Keelin. "Fetal Microchimerism and Maternal Health during and after Pregnancy." *Obstetric Medicine* 1.2 (2008): 56–64.

O'Keefe, John J. "Impassible Suffering: Divine Passion and Fifth-Century Christology." *Theological Studies* 58.1 (1997): 39–60.

O'Keefe, Mark. *What Are They Saying about Social Sin?* New York: St. Meinrad Archabbey, 1990.

O'Neill, John Cochrane. *Who Did Jesus Think He Was?* Leiden: E. J. Brill, 1995.

O'Regan, Cyril. "Theological Epistemology and Apophasis," in *The Oxford Handbook of Mystical Theology*, ed. Edward Howells and Mark A. McIntosh. Oxford: Oxford University Press, 2020: 369–387.

Pannenberg, Wolfhart. *Systematic Theology*, Vol. 1, trans. G. W. Bromiley. Grand Rapids, MI: Wm. B. Eerdmans, 1991.

Pascal, Blaise. *Penseés*, trans. A. J. Krailsheimer. London: Penguin Books, 1995.

Œuvres Completes II, ed. Michel Le Guern. Paris: Gallimard, 2000.

Patterson, Orlando. *Slavery and Social Death: A Comparative Study.* Cambridge, MA: Harvard University Press, 1982.

Pawl, Timothy. *In Defense of Conciliar Christology: A Philosophical Essay.* Oxford: Oxford University Press, 2016.

Pecknold, Chad C. and Tarmo Toom (eds.). *The T&T Clark Companion to Augustine and Modern Theology.* London: Bloomsbury T&T Clark, 2013.

Perriman, Andrew. "The Pattern of Christ's Sufferings: Colossians 1:24 and Philippians 3:10–11." *Tyndale Bulletin* 42.1 (1991): 62–79.

Pfeil, Margaret. "Doctrinal Implications of Magisterial Use of the Language of Social Sin." *Louvain Studies* 27 (2002): 132–152.

Plantinga, Alvin. *Does God Have a Nature?* Milwaukee, WI: Marquette University Press, 1980.

Plantinga, Cornelius Jr. "Social Trinity and Tritheism," in *Trinity, Incarnation, and Atonement: Philosophical and Theological Essays*, ed. Ronald J. Feenstra and Cornelius Plantinga, Jr. Notre Dame, IN: University of Notre Dame Press, 1989: 21–47.

Plaskow, Judith. *Sex, Sin, and Grace: Women's Experience and the Theologies of Reinhold Niebuhr and Paul Tillich*. Washington, DC: University Press of America, 1980.

"Feminist Anti-Judaism and the Christian God," in *The Strength of Her Witness: Jesus Christ in the Global Voices of Women*, ed. Elizabeth A. Johnson. Maryknoll, NY: Orbis Books, 2018.

Ployd, Adam. *Augustine, the Trinity, and the Church: A Reading of the Anti-Donatist Sermons*. Oxford: Oxford University Press, 2015.

Prevot, Andrew. *Thinking Prayer: Theology and Spirituality among the Crises of Modernity*. Notre Dame, IN: University of Notre Dame Press, 2015.

Radde-Gallwitz, Andrew. *Basil of Caesarea, Gregory of Nyssa, and the Transformation of Divine Simplicity*. Oxford: Oxford University Press, 2009.

Radner, Ephraim. *Leviticus*. Grand Rapids, MI: Brazos Press, 2008.

Rambo, Shelly. *Spirit and Trauma: A Theology of Remaining*. Louisville, KY: Westminster John Knox, 2010.

Ratzinger, Joseph. ""Instruction on Certain Aspects of the 'Theology of Liberation.'" (1984): www.vatican.va/roman%5Fcuria/congregations/cfaith/documents/rc%5Fcon%5Fcfaithdoc%5F19840806%5Ftheology-liberationen.html.

Rebera, Ranjini Wickramaratne. "The Syrophoenician Woman: A South Asian Feminist Perspective," in *A Feminist Companion to Mark*, ed. Amy-Jill Levine with Marianne Blickenstaff. Sheffield, AL: Sheffield Academic Press, 2001: 101–110.

Reed, Jonathan L. *Archaeology and the Galilean Jesus: A Re-Examination of the Evidence*. Norcross, GA: Trinity Press International, 2000.

"Mortality, Morbidity, and Economics in Jesus' Galilee," in *Galilee in the Late Second Temple and Mishnaic Periods*, Vol.1, ed. David A. Fiensy and James Riley Strange. Minneapolis, MN: Fortress Press, 2014: 242–252.

Riches, Aaron. *Ecce Homo: On the Divine Unity of Christ.* Grand Rapids, MI: Wm. B. Eerdmans Publishing Co., 2016.

"A Gentile Woman's Story," in *Feminist Interpretations of the Bible,* ed. Letty M. Russell. Philadelphia, PA: Westminster Press, 1985: 65–72.

Ringe, Sharon H. "A Gentile Woman's Story, Revisited: Rereading Mark 7.24–31," in *A Feminist Companion to Mark,* ed. Amy-Jill Levine with Marianne Blickenstaff. Sheffield, AL: Sheffield Academic Press, 2001: 79–100.

Rivera, Mayra. *Poetics of the Flesh.* Durham, NC: Duke University Press, 2015.

Rivière, Jean. "Notre Vie dans le Christ selon Saint Augustin." *La Vie Spirituelle* 24 (1930): 112–134.

Roberts, Tyler. *Encountering Religion: Responsibility and Criticism after Secularism.* New York: Columbia University Press, 2013.

Roche, William J. "Measure, Number, and Weight in St. Augustine." *The New Scholasticism* 15.4 (1941): 350–376.

Rodríguez, Rafael. "Authenticating Criteria: The Use and Misuse of a Critical Method." *Journal for the Study of the Historical Jesus* 7 (2009): 152–167.

Rogers, Eugene F. Jr. *Sexuality and the Christian Body: Their Way into the Triune God.* Oxford: Blackwell Publishers, 1999.

Jr. *After the Spirit: A Constructive Pneumatology from Resources outside the Modern West.* Grand Rapids, MI: Wm. B. Eerdmans, 2005.

Rogers, Katherin A. "Eternity Has No Duration." *Religious Studies* 30.1 (1994): 1–16.

"St. Augustine on Time and Eternity." *American Catholic Philosophical Quarterly* 70.2 (1996): 207–223.

"Augustine's Compatibilism." *Religious Studies* 40.4 (2004): 415–435.

Rosheger, John P. "Augustine and Divine Simplicity." *New Blackfriars* 77.901 (1996): 72–83.

Rubio, Julie Hanlon. *Hope for Common Ground: Mediating the Personal and the Political in a Divided Church.* Washington, DC: Georgetown University Press, 2016.

Ruddy, Deborah Wallace. "The Humble God: Healer, Mediator, Sacrifice." *Logos: A Journal of Catholic Thought and Culture* 7.3 (2004): 87–108.

Ruether, Rosemary Radford. *Sexism and God-Talk: Toward a Feminist Theology.* Boston, MA: Beacon Press, 1993.

Saiving, Valerie. "The Human Situation: A Feminine View." *The Journal of Religion* 40.2 (1960): 100–112.

Schäfer, Peter. *The Jewish Jesus: How Judaism and Christianity Shaped Each Other.* Princeton, NJ: Princeton University Press, 2012.

Schiffman, Lawrence H. "Was There a Galilean Halakhah?," in *The Galilee in Late Antiquity,* ed. Lee I. Levine. New York: The Jewish Theological Seminary of America, 1992: 143–156.

Schumacher, Lydia. *Divine Illumination: The History and Future of Augustine's Theory of Knowledge.* Oxford: Wiley-Blackwell, 2011.

Serrano, Andrés García. *The Presentation in the Temple: The Narrative Function of Lk 2:22–39 in Luke-Acts.* Rome: Gregorian & Biblical Press, 2012.

Shults, F. LeRon. *Reforming Theological Anthropology: After the Philosophical Turn to Relationality.* Grand Rapids, MI: Wm. B. Eerdmans, 2003.

Skye, Lee Miena. "Australian Aboriginal Women's Christologies," in *The Strength of Her Witness: Jesus Christ in the Global Voices of Women,* ed. Elizabeth A. Johnson. Maryknoll, NY: Orbis Books, 2016: 162–171.

Slee, Nicola. "Visualizing, Conceptualizing, Imagining and Praying the Christa: In Search of Her Risen Forms." *Feminist Theology* 21.1 (2012): 71–90.

Smith, J. Warren. "Suffering Impassibly: Christ's Passion in Cyril of Alexandria's Soteriology." *Pro Ecclesia* 11.4 (2002): 463–483.

Sobrino, Jon. *Christology at the Crossroads,* trans. John Drury. Maryknoll, NY: Orbis Books, 1978.

Jesus the Liberator: A Historical-Theological Reading of Jesus of Nazareth, trans. Paul Burns and Francis McDonagh. Maryknoll, NY: Orbis Books, 1991.

Christ the Liberator: A View from the Victims, trans. Paul Burns. Maryknoll, NY: Orbis Books, 2001.

"Jesus' Approach as a Paradigm for Mission," in *Jesus of Galilee: Contextual Christology for the 21st Century,* ed. Robert Lassalle-Klein. Maryknoll, NY: Orbis Books, 2011: 85–98.

Sokolowski, Robert. *The God of Faith and Reason: Foundations of Christian Theology*, 2nd ed. Washington, DC: The Catholic University of America Press, 1995.

Stalnaker, Aaron. "Spiritual Exercises and the Grace of God: Paradoxes of Personal Formation in Augustine." *Journal of the Society of Christian Ethics* 24.2 (2004): 137–170.

Stark, Judith Chelius (ed.). *Feminist Interpretations of Augustine*. University Park, PA: The Pennsylvania University Press, 2007.

Stefano, Troy A. "Christology after Schleiermacher: Three Twentieth-Century Christologies," in *The Oxford Handbook of Christology*, ed. Francesca Aran Murphy and Troy A. Stefano. Oxford: Oxford University Press, 2015: 362–377.

Stewart-Kroeker, Sarah. *Pilgrimage as Moral and Aesthetic Formation in Augustine's Thought*. Oxford: Oxford University Press, 2017.

Strauss, David Friedrich. *The Life of Jesus, Critically Examined*, 3 Vols., trans. George Elliot. London: Chapman Brothers, 1846.

Straw, Carole. "Timor Mortis," in *Augustine through the Ages: An Encyclopedia*, ed. Allan D. Fitzgerald. Grand Rapids, MI: Wm. B. Eerdmans, 1999: 838–842.

Studer, Basil. "Sacramentum et Exemplum chez saint Augustin." *Recherches Augustiniennes* 10 (1975): 87–141.

The Grace of Christ and the Grace of God in Augustine of Hippo: Christocentrism or Theocentrism? Trans. Matthew J. O'Connell. Collegeville, MN: The Liturgical Press, 1997.

"Loving Christ According to Origen and Augustine," in *In the Shadow of the Incarnation: Essays on Jesus Christ in the Early Church in Honor of Brian E, Daley, SJ*, trans. Peter W. Martens. Notre Dame, IN: University of Notre Dame Press, 2008: 149–175.

Stump, Eleonore. "Aqunas's Metaphysics of the Incarnation." in *The Incarnation*, ed. Stephen T. Davis, Daniel Kendall, and Gerald O'Collins. Oxford: Oxford University Press, 2004: 197–218.

Sumney, Jerry L. "'I Fill up What Is Lacking in the Afflictions of Christ': Paul's Vicarious Suffering in Colossians." *The Catholic Biblical Quarterly* 68.4 (2006): 664–680.

Swetnam, James. "A Note on *in Idipsum* in Augustine." *The Modern Schoolman* 30.4 (1953): 328–331.

Swinburne, Richard. *The Christian God*. Oxford: Oxford University Press, 1994.

Swinton, John. *Raging with Compassion: Pastoral Responses to the Problem of Evil*. Grand Rapids, MI: Wm. B. Eerdmans, 2007.

Tanner, Kathryn. *God and Creation in Christian Theology: Tyranny or Empowerment?* Minneapolis, MN: Fortress Press, 1998.

Jesus, Humanity, and the Trinity: A Brief Systematic Theology. Minneapolis, MN: Fortress Press, 2001.

Christ the Key. Cambridge: Cambridge University Press, 2010.

Taylor, Charles. *Sources of the Self: The Making of the Modern Identity*. Cambridge, MA: Harvard University Press, 1989.

TeSelle, Eugene. *Augustine the Theologian*. Eugene, OR: Wipf and Stock, 1970.

Teske, Roland J. "Divine Immutability in Augustine," in *To Know God and the Soul: Essays on the Thought of Saint Augustine*. Washington, D.C.: The Catholic University of America Press, 2008: 131–152.

Teubner, Jonathan D. *Prayer after Augustine: A Study in the Development of the Latin Tradition*. Oxford: Oxford University Press, 2018.

Theissen, Gerd and Dagmar Winter. *The Quest for the Plausible Jesus: The Question of Criteria*, trans. M. Eugene Boring. Louisville, KY: Westminster John Knox Press, 2002.

Theodore the Studite. *On the Holy Icons*, trans. Catharine P. Roth. Crestwood, NY: St. Vladimir's Seminary Press, 2001.

Ticciati, Susannah. *A New Apophaticism: Augustine and the Redemption of Signs*. Leiden: Brill, 2015.

On Signs, Christ, Truth, and the Interpretation of Scripture. London: T&T Clark, 2022.

Tonstad, Linn Marie. "The Limits of Inclusion: Queer Theology and Its Others." *Theology and Sexuality* 21.1 (2015): 1–19.

God and Difference: The Trinity, Sexuality, and the Transformation of Finitude. New York: Routledge, 2016.

Torchia, Joseph. "'*Pondus meum amor meus*': The Weight-Metaphor in St. Augustine's Early Philosophy." *Augustinian Studies* 21 (1990): 163–176.

Totleben, Peter. "Thomas Aquinas and Maximus the Confessor on Free Choice in Christ." Academia.edu, www.academia.edu/35580907/Thomas%5FAquinas%5Fand%5FMaximus%5Fthe%5FConfessor%5Fon%5FFree%5FChoice%5Fin%5FChrist.

Townes, Emilie. *Womanist Ethics and the Cultural Production of Evil*. New York: Palgrave Macmillan, 2006.

Trudinger, Paul L. "A Further Brief Note on Colossians 1:24." *The Evangelical Quarterly* 45 (1973): 36–38.

Turner, Denys. *The Darkness of God: Negativity in Christian Mysticism*. Cambridge: Cambridge University Press, 1998.

Julian of Norwich, Theologian. New Haven, CT: Yale University Press, 2011.

Verghese, T. Paul. *The Freedom of Man: An Inquiry into Some Roots of the Tension between Freedom and Authority in Our Society*. Philadelphia, PA: The Westminster Press, 1972.

Vermes, Géza. *The Religion of Jesus the Jew*. Minneapolis, MN: Fortress Press, 1993.

"The Son of Man Debate Revisited (1960–2010)." *Journal of Jewish Studies* 61.2 (2010): 193–206.

Verwilghen, Albert. "Le Christ médiateur selon Ph 2, 6–7 dans l'oeuvre de saint Augustin." *Augustiniana* 41.1/4 (1991): 469–482.

Vidu, Adonis. "Opera Trinitatis ad Extra and Collective Agency." *European Journal for Philosophy of Religion* 7.3 (2015): 27–47.

Ward, Graham. *Christ and Culture*. Oxford: Blackwell, 2008.

Ward, Kate. "Porters to Heaven: Wealth, the Poor, and Moral Agency in Augustine." *Journal of Religious Ethics* 42.2 (2014): 216–242.

Webster, John. "The Church and the Perfection of God," in *The Community of the Word*, ed. Mark Husbands and Daniel J. Treier. Downers Grove, IL: InterVarsity Press, 2005: 75–95.

"Rowan Williams on Scripture," in *Scripture's Doctrine and Theology's Bible: How the New Testament Shapes Christian Dogmatics*, ed. Markus Bockmuehl and Alan J. Torrance. Grand Rapids, MI: Baker Academic, 2008: 108–123.

"'In the Society of God': Some Principles of Ecclesiology," in *God without Measure: God and the Works of God*, Vol. 1. London: Bloomsbury T&T Clark, 2016: 177–194.

Wells, Samuel. *God's Companions: Reimagining Christian Ethics*. Oxford: Blackwell, 2006.

Wenham, John William "Mark 2[26]." *The Journal of Theological Studies* 1.2 (1950): 156.

Wetzel, James. *Augustine and the Limits of Virtue*. Cambridge: Cambridge University Press, 1992.

"The Force of Memory: Reflections on the Interrupted Self," *Augustinian Studies* 38.1 (2007): 147–159.

Augustine: A Guide for the Perplexed. London: T&T Clark, 2010.

Parting Knowledge: Essays after Augustine. Eugene, OR: Cascade Books, 2013.

White, Thomas Joseph. "Dyothelitism and the Human Consciousness of Jesus." *Pro Ecclesia* 17.4 (2008): 396–422.

The Incarnate Lord: A Thomistic Study in Christology. Washington, DC: Catholic University of America Press, 2015.

Wilhite, David E. "Augustine the African: Post-colonial, Postcolonial, Post-Postcolonial Readings." *Journal of Postcolonial Theory and Theology* 5.1 (2014): 1–34.

Wilkins, Jeremy. "Love and Knowledge of God in the Human Life of Christ." *Pro Ecclesia* 21.1 (2012): 77–99.

Williams, Bernard. *Shame and Necessity*. Berkeley, CA: University of California Press, 2008.

Williams, Delores S. *Sisters in the Wilderness: The Challenge of Womanist God-Talk*. Maryknoll, NY: Orbis Books, 1993.

Williams, Rowan. *On Christian Theology*. Oxford: Blackwell, 2000.

Arius: Heresy and Tradition, revised ed. Grand Rapids, MI: Wm. B. Eerdmans, 2001.

"Augustine and the Psalms." *Interpretation* 58.1 (2004): 17–27.

"Redeeming Sorrows: Marilyn McCord Adams and the Defeat of Evil," in *Wrestling with Angels: Conversations in Modern Theology*, ed. Mike Higton. London: SCM Press, 2007: 255–274.

"Augustine's Christology: Its Spirituality and Rhetoric," in *In the Shadow of the Incarnation: Essays in Honor of Brian E. Daley, S.J.* Notre Dame, IN: University of Notre Dame Press, 2008: 176–189.

The Edge of Words: God and the Habits of Language. London: Bloomsbury, 2014.

On Augustine. London: Bloomsbury Continuum, 2016.

Christ the Heart of Creation. London: Bloomsbury Continuum, 2018.

"Negative Theology: Some Misunderstandings." *Modern Theology* (Early View, 6 March 2023), https://doi.org/10.1111/moth.12852.

Williams, Thomas. "Augustine vs. Plotinus: The Uniqueness of the Vision at Ostia," in *Medieval Philosophy and the Classical Tradition: In Islam, Judaism, and Christianity*, ed. John Inglis. London: RoutledgeCurzon, 2002: 143–151.

Winner, Lauren F. *The Dangers of Christian Practice: On Wayward Gifts, Characteristic Damages, and Sin.* New Haven, CT: Yale University Press, 2018.

Wirzba, Norman. *This Sacred Life: Humanity's Place in a Wounded World.* Cambridge: Cambridge University Press, 2021.

Wittgenstein, Ludwig. *Philosophical Investigations*, 4th ed., ed. P. M. S. Hacker and Joachim Schulte, trans. G. E. M. Anscombe, P. M. S. Hacker and Joachim Schulte. Oxford: Wiley-Blackwell, 2009.

Wood, Jordan Daniel. *The Wholy Mystery of Christ: Creation as Incarnation in Maximus Confessor.* South Bend, IN: University of Notre Dame Press, 2022.

"Against Asymmetrical Christology: A Critical Review of Rowan Williams, *Christ the Heart of Creation*," in *Eclectic Orthodoxy*, August 2019: https://afkimel.wordpress.com/2019/08/04/against-asymmetrical-christology-a-critical-review-of-rowan-williamss-christ-the-heart-of-creation/.

Wood, William. *Blaise Pascal on Duplicity, Sin, and the Fall: The Secret Instinct.* Oxford: Oxford University Press, 2013.

Analytic Theology and the Academic Study of Religion. Oxford: Oxford University Press, 2021.

Yadav, Sameer. "Toward an Analytic Theology of Liberation," in *Voices from the Edge: Centring Marginalized Perspectives in Analytic Theology*, ed. Michelle Panchuk and Michael Rea. Oxford: Oxford University Press, 2020: 47–74.

Yates, Roy. "A Note on Colossians 1:24." *The Evangelical Quarterly* 42 (1970): 88–92.

Zachhuber, Johannes. *The Rise of Christian Theology and the End of Ancient Metaphysics: Patristic Philosophy from the Cappadocian Fathers to John of Damascus.* Oxford: Oxford University Press, 2020.

Zhang Jing. "Beyond What She Said: On the Syrophoenician Woman." *Chinese Theological Review* 20 (2007): 102–136.

Zizioulas, John D. *Being as Communion: Studies in Personhood and the Church.* Crestwood, NY: St. Vladimir's Seminary Press, 1985.

Index

Printed in the United States
by Baker & Taylor Publisher Services